The Diary of James A. Garfield
Volume II 1872-1874

The Diary of
James A. Garfield

Volume II 1872-1874

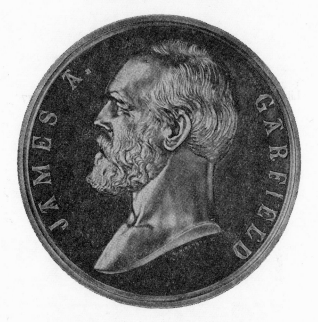

Edited with an Introduction by

Harry James Brown
Frederick D. Williams

MICHIGAN STATE UNIVERSITY PRESS
1967

Copyright © 1967
Michigan State University Press
Library of Congress Catalog Card Number: 67-12577
Manufactured in the United States of America

The Editors Dedicate Their Work
to the Memory of
ABRAM GARFIELD (1872–1958)
Whose Help Was Indispensable

Contents

Contents

The Diary of James A. Garfield
Volume II 1872-1874

1872

January

MONDAY, 1. Returned to Washington from New York, whither Crete and I had gone, partly to attend the banquet of the Williams Alumni Association and do some shopping, and partly to escape the necessity of New Year's calls. The day was fearfully stormy and uncomfortable outside. Found the family in good condition. While in New York, we heard Booth[1] in *Julius Caesar*. It was put on the stage in magnificent style. We were also at the 5th Avenue Theatre and saw the new play called *Divorce*.[2] A quiet but terrible criticism on the times. A mild Juvenal.

TUESDAY, 2. Wrote my fourteenth [sixteenth] New Year's letter to B. A. Hinsdale.[3] All day at work bringing up correspondence.

WEDNESDAY, 3. Continued the work of clearing up accumulated correspondence.

THURSDAY, 4. Worked out the tangled question of ownership of the paint patents of H. W. Bradley,[4] 1867–8. Answered the telegram

---

[1] Edwin Thomas Booth (1833–1893) played the role of Marcus Brutus in *Julius Caesar*, which was presented at Booth's Theater from December 25, 1871 to June 29, 1872.

[2] A dramatization of Anthony Trollope's novel, *He Knew He Was Right*, which opened at the Fifth Avenue Theater on September 5, 1871, and ran for two hundred nights.

[3] Hinsdale wrote a letter to Garfield on New Year's Day, 1857; Garfield responded on January 15. Thereafter as long as Garfield lived the two friends exchanged letters early in the new year.

[4] Henry W. Bradley of New York and New Jersey was associated with the Cleveland Chemical Paint Company, an Ohio corporation which was sued by

addressed me by the seven Republican members in the General Assembly from the 19th District in regard to the senatorial question. I have reason to believe that I could be made Senator next Tuesday, by asking a few friends to bolt the Republican Caucus, but I will not ask it. Thus far in my life I have asked for no office. I may sometime do so but will not begin now.[5]

FRIDAY, 5. Still writing letters and working off accumulated Department business. Criticised additional chapter of Hinsdale's forthcoming book, on the genuineness and authenticity of the Gospels. Answered Prof. Demmon's[6] inquiry on the meaning of "*Monstra Natantia*" in the third of the first book of Horace's Odes. The Professor thought the words meant ships. I say it means animals; marine monsters.

SATURDAY, 6. As the result of two days' studies, I have written a long letter to Hinsdale, giving him the grounds of the argument for

---

the Averill Paint Company of New York for infringement of patent rights. The case went before the U.S. Circuit Court in Cleveland but was compromised in 1873. Garfield was retained in the case by the Cleveland concern.

[5] In 1872 John Sherman was a candidate to succeed himself in the U. S. Senate. Since there was some opposition to him among Republicans in the Ohio legislature, Garfield's name was mentioned as an alternative. If some of the Republicans bolted the Republican caucus and refused to be bound by its decision, Sherman could be defeated with the aid of the Democrats. As the election approached, seven legislators telegraphed Garfield asking whether he desired them to consider him a candidate. Although Garfield had no enthusiasm for Sherman and was willing to be promoted to the Senate, he was unwilling to take the risks involved in an outright declaration of candidacy. "I believe the law of 1866," he telegraphed the seven, "was designed to remove the choice of senators from the caucus to the legislature, but of that you must judge. Do as you think about presenting my name." Since he had been assured of Democratic support, it is likely that he could have been elected at this time. His decision not to make the fight was a crucial one in his political career. The telegram is quoted in a letter to Halsey Hall, January 5, 1872, in Garfield's letterbook.

[6] Isaac Newton Demmon (1848–1920) taught Greek and Latin at Hiram College, 1870–72; in 1876 he went to the University of Michigan and had a long career there as a professor of rhetoric and English. He became an intimate friend of Burke Hinsdale.

the genuineness and integrity of the received text of Shakespeare's plays. He desires to use it to illustrate the argument for the genuineness of the text of the Gospels.

SUNDAY, 7. At church with the family. The sermon was an attempt to draw a mathematical line across the world, with Hell bound on one side and Heaven bound on the other. The issues of life and and death and the exact scope of moral worth cannot be mapped out like counties on a blackboard.

MONDAY, 8. Congress assembled again today and resumed the work which will not let up on me until the last appropriation bill has passed, in the wee sma' hours of the last night of the session. Twenty-five letters is a part of the day's work. Among others a long letter to E. I. Garfield of Detroit, Mich., on the history of the Garfield family, so far as known to me. I have lately been much interested in the genealogy of our family. See letter of this date in my letter-book.

TUESDAY, 9. Begin to get my shoulders under the appropriation bills. Pleasant visit with Judge Black.[7] Answered Elizabeth Cady Stanton's[8] letter, inviting me to speak at the Woman's Rights Convention, saying no and giving the reasons why.[9]

[7] Jeremiah Sullivan Black (1810–1883), of Pennsylvania, prominent lawyer, jurist and Democrat; served in President Buchanan's cabinet as attorney general, 1857–60, and as secretary of state, 1860–61. Garfield was associated with him in a number of law cases, including *Ex parte Milligan*; like Garfield he was a Disciple of Christ. Although Garfield had long been an admirer and friend of Black, communication between them ended in 1880 as a result of letters written by Black during the campaign which were offensive to the Republican presidential candidate and his friends.

[8] Elizabeth Cady Stanton (1815–1902), reformer and leader of the women's rights movement, was president of the National Woman Suffrage Association.

[9] "In answer to your letter of today, inviting me to address the Suffrage Convention, now in session in this City, I beg leave to say that while I heartily sympathize with all efforts that will elevate women and better her condition, I do not believe that suffrage will accomplish that result.

Had I no other reason for this opinion the recent tendencies of the suffrage movement in this country would confirm me in the correctness of my conclusion.

WEDNESDAY, 10. Meeting of Committee on Appropriations, and ten pages progress in Legislative Appropriation Bill. The Venerable Virgin Susan B. Anthony,[10] on the reading of my letter yesterday in the Convention, said, "In writing that letter, he has written his epitaph." Perhaps Susan is right. We shall see.

THURSDAY, 11. Received the Preface of Burke's book, and returned it with criticisms, for which see letter-book of this date. Also answered his New Year's letter. Curious debate in the House on Roger Williams. Mr. Eames[11] of R.I. made a speech on presenting the statue of R. W. to the nation and Gen. Banks[12] criticised that portion of it that related to Williams' banishment from Mass., and claimed that liberty of conscience was not then in debate, but was an afterthought of Williams, after he had left Mass. I quoted [George] Bancroft in refutation of Banks.

FRIDAY, 12. Committee meeting, a dozen pages more of the bill gone over. Sec'y Boutwell[13] before the Committee to explain his estimates. Answered Burke's letter asking permission to dedicate his book to me. Worked on Legislative Bill four hours, besides three hours with the Committee. Went to Sec'y Delano's[14] to meet with Commissioners on Indian Affairs. I fear the most they can accomplish is to let the

---

I, therefore, respectfully decline your invitation." Letterbook, January 9, 1872.

[10] Susan Brownell Anthony (1820–1906), reformer, was chairman of the executive committee of the National Woman Suffrage Association.

[11] Benjamin Tucker Eames (1818–1901), Republican member of the House from Rhode Island, 1871–79.

[12] Nathaniel Prentice Banks (1816–1894) was elected ten times to the House as a representative from Massachusetts between 1852 and 1888 under various party labels. During Garfield's years in Congress he was a member from 1865 to 1873 and from 1875 to 1879, as a Union Republican, a Republican and a Liberal Republican. He was speaker of the House, 1856–57, governor of Massachusetts, 1858–60, and a major general during the Civil War.

[13] George Sewall Boutwell (1818–1905), Republican member of the House from Massachusetts, 1863–69, secretary of the treasury, 1869–73, U. S. senator, 1873–77.

[14] Columbus Delano (1809–1896), a Whig member of the House from 47, Republican member, 1865–69, commissioner of internal –70, secretary of the interior, 1870–75.

Indian races [sink] as gently and easily as possible in oblivion, for there they will go in spite of all efforts.

SATURDAY, 13. Seven hours' hard work on Legislative Appropriation Bill.

SUNDAY, 14. Too ill to go out. Staid at home, read a chapter from Emerson's book on *Society and Solitude* [1870]. His chapter on art, the calm spirit which he breathes around him, makes me desire greatly to get up and out of the smoke and dust and noise of politics into the serene air of literature. Still, I suppose, if I were there, I should grow weary of the silence. Emerson is now in the city, and though over seventy, looks young.

MONDAY, 15. Meeting of the Committee on Appropriations. The Sec'y of the Treasury and the Commissioner of Internal Revenue were before us, and we studied the probabilities of future reduction in the Internal Revenue establishment. Hon. James Brooks[15] returned to his seat today from a trip around the world which he has made since I saw him last spring. Am reading an article in the *Revue des Deux Mondes,* for Nov. 15th, 1871, entitled *"L'Impôt Radical,"*[16] in which occurs this sentence. "Given the two terms of the whole social problem; tradition and movement; religion and philosophy; authority and liberty; capital and labor; usually one of these two terms are summarily abolished or excessively subordinated under the tyranical yoke of its rival."

TUESDAY, 16. Another hard day's work on the Legislative Bill. Answered a letter from Cox in which I discussed the arbitrary and illegal conduct of the Lieut. Governor of Ohio in counting the votes at the senatorial election last week.[17] House passed a bill appropriat-

---

[15] James Brooks (1810–1873), journalist and politician, was editor of the *New York Express,* 1836–73, Whig member of the House from New York, 1849–53, and Democratic member, 1863–66, 1867–73. In 1867 he was named government director of the Union Pacific Railroad and thereafter secured 150 shares of Credit Mobilier stock. The House committee investigating the Credit Mobilier scandal concluded that he had taken the stock as a bribe (he claimed that it had been bought by his son-in-law) and recommended his expulsion; the House censured him instead.

[16] M. Henri Baudrillart, *"Du Radicalisme en Matière d'Impôt,"* *Revue des Deux Mondes,* 96 (Paris, 1871), 346–378.

[17] Some Democratic members of the legislature voted for their party's candidate for senator but planned to transfer their votes to Jacob D. Cox, a

ing $50,000 for a resurvey of our North Western Boundary Line.[18] Ralph Waldo Emerson lectured this evening in the city, but I could not get the time to attend. Called on Sec'y Boutwell and discussed some points in the Legislative and Judicial Appropriation Bill. Received a long letter on financial subjects from Prof. Bonamy Price,[19] Oxford, England.

WEDNESDAY, 17. Finished the preliminary preparations of the Legislative, Judicial and Executive Bill in Committee this morning, and at 1 o'clock introduced it into the House and had it set for consideration next Tuesday. The first regular speech of the session against Civil Service was made today by Mr. Snapp[20] of Illinois. It was mere politics and low down at that. Secretary Fish[21] called on me to secure an appropriation to show the courtesies of the Nation to a party of Japanese just landed in San Francisco.[22]

Republican, before the result of the ballot was announced, expecting that all the Democrats and a few anti-Sherman Republicans would join them, thus defeating Sherman. But they reckoned without Lieutenant Governor Jacob Mueller, who announced the result of the ballot while numerous Democrats were trying to get the floor to change their votes. Cox believed that had it not been for Mueller's action he would have have been elected. Garfield wrote to Cox: "No defense of the Lieut. Governor's conduct is possible." He indicated that if he were in the legislature he would demand "an overhauling of the whole transaction," and pointed out that those who felt outraged could ask the U. S. Senate to declare the proceedings invalid. Letterbook, January 16, 1872.

[18] The bill, which became law in March, authorized the survey and marking of the boundary line between the United States and British possessions from the Lake of the Woods to the summit of the Rocky Mountains.

[19] Bonamy Price (1807–1888), English economist, free trader, and author of tracts on money and banking, was a professor at Oxford University.

[20] Henry Snapp (1822–1895), a Republican member of the House from Illinois, 1871–73.

[21] Hamilton Fish (1808–1893) of New York, was secretary of state, 1869–77. His wife, Julia Kean Fish, and some of his children, the most prominent of whom were Hamilton and Nicholas, also appear in the diary.

[22] Tomomi Iwakura (1835–1883) headed a large Japanese embassy, 1871–73, which visited Europe and America to inform governments of conditions in Japan and to pave the way for treaty revisions.

THURSDAY, 18. The Committee finished examination of the Post Office Bill, and also of the Pension Bill and ordered them reported. Have been doing what I could today to resist the loose legislation asked for by the Pension Committee, but without much avail. I appreciate more than I formerly did the resistance of Elihu Washburne to legislation in regard to claims. Curious and delicate investigation, in an informal way, of some charges against Mr. Hulburd,[23] Comptroller of the Currency. Had the following friends at dinner: Mr. and Mrs. Riddle, the widow of ex-Gov. [Seabury] Ford of Ohio, Representative Packard[24] and wife of Indiana and Mrs. Warren Packard of Warren, Ohio. Also, Ensign Harber[25] came tonight to pay us a visit.

FRIDAY, 19. The Appropriation Committee heard General Banks today in favor of appropriating money to entertain the Japanese Delegation now on its way to this city. The Committee concluded to recommend a $50,000 appropriation. At half-past two o'clock I went to the Treasury Department and spent an hour or two gathering statistics for a speech on the General Appropriation Bill. Have been at work this evening with an officer of the Treasury on the same subject. I am trying to find approximately the laws by which expenditures increase and decrease. Ignorance is my greatest difficulty, in this, as in any other thing.

[23] Hiland R. Hulburd, of Ohio, was comptroller of the currency, 1867–72. He was carrying a letter just received from Garfield when he lost his life in June 1880 as a result of the burning of the steamship *Savannah* at Hell Gate, East River.

[24] Jasper Packard (1832–1899), a Republican member of the House from Indiana, 1869–75. His brother, Warren Packard, was a prominent businessman in Warren, Ohio.

[25] Giles B. Harber (1849–1925) of Youngstown, Ohio, was Garfield's first appointee to the U. S. Naval Academy. In making his appointments to Annapolis and West Point Garfield usually followed the custom of his predecessor from the Nineteenth District, basing his choices on the results of competitive examinations open to all who could meet the requirements for admission. Harber is an excellent illustration of the merits of Garfield's method of selection. He graduated in 1869 and had a distinguished career in the service, retiring as a rear admiral in 1911. He became a close friend of Garfield and his family.

SATURDAY, 20. Have spent the day in preparing the materials for a speech on the introduction of the Legislative Appropriation Bill, next Tuesday morning. I am trying to discover, if I can, the normal law by which expenditures increase in time of peace and also the effect of war on expenditures. The subject is full of interest and I feel the need of more knowledge.

SUNDAY, 21. Attended church in the morning. At half-past three in the afternoon spoke at the Young Men's Christian Association.

MONDAY, 22. Committee took up the Naval Appropriation Bill and made good progress on it. In the House I introduced and carried through an appropriation of $50,000 to entertain the Japanese Embassy, but so worded the bill that it should not assume all the expenses. Also a resolution to appropriate money for the Committee to investigate the troubles in New Orleans which occasioned a long and partisan debate.[26] In the evening continued my work on the speech.

TUESDAY, 23. Committee continued the work on the Naval Appropriation Bill, and nearly completed it. In the House at half-past one went into Committee of the Whole and spoke an hour. Some parts of my speech were too crude, but on the whole it was a fair success. After an hour and a half of general debate including my own speech, proceeded with the bill by paragraphs and completed 14 pages without any amendment; this I believe is an unusual progress. In the evening worked until midnight revising notes of my speech.

WEDNESDAY, 24. Committee heard the Sec'y of the Interior, Commissioners of the General Land Office, Patent Office, and Pensions, on increased appropriations for their Departments in the pending bill. In the House at 2 o'clock resumed debate on the bill and

[26] In 1871 opposition to the administration of Governor Henry Clay Warmoth resulted in an open rupture between two wings of the Republican party in Louisiana. By January, 1872, factional strife had become so fierce that a congressional committee was appointed to investigate the matter. Garfield's resolution of January 22 provided for payment of the committee's expenses and was passed after a lengthy and heated debate. The committee conducted its investigation and submitted a report containing a resounding condemnation of Warmoth and his supporters.

reached the 30th page with no amendments but such as the Committee approve. Corresponded in the evening and played billiards with Swaim. Disgracefully beaten at the latter, and reasonable success at the former.

THURSDAY, 25. Committee finished the Naval Appropriation Bill this morning and ordered it reported in the House. Reached 41st page of the Legislative Appropriation Bill, without material change. The House is treating me very kindly. In the evening attended the Burns Club, which celebrated the 112th [113th] anniversary of the poet Burns's birth. Responded in place of Speaker Blaine to the Toast, "The Day we celebrate and a' wha honor it." Compared Burns with Horace. Horace softened the stately Latin into song. Burns lifted into immortal song the barbarous dialect of Scotland.

FRIDAY, 26. In Committee this morning finished the Indian Appropriation Bill and ordered it reported to the House. Also added three sections and an amendment to the Legislative Bill. In the House finished Legislative Bill, adding sections on public printing. Also finished Pension Bill. Got both bills out of Committee of the Whole into the House and passed them, with only the loss of the second section. This I believe is the most rapid work of the kind I have known since I have been in Congress. Harber left this evening. Went with Swaim and the ladies to Gen'l [David] Hunter's.

SATURDAY, 27. Not feeling very well today, staid at home working up my letters. Among other things wrote a letter to Professor Demmon, on the construction of the 7th and 8th verses of Ode VII, book 4, Horace.

In the evening called at Judge Holt's[27] with Major Swaim and afterwards spent two hours at Major Brown's with Swaim and General Shiras.[28]

SUNDAY, 28. Quite unwell. At church in the morning.

MONDAY, 29. In Committee worked on the Civil [Consular] and Diplomatic Bill. In the House attacked the Pension Bill, which has lately passed the House, and pointed out its reckless extravagance.

[27] Brigadier General Joseph Holt (1807–1894) was judge advocate general, 1862–75.

[28] Alexander Eakin Shiras (1812–1875) was an assistant commissary general in the War Department; he was later commissary general.

Tried to secure its recall from the Senate, but the shadow of the coming elections obscured the minds of members, and they voted me down. Introduced [January 30] a proposition for a new rule to be added to the appropriation bill[s]—one for the construction and repair of public buildings.[29]

TUESDAY, 30. In Committee finished the Consular and Diplomatic Bill. In the House commenced the consideration of the Indian Bill, Mr. Sargent[30] of California having charge of it. Got through with six pages.

WEDNESDAY, 31. In Committee heard the Postmaster General and Mr. [Richard B.] Irwin of the Pacific Mail Steamship Co., in favor of an increased subsidy of half a million for the China Line.

In the House the day was spent in discussing the legality of Mr. Boutwell's operations with the syndicate: I am willing that Congress shall condone his operations, but I cannot vote to declare them legal.[31]

February

THURSDAY, 1. In Committee commenced the consideration of the Deficiency Bill. In the House the debate on the syndicate was ended. I declined to vote either way, neither wishing to injure the credit of the Government nor to ratify an illegal act. Proceeded with the Indian Bill, the House was in admirable temper, and after forty pages had been read, unanimous consent was obtained to rise and

[29] Garfield's proposal, which was not accepted, was to increase by one (from 10 to 11) the number of regular appropriation bills provided for by House Rule 77.

[30] Aaron Augustus Sargent (1827–1887), a Republican member of the House from California, 1861–63, 1869–73, and U. S. senator, 1873–79.

[31] Under a funding act of 1870 Secretary George S. Boutwell secured a loan from American and European bankers, who were soon referred to as the syndicate. On the floor of the House Boutwell was charged with violation of the funding act by increasing the public bonded debt and by exceeding the amount allowed for expenses in placing the loan. After considerable debate the House refused to support these charges.

report it to the House, though thirty pages remained unread. About five o'clock the previous question was seconded and the House adjourned.

We had Mr. Monroe[32] and his wife, Gen'l Sheldon and his wife and Major Clapp[33] at dinner.

FRIDAY, 2. In Committee continued work on Deficiency Bill. House passed the Indian Bill. Balance of the day giving [given] to the Committee on Education and Labor. Adjournment till Monday.

Took dinner with Mr. Mori,[34] the Japanese representative here. The party consisted of Senators Cameron[35] and Cole,[36] Admiral [Thornton Alexander] Jenkins, Professor Henry,[37] General Banks and myself. Had interesting accounts of that strange old country,

[32] James Monroe (1821–1898), college professor and politician, made the acquaintance of Garfield when both men were members of the Ohio Senate in 1860. Monroe taught at Oberlin, 1849–62, and 1883–96, was U. S. consul in Rio de Janeiro, 1863–69, and a Republican member of the U. S. House of Representatives, 1871–81.

[33] William H. Clapp studied under Garfield at the Western Reserve Eclectic Institute, served under him as an officer in the 42nd Ohio Infantry Regiment, and had a long career after the war as an officer in the army. His father, Thomas Clapp of Mentor, and his sister Eliza, are also mentioned in the diary.

[34] Arinori Mori (1847–1889), Japanese statesman and diplomat, was at this time chargé d'affaires of the Japanese legation in Washington. In response to his request for suggestions for improving Japanese education, Garfield wrote him a long letter. In 1885 Mori became Japan's first minister of education and introduced many educational reforms.

[35] Simon Cameron (1799–1889), of Pennsylvania, a founder of the Republican party, was U. S. senator, 1857–61, secretary of war, 1861–62, minister to Russia, 1862, and U. S. senator, 1867–77.

[36] Cornelius Cole (1822–1924), of California, a Republican member of the House, 1863–65, and U. S. senator, 1867–73. On June 26, 1922, shortly before his hundreth birthday, he visited Washington and addressed the House.

[37] Joseph Henry (1797–1878), distinguished physicist, known for his work in electromagnetism, headed the Smithsonian Institution from its beginning in 1846 until his death; he was a member of the Light House Board from 1852 and its president from 1871. Garfield, a regent of the Smithsonian for many years, was a strong supporter of scientific research, and a great admirer of men of science.

which is just awakening into life. With Crete and Julia[38] attended Delano's reception.

Swaim left tonight.

SATURDAY, 3. Have spent the whole day partly in correspondence, but mainly in preparing the case of the *U. S. vs. John Henderson*,[39] No. 104, Supreme Court Docket. The amount in controversy is not large, but it bristles with law points.

Sent Charlotte[40] and the children to hear Maggie Mitchell[41] in *Fanchon*.

SUNDAY, 4. In accordance with previous arrangement, went at 10 o'clock with Dr. Hayden[42] to the Smithsonian Institution to see the

[38] Julia Morgan Choate, a young widow from Newburgh, Ohio, who was a friend of the Garfields. Her father, Caleb Morgan, is also mentioned in the diary.

[39] In this case John Henderson of New Orleans was represented before the Supreme Court by Garfield. Henderson had bought and paid the tax on 100 barrels of liquor which the U. S. government later seized, claiming that the sale was invalid since the previous owner had intended to defraud the government of the tax and hence had forfeited the liquor. Despite an impressive argument presented by Garfield on February 8 and 9, the court decided against Henderson, reversing a decision of a lower federal court. Justice Swayne told Garfield that it was the best argument he had ever made before the Supreme Court. *Henderson's Distilled Spirits* (81 U. S. 44).

[40] Charlotte Bachelard came from Switzerland in 1871 to work for the Garfields. Her services were secured with the help of John Hitz, consul general of Switzerland in Washington. Garfield advanced $78.50 in currency to pay for transporting her from Geneva to Hiram. She looked after the children and gave some instruction in French.

[41] Margaret Julia Mitchell (1837–1918), affectionately known as "Maggie" Mitchell to playgoers of four decades, was best known for her title role in *Fanchon the Cricket*.

[42] Ferdinand Vandiveer Hayden (1829–1887) as a geologist long in the service of the United States made geological and natural history surveys which added much to the knowledge of the West. His work led to the establishment by Congress in 1872 of the Yellowstone National Park. When the U. S. Geological Survey was created in 1879 he became the geologist for the Montana section. Of Hayden Garfield wrote in March, 1872: "He is under many obligations to me for securing the support of the Gov't in this work. . . ." To Hinsdale, letterbook, March 12, 1872.

results of his geological explorations in the Valley of the Yellowstone.

James Mason[43] of Cleveland took dinner with us and Dr. Streator[44] called. Was compelled to work on Supreme Court case in the evening.

MONDAY, 5. In Committee heard the Sec'y of War, Quartermaster-General, and Chief of Ordnance on the military items of Deficiency Bill. Went over most of the bill.

House spent nearly all day in a struggle over proposed drawing of seats. An unmanly exhibition of the merest selfishness. To relieve myself of the disgust I felt for it, I went to the Senate and heard an exceedingly personal debate between Sumner and Carpenter.[45] Sumner is lofty, strong, cumulative, full of self-consciousness, but devoted to his idea. Carpenter is clear, of athletic mind, and a practical lawyer.

Law case in the evening.

TUESDAY, 6. In Committee made further progress on the Deficiency Bill.

In the House, Perce's[46] Educational Bill was discussed and I made a speech defending the bill, but emphasizing the fact that it did not interfere with our American system of education. Quoted authority to show the tendency of European thought in favor of our system, the

---

[43] James Mason (1817–1885), a prominent Cleveland lawyer associated with the Lake Shore and Michigan Southern Railway. He was a cousin of Lucretia Garfield; his daughter Belle married Harry A. Garfield in 1888.

[44] Worthy S. Streator (b. 1816), a New Yorker who practiced medicine in Ohio for a number of years before abandoning it for business. He became a prominent Cleveland businessman, best known as a railroad builder; in 1872 he was president of the Lake Shore and Tuscarawas Valley Railroad Company. A Disciple of Christ, he was an intimate friend of Garfield, and member of the Quintinkle Club, composed of Garfield and a few of his close friends, and their wives.

[45] Matthew Hale Carpenter (1824–1881), Republican member of the Senate from Wisconsin, 1869–75, 1879–81.

[46] Legrand W. Perce (1836–1911), a Republican member of the House from Mississippi, 1870–73, proposed that the proceeds from the sale of public lands be used to aid the states in the establishment of free education for all children regardless of color. Although the bill passed the House it was not considered in the Senate.

autonomy of the states and their schools. In the evening dined with Thomas Nast,[47] the Caricaturist. The rest of the party were Senator Morrill[48] of Maine; Mr. Belknap,[49] the Sec'y of War; Mr. Kerr[50] of Indiana; Gen'l Chipman[51] and Gardiner Hubbard.[52] Nast says he does not know how he sketches his pictures; his only wonder is that everybody else can't do the same. Law case in the evening.

WEDNESDAY, 7. In Committee continued work on Deficiency Bill. Heard the Board of Health of this District in favor of fixing their salaries. Dr. Verdi[53] made a fine speech. In the House spent the whole day in voting on amendments to Educational Bill. In the evening finished proof in the law case. Have satisfied myself tolerably well on the argument. Sheldon of Louisiana wrote up one point in the brief.

THURSDAY, 8. Read the proofs of my brief at ten o'clock. Met Appropriation Committee at 11. Made further progress with the Deficiency Bill and nearly completed Army Appropriation Bill. In

[47] Thomas Nast (1840–1902), German-born American cartoonist and caricaturist, was then concluding his famous campaign in *Harper's Weekly* against the corrupt Tweed Ring in New York City.

[48] Lot Myrick Morrill (1813–1883), of Maine, was governor of his state, 1858–60, Republican member of the U. S. Senate, 1861–69, 1869–76, secretary of the treasury, 1876–77, collector of customs in Portland, 1877–83.

[49] William Worth Belknap (1829–1890), Union general, was secretary of war, 1869–76. He resigned before the House voted to impeach him for malfeasance in office; at the trial before the Senate the two-thirds vote necessary for conviction was not secured. After leaving office he practiced law in Philadelphia and Washington.

[50] Michael Crawford Kerr (1827–1876), Democratic member of the House from Indiana, 1865–73, 1875–76 (during which he was speaker).

[51] Norton Parker Chipman (1834–1924), Washington lawyer and delegate to Congress from the District of Columbia, 1871–75.

[52] Gardiner Greene Hubbard (1822–1897), of Massachusetts and Washington, D. C. (from 1879), practiced law and promoted science, education, and industry; he organized the Bell telephone industry and founded the National Geographic Society; his daughter married Alexander Graham Bell. Hubbard was the host of the dinner here mentioned, held at Wormley's Hotel.

[53] Tullio S. Verdi was secretary of the Board of Health of the District of Columbia and a practicing physician.

the House the Educational Bill passed by a close vote. Then drew seats. In the 38th Congress I drew the first choice; today almost the last. At a quarter-past two commenced my argument in the Supreme Court. Spoke until adjournment at 3 o'clock. I satisfied myself better in the management of my voice than I usually do. Had the close attention of the Court. In the evening brought up my correspondence. Harry and Jimmy are doing exceedingly well in school. Harry needs a little spurring and encouragement, Jimmy, the recognition is [of] a success. Am very tired tonight. Visited Gilfillan[54] in the evening.

FRIDAY, 9. Spent half an hour in the Committee. Then Court where I finished my argument in three-quarters of an hour, and listened to the Solicitor General in response. I'm pretty well satisfied with the case as I have presented it.

SATURDAY, 10. Worked off large batch of correspondence. In the evening attended Press dinner. Responded to a toast, "The Independent Congressman." Shortly after I had spoken the President entered the room and was called up on a toast "To a Sword." He arose and acknowledged the toast and called upon me to answer for him. I took the sword and pen in their relation to each other for a five minutes' speech. The Corps of Washington Correspondents has become a powerful body in this country. The dinner was one of Welcker's[55] best. About fifty guests present.

SUNDAY, 11. Church in the afternoon. Prof. Brown, late of Indianapolis, spoke. In the afternoon read Onslow York's,[56] supposed to be Hepworth Dixon, *Secret History of the International.* Dined

---

[54] James Gilfillan (1836–1929), a Williams College classmate and Washington neighbor of Garfield, was chief of the Loan Division in the office of treasurer of the United States; from 1877 to 1883 he was himself treasurer.

[55] The most famous restaurant of its day in Washington, kept by John Welcker on the east side of 15th Street between New York Ave. and H. St., N. W. It was the scene of much elegant and expensive entertaining. ". . . There is no dinner like Welcker's," wrote the journalist George Alfred Townsend in his *Washington, Outside and Inside* (1873).

[56] Onslow York (William Hepworth Dixon), *Secret History of "The International" Working Men's Association* (1872).

with the Sec'y and Mrs. Fish and Mr. Hale,[57] the new Sec'y of State. Had a long conversation on the present position of the *Alabama* Treaty with England. Mr. Fish told me he had been trying to trace the origin of our national motto, *"E Pluribus Unum"* but could find no earlier trace than the *Gentleman's Magazine* established in 1754, on the title page of which was a hand grasping a bunch of flowers, and under it the motto. At the conclusion of the dinner, the Sec'y and Mrs. Robeson[58] came.

MONDAY, 12. Had no Committee meeting this morning and worked until nearly 12 in clearing up private correspondence. Kelley[59] of Pennsylvania attempted to get a resolution through the House to allow the Woman's Rights women in to address the House next Saturday. I voted against it on two grounds. First. They have already had enough attention of the committees of Congress. Second. It is improper for the House to break down the old rule of making committees its organs of communication with suitors and petitioners. There is no more reason for letting these people in than others who have business with Congress. The resolution was defeated. Mr. Jones, late U. S. Consul from some Chinese Port, called to see me on the proposition to use the Chinese Indemnity Fund for the establishment of a college at Pekin to educate interpreters.[60]

[57] Charles Hale (1831–1882), journalist and politician of Massachusetts, and brother of Edward Everett Hale, was U. S. consul general in Egypt, 1864–70, and assistant secretary of state, 1872–73.

[58] George Maxwell Robeson (1827–1897), of New Jersey, secretary of the navy, 1869–77, and a Republican member of the House, 1879–83.

[59] William Darrah Kelley (1814–1890), a Republican member of the House from Pennsylvania, 1861–90, was best known for his long advocacy of protection for home industries; his devotion to the iron industry won him the sobriquets "Old Pig" and "Pig-Iron." He was regularly a member of the Committee of Ways and Means. He was also a leading inflationist.

[60] William Patterson Jones (1831–1886) served during the 1860's as U. S. consul at Macao, Amoy and Canton. In accordance with the treaty of 1858 the United States received from China funds for the payment of certain losses sustained by American citizens. In May, 1872, a bill related to the unexpended balance was reported in the House. After certain claims against it had been investigated and paid if found proper, the United States was to offer to return the unused portion of the fund. If China refused, the

TUESDAY, 13. No committee meeting this morning. Set for portrait at Thorp's Gallery on the roof of the Capitol, on the Senate wing. In the House unsuccessfully resisted a bill to begin a new U. S. building at Albany, N. Y. After the morning hour took up Invalid [Naval] Appropriation Bill, and Mr. Hale[61] of Maine in charge of it. General debate for two hours and a half. Am troubled about Harry's school. Scholars are a rough set. Must try to find a private school, though the rough and tumble of a public school is good for a boy.

WEDNESDAY, 14. Went with Crete to the Depot at 10 o'clock to meet Dr. and Mrs. Robison. They did not arrive. In Committee went forward with the Deficiency Bill. Heard Mr. Negus[62] in favor of an increased appropriation for hydrographic charts. Heard the Sec'y of the Navy in regard to the sale of old ships. In the House, debate in the morning hour on public buildings. Tried to resist the appropriation of $150,000 for Quincy, Ill. Reported to the House and passed Post Office Deficiency and Pension bills, with Senate amendments. Proceeded with the Naval Appropriation Bill. On reaching home found the Dr. and Mrs. Robison here.

THURSDAY, 15. In Committee heard the Ass't Supervising Architect of the Treasury. Made further progress with the Deficiency Bill, also concluded the Army Bill and ordered it reported to the House.

After the morning hour, proceeded with the Navy Bill. Succeeded in adding a section to sell off old and useless ships of war and a little after four o'clock passed the bill. Sent Harry to private school kept in the basement of the Congregational Church. Mollie is beginning to make some progress.

FRIDAY, 16. Went to the Post Office Department this morning with Mr. Udell. In Committee continued consideration of the Deficiency

---

fund would be used to train American youths in the Chinese language and literature and Chinese youths in the English language and literature and in the natural sciences and arts, with a view to their use as interpreters and assistants in Sino-American intercourse. The bill was not debated.

[61] Eugene Hale (1836–1918), of Maine, a Republican member of the House, 1869–79, and U. S. senator, 1881–1911. He was the son-in-law of Zachariah Chandler of Michigan.

[62] T. S. and J. D. Negus were publishers of a nautical almanac in New York.

Bill and finished. Was authorized to report it to the House. Antagonized the Diplomatic Bill with the bill to pay $65,000 to William and Mary's College,[63] and succeeded in getting into Committee, but it being late in the day House adjourned. Listened to Tipton[64] in the Senate. The political elements are full of nitre just now. If the opposition to Grant were to concentrate he would stand a good chance to be beaten. Home in the evening, very tired.

SATURDAY, 17. Worked off a large lot of letters. Went to the Executive Mansion, Treasury Department, Post Office, and Patent Office on business.

SUNDAY, 18. Attended church in the forenoon with family and friends. Quite ill in the evening.

MONDAY, 19. In Committee made some additions to the Deficiency Bill and prepared it for report to the House, which I did later in the day, making it a special order for early action. It was a stormy unsatisfactory day. Tea and coffee were voted on the Free List, under a suspension of the rules, with thirty-eight dissenting votes, my own among the number. There can be no proper adjustment of the tariff with such action as this. It is a terrible thing for men to live in the fear of their constituents to the extent which many members do. I would rather be defeated every day in the year, than suffer such fear. It is pleasant to have the approval of the public, but it is vital and necessary to have the approval of one's self.

TUESDAY, 20. In Committee considered and completed the Appropriation Bill for the Military Academy and ordered it reported to the House. In the House under the leadership of Governor Swann,[65] the Consular and Diplomatic Bill was taken up; general debate continued until near the close of the day, when we made a little progress on the bill by paragraphs. The House was thin in conse-

---

[63] A bill to reimburse the College of William and Mary for property destroyed during the Civil War; it did not come to a vote during the 42nd Congress.

[64] Thomas Weston Tipton (1817–1899), a Republican member of the Senate from Nebraska, 1867–75. On this occasion he delivered an anti-administration speech in response to remarks by Senator Morton of Indiana, a supporter of Grant.

[65] Thomas Swann (1809–1883), governor of Maryland, 1865–69, Democratic member of the House, 1869–79.

quence of the excitement in the Senate. Carl Schurz[66] made the most brilliant senatorial speech of his life on the resolution concerning the sale of arms.[67] I did not hear it, but all the reports concur in pronouncing it exceedingly brilliant. Cultivated foreigners who have mastered our tongue seem to have a power of speech superior to our native people. We are educated in the streets.

WEDNESDAY, 21. In Committee heard Gen'l Humphreys[68] and Col. Casey[69] on the condition of our fortifications. The science of defence consists in determining the relative force of projectile and strength of targets or fortifications. In building fortifications we are on the target side of the question. It seems to be demonstrated that iron and masonry are inferior to earthworks for defense against heavy artillery. In the House we finished the consideration of the Consular and Diplomatic Bill and got it out of Committee of the Whole and into the House under the previous question. Raised the Russian Mission to the 1st class and the Japan to the second. Unsuccessfully resisted the motion to adjourn over for Feb. 22d. This adjournment has not usually been made since I have been in Congress. Heard Mr. Dimmick [Dimock][70] on the Atlantic mail subsidy.

[66] Carl Schurz (1829–1906), a German immigrant to the United States after the Revolution of 1848, was a Republican member of the Senate from Missouri, 1869–75, and secretary of the interior, 1877–81. He was prominent in the civil service reform movement.

[67] On February 12 Charles Sumner introduced a resolution calling for the appointment of a select committee to investigate the sale of ordnance stores by the government during the Franco-Prussian War. The resolution resulted from rumors of improper action on the part of government officials in sales to France. It had strong political overtones since Sumner was an anti-Grant Republican, as was Carl Schurz, who was also critical of the government's policy in the arms case. The committee appointed in accordance with the resolution reported that the transactions had been entirely proper.

[68] Thomas Atkinson Humphreys (1810–1883) served as chief of the Corps of Engineers, 1866–79, with the rank of brigadier general.

[69] Thomas Lincoln Casey (1831–1896), now an assistant to Humphreys, was later superintending engineer of public buildings, grounds and works, and chief of the Corps of Engineers. He had charge of the construction of the State, War and Navy Building, and of the completion of the Washington Monument, and at his death was engaged in the construction of the Library of Congress.

[70] A. W. Dimock was president of the Atlantic Mail Steamship Company.

THURSDAY, 22. No session today. Staid at home working on the correspondence. In the evening dined with Ingersoll of Illinois. Present, Speaker Blaine, Hooper, Blair,[71] Eldredge,[72] Kerr, Niblack,[73] Buckley,[74] Myers,[75] Robinson,[76] and a few others, fourteen in all. A good deal of free talk on the political situation, which all admitted is becoming more and more complicated. Father and Mother Rudolph arrived today.

FRIDAY, 23. In Committee concluded the consideration of the Fortification Bill. Kept the amount a little below two millions, and ordered the bill reported to the House. In the House passed the Consular and Diplomatic Bill, and then debated the bill for the relief of William and Mary's College. Opposed the bill without abusing the South.[77] Heard part of Trumbull's[78] speech on the proposed investi-

[71] There were two Blairs in the House at this time:

Austin Blair (1818–1894), Republican governor of Michigan, 1861–65, member of the House, 1867–73, and unsuccessful Liberal Republican candidate for governor of Michigan, 1872.

James Gorrall Blair (1825–1904), Liberal Republican member of the House from Missouri, 1871–73.

[72] Charles Augustus Eldredge (1820–1896), a Democratic member of the House from Wisconsin, 1863–75.

[73] William Ellis Niblack (1822–1893), a Democratic member of the House from Indiana, 1857–61, 1865–75, and judge of the Supreme Court of Indiana, 1877–89.

[74] Charles Waldron Buckley (1835–1906), a Republican member of the House from Alabama, 1868–73.

[75] Leonard Myers (1827–1905), a Republican member of the House from Pennsylvania, 1863–69, 1869–75.

[76] James Carroll Robinson (1823–1886), a Democratic member of the House from Illinois, 1859–65, 1871–75.

[77] The bill provided for reimbursing William and Mary College in the amount of $65,000 for property destroyed during the Civil War. In his speech, Garfield spoke of the college as "an ancient, venerable, and honorable institution," but insisted that passage of the bill would establish a "fatal precedent," the result of which would be a "vast, limitless body of claims of all sorts" against the federal government.

[78] Lyman Trumbull (1813–1896), U. S. senator from Illinois, 1853–73. He started his political career as a Democrat and then became a leading Republican. In 1872 he was a severe critic of the Grant administration and a leader of the Liberal Republican movement; he later returned to the

gation for the sale of arms. He favored the Cincinnati Convention. Wells[79] called in the evening.

SATURDAY, 24. At home working up the correspondence; commenced a letter to the Japanese Minister, in answer to his letter asking me to submit my views on the subject of popular education, especially as [it] applies to Japan, its value to the material, social and political prosperity of the state. I am interested in the great awakening in that country. I look for remarkable developements in the commerce and trade between our country and Japan and China.

SUNDAY, 25. Attended church in the forenoon.

MONDAY, 26. In Committee considered some further items of the Deficiency Bill. In the House passed the morning hour in the usual manner. Succeeded at three o'clock in getting the Committee of the Whole on the Deficiency Bill. Made a general statement of the character of the appropriations in the bill, and the reasons for them. Got to the middle of the third page in the discussion of the bill by paragraphs. Most of the family went to Mount Vernon today, but was delayed so that they did not get home before eight o'clock.

TUESDAY, 27. In Committee considered some additional deficiency estimates. In the House after the morning hour got into Committee of the Whole and proceeded with the Deficiency Appropriation Bill. Beck[80] of Kentucky made a political attack on some of the army deficiencies, but after a lengthy and exciting discussion he was beaten. In the evening dined with Ward,[81] Banks, Wells, and Thurman,[82]

Democratic party. In the speech referred to by Garfield, Trumbull defended the Missouri movement for a convention in Cincinnati to nominate an independent national ticket, an action which would split the Republic party.

[79] David Ames Wells (1828–1898), a leading economist of the day and a prolific writer on economic matters, was best known for his attacks on the protective tariff system, attacks which cost him his position as special commissioner of the revenue in 1870. He was an alumnus of Williams College and a close friend of Garfield, whom he sometimes counseled on tariff matters. He became an active Democrat and in 1876 and 1890 he was a candidate for Congress from Connecticut.

[80] James Burnie Beck (1822–1890), a Democratic member of the House from Kentucky, 1867–75, and U. S. senator, 1877–90.

[81] Samuel Ward (1814–1884), "King of the Lobby," was well known for his social qualities, elegant dinners, and Congressional lobbying in behalf of private interests. He was the brother of Julia Ward Howe and uncle of

[Simeon M.] Johnson, MacFarland,[83] a lawyer of New York, and Russell of the same place. The political warfare is still going on in the Senate.

WEDNESDAY, 28. Dr. Robison and wife left this morning at 7 o'clock for Florida. In committee considered some additional deficiency estimates. Heard General Leggett, Commissioner of Patents, in favor of establishing an Official Gazette in the Patent Office. In the House, after the morning hour was over, went to the Speaker's table and consumed the whole day. Heard part of Sumner's speech on the sale of arms to France. He is the acknowledged authority in Congress on questions of international laws. Crete and Mother, Mr. and Mrs. Rudolph and Miss Willson went to the Senate to hear Sumner. Dined this evening at S[imeon] M. Johnson's with Wells, Ward, and others, and after dinner called at Freeman Clarke's,[84] corner 15th and I St., where we had a conference with him, Amasa Walker[85] and a Mr. Sherman[86] of New York on questions of currency and exchange.

THURSDAY, 29. In Committee discussed additional items for Deficiency Bill and adjourned until Monday morning. The House spent the whole day on the Saint Croix and Bayfield Railroad. It suffered

---

the novelist F. Marion Crawford, whose career he advanced. He and Garfield first met in 1865 and they were on friendly terms thereafter.

[82] Allen Granberry Thurman (1813–1895), of Ohio, was a Democratic member of the House, 1845–47, a judge of the Supreme Court of Ohio, 1851–56, U. S. senator, 1869–81, member of the Electoral Commission, 1877, and candidate for vice president with Cleveland in 1888. After he had failed to win re-election to the Senate in 1881, Garfield appointed him an American representative to the International Monetary Conference in Paris.

[83] William W. MacFarland, a New York lawyer who had clients with claims against the government; Garfield was of some service to him during this session of Congress.

[84] Freeman Clarke (1809–1887), Republican member of the House from New York, 1863–65, 1871–75; at this time he was a member of the Committee on Appropriations.

[85] Amasa Walker (1799–1875), political economist; Republican member of the House from Massachusetts, 1862–63; father of Francis A. Walker.

[86] Probably Thomas G. Shearman (1834–1900), New York lawyer and economist.

defeat in several shapes but was not finally killed. I am greatly in doubt about the bill, not being quite satisfied that it should be defeated, and yet not quite willing to see it pass. The fact is that a large number of settlers have acquired equity rights, which will suffer if the bill does not pass. And yet it is high time to arrest the policy of granting lands to railroads.

March

FRIDAY, 1. Five o'clock this morning S. M. Johnson, with whom I dined night before last, fell dead in his wife's arms. He was a prominent lawyer and a strong personal and political friend to [Lewis] Cass. This morning finished the letter on education to Mr. Mori, Chargé d'Affaires of Japan. In the House at half-past two, got into Committee on Deficiency Bill, and advanced four pages on it. It is full of items and was a good deal debated. In the evening called with Mr. Sargent on Mr. [Charles E.] DeLong, our Minister to Japan. Received an interesting letter on the currency from Prof. Bonamy Price, Oxford, England.

SATURDAY, 2. Worked off a large amount of correspondence. At 11 o'clock went with Mrs. Garfield to visit the Columbia Hospital with a view to ascertaining how much Congress ought to appropriate for maintaining it. On my return called at the Treasury Department and looked after some tariff statistics. Very heavy snowstorm raged all day, quite unusual for Washington. I enjoy such a storm for it brings out the contrast between cheerfullness within and the forbidding aspect of the world without.

SUNDAY, 3. Attended church in the forenoon. Read and wrote in the afternoon and evening.

MONDAY, 4. In Committee heard Gen'l Whittlesey[87] in regard to the appropriation of $34,000 for the deficiency in the Freedmen's Bureau accounts. Also went over several other items for the Deficiency Bill, among them an appropriation of $100,000 for the relief of seamen

[87] Eliphalet Whittlesey (1821–1909) served for a time as acting assistant adjutant general in the Bureau of Refugees, Freedmen, and Abandoned Lands.

rescued from the whaling fleet lost in the North Pacific.[88] In the House at half-past two o'clock, after some struggle, got into Committee of the Whole and made progress on the Deficiency Bill as far as the 23rd page. In the evening read a book of Pope's *Dunciad*. I find it very difficult to expel the impression that a good deal of it is slang. I fear I shall never be able to consider Pope a great poet.

TUESDAY, 5. In Committee heard an argument from Gen'l Paine[89] of Wisconsin in favor of returning to private owners the cotton seized from them after the war had ended. In the House after the morning hour proceeded with the Deficiency Bill. Got in, and carried all the amendments authorized by the Committee. On the Judicial Fund a brisk debate sprung up, which drifted off into questions of Ku Klux, in which an amusing passage at arms occurred between Cox[90] of N. Y. and Rainey,[91] a colored member from South Carolina. Cox got the worst of it.

WEDNESDAY, 6. No Committee meeting this morning. At 11 o'clock, the House received the Japanese Embassy. The Speaker made a very fine address of welcome, and Iwakura, Chief of the Embassy, read a response in [the] Japanese language, a translation of which was read to the House by Gen'l Banks. The address in Japanese was delivered

[88] In 1871 a fleet of more than thirty whaling vessels was trapped and crushed by ice floes off the northern coast of Alaska; a heroic rescue mission saved the more than 1,200 persons aboard the vessels.

[89] Halbert Eleazer Paine (1826–1905), a Republican member of the House from Wisconsin, 1865–71, was now practicing law in Washington.

[90] The debate was over a proposed appropriation of $1,000,000 to defray the cost of enforcing the so-called Ku Klux Act of 1871. In a speech opposing the appropriation Samuel Sullivan Cox, who professed to be a friend of the Negro, said that "if there ever was a corporate body thoroughly and disgracefully corrupt with detestable putrescence, it is the State government of South Carolina, both black and white, and especially the black." Rainey countered with an impassioned plea for justice for the Negro. He accused Cox and his Democratic colleagues of voting against all recent measures which proposed to elevate the position of the Negro, whose cause he identified with the Republican party. *Congressional Globe*, 42 Cong., 2 Sess., Part II, 1440, 1442–1443.

[91] Joseph Hayne Rainey (1832–1887), first Negro to be elected to the House, was a Republican member from South Carolina, 1870–79.

in chanting tones and had the appearance of being in some sort of meter, like that in which the Hebrew Psalms were written. The translation exhibited a fine vein of thought, lighted up with the imagery for which the Orientals are distinguished. In the House after the morning hour resumed the consideration of the Deficiency Bill, and after a long and turbulent debate succeeded in getting the bill reported from the Committee into the House; then adjourned. Dined with Messrs. Ward, Davinge [Davidge][92] and another whose name I forget.

THURSDAY, 7. After a brief meeting, Committee went into the House and after an hour's struggle, the Deficiency Bill passed. I allowed Mr. Dawes's[93] eight hour appropriation to be offered as an amendment, but allowed Farnsworth's[94] amendment to the amendment.[95] Both prevailed. Dawes was somewhat offended at me for allowing Farnsworth's motion, but justice required that both should be heard. In the evening dined at Welcker's with Piatt,[96] Townsend,[97] John A. Smith[98] and Henry Reed[99].

[92] Walter Dorsey Davidge (1823–1901), prominent Washington lawyer. See entry for May 16, 1872.

[93] Henry Laurens Dawes (1816–1903), Republican member of the House from Massachusetts, 1857–75, and U. S. senator, 1875–93. At this time he was chairman of the Committee on Ways and Means.

[94] John Franklin Farnsworth (1820–1897), a Republican member of the House from Illinois, 1857–61, 1863–73. He practiced law in Washington from 1880.

[95] In June, 1868, Congress passed an act providing for an eight-hour day for laborers and mechanics employed by or on behalf of the government; in May, 1869, the President issued a proclamation concerning pay adjustments under the law. The amendment offered by Dawes provided that in settling accounts for the period between the date of the law and the date of the proclamation, the government should make no reductions in wages on account of the reduction in hours. Farnsworth offered an amendment to the amendment which provided that no money should be paid those who had already been paid for eight hours of work four-fifths as much as the amount paid to like workers for ten hours of work.

[96] Donn Piatt (1819–1891), Ohio-born journalist, became the Washington correspondent of the *Cincinnati Commercial* in 1868; in 1871 he founded, along with George Alfred Townsend, the weekly Washington *Capital*, and edited it until 1880. He wrote several books, including the con-

FRIDAY, 8. In Committee offered, and was authorized to add to the Post Office Bill, a section prohibiting officers of the Executive Dep'ts from practicing before those departments as agents and attorneys within two years after ceasing to be officers, that a repetition of such scoundrelism as that of Giles A. Smith[100] may not be repeated. After the morning hour, got the Post Office Appropriation Bill well under way. At four o'clock joined Mrs. Garfield and took the steamer *Lady of the Lake* going down to Fortress Monroe with Gen'l Butler[101] and party.

SATURDAY, 9. Reached Fortress Monroe at 7 o'clock in the morning, went up to Hampton in the steamer *Mystic*. Invited the Board of Managers of the Soldiers' Home to visit Hampton Normal School.[102] We went in small boats and had a delightful visit. I presided at the meeting and several speeches were made, Gen'l Butler and Senator

---

troversial *Memories of the Men Who Saved the Union* (1887). In his newspaper he sometimes gave generous support to Garfield.

[97] George Alfred Townsend (1841–1914), journalist and author, who sometimes wrote under the name "Gath," was a correspondent for the *Chicago Tribune* and scores of other papers during his long career. He helped Piatt found the *Capital* and was for a very brief time co-editor. His *Washington, Outside and Inside*, was published in 1873. He was one of the best known correspondents of his day.

[98] John Armstrong Smith (1814–1892), a Republican member of the House from Ohio, 1869–73.

[99] Henry Reed, of Ohio, was associated with Donn Piatt on the Washington *Capital*.

[100] Giles A. Smith (1829–1876) was second assistant postmaster general, 1869–72.

[101] Benjamin Franklin Butler (1818–1893), Union general in the Civil War, was a Republican member of the House from Massachusetts, 1867–75 and 1877–79. He was president and treasurer of the National Asylum for Disabled Volunteer Soldiers, the inspection of whose establishment at Hampton, Virginia, was the object of this trip. During his political career, which was as colorful as his military career was controversial, he occasionally clashed with Garfield, who grew to dislike him intensely.

[102] From 1870 to 1875 Garfield was a member of the Board of Trustees of Hampton Normal and Agricultural Institute, opened in 1868 for the education of Negroes.

Wilson participating. At two o'clock the whole party dined at National Asylum. In the evening went to Fortress Monroe. Gov. Fairchild,[103] Mrs. Garfield and myself returned to Hampton and spent the night.

SUNDAY, 10.   At 8 o'clock Gen'l Armstrong[104] in his yacht took us to Fortress Monroe. Time, 19 minutes. At nine o'clock whole party left in steamer *Lady of the Lake* for Washington. The Potomac is a wonderfully fine river, twelve miles in width for nearly fifty miles of its length. Remained on board till morning.

MONDAY, 11.   Worked off a large amount of correspondence. Had no Committee meeting. In the House brought up no appropriation bills, but introduced a bill and referred it to the Judiciary Committee to require full detailed reports from the Dep't of Justice showing the appropriations and expenditures for each fiscal year. In the evening read a few chapters from Bryce's *Holy Roman Empire*.[105]

TUESDAY, 12.   In Committee heard an argument from Clarkson N. Potter[106] in favor of building a monument to General Herkimer of the War of Independence. Also heard ex-Senator Wade in favor of increasing the appropriation for surveying the Northern Pacific R.R. lines. In the House after the morning hour went forward with the Post Office Appropriation Bill on the amendment to increase the subsidy to the Pacific Mail Steamship Co. Made a short speech in its

[103] Lucius Fairchild (1831–1896) was governor of Wisconsin, 1866–72, and in the foreign service of the United States during the following decade.

[104] Samuel Chapman Armstrong (1839–1893), founder and head of the Hampton Normal and Agricultural Institute, was a friend of Garfield. When the war broke out he was at Williams College, living in the home of President Mark Hopkins; he joined the army and at the end of the war received the brevet rank of brigadier general. Successful with colored troops during the war, he became in 1866 an agent of the Freedmen's Bureau, and soon launched his plan for a school for Negroes. On this occasion he was eager to have the visiting dignitaries at the National Asylum pay his school a visit also, and received the help of Garfield in bringing it about.

[105] James Bryce, *The Holy Roman Empire* (1864). Burke Hinsdale had called it to Garfield's attention.

[106] Clarkson Nott Potter (1825–1882), a Democratic member of the House from New York, 1869–75 and 1877–79.

favor. Dined with Ward, Burchard,[107] Banks, Casserly[108] and Russell in the evening.

WEDNESDAY, 13. In the Committee commenced the discussion of Sundry Civil Bill. Heard Mr. Campbell [Kimball][109] of the Treasury Department on Life Saving Stations, Revenue Cutter Service, and Marine Hospital. In the House debate continued on Pacific Mail subsidies. Harber came this evening. Also Mr. Servis of Mahoning County. With him I called on Mr. Clagett,[110] the Delegate from Montana.

THURSDAY, 14. In Committee heard Admiral [Charles Stuart] Boggs and Major [George H.] Elliot on the Light House Board, its organization and work and the appropriations asked for to maintain it during the coming year. Also heard the Att'y General on the appropriations asked for in his Department. The House spent the day after the morning hour on the Saint Croix land grant. In the Senate after many days' debate, the Legislative and Judicial Appropriation Bill passed. As Chairman of the Conference Committee on the part of the House agreed to amendments to the Saint Louis Public Building Bill and reported it to the House where the report was sustained.

FRIDAY, 15. In the morning called on the President with Servis, Clagett, Ambler and Upson.[111] In Committee heard Gen'l [Willis]

---

107 Horatio Chapin Burchard (1825–1908), a Republican member of the House from Illinois, 1869–79.

108 Eugene Casserly (1820–1883) was a Democratic member of the Senate from California, 1869–73. In the text the name was correctly written, but someone, doubting its accuracy, drew a line through the last four letters and wrote above them "ady (?)."

109 Sumner Increase Kimball (1834–1923), organizer and for many years general superintendent of the U. S. Life Saving Service. He was chief of the Revenue Marine Division of the Treasury.

110 William Horace Clagett (1838–1901) was delegate from the Territory of Montana, 1871–73; a restless lawyer, he practiced over the years in a number of Western states and territories.

111 William Hanford Upson (1823–1910) was a Republican member of the House from Ohio, 1869–73. Garfield's friend, Francis G. Servis, of Canfield, Ohio, was seeking a federal judgeship in Montana Territory; accompanying him to the White House on this occasion were three Ohio

Drummond, Commissioner of the Gen'l Land Office, on appropriations for surveys of public lands. House spent nearly the whole day
on the Saint Croix Bill. Legislative and Judicial Appropriation Bill
came back from the Senate with ninety-three amendments. Had it
referred to the Committee and ordered to be printed.

SATURDAY, 16.   After working on correspondence until half-past ten
o'clock, went to the Treasury with a sub-committee of the Appropriation Committee, and spent three hours with the Light House Board
examining the estimates for the construction, repairs and maintenance
of light houses during the coming year. At two o'clock went to the
Smithsonian with the family to see [George] Catlin's Indian pictures. Also visited Prof. [Joseph] Henry in regard to the subject of
light houses.

SUNDAY, 17.   Tired out. Home all day. Snowed heavily.

MONDAY, 18.   In Committee heard Senator Hitchcock[112] from Nevada
[Nebraska] on Western surveys, and Gen'l Babcock[113] on public
buildings and grounds in Washington. The House consumed nearly
the whole day on the Senate bill to provide for the printing of the
Globe during the present Congress. Made a short speech criticising
the bill. House adjourned without action. In the evening visited Senator Sherman, met a number of members of the Ohio Legislature.

TUESDAY, 19.   In the morning before going to the Committee, went
with Governor Potts[114] of Montana, and Mr. Servis and some others

congressmen and the delegate from Montana. Garfield appears to have
been the most important influence in securing his appointment.

[112] Phineas Warren Hitchcock (1831–1881), delegate from Nebraska
Territory, 1865–67, Republican member of the U. S. Senate from Nebraska,
1871–77.

[113] Orville E. Babcock (1835–1884), secretary to President Grant and
superintending engineer of public buildings, grounds and works in Washington. In 1875 he was indicted by a grand jury in St. Louis for conspiring
(Whisky Ring scandal) to defraud the U. S. government, but, aided by a
desposition of the President, was acquitted.

[114] Benjamin Franklin Potts (1836–1887), of Ohio, Union officer in
the Civil War, lawyer and politician, was governor of the Territory of
Montana, 1870–83. There are more than forty letters from him to Garfield
in the Garfield Papers.

31

to the Att'y General's, asking for the appointment for Mr. Servis as U. S. Judge in Montana. In Committee heard Gen'l Walker[115] in regard to the new invention for tabulating census returns, which the inventor asks pay for. Then considered the Senate amendments to the Legislative Appropriation Bill. In the House after the morning hour the day was spent on the Pacific Mail subsidy. Home in the evening. Work as usual.

WEDNESDAY, 20.   In the morning visited the Agricultural Dep't with J. H. Robinson. In Committee heard the Delegates Clagett, McCormick[116] and Garfielde[117] in regards to surveys of Western lands. Continued examination of Senate amendments to Legislative Bill. In the House after the morning hour resumed the consideration of the Post Office Appropriation Bill, and at 4 o'clock, after voting on several amendments, the increase of Pacific Mail service was beaten by a vote of four. Finally the bill was reported to the House and passed. No amendment was made changing the amount of the appropriation. In the evening called with Servis on Foster[118] of Pennsylvania in regard to Servis' claim to the Pegg Estate in Philadelphia. I have been retained as his attorney in that case. Very cold weather today.

THURSDAY, 21.   In Committee concluded consideration of Senate amendments to Legislative [Bill]. In the House after the morning hour took up the Army Bill and general debate continued an hour and a half. Am studying up the subject of light houses, also of the fish culture. Every day shows new elements in the great interests and

---

[115] Francis Amasa Walker (1840–1897), educator, economist and statistician, was chief of the Bureau of Statistics, 1869–71, superintendent of the censuses of 1870 and 1880, and commissioner of Indian affairs, 1871–72.

[116] Richard Cunningham McCormick (1832–1901), journalist, politician and businessman, was secretary and governor of the Territory of Arizona before becoming delegate, a position which he held, 1869–75. He later returned to New York City, where he was born, and served one term as a Republican member of the House, 1895–97.

[117] Selucius Garfielde (1822–1881), delegate from the territory of Washington, 1869–73.

[118] Henry Donnel Foster (1808–1880), Pennsylvania lawyer, was a Democratic member of the House, 1843–47, and a Republican member, 1871–73.

forces that compose the Government of the United States. General Hazen[119] took dinner with us today. He has completed the manuscript of his book on the Franco-Prussian War, and it is now passing through the press. Mr. Hawley completed his pamphlet on salt.[120]

FRIDAY, 22. In the Committee heard Professor Baird,[121] Hon. Mr. Frye[122] of Maine and Mr. Page of N.J., on fish culture and the importance of Congress making an appropriation to aid it. In the House after the morning hour the Committee on the District of Columbia spent the whole day in an effort to grant 120,000 [square] feet of ground to a railroad company to bring their depot close up to Pennsylvania Avenue. The power of great corporations has never been more strikingly exhibited in the House than today. They had more than two-thirds of the House for passing the bill in manuscript, and thus blasting all the possibilities of a National Park from the Capitol to the President's House. I am greatly disheartened by the manifestations of the House on this subject.[123] Home in the evening.

[119] William Babcock Hazen (1830–1887), controversial army officer who, after observing the German army in the Franco-Prussian War, wrote *The School and the Army in Germany and France, with a Diary of the Siege Life at Versailles* (1872). As a result of service in the West he helped to expose War Department corruption and the exaggerated claims of railroads concerning Western lands. In 1880 Garfield, who had been his friend for a generation, secured from President Hayes his appointment as chief signal officer and promotion to the rank of brigadier general.

[120] Garfield's Detroit friend, Richard Hawley, who was associated with the production of salt in Goderich, Ontario, was now in Washington to present to the Committee of Ways and Means the case for free salt.

[121] Spencer Fullerton Baird (1823–1887), naturalist, assistant secretary of the Smithsonian Institution, 1850–78, secretary, 1878–87, performed outstanding service as unpaid head of the U. S. Commission of Fish and Fisheries, 1871–87.

[122] William Pierce Frye (1830–1911), Republican member of the House from Maine, 1871–81, U. S. senator, 1881–1911.

[123] The bill referred to was designed to confirm a grant made to the Baltimore and Potomac Railroad Company (an affiliate of the Pennsylvania Railroad) by the government of the District of Columbia. The new road was welcomed by many as a means of breaking the monopoly of the Baltimore and Ohio. The bill was passed promptly, becoming law in May, 1872. Garfield voted against it. The company laid its tracks on the Mall and

SATURDAY, 23. At 10 o'clock by previous arrangement Committee met at [the] Executive Mansion and with General Babcock proceeded to examine into the condition of the public buildings and grounds in Washington in view of making appropriations for their repair and protection. Passing down by Monument Square and Smithsonian, across the Mall to the Capitol, thence to Lincoln Park and Stanton Place, around by Vermont and Massachusetts Ave. and Franklin Square. Took a lunch at Welcker's. Then visited other reservations, making in all five hours' work. Home in the evening. Miss Booth came.

SUNDAY, 24. Attended church. Gen'l McDowell[124] and C. H. Hill[125] with us at tea in the evening.

MONDAY, 25. In Committee reviewed the estimates for public buildings and grounds around Washington and also the estimates of light houses. In the House another struggle over the location of a railroad depot, and some struggle over the order of business. Major [Charles H.] Hoyt of San Francisco and General McDowell called in the evening. Had a long conversation on Yerba Buena Island and was glad to find that there was much opposition to the bill in California.[126]

---

built on the site of the present National Gallery a Gothic stone depot which opened in 1873 and became a city landmark. This was the station in which Garfield was shot on July 2, 1881.

[124] Irvin McDowell (1818–1885), Union general in the Civil War, was a close friend of Garfield. From 1868 to 1872 he commanded the Department of the East; in the latter year he was promoted to major general and succeeded George C. Meade as commander of the South; from 1876 until his retirement in 1882 he served on the Pacific coast. Garfield's third son was named for him.

[125] Clement Hugh Hill (1836–1898) was assistant attorney general of the United States, 1870–75. He came to this country from England as a boy, graduated at Williams College with Garfield in 1856 and practiced law and journalism in Boston before going to Washington in 1870. From 1877, having inherited wealth, he lived a life of leisure, spending much of his time abroad. He was a friend of Francis Parkman and other notables in Boston.

[126] Desiring to extend its line to San Francisco, the Central Pacific Railroad Company first sought from the California legislature an eight mile

TUESDAY, 26. In Committee discussed further items of the Sundry Civil Bill. Heard Mr. Biggs[127] of Delaware on the light house appropriation for his state. House spent the whole day in filibustering on the proposition to grant part of the Public Park to a railroad company for a depot. Rainy dreary day. Home in the evening.

WEDNESDAY, 27. Called at the Pension Office to secure restoration of the pension of Widow Camps [Gans] at the request of General Schenck. In Committee heard Mr. Gallaudet[128] concerning the estimate for appropriation for the Columbia Institution for the Deaf and Dumb. Had a long and painful discussion of the Institution and its relations to the Government. In the House the whole day was wasted on the Depot question. The Senate still at work on the tariff. Meeting at the Smithsonian Institution in the evening. Went with the Committee at 11 o'clock to Gen'l Myer's[129] and examined his method of taking the reports of the weather and various signals used.

THURSDAY, 28. In Committee heard William Orton,[130] President of

---

strip along the San Francisco waterfront. Defeated in this attempt, it turned to Congress for help. The bill to which Garfield refers provided for the grant of half of Yerba Buena Island in San Francisco Bay to the railroad for a terminal. Aroused San Franciscans, fearing a Central Pacific monopoly, fought the measure vigorously and with success.. The company was able to achieve its objective by buying and linking with the Central Pacific two east bay railroads which owned trans-bay ferries. See Oscar Lewis, *The Big Four* (1938).

[127] Benjamin Thomas Biggs (1821–1893), Democratic member of the House from Delaware, 1869–73, governor of Delaware, 1887–91.

[128] Edward Miner Gallaudet (1837–1917) was head of the Columbia Institution for the Deaf and Dumb, incorporated by Congress in 1857. Its advanced division, National Deaf Mute College, became Gallaudet College in 1894. The school was supported by public and private funds. As a memorial to Garfield whose "support of the college in Congress had been so constant and so effective," a bust of Garfield by Daniel Chester French was unveiled in the College Chapel in 1883.

[129] Albert James Myer (1829–1880), soldier and signal officer, founded the Weather Bureau in 1870 and supervised it during its first decade; he was familiarly known as "Old Probabilities."

[130] William Orton (1826–1878) resigned in 1865 as commissioner of internal revenue to become president of the recently organized United States

the Western Union Telegraph Co., the Postmaster Gen'l, Gen'l Myer
and Solicitor Whiting[131] on the matters at issue between the Signal
Service Bureau and the Western Union Telegraph Company. A long
and interesting discussion, to be continued tomorrow. The House,
after further filibustering on the Depot question, took up the Steamboat Inspectors Bill, and made progress of fifty pages in its discussion.
I presided in the Chair for two hours. At seven o'clock met with the
Board of Regents,[132] but after waiting an hour and a half there was
no quorum. Senate passed the Tariff Bill with internal revenue clauses
added. No meeting of the House till Monday.

FRIDAY, 29.   House not in session today. The Committee sat nearly
four hours on the matter of difference between the Signal Service
Office and the Western Union Telegraph Company. The discussion
was very interesting and as the result of it I am almost led to the conclusion that the U. S. must ultimately take control of the telegraph, or
at least must have telegraph lines of its own. Whether the Post Routes
of the Constitution may not be a route consisting of a single wire

---

Telegraph Company. The following year he merged his company with
the Western Union Telegraph Company, of which Jeptha Wade of Cleveland was head. In 1867 the American Telegraph Company also joined
Western Union, and Orton became president of the enlarged company,
a position he held until his death. He frequently appeared before congressional committees in opposition to bills designed to put the government into
the telegraph business.

[131] William Whiting (1813–1873), noted Boston lawyer, was solicitor of
the War Department during the Civil War. In 1872 as assistant to the
attorney general he published *Certain Matters between the United States
and the Telegraph Companies upon the Construction of the Act Approved
July 4, 1866.*

[132] Garfield was appointed a member of the Board of Regents of the
Smithsonian Institution in 1865 and served until 1873; he was again
appointed in 1877 and served until 1880. With his inauguration as President of the United States he became *ex officio* the presiding officer of the
Institution. In 1880 Asa Gray, a regent, wrote to William J. Rhees of the
Smithsonian: "While one does not like to lose from our Board so old and
extremely useful and wise a member as General Garfield, it is a satisfaction
to know that one of the ablest and best friends of the Institution will be
in the Presidential chair." Quoted in a letter of Rhees to Garfield, December 29, 1880.

and have the lightning for its post rider is a grave question. At home in the evening, with many callers.

SATURDAY, 30. After working off letters, went with Mother, and Father and Mother Rudolph, Miss Booth and the two boys to the Naval Observatory and to Arlington. Home in the evening. Read up the subject of the transit of Venus.

SUNDAY, 31. At home with the children during the day. In the evening attended Dr. [Samuel S.] Mitchell's [Presbyterian] church, N. Y. Ave. and H. St.

April

MONDAY, 1. In Committee concluded the hearing of Solicitor Whiting and Mr. Orton on Signal Service and Telegraphy. In the House Washington Depot Bill was finally passed under a suspension of the rules by a two-thirds vote, to my great regret. In the evening attended the dinner of the ambassadors of Japan. Twenty-nine covers. Dinner lasted until near midnight. The more I know of that singular people the more I am interested in the curious problem of our future relations with them. Senators Cole and Hamlin,[133] and Representatives Banks, Brooks[134] and myself were there. The Vice President and more than half of the Cabinet were present.

TUESDAY, 2. In Committee considered further items in the [Sundry] Civil Bill. In the House had a long discussion on the right of the House to originate money bills, and the Senate's action on our bill, abolishing the duty on tea and coffee, was considered an infringement of their rights and laid on the table. I spoke. In the evening dined with Ward, Thurman, Anthony,[135] Burchard, Cox and several others.

[133] Hannibal Hamlin (1809–1891), of Maine, who had a political career as a Democrat before the formation of the Republican party, was vice president of the United States, 1861–65, and U. S. senator, 1869–81.

[134] George Merrick Brooks (1824–1893), Republican member of the House from Massachusetts, 1869–73, resigned to take a judicial position in Massachusetts.

[135] Henry Bowen Anthony (1815–1884), a Republican member of the Senate from Rhode Island, 1859–84.

WEDNESDAY, 3. In Committee continued work on Sundry Civil Bill. Finished portions relating to the construction of light houses, also Prof. Hayden's survey and several other items. In the House the day was spent on the Steamboat Inspection Bill, which was nearly finished at the time of adjournment. Had Judge Black and Prof. Newcomb[136] at dinner and discussed until a late hour the transit of Venus, and its value to science.

THURSDAY, 4. In Committee finished the consideration of surveys of public lands. In the House the Steamboat Inspectors Bill was finished, and the Shipping Commissioners Bill discussed during the remainder of the day.[137] Have been feeling quite ill all day. The result of overwork I think, and, what is unusual with me, my appetite has failed.

FRIDAY, 5. In Committee considered the estimates for appropriations for Rock Island arsenal. Heard Gen'l Benét,[138] Col. [Daniel W.] Flagler in command of Rock Island Arsenal and Mr. Hawley,[139] Representative from that District, on the subject. In the House, after the morning hour, finished general debate on the Military Appropriation Bill and run through the sections. I moved a new section to root out the old relic of barbarism from the army which permitted tattooing and branding the body of a soldier. The bill was reported to the House and passed and thus ends the legislative week. I am better today but still not well. Have not smoked for ten days. Called on Dr. McDonald.

SATURDAY, 6. After closing up a large amount of correspondence, went to the Post Office Department and thence to the Deaf and Dumb

136 Simon Newcomb (1835–1909), astronomer, was professor of mathematics in the U. S. Navy, 1861–97. The third transit of Venus known to have been observed occurred in 1874. Newcomb was involved in the preparations and observations relating to it, and Garfield supported congressional appropriations to make them possible.

137 A bill to authorize the appointment of shipping commissioners by federal circuit courts to superintend the shipping and discharge of seamen engaged on U. S. merchant ships.

138 Stephen Vincent Benét (1827–1895) was in the Ordnance Department; he did not attain the rank of brigadier general until 1874 when he became chief of the Department.

139 John Baldwin Hawley (1831–1895), a Republican member of the House from Illinois, 1869–75, assistant secretary of the treasury, 1877–80.

Asylum and to the Capitol. Correspondence again in the evening and then went visiting. Very tired.

SUNDAY, 7.   Attended church in the forenoon. Home during the rest of the day and evening. Prof. Henry spent the evening with me and explained his discoveries in connection with Morse's telegraph.[140]

MONDAY, 8.   In Committee finished the consideration of the different arsenals. In the House, after the morning hour, reported the River and Harbor Bill in the same shape as it was introduced by the Committee on Commerce, and had it referred to the Committee of the Whole. Later in the day introduced the Legislative, Executive and Judicial Bill, with the ninety-three Senate amendments. Recommended concurrence in twenty-nine and non-concurrence in fifty-nine and concurrence with an amendment of five others. Got half through the amendments when the Committee arose and the House adjourned.

TUESDAY, 9.   In Committee heard Dr. Ingalls[141] on the appropriations for the Asylum for the Insane, and also heard an officer of the Navy Department on appropriations for navy yards. In the House a bill

[140] Samuel F. B. Morse, the inventor of the telegraph, died on April 2, 1872. A memorial service in the hall of the House of Representatives was planned, at which Garfield was invited to speak. Knowing that there had been a rupture of relations between Morse and Garfield's friend Joseph Henry, whose experiments in the field of electromagnetism and assistance to Morse are part of the history of the telegraph, Garfield wrote to Henry before accepting the invitation. Indicating that he had not known the precise nature of the controversy between the two men, he wrote: "If you have suffered personal injustice at the hands of Prof. Morse, I will at once decline to have anything to do with the celebration; for however much I honor the genius and labors of Prof. Morse, I will give no countenance to anything that has directly or indirectly wronged you personally. Or if, by speaking, I might without violating the proprieties of the occasion, do justice to you as well as to Prof. Morse, it might induce me to accept the invitation." Letterbook, April 6, 1872. After the evening with Henry, Garfield undertook to write a speech for the Morse observance. A crude drawing made by Henry that evening to illustrate the nature of his own work in relation to the telegraph is preserved among the Garfield Papers.

[141] Charles H. Nichols, M.D., was superintendent of the Government Hospital for the Insane. Garfield's stenographer presumably misunderstood the name.

was passed to establish the postal card system. I proposed an amendment requiring a flap to cover the face of the writing, fearing lest the open card would offer an opportunity for libelous letters.

In the evening took dinner with Donn Piatt, Senators West[142] and Caldwell,[143] Messrs. Flaschman and Thompson.

WEDNESDAY, 10. In Committee heard [William] Saunders of the Agricultural Department and Dr. [James] Thompson of the Columbia Hospital and settled those two subjects in the Sundry Civil Bill, also the Rock Island arsenal question. In the House, after the morning hour, took up the Senate amendments to the Legislative Bill and went through from the 34th to the 90th, which last was the civil service appropriation, on which arose a brisk debate, I defending, many others assailing "Civil Service Reform." House adjourned without concluding the subject.

THURSDAY, 11. In Committee made further progress in the working up of the Sundry Civil Bill. Disposed of an appropriation for the Deaf and Dumb Asylum, also for Capitol extension. In the House, after the morning hour, took up the Senate amendments to the Legislative Bill. Continued the discussion of the civil service and saved a part of the appropriation after a hard fight. Committee of the Whole seemed disposed to buy the two squares on the East Front of the Capitol. A little after 5 o'clock the Committee rose and reported the bill to the House. After a struggle with a drunken Democrat who attempted to adjourn the House, succeeded in getting the previous question ordered, when on my motion House adjourned.

Called at Rose's[144] in the evening.

[142] Joseph Rodman West (1822–1898), a Republican member of the Senate from Louisiana, 1871–77.

[143] Alexander Caldwell (1830–1917), Kansas businessman, was a Republican member of the Senate, 1871–73.

[144] George U. Rose, a government clerk, served Garfield as part-time stenographer and secretary for about thirteen years before Garfield entered the White House. Much of the diary from 1872 is in his handwriting. He was bitterly disappointed because Garfield did not make him his private secretary when he became President. After Garfield's death, Rose, claiming that he had never been adequately compensated for his service, sought additional money from Mrs. Garfield; although she gave him something

FRIDAY, 12. In Committee discussed and adopted an appropriation of $15,000 for the Soldiers' Orphan Asylum, also heard the Supervising Architect of the Treasury on the public buildings now in progress. After the reading of the Journal in the House, took up the Senate amendments to the Legislative Bill; the debate was directed to the purchase of two squares east of the Capitol and to the Civil Service amendment. I made a speech of 15 minutes, at the end of the debate, reviewing the points that had been made against us and asserting the necessity of civil service reform in some way. The exhibition in the House on the subject is itself the most striking commentary on the wretched tone of public feeling in regard to civil service. After a long struggle the bill passed.

SATURDAY, 13. Worked up my correspondence and made some studies preparatory to a speech on the life and services of Prof. Morse. At two o'clock met with the Committee at the room of the Supervising Architect in the Treasury, and went thence to visit the new State Department building with a view to making an appropriation for the coming year.[145] Home in the evening. The Committee of Ways and Means badly broken up in regard to the Tariff Bill, and some regrets are being expressed that a different slate was not made.[146]

SUNDAY, 14. Attended church in the forenoon, drove out with Mr. S. S. Sumner[147] in the afternoon. Home in the evening.

MONDAY, 15. In Committee determined the appropriations to be

---

more she refused to concede that his claims were just. Rose's only daughter was born in the Garfield house in Washington in January, 1881, and was named for Mrs. Garfield.

[145] The State, War and Navy Building, adjacent to the White House, was then under construction; it was designed by Alfred B. Mullett (1834–1890), the supervising architect of the Treasury. It is now given over to executive offices.

[146] Speaker of the House James G. Blaine had appointed a Committee of Ways and Means with Henry L. Dawes of Massachusetts, a strong protectionist, as chairman, but with a committee majority leaning towards tariff reform. Dawes refused to support the bill prepared by his committee.

[147] Samuel S. Sumner, a clerk in the Treasury Department with whose family the Garfields were on friendly terms; he sometimes looked after their house in their absence.

granted for the public buildings and also finished consideration of appropriations for light houses. Also an appropriation to provide against spoilation of timber on public lands. In the House, after the morning hour, took up the River and Harbor Bill put in charge of Mr. Sawyer[148] of Wisconsin, and at half-past four o'clock finished its consideration and passed it. This is the 9th of the 12 regular bills that have passed the House. In the evening, at home preparing an address on the life and services of Prof. Morse. I am greatly troubled with the relative merits of Professors Morse and Henry.

TUESDAY, 16. In Committee considered the appropriation for continuing Major Powell's[149] exploration of the Colorado River. Heard a statement from the Major in regard to his work. Also heard the Chief of the Metropolitan Police on the appropriation for that service. The work of the House was full of miscellany. Introduction of the Tariff Bill. Contest between the Speaker and Gen'l Beatty[150] of Ohio on the rights of the Committee on Printing. Adjourned at three o'clock. In the evening Morse memorial meeting in the Hall of the House. One senator and five members made addresses. I spoke and attempted to do justice to the discoverers who had preceded Morse. Not well satisfied with my effort. Meeting was an immense one.

WEDNESDAY, 17. In Committee considered further items of the

[148] Philetus Sawyer (1816–1900), a Republican member of the House from Wisconsin, 1865–75, and of the Senate, 1881–93.

[149] John Wesley Powell (1834–1902), geologist, explorer and administrator, won fame in 1869 by leading an expedition financed by Congress and the Smithsonian down the Colorado River through the Grand Canyon; he afterwards made further explorations in the region. He was director of the Second Division of the U. S. Geological and Geographical Survey of the Territories (known from 1877 as the Survey of the Rocky Mountain Region), 1875–79. Instrumental with the strong support of Garfield in getting the various western surveys consolidated into the U. S. Geological Survey in 1879, he served as its director, 1880–94.

[150] John C. Beatty (1828–1914), a brigadier general in the Civil War, was a Republican member of the House from Ohio, 1868–73, and a banker in Columbus for thirty years thereafter. In 1879 he published his Civil War diary under the title *The Citizen Soldier*. He is not to be confused with John C. Beatty, Ravenna merchant, postmaster, and Portage County treasurer, who was one of Garfield's active political supporters.

Sundry Civil Bill in connection with expenses for the public buildings. In the House, after the morning hour, took up and passed the appropriation bill for the Military Academy. This is the tenth of our twelve regular bills. Mrs. Garfield and I took dinner at Gen'l Myer's, with his family, Mr. and Mrs. Williams, Mr. and Mrs. Paine and some others.

THURSDAY, 18. Committee considered further items in the Sundry Civil Bill, but did not finish it. Heard Prof. Hilgard[151] concerning appropriations for the Coast Survey, and Mr. Mullett in regard to new public buildings. In the House, after the morning hour, further discussion of the civil service. In the evening, with Mrs. Garfield and Mrs. Choate, took dinner with Mrs. Chipman. Large company present. In company with Aaron F. Perry,[152] called on the President and urged him to speak decisively to his special champions in Congress in favor of Civil Service Reform so that they might not represent him as covertly opposed to the policy he officially advocates.

FRIDAY, 19. In Committee considered further items of the Sundry Civil Bill. In the House, debate on the Civil Service Reform concluded. I made a speech of twenty minutes in reply to Butler's speech of yesterday, in which I reviewed his assumption that the President was opposed to this measure. I tried to show that the President was wholly in earnest in this matter. A point of order was made upon me against my repeating any expressions of the President's. The point was no doubt correctly made. But I think it was no worse to represent him correctly, than to misrepresent him, as Butler has done. Dined with Piatt and G. Q. Cannon,[153] a Mormon apostle.

SATURDAY, 20. At ten o'clock, met in conference on the disagreeing votes of the two houses on the Legislative Appropriation Bill. Con-

---

[151] Julius Erasmus Hilgard (1825–1891), a scientist long associated with the U. S. Coast Survey; he was superintendent, 1881–85. In 1872 he was the American delegate to an international convention in Paris concerned with forming the International Bureau of Weights and Measures.

[152] Aaron Fyfe Perry (1815–1893), a Republican member of the House from Ohio, 1871–72.

[153] George Quayle Cannon (1827–1901) was in Washington in behalf of statehood for the Territory of Utah; he was the Territory's delegate in Congress, 1873–81.

ferees on the part of the Senate, Senators Cole, Morrill of Vermont, and Sawyer.[154] Conferees with me on the part of the House, Clark[155] and Niblack. After four hours' session, concluded the conference satisfactorily. Home in the evening.

SUNDAY, 21. At home all day, not well. In the evening, read "Oenone."

MONDAY, 22. In Committee took up Mr. Palmer's[156] bill for postal telegraph service and heard Mr. Hubbard of Massachusetts during the hour in defense of the measure. I am inclined to believe that some way or other the Government must take charge of the telegraph lines.[157] In the House nearly all day was occupied on an election case. Met with Committee on Rules and agreed to report a more stringent rule in regard to ex-members of Congress enjoying the privileges of the floor. It was reported by Cox of N.Y. but met with some opposition, and was recommitted. If I ever return to Washington as a lobbyist after I leave Congress, I hope some friend will shoot me.

[154] Frederick Adolphus Sawyer (1822–1891), a Republican member of the Senate from South Carolina, 1868–73.

[155] William Thomas Clark (1831–1905), a Republican member of the House from Texas, 1870–72; his election was contested and he lost his seat in May.

[156] Francis Wayland Palmer (1827–1907), a Republican member of the House from Iowa, 1869–73, postmaster of Chicago, 1877–85, public printer of the United States, 1889–94, 1897–1905. During his lifetime he was associated with a number of newspapers, including the Chicago *Inter Ocean.*

[157] After a generation of the telegraph, the transmission of telegraphic messages was in the hands of private corporations, the most powerful of which was the Western Union Telegraph Company. In the interest of bringing about greater use of the telegraph at lower rates and with improved service two major proposals had been put forward. One plan (referred to by Garfield as the Washburn plan) involved government ownership and operation of the telegraph lines of the nation as part of the postal system. The other involved the chartering of a new corporation by Congress, the Postal Telegraph Company, which would serve the country under contract with the Post Office Department, using the facilities of the postal system, and at rates set by Congress. Gardiner Greene Hubbard and numerous others were to be the incorporators. Western Union, of course, did not favor either proposal.

TUESDAY, 23. In Committee continued the hearing on the subject of postal telegraphy. Mr. Lines[158] spoke in favor of the Washburn plan and against that of Mr. Hubbard. Mr. Prescott[159] of the Western Union Telegraph spoke against the Hubbard Bill and against the Washburn Bill also. In the House miscellaneous business.

I am opposed to allowing the Government to take charge of the telegraphs. 1st, because it would too greatly increase the centralizing tendency. 2nd, because the evils of our present civil service would be greatly aggravated. 3rd, because this class of business can be better done by private enterprise. But I think we must find some method of utilizing telegraphs for postal purposes.

WEDNESDAY, 24. In Committee considered subject of new public buildings. Ordered appropriations for Cincinnati, Indianapolis, Hartford, Albany. Senate recommitted Conference Report because new matter had been introduced, namely, Judge of Supreme Court of the District of Columbia, in addition to other judges. That is a close and an unusual one.[160] In the evening dined with Clarkson Potter and his friends, Bingham,[161] Poland,[162] Eldredge, Beck, Scofield,[163] and a

---

[158] R. B. Lines, a government clerk who had been gathering statistical data relative to the controversy over the telegraph system.

[159] George Bartlett Prescott (1830–1894), an engineer with the Western Union Telegraph Company, was for a decade after 1869 the company's expert witness before congressional committees. It has been said that he "probably did more than any other single individual to prevent the proposed acquisition of the telegraph by the government." *Dictionary of American Biography*, Vol. 15, p. 194.

[160] The Senate had been more generous in respect to salary increases than the House; the conference reached a compromise increasing the salaries of fewer officials, but including judges of the Supreme Court of the District of Columbia, who had not been specifically included in the bill before the Conference Committee. The bill was sent back to the committee by the Senate on the ground that new matter had been introduced in conference. The bill finally agreed on did not provide for these judges.

[161] John A. Bingham (1815–1900), Republican member of the House from Ohio, 1885–63, 1865–73, minister to Japan, 1873–85.

[162] Luke Potter Poland (1815–1887), of Vermont, who served on the Supreme Court of his state, 1848–65, was a Republican member of the

gent from N.Y. Singular unanimity of opinion concerning a certain prominent member of the House.

THURSDAY, 25.   In Committee considered Freedmen's Bureau appropriations, also Senate amendments to Indian Appropriation Bill. Conference Committee reassembled, sat for an hour, but failed to agree. In the House the case of Dr. Houard, a Cuban prisoner, was discussed.[164] Towards evening, Committee spent another hour on Conference Report. Partly agreed to report. Dined at Wormley's[165] with Mr. Hooper of Mass. and Senators Morton,[166] Chandler,[167] Howe,[168] and Hamlin, Representatives Blaine, Peters,[169] Dawes, and Butler. At

---

Senate, 1865–67, and of the House, 1867–75, 1883–85. He was chairman of the House committee which in 1873 investigated Credit Mobilier.

[163] Glenni William Scofield (1817–1891), a Republican member of the House from Pennsylvania, 1863–75, register of the Treasury, 1878–81, associate justice of the U. S. Court of Claims, 1881–91.

[164] Dr. John Emilio Houard, an American citizen who had lived in Cuba most of his life, had had his property confiscated and had been sent to a penal colony after trial and conviction by Spanish authorities on the charge of giving aid and comfort to Cuban insurrectionaries. The House passed a resolution indicating that in its opinion the President should demand his release and the restoration of his property, unless it appeared on investigation that he had been properly tried, and that privileges secured to American citizens by treaty with Spain had not been denied or disregarded.

[165] Wormley's Hotel, at the southwest corner of Fifteenth and H streets, was opened in 1871 by James Wormley, a Negro, who had been in the hotel and catering business in Washington for a number of years; it became one of the most famous of the city's hostelries.

[166] Oliver P. Morton (1823–1877), Civil War governor of Indiana, was a Republican member of the Senate, 1867–77.

[167] Zachariah Chandler (1813–1879), a founder of the Republican party, was senator from Michigan, 1857–75, 1879, and secretary of the interior, 1875–77. In 1868 and 1876 he was the chairman of the Republican National Executive Committee. Garfield delivered a tribute to him in the House on January 28, 1880. "As a political force," he declared, "Mr. Chandler may be classed among the Titanic figures of history."

[168] Timothy Otis Howe (1816–1883), a Republican member of the Senate from Wisconsin, 1861–79, postmaster general, 1882–83.

[169] John Andrew Peters (1822–1904), a Republican member of the House from Maine, 1867–73, judge of the Supreme Judicial Court of Maine, 1873–83, chief justice, 1883–1900.

ten o'clock went with Crete and Julia to Senator [William] Sprague's. The broken health of the venerable Chief Justice presents a strange contrast to the great finance minister, as I knew him when I was his guest in the same house ten years ago.[170]

FRIDAY, 26. In Committee considered appropriations for surveys on the northern lakes, also for explorations of western territories under War Department. Sat again in Committee of Conference on the Legislative Bill and came to agreement. After a long struggle on question of final adjournment, House went into Committee of the Whole on the Tariff Bill and Finkelnburg[171] made an able speech. At half-past four o'clock I made the Conference Report on the Legislative Bill, the Senate having agreed to it. Home in the evening thoroughly tired out.

SATURDAY, 27. Correspondence in the morning. Committee did not meet. In the House discussion of the Tariff Bill. In the evening dined with W. C[W]. MacFarland of N.Y., also Peters and Ward. Cincinnati Convention looms up formidably.[172] Was there ever so strange

[170] Garfield was the guest of Salmon P. Chase for about six weeks of the period he spent in Washington (September, 1862-January, 1863) awaiting a field assignment in the army. On November 13, twelve days before his appointment to the Fitz John Porter court-martial, he left Chase's home and roomed at 119 Pennsylvania Avenue until he departed the capital on orders assigning him to the Army of the Cumberland. Chase at the time was secretary of the treasury. His daughter Kate, who later married Senator William Sprague of Rhode Island, was then the belle of Washington society.

[171] Gustavus Adolphus Finkelnburg (1837–1908), a member of the House from Missouri, 1869–73, first elected as a Republican and then as a Liberal Republican. Since Henry L. Dawes, chairman of the Committee on Ways and Means, refused to defend the tariff bill of the committee, Finkelnburg assumed the responsibility of doing so.

[172] During Grant's first administration strong opposition developed within the Republican Party to the southern, tariff, and civil service policies of the administration. On May 1, 1872, the Liberal Republican movement was launched nationally at Cincinnati. The platform adopted was a liberal document favoring racial equality before the law, Negro suffrage, the supremacy of the civil over the military, civil service reform, a return to specie payment, and the end of land grants to railroads and other corporations. For President the new party passed over Charles Francis Adams and Lyman Trumbull, either of whom might have been a real threat to Grant,

a freak in the history of politics! The platform is one of the most striking and, in some respects, the most admirable political declarations I have known. But the nomination is so at variance with the spirit of the platform. The movement was a revolution but the revolution has revolted. The result is obscured by clouds.

SUNDAY, 28. Church in the forenoon. In the afternoon drove wtih the family to Soldiers' Home and back through Glenwood.

MONDAY, 29. In Committee considered the Senate bill appropriating $110,000 for the Reform School. Heard statements of the Trustees and recommendations of the Committee on the District of Columbia. In the House, after the morning hour, debated the Report of the Conference Committee on the Legislative Bill, and after a sharp struggle House divided and reported [rejected] by a vote of 81 to 80 the clause empowering the Sec'y of the Treasury to employ agents to recover concealed and unpaid taxes, for contingent fees. This opposed the informer and moiety system, in which I concur, but was anxious to save the report. House recommitted the Report to the same Conference Committee. Home in the evening with a severe headache.

TUESDAY, 30. In Committee heard Mr. Poland of Vermont on the bill for the Reform School and his proposed amendments thereto. At half-past eleven Conference on the part of the House went to the President's Room in the Senate and met Senate Conference on the Legislative Bill, and after an hour's interview reached no conclusion. House consumed the day on the tariff debate. In the evening at half-past 6 went to dinner given to the Committee on Appropriations by Mr. Sargent of California. Speaker Blaine and all the members of the Committee present, except Messrs. Swann and Marshall.[173] A good dinner. Sat late, and the party told ghost stories for nearly the whole of the last hour. Sargent said that when he was going home one night in Newburyport, when he was courting his wife, a heavy

---

and nominated Horace Greeley, editor of the *New York Tribune,* who had long been a leading protectionist, and who would scarcely arouse the enthusiasm of the Democrats, whose support was necessary for success.

The original entry for April 27, in the handwriting of Garfield's secretary, ended at this point. Some time later, after the results of the Cincinnati Convention were known, Garfield himself added the commentary.

[173] Samuel Scott Marshall (1821–1890), Democratic member of the House from Illinois, 1855–59, 1865–75.

shower of rain came up and a man suddenly appeared beside him with a large umbrella which he held over their heads and walked two squares with him. Sargent heard the rain patter on the umbrella but on reaching out his arm it passed directly through the substance of the man beside him, without resistance. At the end of the two squares the apparition vanished.

May

WEDNESDAY, 1.   In Committee made further progress with the Sundry Civil Bill. In the House, debate on the tariff continued. House met in the evening on reports from the territories. Committee on Appropriations met at 8 o'clock and sat until 11 o'clock on the Hubbard Postal Telegraph Bill, went over half the bill making amendments. I begin to think it will be best to report the bill to the House and let it draw the fire of public opinion during the coming recess. It may pioneer the way to a solution of the difficult problem to which it relates.

THURSDAY, 2.   In Committee finished consideration of Reform School Bill and made additions to the Sundry Civil Bill. Concluded to transfer the Freedmen's Bureau to the War Department.[174] Conference on the Legislative Bill, came to an agreement on Conference report. After sitting in the House three hours Committee on Appropriations met and spent an hour and a half on Postal Telegraph Bill and ordered it reported to the House and recommitted. In the evening dined with Messrs. Ward and Craig[175] of N.Y. and following members of the House: Kerr, Slocum,[176] Dickey,[177] Cox. Some of the best men socially in the Congress are political adversaries.

[174] The Sundry Civil Act of 1872 provided for the discontinuance of the Bureau of Refugees, Freedmen and Abandoned Lands but made the secretary of war (in whose Department the Bureau was located) responsible for carrying on certain of its functions.

[175] Probably Daniel H. Craig (1814–1895), one-time journalist and associate of Ezra Cornell in the development of telegraphic facilities, author of several pamphlets on telegraphy.

[176] Henry Warner Slocum (1827–1894), a Democratic member of the House from New York, 1869–73, 1883–85.

[177] Oliver James Dickey (1823–1876), a Republican member of the House from Pennsylvania, 1868–73.

FRIDAY, 3. In Committee made further progress. Heard the Board of Public Works in the District on their request for appropriations. In the House, after the close of the tariff debate, introduced and carried Conference Report on the Legislative Appropriation Bill. Thus ends a hard fight. The nomination of Greeley at the Cincinnati Convention was a surprise to members of the House. It appears tonight as though it insures a regular Democratic nomination. I am puzzled to know why the Convention made that choice but I recognize the fact that none of us can estimate the strength of the nomination tonight without further reflection and knowledge of facts.

SATURDAY, 4. House not in session today. After finishing correspondence in the morning, went to the Assessor of Internal Revenue and swore to my income statement for last year and forwarded the same to the Assessor at Ravenna.[178] Also called at the Post Office Department on business. Then went to the Committee Room and Congressional Library[179] and worked until four o'clock. Home in the evening, very tired. Harry, Mollie and Irvin[180] very sick with the measles.

---

[178] A letter from Garfield accompanying his statement gives full information concerning his income for 1871:

Congressional salary	$5,000.00
Law fees	600.00
Interest on notes	182.00
Rents	24.00
Coupons on U. S. bonds	51.00
Gross income	$5,857.00

Exemption	$2,000.00	
Deductions:		
Taxes	141.61	
Repairs	263.00	
Interest on notes	295.62	2,700.23
Taxable income		3,156.77

To F. W. Coffin, letterbook, May 4, 1872. Although Garfield did not indicate it in this letter, the tax on this amount was $78.92 (2½% of the net income). No further federal income tax was levied in his lifetime.

[179] The Library of Congress was then housed in the center of the west front of the Capitol.

[180] Irvin McDowell Garfield (1870–1951), Garfield's third son, named for General Irvin McDowell, was born in Washington, D. C., attended

Have spent much of the evening in reading up the history of the Ballou family. I have traced it back to Maturin Ballou, who appeared in Rhode Island as early as 1646.

SUNDAY, 5. At home all day. Children still sick with the measles. *Alabama* Claims still in doubt.[181]

MONDAY, 6. In Committee reviewed the 64 Senate amendments to the Deficiency Bill. The Committee continued its session until near one o'clock. Ordered the bill reported to the House. At two the House considered these amendments of the Committee. Recommended the adoption of them to the 61st, when the House adjourned. Eight hour clause occasioned long debate. I expressed the opinion that the eight hour movement had been a blunder from the first and unwarrantable interference with the rights of the laborers.

St. Paul's School in Concord, New Hampshire, graduated at Williams College in 1896, and joined the Boston law firm of Procter and Warren, of whose successor, Warren and Garfield, he became head. In 1906 he married Susan Emmons of Boston.

[181] During the Civil War several ships, notably the *Alabama*, had been built, armed, or manned for the Confederacy in Britain or in British possessions, and had gone forth to prey on Union shipping. In the treaty of Washington (1871) the United States and Great Britain agreed to the establishment of a Tribunal of Arbitration at Geneva to pass on American claims for damages. The American Case included not only claims for direct damages done by the ships in question, but also for indirect ("consequential") damages as well—the most important of the latter claims being for compensation because the war had been prolonged by the activities of the Confederate ships. The British strongly objected to the inclusion of such claims and for several months the whole arbitration was threatened. Finally the British government proposed that a new provision be added to the treaty in which both powers would agree never in the future to make a claim for consequential damages against the other and the United States would agree to drop its indirect claims. Grant, eager for settlement, asked the Senate for advice. The Senate voted approval of the proposed addition to the treaty with some modifications unacceptable to Great Britain. Fortunately, on June 19, a solution was reached at Geneva. The Tribunal gave in effect an advisory opinion that these claims for indirect damages did not constitute in international law "good foundation for an award of compensation or computation of damages between nations." The United States accepted this statement. See Allan Nevins, *Hamilton Fish, the Inner History of the Grant Administration*, 2 vols., Revised Edition (1957).

TUESDAY, 7.   Went to the Treasury Department with General Banks to get Mrs. Reed[182] promoted. In Committee considered some amendments to the Deficiency Bill and others to the Sundry Civil Bill. In the House fought the battle against the Morrill amendment, and was successful. I do not believe in perpetuating forever the word "rebel" in our politics and making it the basis of robbery on the part of the Government.[183] Finished Deficiency Bill and asked for a Conference Committee. Also took up and finished Indian Appropriation Bill and asked for a conference. Curious fight on the tariff. Kelley undertook to trade off the tax on tobacco for the support of the free traders to help him kill the tariff bill. He failed at the last moment for want of parliamentary tact. Had he moved the previous question on his motion to recommit with instructions, it would have been successful. As it was Dawes won it from him. Attended evening session.

WEDNESDAY, 8.   In Committee considered Senate amendments to the Naval Appropriation Bill and ordered them reported to the House. Also made further progress in the Sundry Civil Bill. The whole day consumed in the tariff debate. I spoke a few moments in favor of reducing the duty on salt. Mr. Dawes remarked to me today that he felt grieved when he saw such men as Banks, Scofield and some others he named, capable of great things, and by indolence or other causes, accomplish so little, when mediocre men by industry could become leaders. Took dinner with MacFarland of N.Y. with several senators and members. Evening session on military matters. Home at ¼ to 11 o'clock.

THURSDAY, 9.   In Committee finished preparation of the Sundry Civil

---

182 Emily Reed, a friend of the Garfield family, was often referred to as "Aunt Em." Over the years Garfield helped her on more than one occasion in connection with her employment as a government clerk.

183 Numerous claims were filed against the government for property confiscated during and after the war. The Supreme Court opened the door to certain claims regardless of whether the claimant had been loyal to the Union. The amendment proposed by Senator Justin Smith Morrill was designed to limit the jurisdiction of the Court of Claims to cases in which it was established that the owners never gave aid or comfort to the Confederacy. The substitute for the amendment which was adopted authorized the Treasury to settle certain cotton claims; the issue of loyalty was not introduced.

Bill and ordered it reported to the House. After the morning hour, reported it to the House. Had it set for Tuesday morning next. Spent two hours with the Senate conference on the Deficiency Bill. After the tariff discussion closed, reported to the House and passed the Reform School Bill. Dined at Mr. Hooper's of Mass. at 6 o'clock with 6 ladies, no gentlemen being present but myself. Mr. Hooper was too ill to come down stairs. The ladies were Mrs. Hooper and her daughter, Mrs. Senator Conkling, and three Boston ladies, relatives of the Hoopers, I believe.

FRIDAY, 10. In Committee considered the claim of Dempsey and O'Toole on the Post Office Dep't and recommended an appropriation of $29,000.[184] In the House after the morning hour, passed the Fortification Appropriation Bill, the eleventh of our regular bills. At 2 o'clock went to the Senate and held a further conference on the Deficiency Bill and staid until five o'clock without concluding the conference. At half-past six dined with ex-Governor Swann of Md., who gave a dinner to the Committee. There were present all the members of the Appropriation Committee, the clerk, Col. [Robert] Stevens, and Gen'l Babcock, private sec'y to the President.

SATURDAY, 11. Called on Judge Black at the Arlington, had an interesting visit. Committee did not meet. House continued discussion of the Tariff Bill. Made slow progress. From three to five o'clock P.M. sat in conference on the Deficiency Bill. Have nearly concluded to report. The Senate Conference gave way on the Morrill amendment and adopted the House amendment to pay for private property taken unlawfully. I am glad to have foiled this attempt to project the word rebel forward into the indefinite future. The nation cannot prosper with stolen money in its Treasury.

SUNDAY, 12. At home all day trying to rest, and reading a little.

MONDAY, 13. In Committee finished the consideration of the Hubbard Postal Telegraph Bill and authorized Mr. Palmer to report to the House for passage. I consent to this bill with some misgivings. Finished the conference on the Deficiency Bill, having arranged for killing the Morrill amendment and carrying the House amendment

---

[184] This appropriation was to satisfy the claim of the firm of Dempsey and O'Toole for loss caused by the annulment of a contract with the Post Office Department for furnishing stamped envelopes and newspaper wrappers.

which I offered in its place. Voorhees[185] made an assault on Greeley for the Presidency which was able but imprudent. It offended many of his associates and the last paragraphs subjected him to the charge of making it in Grant's interest. Dined with Speaker at ½ past six.

TUESDAY, 14. In Committee considered the Military Academy Bill and ordered bill to be reported back to the House. Also ordered several items added to the Sundry Civil Bill. In the House acted on the Senate amendments to the Naval Bill and asked for a Committee of Conference on the disagreements. The tariff dragged its slow length along with but little progress. Drs. Robison and Streator dined with me in the evening. Evening session on business of the Judiciary Committee. Home at 11 o'clock. Streator and Robison are here to secure the pardon of G. W. N. Yost, who has been convicted of perjury and sentenced to the penetentiary for two years. Cause, patent business.

WEDNESDAY, 15. In Committee considered amendments to the Post Office Appropriation Bill. In the House acted on sundry amendments to the Military Academy and Diplomatic Bills. Rest of the day spent on the tariff.

The pendency of the presidential election, and the nomination of Mr. Greeley by the convention called in the interest of Revenue Reform, have greatly unsettled the opinions of men in regard to the tariff. It is difficult to get a quorum to vote on many questions that arise in the course of debate. It is becoming apparent that men act on the tariff mainly as local interest requires and without a general, consistent principle.

THURSDAY, 16. In Committee heard Messrs. Garrison[186] and Davidge in favor of a subsidy to the Brazilian line of steamers. At the close of the hour the Committee resolved to report in favor of that subject and so the Post Office Bill was ordered reported back to the House. All day in the House spent in slow progress on the tariff. I made a short speech supporting an amendment which I offered in

[185] Daniel Wolsey Voorhees (1827–1897), a Democratic member of the House from Indiana, 1861–66, 1869–73, U. S. senator, 1877–97.

[186] Cornelius Kingsland Garrison (1809–1885), New York financier with large shipping interests, initiated a steamship service between New York City and Brazil.

favor of free books in foreign languages and free English books 20 years old. The amendment was adopted, but I fear the last clause may be too broad and will be assailed by the book manufacturers.

FRIDAY, 17. In Committee heard Mr. Brisbane[187] on his scheme for a pneumatic railway. The Committee were so far satisfied as to resolve to appropriate $15,000 to try the experiment between the Capitol and the Public Printing House. We run some risks of being laughed out of the House, but remembering the example of the appropriation for Morse I shall take the risk, believing that this will develop into a great invention. In the House carried the Conference on the Naval Appropriation Bill and thus finished that work. Rest of the day spent on the tariff, which is to be only a patch-work bill, with no great step toward reform.

SATURDAY, 18. Committee did not meet this morning. The House spent the day mainly on claims. My Committee carried through the conferences on the Diplomatic and Indian bills. Drs. Robison and Streator left this evening having secured Yost's pardon. At home in the evening but desperately tired. It looks now as though our session would be much longer than we thought it would be a few days since. The Senate is struggling over the proposed additional clause to the *Alabama* Treaty, and also over the attempt to continue the suspension of the Habeas Corpus.[188] This last I oppose but I am in favor of withdrawing our absurd claim for consequential damages.

SUNDAY, 19. Attended the New York Avenue church with Crete and Julia Choate, and heard [William H.] Roberts, a young Welshman, late clerk in the Congressional Library, preach.

---

[187] Albert Brisbane (1809–1890), best known as a social reformer, hoped to revolutionize transportation by means of hollow spheres propelled in pneumatic tubes. The experiment in constructing a tube from the Capitol to the Public Printing Office on North Capitol and H streets, which he was able to undertake because of Garfield's support, was not successful.

[188] An act of Congress of April, 1871, known as the Ku Klux Act since it resulted from disturbances in the South, authorized the President for a limited period to suspend under certain circumstances the privilege of the writ of habeas corpus. The bill which passed the Senate and which Garfield helped to defeat in the House provided for the continuance of this authorization until the end of the next session of Congress.

MONDAY, 20. Called at the Land Office on business. Thence to the Committee, where we considered miscellaneous items. In the House, Mr. Dawes moved to reopen discussion on the tariff for an hour. I resisted and suggested that the rules had better be suspended and the bill passed. After a little while Mr. Dawes adopted that suggestion and tried the motion, and the bill was passed under a suspension of the rules. We then passed the Senate resolution to adjourn on the 29th inst. After some other business, I took up the Sundry Civil Bill and finished nine pages. House met in the evening on the foreign affairs.

TUESDAY, 21. In Committee heard the Sec'y of the Navy on the appropriation for League Island; also considered several other items to be put in the Sundry Civil Bill. In the House after the reading of the Journal, took up and acted on the Senate amendments to the Post Office Bill, occupying three hours. The chief points of interest were the subsidies to Japanese and Brazilian steamship lines. The former was adopted by a large majority and the latter failed through the folly of the pig iron men in attempting to force iron ships on the line. Spent an hour and a half on the Sundry Civil Bill and made considerable progress. Had an unpleasant debate with Farnsworth on the Supervising Architect of the Treasury.[189]

WEDNESDAY, 22. Committee considered and concluded the consideration of the Senate amendments to the Army Bill.

THURSDAY, 23. In Committee added a few remaining items to the Sundry Civil Bill, and as soon as the Journal was read in the House, took the floor. Discussion continued without interruption on the Sundry Civil Bill until ¼ past five, when the Committee rose

[189] Representative Farnsworth of Illinois, a severe critic of A. B. Mullett, supervising architect of the Treasury, for what he considered unjustified and even corrupt practices, sought to impose additional restrictions on the expenditures of money for public buildings appropriated under the Sundry Civil Bill under discussion. The next day Garfield introduced a resolution to inform the secretary of the treasury of Farnsworth's charges and request him to investigate them and to take appropriate action. Farnsworth proposed an amendment to this to request the secretary of the treasury to report to the House specific answers to the charges made by him. The amended resolution was passed.

and reported the bill and under a suspension of the rules was put on its passage. It was carried by a ⅔ majority. Got in Brisbane's pneumatic experiment. The day has been a hard one, and I must have spoken forty times. Managed to keep my temper though there were many annoyances, and I believe I held control of the House better than ever before. In the evening House met on business of the Naval Committee.

FRIDAY, 24. Committee did not meet. In the House acted on the Senate amendments to the Army Appropriation Bill, most of the recommendations of the Committee being adopted. Conference Committee on the Post Office Appropriation Bill. Made a partial report covering the whole subject, except the subsidy to Brazil. The report was adopted and the Brazilian clause brought under discussion. Not completed. In the evening Committee on Claims had the floor. Continued until ¼ past 11, passing the bills with such rapidity that about seventy were got through. A contest having arisen over one resulted in ill feeling and a call of the House and the session continued until 8 o'clock the following morning. I am greatly distressed at the growing tendency to extravagant appropriations and the admission of dangerous and doubtful claims. House adjourned until Monday.

SATURDAY, 25. Saturday went to bed at ½ past nine o'clock in the morning and slept until half-past two. House did not meet. At three o'clock went to the Capitol. Sat with the Senate Committee on Appropriations while they examined Sundry Civil Bill. In the evening visited Mr. Brisbane. Mrs. Chorpening [Chorpenning] was there and claimed to be a medium under the control of the spirit of a little Indian girl. In that state she told me many things about my past life and prophesied extravagantly of what my future is to be. I pay no heed to these predictions, but the manifestations are very wonderful. Somewhere in that direction is a great series of truth yet to be developed but what and how, who knows?

SUNDAY, 26. Attended church. Bartholomew[190] spoke on the glory

---

[190] Othniel A. Bartholomew (b.1837) was pastor of the Disciples of Christ Church on Vermont Avenue, above N St., N.W., 1869–73. He was a graduate of North Western College (now Butler University) and became prominent in the church.

of the church. Don't agree with him. The Church is the trellis. True life the vine. Glory to the vine rather than the trellis.

MONDAY, 27. In Committee considered a few odds and ends of appropriations. In the House finished the debate on the Brazilian subsidy which was beaten. New Conference appointed. New report made and the bill goes to the President. Thus nine of the appropriation bills are out of the way. House adjourned over. Members have learned to dread evening sessions after the experience of last Friday. Home in the evening. It is amazing how the *Tribune* has toned down on the tariff. The strongest thing that has appeared in it for weeks is a heading about the legislation in the House which speaks of the Tariff Tinkering.[191]

TUESDAY, 28. Committee did not meet this morning. The business of the Senate will not permit us to adjourn before Monday, June 3d. They seem determined to push us into the passage of the Ku Klux Bill, and threaten us with an extra session in case we do not pass it. Their performances, however, the House checked this morning by a vote of 112 for and 98 [94 for and 108] against taking the Ku Klux Bill from the table and passing it. I voted against the passage with 22 other Republicans. If we suspend the writ of habeas corpus when there is no rebellion or invasion, it asserts the doctrine that Congress may suspend that right at its pleasure, a doctrine subversive of our Government. I introduced and passed a bill transferring the pension [appropriation] from one fund to another.[192] My chief effort during the day was to prevent legislation and to secure the adjournment without an evening session.

[191] Horace Greeley had been one of the foremost advocates of protection in the United States. Now that he had been nominated for the presidency by the Liberal Republicans and the Democrats, both of whom favored revenue reform, his protectionist views were less in evidence in his paper.

[192] Three separate war pension funds were provided for by Congress: (1) for invalids; (2) for widows and dependent relatives; (3) for pensioners of the War of 1812. At this time it was clear that the first lacked money to fulfill its obligations while the others had a surplus. Garfield's bill authorized the secretary of the treasurer to transfer to the first fund from the others such an amount as might be necessary to meet any deficiency in the appropriation for invalid pensions for the year.

WEDNESDAY, 29. Called at the War Department on business with the Quartermaster General. Committee did not meet. House practically waiting on the Senate with nothing to do. Conference report on the Army Appropriation Bill agreed to accept [except] the appropriation for Fort Leavenworth. Niblack reported from the Committee on Appropriations bill for the relief of Dempsey and O'Toole, which was passed. Attempt of Butler to get up the election and Ku Klux bill. Resisted by the Democrats filibustering to the hour of adjournment.[193] Home in the evening. Selucius Garfielde called and spent two hours. Am reading an interesting article of Herbert Spencer's in *Contemporary Review* for May, 1870, on the question "Is there [a] Social Science."

THURSDAY, 30. Committee did not meet this morning, and as the Senate did not return any of the appropriation bills nor the tariff, the House adjourned at half-past one, partly in honor of Decoration Day, but chiefly because we had nothing to do but mischief. I heard with pleasure a remark today that the President will veto several of the bills that were passed so hastily last Saturday night. I hope this may be done as a check to hasty legislation. Session in the evening. The Tariff Bill did not reach the House and nothing was done in the House but general debate on the Ku Klux.

FRIDAY, 31. Committee did not meet for reasons stated yesterday. Chief business in the House has been to prevent reckless legislation. During the day the Tariff and Tax Bill came back from the Senate and we non-concurred in almost all the amendments and asked for a Committee of Conference. In the Senate, Sumner moved

---

193 A bill to amend an act of 1871 concerned with the enforcement of the right to vote passed the Senate on May 10. On May 28 there was insufficient support in the House to suspend the rules and pass the bill. Accordingly on May 29 Benjamin F. Butler of Massachusetts reported from the Joint Select Committee on the Insurrectionary States a similar bill, intending to call the previous question and get it passed; he failed because of dilatory tactics of the Democrats. The supporters of these proposals incorporated them in the Sundry Civil Bill, which passed the House on June 10 after amendments to the enforcement provisions had been made in the Conference Committee.

to postpone indefinitely the Sundry Civil Bill and then made a speech of four hours against Grant. It was marked by great ability, greater bitterness and indiscretions in quoting conversations of dead men, and other similar features. In the evening Schurz followed in a speech of great ability on the sale of arms to France.

June

SATURDAY, 1. Introduced and carried a joint resolution to extend the session to Tuesday evening. Senate spent the whole day in struggling over the question of adjournment. They are determined to force on us an extra session. They sent us a resolution to rescind our resolution for adjournment in the evening. The House amended their resolution by fixing the adjournment for Monday, June 10th. House then adjourned and left the responsibility to the Senate. After a long struggle they concurred. This holds us a week longer and may prevent an extra session.

SUNDAY, 2. Attended church. Heard a sermon addressed to children. A dry history of Josiah's godliness utterly unfitted to children's minds. In the afternoon drove out to A. R. Shepherd's[194] five and a half miles in the country.

MONDAY, 3. Called at the office of the Board of Public Works in regard to improvements around my house. The House has passed another day waiting on the tardiness of the Senate. At ½ past 12 o'clock took a recess until three, and at ½ past four adjourned for the day. In Senate Carpenter of Wisconsin made a four hours' speech of great ability in reply to Schurz's and Sumner's attack of Saturday. In the evening went to the Senate to see the progress of the Sundry Civil Bill, but finding the evening devoted to private bills, returned home.

TUESDAY, 4. Conference Report on the Tariff Bill came in from the Senate and after two hours' debate was adopted by the House. The new tariff is a short step in the right direction. It must be followed

[194] Alexander Robey Shepherd (1835–1902) was at this time the leading figure on the Board of Public Works of the District of Columbia; in 1873 he succeeded Henry D. Cooke as governor of the District. See note 198.

up by more such hereafter, when the public sentiment works up to it. The Senate is so much behind in work that on my motion the House adjourned until Friday. Went to the Senate in the evening to watch the progress of the Sundry Civil Bill.

WEDNESDAY, 5. Brought up correspondence. Went to the Senate to watch the progress of the Sundry Civil Bill. Went to the Treasury Dep't, Post Office and Patent Office on Dep't business.

Crete quite sick. The air is full of malaria. Spent two hours and a half in the evening with Capt. [William B.] Chapman, postmaster at Conneaut, in regard to his threatened removal. Not well. Philadelphia Convention organized today.[195] I have but little enthusiasm for the coming campaign. The dissolution of parties is near at hand. A new birth is needed.

THURSDAY, 6. Worked up correspondence. Went to the Post Office and Patent Office and thence to the Senate to watch the progress of the appropriation bills. The Fortification Bill passed as it left the House without amendment. The River and Harbor Bill passed late in the afternoon. Wilson nominated for the Vice Presidency over Colfax.[196] The newspapers formerly made and have now unmade a hero. Crete still sick.

FRIDAY, 7. The Fortification Bill and the River and Harbor Bill came back from the Senate with amendments. Considered them in the House, agreeing with some and disagreeing with others. Disagreed to the only amendment made to the Fortification Bill and asked for conferences. House met at 8 o'clock in the evening, still waiting for the Senate. At ten when that body had nearly finished the Sundry Civil Bill, the enforcement act was offered as an amendment and the Senate sat all night. The result I do not know.

SATURDAY, 8. Committee held its last regular meeting for the session and agreed to ask the House for authority to sit during the recess to prepare for next winter's work. At 7 o'clock this morning Senate passed the Sundry Civil Bill with the Election Act added. When I

[195] The Republican National Convention met at Philadelphia on June 5, and renominated President Grant on the first ballot, with Senator Henry Wilson of Massachusetts as his running mate.

[196] Schuyler Colfax (1823–1885), a Republican member of the House from Indiana, 1855–69, and Vice President of the United States, 1869–73.

moved to take it up in the House the Democrats commenced filibustering and continued from 11 in the morning until ten o'clock,
at which time after exhausting all ordinary forms of motion to
prevent the consideration of the bill, I offered a motion which
succeeded, to nonconcur with the Senate amendment, and asked
for a Committee of Conference, and then to take a recess until
8 o'clock Monday morning. A little past ten met with the Senate
Conference and sat until midnight discussing the mode of procedure.
Adjourned to meet at one o'clock on Sunday.

SUNDAY, 9. In the morning visited Speaker Blaine and Senator
Edmunds.[197] From 1 o'clock P.M. until 9 P.M. sat in conference on
the Appropriation Bill. Majority agreed to report.

MONDAY, 10. House met at 8 o'clock. I delivered the Conference
Report and filibustering commenced on Kelley's motion to recommit. I spoke, exhibiting the revolutionary proceedings of the minority. After a turbulent debate the report was recommitted. At three
o'clock second report was made that the Committee failed to agree.
Third Conference asked for. By studying carefully all the conflicting
elements a compromise was effected by which the most objectionable
features of the election law were removed. Thus amended, the
responsibility was thrown on the Senate. At 5 o'clock they agreed
to the report. At half-past 5 I presented it to the House, and after
debate and calling out the expressions of the leaders of the opposition
against further filibustering, at 6½ report was adopted by 102 yeas
and 79 nays. Pretty well satisfied with my day's work. Final adjournment at 9 P.M. Home at 12.

TUESDAY, 11. Very tired this morning. After working up a large
amount of correspondence went to the War Department on business
and at 1 o'clock met Committee on Appropriations to make arrangements for our meetings during the recess. Telegraphed to General
Armstrong that I could not be with him at the meeting of the
trustees at Hampton. Finished that portion of my census article
relating to Great Britain. Continued correspondence and at 11 o'clock

[197] George Franklin Edmunds (1828–1919), a Republican member of
the Senate from Vermont, 1866–91, member of the Electoral Commission,
1877, president pro tempore of the Senate, 1883–85.

met the Committee on Appropriations. Discussed several deficiencies and ordered a partial deficiency bill. Listened to the request of the Governor of the District of Columbia and Board of Public Works for a hearing. Set tomorrow for that purpose. Several callers in the evening, Judge Black among the number. Sat until midnight over the first quarto of our Ninth Census just out.

WEDNESDAY, 12. Made further progress in working up correspondence. Called on Judge Black at the Arlington. Transacted a good deal of miscellaneous business and came about as near melting as is consistent with life. The President left for Long Branch at 8 o'clock yesterday, leaving a great many Congressmen with fingers in their mouths, waiting to complete business at the Executive Mansion. The President has done much to show with how little personal attention the Government can be run. Perhaps this is the drift of modern thought. It is said that Queen Victoria's retirement from public affairs has proved to England how unnecessary a sovereign is to the wants of a people. We can say as the Methodist shouter did in Bedford, "The same thing over here."

THURSDAY, 13. Worked up correspondence. Did further business at the Departments and sweltered all day under the burning heat, while sighing for the breezes of the northern lakes. The adjournment of Congress seems to have laid to rest all the winds of heaven and the still air and still life of Washington swelter and melt together. Have been working up the De Golyer Patent Pavement and laying its claims before the Board of Public Works.[198]

---

[198] The vast and costly program of public improvements begun in 1871 by the District of Columbia under the guidance of Alexander Robey ("Boss") Shepherd of the Board of Public Works included construction of new pavements, contracts for which were awarded by the Board. The DeGolyer-McClelland Company of Chicago, makers of a patented wooden paving block, agreed to share profits with another Chicagoan, George R. Chittenden, if he could get a contract for them. In Washington Chittenden committed the company to payments of $97,000 to individuals for aid in getting a contract. He employed as an attorney Richard C. Parsons of Cleveland, then marshal of the U. S. Supreme Court, who made an argument before the Board. As Parsons subsequently told the story, he was called to Cleve-

Had a long visit with Judge Black at the Arlington. He is a wonderful man in his grasp of mind and his scholarly attainments. In his perplexity about the political situation he likens himself to Lear between Goneril and Regan, but says he shall look for Cordelia. I wrote a note on it for the *Washington Chronicle*.[199]

FRIDAY, 14.   Visited the Treasury Department. Spent several hours with Judge Black. Worked up further correspondence and made further preparations for leaving the city. And now at 9 in the evening the blessed rain is falling, bringing down cool refreshment to

---

land before he could complete his work for Chittenden, and asked his friend Garfield to finish it for him. The diary entry for June 2 indicates that on that Sunday Garfield paid a visit to Shepherd at his country estate; Parsons appears to have been with him. Other entries indicate that he gave some attention to the matter. The contract was awarded. Parsons received altogether $15,000, of which he paid Garfield $5,000. Since Garfield did some law work, there was nothing strange about his willingness to assist his friend Parsons. But the size of the fee (equal to a year of his congressional salary) in relation to the small amount of work he did, and testimony before a congressional investigating committee in 1877, suggest that Garfield's employment resulted rather from his commanding position in Congress than from his legal ability. The Sundry Civil Bill, which included appropriations to reimburse the District for paving in front of federal buildings and for other things, had not been passed when Garfield made his Sunday visit to Shepherd, and more bills involving District appropriations would come out of Garfield's committee in the future. As a matter of fact a deficiency bill passed Congress early in January, 1873, which included an appropriation for nearly one and one quarter millions of dollars to cover expenditures made by the Board of Public Works for paving and related activities on and adjoining federal property. Garfield was highly indignant at charges that he had been corruptly involved, maintaining that he had simply acted as a lawyer. His involvement in the DeGolyer pavement affair was a weapon in the hands of his political foes during the campaign of 1880.

[199] Garfield's note appeared as a news item in the *Chronicle* on June 14. Contrary to Black's earlier expectations, he at length came reluctantly to the support of Greeley. Before Garfield had seen Black's statement in support of Greeley, he wrote to him: "I suppose you have gone for Greeley only on the strength of what Butler says that everybody in this campaign is going for somebody he don't want." Letterbook, September 16, 1872.

man and earth. Charlotte [Bachelard], Lizzie[200] and Frank[201] have gone with Harry, Jimmie and Mary to the theatre to see *Humpty Dumpty*. This brings the suggestion of old age. How much more these little fellows have seen and heard at their age than I did when I was twice as old as they! I wonder if it will prove better or worse for them? I may know sometime and may not.

SATURDAY, 15. At half-past 8 o'clock went with Judge Black to Alexandria and thence to Hunter's Station to see about getting our fee from Alexander Hunter for the case we tried for him two years ago. He wanted to sell us 44 acres of land at $150 an acre and from the selling price subtract our fee, $1,500. We visited the land and concluded we could not take it, and after dining at his house came home by rail.[202] Settled other miscellaneous matters. Dined at Welcker's with Hill, Ass't Att'y Gen'l and [Charles] Hale, Ass't Sec'y of State and Francis A. Walker, and Ben Perley Poore.[203] Home at 9½, oppressed with the heat and the day's work.

SUNDAY, 16. At home preparing to leave for Ohio. At 4½ P.M. went with Crete to the Deaf Mute College and took tea with Mr.

[200] Lizzie Ladd, an Ohio girl who was living with the Garfields. See entries for June 19, 1872, and May 12 and 15, 1873.

[201] Joseph F. (Frank) Boston was employed for a time in the Garfield household. In 1873 Garfield secured a job as nightwatchman for him in the Treasury Department, but he did not prove satisfactory.

[202] Garfield and Jeremiah Black had represented Alexander Hunter in a suit brought by Hunter to recover title to land in Virginia which had been taken from him by the federal government and sold to another party after Hunter had allegedly failed to comply with a federal law providing for the collection of taxes in insurrectionary districts. On appeal the Supreme Court ruled (1870) in favor of Hunter. Since Hunter was land poor his lawyers experienced considerable difficulty in collecting their fee. They eventually acquired some of his land.

[203] Benjamin Perley Poore (1820–1887), Washington correspondent for the *Boston Journal* and other papers, was one of the best known newspapermen of his day. He was an early columnist, signing himself "Perley." For the government he made many compilations, including the annual *Congressional Directory*, first published in 1869. His numerous writings include *Perley's Reminiscenses of Sixty Years in the National Metropolis*, 2 vols. (1866).

and Mrs. Gallaudet. They go to Europe in a few weeks. Called on the way back at Mr. and Mrs. Spencer's.[204]

MONDAY, 17. Worked hard to get away for home this evening, but found it necessary to stay over at least another day to work up the pavement case. Went to Interior Department to consult about the commissionership to which the Secretary has appointed me, to remove the Flathead Indians from the Bitter Root Valley, Montana.[205]

[204] Henry C. Spencer, a son of Platt Rogers Spencer, operated the Washington Business College at the corner of Seventh and L streets, N.W. His wife, Sara Andrews Spencer (1837–1909), principal of the Ladies' Department, became well known as a reformer. In 1871 she tried without success to vote in Washington, and with others forced the Supreme Court to rule on the subject. From 1874 to 1881 she was secretary of the National Woman Suffrage Association. She was also active in the Red Cross, in support of the National Homeopathic Hospital, and in behalf of outcast girls. In 1876 she became the first woman ever to address a national presidential convention. She had a high regard for Garfield despite his opposition to woman suffrage.

[205] By a treaty between the United States and the Flathead, Pend d'Oreille and Kootenay Indians made in 1855 and ratified by the Senate in 1859, the Indians ceded a vast area to the United States and agreed to the establishment of the Jocko Reservation in northwestern Montana. Since the Flatheads, who lived in the Bitter Root Valley, objected to removal, the treaty provided that if the President, after having had the Bitter Root Valley above the Lolo Fork carefully surveyed and examined, should determine that it was a better place for the Flatheads than the Jocko Reservation, a separate reservation for them would be created there. During the years following the treaty the Pend d'Oreilles and the Kootenays moved to the reservation; the Flatheads remained in the Bitter Root Valley. Although the treaty provided that the valley should not be open to white settlement until after the President's determination of the more suitable site for the Flatheads, white men settled as squatters in the valley in considerable numbers, sometimes at the invitation of the friendly Indian chief Victor. As the white men established themselves, pressures for the removal of the Flatheads to the Jocko Reservation began. William Clagett, the territorial delegate to Congress (1871–1873), mentioned a number of times by Garfield, was an advocate of removal. On November 14, 1871, President Grant issued a removal order, claiming that the Bitter Root Valley above the Lolo Fork had been carefully surveyed and examined in accordance with the treaty of 1855, and declaring that no por-

Went also to the Capitol and closed up some matters there, took back books to the library, etc. Also went with Crete to make purchases preparatory to going home. Paid $543 for the coal vault, sewage, and other improvements around the place. Bought Taine's *Notes on England* and resolved to read the reflections of that remarkable Frenchman who has written perhaps the best treatise on English literature.[206]

TUESDAY, 18.   Still detained by the Chicago business. Went to the Post Office Dep't, settled several post office and post route questions. Went to the Capitol. Got off correspondence. Got library books for Burke [Hinsdale]. In short it has been a day of general miscellany, which is always more laborious than steady work.

WEDNESDAY, 19.   Another day of miscellany. Waiting to close up the Chicago matter and yet struggling all the while to get off. Lunched at one o'clock with Brisbane. Pneumatic tube progresses favorably. He is enthusiastic over its prospective success. Went to the War Dep't to secure the transfer of Lieut. Atwood[207] from the Infantry to the Artillery. At 6 o'clock called on A. R. Shepherd and substantially concluded arrangements for Chicago plans. At 7.45 with all my family, except Lizzie, took the train for Baltimore, Harrisburg and the West.

---

tion of it needed to be set apart as a separate reservation for the Flatheads. In June, 1872, Congress passed a removal act, making provision for the opening of the valley above the Lolo Fork to sale and settlement; Indians who were heads of families or who had cultivated lands were to be allowed to get title to lands in the valley if they chose to stay and leave their tribe. The secretary of the interior appointed Garfield to act as special commissioner to secure the consent of the Flatheads to removal and to make necessary arrangements. He was paid nearly eleven hundred dollars, only a small fraction of which he expended on his trip. His report and related documents are in the Report of the Commissioner of Indian Affairs for 1872, in *House Ex. Docs.,* Serial 1560, pp. 494–503.

[206] Hippolyte A. Taine, *Notes on England,* translated by W. F. Rae (1872). His *History of English Literature* was published in a translation by H. Van Lau in two volumes in 1871.

[207] Edwin B. Atwood of Portage County had served during the Civil War in the 41st Ohio Infantry Regiment and was now stationed in the West with the 6th Infantry. Garfield was unable to effect his transfer.

THURSDAY, 20.   Reached Pittsburgh at 10 A.M. Waited until 2.40.
Took the train for Cleveland, where we arrived at 8 P.M. and stopped
at Dr. Robison's. A very hot disagreeable day. Found the Doctor
had gone to Hiram to meet me.

FRIDAY, 21.   Spent the day at Dr. Robison's. With him, [Isaac]
Errett, and [Jefferson Harrison] Jones visited the Fair Grounds, and
in the evening had a session of the Quintinkle Association. Crete
was admitted.[208]

SATURDAY, 22.   Went to Hiram by the morning train leaving Mother
at Solon. Reached Hiram at 10. Spent the day and evening with
Burke and among home friends. The sweet breath of the country
air is reviving.

SUNDAY, 23.   Attended church and heard Burke preach.

MONDAY, 24.   Went by morning train to Cleveland and wrote on
the paint case at Lockwood's[209] until 3 o'clock. A proposition for
settlement is pending and I recommend my clients to accept it. At

[208] In 1861, just before Garfield and Jefferson Harrison Jones left for
service with the 42nd Ohio Infantry Regiment, they met one night, along
with Isaac Errett, at the home of J. P. Robison. On that occasion the four
men and Mrs. Robison formed the Quintinkle Society, "pledging themselves
to go at call to each other's aid in distress, and to perform all the duties
specified in this covenant of friendship." Other friends joined the group,
which met many times over the years.

[209] Charles Brown Lockwood (b. 1829), formerly a Solon, Ohio, store-
keeper, and now a member of a prominent Cleveland hardware firm and
president of the Cleveland Chemical Paint Company, which Garfield was
representing in the case mentioned in note 4. A New Yorker by birth, he was
brought to Ohio as a young boy. After spending four years in California
during the gold rush, he graduated from a law school in Poughkeepsie, New
York. Returning to Ohio he engaged in business. He was long a Disciple of
Christ although he became a Unitarian in his later years. He was a member
of the Board of Trustees of the Western Reserve Eclectic Institute, 1865–67,
and of Hiram College, 1867–1907; he was president of the Board, 1899–
1907. In 1879 he attended the first session of Bronson Alcott's Concord
Summer School of Philosophy and Literature. He was a friend of Garfield for
many years.

3.45 took the Atlantic and Great Western road with MacFarland of N. Y. for the East.

TUESDAY, 25. Arrived this morning at Binghamton, N.Y., where I left the main line and took the Susquehanna Branch. Passed through Worcester where my father was born. It lies in a beautiful valley surrounded by wild hills. Reached Albany at 2 o'clock, went thence to Troy, where at 5 P.M. took the train for Williamstown, which I reached at 7 o'clock. Staid at President Hopkins' by whose family I was pleasantly greeted.

WEDNESDAY, 26. Presided at the alumni meeting, and was re-elected President for the coming year. Was nominated for Trustee of the College but declined. During the afternoon session an able address was delivered by David A. Wells, class of '47, and a poem by Prof. Carter,[210] and a eulogy on the life and character of the late Professor Albert Hopkins, by the Rev. Henry M. Field.[211]

Took supper with Wells at Mr. Leake's.[212]

THURSDAY, 27. Thursday forenoon commencement exercises at the conclusion of which President Hopkins conferred on me the degree of LL.D. Alumni dinner at Goodrich Hall. At 2 o'clock President Hopkins resigned his office and President-elect Chadbourne[213] was

[210] Franklin Carter (1837–1919), language professor at Williams, 1865–72, professor of German at Yale, 1873–81, and president of Williams, 1881–1901.

[211] Henry Martyn Field (1822–1907), Presbyterian minister, editor and author, graduated at Williams in 1838. For more than forty years he was associated with the publication of *The Evangelist* in New York City, at first as a partner in the enterprise, later as owner and editor. He also wrote several volumes dealing with his travels in Europe, Asia and Africa.

[212] Frederick Leake (1816–1897), a wealthy resident of Williamstown, for many years donated his services to Williams College as a teacher of French.

[213] Paul Ansel Chadbourne (1823–1883), a graduate of Williams College in 1848, was its president from 1872 to 1881. Before becoming president he had been associated as teacher or administrator with Williams, Massachusetts Agricultural College, the University of Wisconsin, and other institutions, and had attracted some attention by his scientific expeditions and lectures.

inaugurated. Dr. Hopkins spoke for himself, Dr. [S. I.] Prim for the trustees, Prof. [John] Bascom for the faculty, Mr. [R. M.] Chamberlain, Jr., for the undergraduates and I for the alumni. Met two [three] classmates, Eldridge[214] and the two Potters.[215] President's levee in the evening.

FRIDAY, 28. At 7½ A.M. left for N.Y. by the way of Troy. The train took us from Troy to N.Y. in four hours, stopping but twice. Stopped at the Metropolitan Hotel. I rejoiced to find that Cousin Abraham Garfield[216] has dissolved partnership with Tweed and has now left the Metropolitan and is now at Saratoga. This probably is my last visit to the Metropolitan Hotel. My friends who have kept it for so many years have now gone. I shall select another, probably the Brevoort House. Received a letter from [George R.] Chittenden that the contract with the Board of Public Works is concluded.

Dined in the evening with Dimmock[217] at Delmonico's.

SATURDAY, 29. In the afternoon transacted some business and made some calls. Took the evening train for Washington.

SUNDAY, 30. Arrived at Washington at 7 A.M. Went to Welcker's, had breakfast, thence to 1227 I St. I am very tired and the weather is very hot.

---

[214] Hamilton Nathan Eldridge (1832–1882) graduated at Williams College in 1856, served as an officer in the Union army, and practiced law in Chicago before and after the war. Although a Democrat he was active in behalf of Garfield during the Republican National Convention in 1880.

[215] Arnold Gardner Potter (1829–1891) and Andrew Potter (1832–1903) graduated at Williams College in 1856 and practiced law for many years, Arnold in North Adams, Massachusetts, and Andrew in Pittsfield, Massachusetts, Bennington, Vermont, and North Adams. Andrew was a Union officer in the Civil War.

[216] Abram Garfield, son of Garfield's Uncle Thomas, had recently sold his interest in the Metropolitan Hotel to William M. Tweed, who wished to vest the title to the property in his own son alone. Garfield then became manager of the Union Hotel in Saratoga, where he died in 1873.

[217] William Reynolds Dimmock (1835–1878), a graduate of Williams College in 1855, was professor of language and literature at Williams, 1868–72, and headmaster of Adams Academy, 1872–78. He had also been awarded the degree of LL.D. at the Commencement from which Garfield was returning.

July

MONDAY, 1.   Busy all day with letters and Department business. Spent some time in the Library studying Indian affairs.

TUESDAY, 2.   A repetition of yesterday.

WEDNESDAY, 3.   Finished business, among other things completed arrangements in relation to my mission to the Flathead Indians. In the evening took the train for Hiram.

THURSDAY, 4.   Reached home after a hot and dusty journey. Found the family all well and a great mass of letters awaiting me.

FRIDAY, 5.   Went to Ravenna as a witness in a divorce case of *Carroll vs. Carroll*. This is the first time I have ever given testimony in a civil court. I returned home in the evening.

SATURDAY, 6.   Worked up my correspondence.

SUNDAY, 7.   At church. Hinsdale preached.

MONDAY, 8.   Went to Warren in company with Hinsdale. Took dinner at Mr. Austin's. Made several calls in the afternoon. Home in the evening.

TUESDAY, 9.   Reading up the history of Western explorations. The travels of Lewis and Clark [and] among others, *The Adventures of Captain Bonneville*,[218] a book full of interest, but it grows tedious and uninteresting with repetition before the close.

WEDNESDAY, 10.   Finished *Bonneville* and read DeSmet's *History of the Oregon Missions*,[219] in which the missionary efforts of the Jesuits among the Flatheads are specially detailed.

THURSDAY, 11.   Little reading but more correspondence preparatory to a journey to Canada. We go with the whole family for the sake of rest and to visit our friends the Hawleys.[220] Full reports of the

[218] Washington Irving, *The Adventures of Captain Bonneville, U.S.A.* (1837).

[219] Pierre Jean de Smet, *Oregon Missions and Travels over the Rocky Mountains in 1845–46* (1847).

[220] When Richard Hawley and his wife invited the Garfields to visit them at their Goderich, Ontario summer residence, Garfield wrote in reply: "Your very kind invitation to visit Goderich with our whole family opens the pros-

Baltimore Convention received, showing that the Democracy has swallowed Greeley and the Cincinnati Platform.[221] This will be a remarkable campaign full of personal bitterness.

FRIDAY, 12. Took the whole family to Cleveland where we staid at Dr. Robison's. During the day called on Mrs. Kent and Mr. and Mrs. Rhodes. At 8 o'clock in the evening took the steamer for Detroit. The evening was calm and pleasant.

SATURDAY, 13. Reached Detroit at 6 in the morning. After breakfast and a delay of an hour, proceeded by rail to Port Huron across to Sarnia and thence by rail to Stratford, where we took another line and reached Goderich before sunset in the evening. Mr. Hawley's people met us at the depot with carriages and took us to his country residence three miles from town.

SUNDAY, 14. Spent the day quietly at Mr. Hawley's resting and reading.

MONDAY, 15. Went to Goderich in the morning. Returned and spent the day in reading and playing croquet. This is a delightful place and the cool breezes from the lake make the temperature very comfortable this weather.

TUESDAY, 16. Went to town with Crete and Mr. Hawley's people and spent part of the day in shopping. Croquet and reading after our return.

WEDNESDAY, 17. The usual program was followed out with this

---

pect of a most delightful retreat from the labor of public life and the hot sun of Ohio, and nothing will prevent us from accepting it unless it be our fear that we shall overwhelm you with our crowd of little ones. I am less sensitive on that subject than Mrs. Garfield and am doing what I can to persuade her to go and take the whole regiment with us." The whole regiment included four children, ranging from one to nine, and a nurse. Letterbook, June 11, 1872.

[221] At their national convention in Baltimore on July 9 and 10 the Democrats, recognizing that their only hope of defeating Grant lay in coalition with the Liberal Republicans, nominated Horace Greeley for President and B. Gratz Brown for Vice President, and accepted verbatim the platform which the Liberal Republicans had adopted at Cincinnati in May.

Thomas D. Hawley, a Detroit lawyer and son of Garfield's friend Richard Hawley, was a delegate to the Democratic convention and accompanied the committee which visited Greeley at Chappaqua, New York, to inform him of his nomination. See entry for July 18.

difference, that I went with Harry and Jimmy on a ramble to the woods and to the Maitland River where they went in swimming.

THURSDAY, 18. Thomas D. Hawley arrived today from the Baltimore Convention by way of New York City and Chappaqua where he visited the Philosopher to inform him of his nomination.

FRIDAY, 19. Resting, reading, visiting and playing croquet.

SATURDAY, 20. Resting, reading, visiting and playing croquet.

SUNDAY, 21. Attended church at Mrs. Brown's Episcopal Chapel.

MONDAY, 22. [No entry]

TUESDAY, 23. Left Goderich by the 9 o'clock train, reached Detroit in the evening. Saw John and Thomas Hawley and the Colonel and his wife. Had a short visit with them on the boat which left Detroit at 9 in the evening.

WEDNESDAY, 24. Reached home and found a heavy mail awaiting me. Spent the day in overhauling correspondence.

THURSDAY, 25. Commence the preparation of a campaign speech which I have agreed to deliver before the nominating convention at Warren, before the 31st. I dread the opening of this campaign. It promises to be full of bitterness and of all that is low and uncomfortable in politics. I shall attempt to make a speech gaged on a higher level than the times seem to furnish for such efforts.

FRIDAY, 26. Wrote letters and prepared speech.

SATURDAY, 27. The work of yesterday continued.

SUNDAY, 28. At church.

MONDAY, 29. Shorthand writer arrived from Cleveland to take my speech for Wednesday the 31st inst. Worked incessantly today and tonight am nearly sick.

TUESDAY, 30. Finished my preparations for leaving home on trip to the Rocky Mountains and in the afternoon left for Freedom where I took the cars to Kent, and in the evening addressed 1,500 people assembled in the public square, on the political issues of the day. Rode with Messrs. Brainerd,[222] Beatty and Meharg[223] to Ravenna, where I spent the night with H. R. W. Hall.

WEDNESDAY, 31. Took the morning train for Warren and stopped

[222] Enos P. Brainerd, a prominent businessman in Ravenna, was for many years chairman of the Republican Central Committee of Portage County.

[223] John Meharg, a Ravanna lawyer, was a member of the Republican Congressional Committee for Garfield's district.

at Harmon Austin's. Congressional Convention assembled at 11 o'clock and as soon as an organization was effected I was nominated by acclamation. I did not attend the convention but they invited me to address them on their re-assembling at 2 o'clock, at which time I spoke for two hours. At four o'clock, took the train for Cleveland and at Garrettsville was joined by Crete, Charlotte, Mollie and Irvin. Spent the night at Dr. Robison's.

August

THURSDAY, 1. Took the morning train for the West and reached Chicago in the evening and stopped at the Sherman House. In the morning rode over the burnt district and saw the wonderful ruin of fire and saw also the exhibition of marvelous energy which is rebuilding the ruined city.

FRIDAY, 2. Took the Chicago, Burlington and Quincy Road at 10 in the morning and reached Quincy in the evening, crossing the Mississippi again at that place.

SATURDAY, 3. Reached Saint Joseph on the Missouri River at 8 o'clock in the morning where I found Capt. Hopkins,[224] son of Dr. Hopkins, who drove us through the town and at 10 o'clock sent us down to Leavenworth in his Director's car and gave us a fine breakfast on board.

Reached East Leavenworth at 10 [1?] o'clock where we were met by Major Swaim and taken to his house at Fort Leavenworth.

SUNDAY, 4. Read and rested during the day.

MONDAY, 5. Went to Leavenworth with several officers of the Post. In the afternoon Gen'l Pope[225] drove me out on the hills.

TUESDAY, 6. Reading, visiting, playing croquet and resting. A large number of officers and their ladies called on us at Major Swaim's in the evening.

[224] Amos Lawrence Hopkins (1844–1912) had a career as a railroad administrator and reorganizer. At this time he was an official of the Kansas City, St. Joseph and Council Bluffs Railroad.

[225] John Pope (1822–1892) commanded the Department of the Missouri, 1870–83. He detailed Garfield's friend Major David G. Swaim to accompany the congressman on his mission to the Flatheads.

WEDNESDAY, 7. Made several calls during the day and in the evening delivered a speech in the Market House at Leavenworth to a very large audience. Returned to the Fort and passed the night.

THURSDAY, 8. Answered letters, made calls, and completed preparations for Western trips. In the evening at ten o'clock accompanied by Major Swaim, took the cars at Leavenworth City westward on the Kansas Pacific Road. Reached Lawrence at midnight where we took sleeping cars. This part of Kansas was the scene of the great contest between the free and slave forces of the country; but as the usual result of all contests a class of violent, and to some extent, corrupt men have been left as a residuum, although the cause of liberty gained in the fight. These results are observable I think in the political morals of the whole state of Kansas.

FRIDAY, 9. Past the cultivated portions of Kansas and [in] the evening reached Fort Harker and the desolate plains of Kansas. Buffalo skeletons are seen here and there along the road and the short buffalo grass covers the plains on all sides as far as the eye can reach. There seems to be a flavor of wildness in the buffalo grass which like the wild nature of the Indian and buffalo refuses to be tamed. They tell me this grass disappears when the prairies are cultivated; that it seems to die out in the presence of our agriculture.

SATURDAY, 10. In the morning reached Denver and immediately changed cars for Cheyenne where we arrived at one P.M. and after dinner took the Union Pacific train for the West. Before evening we had passed Sherman, the highest point of the Rocky Mountains on the track of the Union Pacific. Took supper at Laramie.

SUNDAY, 11. Awoke among the desolate alkali plains of the Rocky Mountains. Reached Ogden at 4 o'clock and Salt Lake a little before 8. Stopped at the Patterson House and immediately went out to one of the Ward meetings and heard Taylor,[226] one of the apostles, preach.

MONDAY, 12. Early in the morning went with Major Doty [Israel O. Dewey] of the Pay Department to the Warm Springs and took a bath. Returned and after breakfast G. Q. Cannon, one of the

[226] John Taylor (1808–1887), chosen an apostle in 1838 by Joseph Smith, succeeded Brigham Young as president of the Church of Jesus Christ of Latter-day Saints.

12 apostles and the Delegate-elect to Congress, took us in a carriage to the various points of interest in the city. The Tabernacle, the Temple, Brigham's house and Camp Douglas. After dinner he took us to the depot, where we met Brigham[227] just coming in from Ogden. Mr. Young held our train 15 minutes for a chat, and after reaching Ogden we took the train for Corinne, where we arrived at 7 in the evening and spent the night at the International Hotel.

TUESDAY, 13. Took the stage, holding nine passengers inside and two outside with the driver. Moved up the Bear River Valley at a spanking trot and took breakfast 16 miles out.[228] Took dinner at the head of Malad Valley 54 miles out and supper at Port Neuf Cañon. The scenery has been one of grandeur constantly varying. Broad level valleys with rough picturesque mountains on each hand. I have greatly enjoyed my study of the drivers. Rode on top beside them nearly all day. They are a wild, rough, warm-hearted, peculiar people and have a distinct place among American characters.

WEDNESDAY, 14. About one o'clock in the morning the shackle supporting the thorough brace broke and delayed us several hours. Swaim and I lay on a buffalo robe spread out on the ground and the sage brush for a pillow. We got an hour's sleep while they were mending the carriage.

THURSDAY, 15. Passed the divide between the waters that flow into Salt Lake and the waters of Snake River. Passed in sight of the mountain Professor Hayden has named after me.[229] It is covered with snow and its peak is the divide between the two oceans. The air is wonderfully pure and invigorating. Saw the three Tetons 150 miles distant. Reached Lyon [Ryon] late in the evening, and took the Jerkie, instead of the stage.[230]

---

[227] Brigham Young (1801–1877), who led the great Mormon migration to Utah, was president of the Church of Jesus Christ of Latter-day Saints, 1847–77.

[228] The Corinne-Virginia City-Helena road, a famous stage road into Montana, was about 480 miles long.

[229] Garfield Mountain is the highest point in the Bitter Root Range of the Rocky Mountains—over 10,900 feet.

[230] To his wife Garfield wrote that at Ryon (Ryan's Station) they changed coaches "and took a two horse stage with but two seats inside, and packed

The wonderful purity of the atmosphere in these high regions affords many surprises to a man accustomed to living in the plains. I am utterly deceived in my judgment of distances. What I would call five miles distant, I frequently find is forty or fifty or even more. The same thing appears in judging of the depth of water. The streams are so very clear and pure, that a stream appearing to be a foot in depth will wet the axle as we go through it.

FRIDAY, 16. Reached Gaffney's at daybreak, where Gov. Potts met us and on his invitation took the stage for Virginia City where we arrived before noon. Met Chief Justice Wade[231] and our old comrade Sanders.[232] Spent the afternoon in visiting the town and the gold diggings and got a good night's rest at the hotel, after taking a bath, at $2.50 apiece. Lewis and Clark named the main stream of the Missouri, above its three forks, Jefferson, and called the other two streams Gallatin and Madison. When they came nearly to this place, they found that the Jefferson itself was formed by three streams, and in order to have a dignified origin for the river named after their Chief, they called the three Wisdom, Philosophy and Philanthropy. The miners have degenerated this into Beaver Head, Big Hole, and Stinking Water.

SATURDAY, 17. Visited the Supreme Court of the Territory, several prominent citizens and places, and in the evening went to Cavanaugh's,[233] in company with Governor Potts and W. F. Sanders, where after waiting until past midnight we took the stage for Helena. Reports are indicating danger of Indian hostilities in removing the Flatheads. I think there is a mercenary purpose on the part of some

---

eight passengers into and upon it. By a happy invention the drivers call the vehicle a 'Jerkie.' " A jerky was usually springless.

[231] Decius Spear Wade (1835–1905), of Ohio, was chief justice of the Territory of Montana, 1871–87.

[232] Wilbur Fiske Sanders (1834–1905), a New Yorker by birth, moved to Ohio in 1854, where he became a lawyer. After a brief service in the army, he settled in the part of the Territory of Idaho which became the Territory of Montana. There he practiced law and engaged in stockraising, mining and politics. He was U. S. senator from Montana, 1890–93.

[233] James M. Cavanaugh (1823–1879) was the delegate to Congress from Montana Territory, 1867–71.

white settlers to secure troops in the valley that has originated these reports. I wrote this suggestion to the Sec'y of the Interior.[234]

SUNDAY, 18. A glorious day's ride among the mountains, and visiting old friends. Reached Helena in the evening and met several friends.

MONDAY, 19. This morning our party filled the stage and Colonel Viall's[235] ambulance. In these two outfits we passed up the valley of the Prickly Pear and over the main ridge of the Rocky Mountains and descended on the other slope to Deer Lodge. We met Mr. Clagett at this place and got two hours' sleep. Our route of today was in the track of Clark's return from the Pacific to the Atlantic slope. The gorge by which he entered the mountains east of Helena he called the gates of the mountain. The country is wonderfully beautiful.

TUESDAY, 20. A little after two o'clock in the morning took the stage for Missoula. Our party consisted of Col. Viall, Sup't of Indian Affairs, Colonel Sanders, the Hon. Mr. Clagett, Major Swaim and myself. Counting out stoppages for meals and change of horses, we made the distance to Missoula, 95 to 110 miles, in 9½ hours. It was not reckless but exhilarating driving. Spent the night at the

[234] In Virginia City Garfield tried to learn as much as he could of the situation in the Bitter Root Valley. The Flatheads, it was said, were showing great opposition to removal, and visiting Nez Perces and Spokanes were espousing their cause. Missionaries were reported to be advising the Indians to stay in the valley. The white settlers, apprehensive of hostilities, had organized home guards and asked the governor to send them arms, which were about to be forwarded. The settlers were also asking for the posting of two or three companies of cavalry in the valley. The sale of whiskey to the Indians by people in Missoula was blamed for some of the feeling among the red men, and the valley people were asking for law enforcement.

To Secretary of Interior Delano Garfield wrote: "It is manifest that there is a good deal of apprehension of trouble. But I am inclined to believe that much of it is groundless—and it is perhaps partly the result of a desire to secure a military post in the Valley. It would be inconsistent with the whole history and character of the Flatheads if they should resort to violence in a case like this." Letterbook, August 17, 1872. A cavalry post would create a considerable market for the agricultural produce of the valley farmers.

[235] Jasper A. Viall was superintendent of Indian affairs in Montana, 1870–72.

hotel at the mouth of Hell Gate. Our ride today was most exhilarating. Its interest was heightened by the spice of danger there was in it from the furious rate at which we went. "Steve," our first driver out of Deer Lodge, was a rare character. His genius as a driver is exhibited in the ratio of his intoxication. He was very drunk and therefore exceedingly brilliant as a driver.[236]

WEDNESDAY, 21. After breakfast our party proceeded in carriages and wagons up the Bitter Root Valley to Fort Owen. I had sent word ahead but the Flatheads had not then assembled, so I postponed a council until the following morning. This is a lovely valley girded by grand mountain scenery. On our way to this place from Missoula we crossed the little stream now known as Lolo fork of the Bitter Root, but named by Lewis and Clark Traveller's Rest Creek. On its banks those intrepid explorers rested for a fortnight on their way west and made another halt on their return. It is a shame that the old name has not been preserved.

THURSDAY, 22. Held a council of six hours' duration with the Chiefs and principal men of the Flatheads. Found them greatly opposed to leaving the Bitter Root Valley.[237] The interview was somewhat tiresome but there were points of great interest to me in the Indian mode of thought. Slept as last night at Fort Owen. This is the valley down which Lewis and Clark passed on their way to the Pacific in 1805. Before John Owen[238] became a bankrupt and sot, his

---

[236] "The proprietors of the stage company had heard of our going on their line and had directed their drivers to make a notably quick trip—and we did distance all former time." Garfield to his wife, from Missoula, August 23, 1872.

[237] The Flatheads argued that Victor (whose son Charlot was now their number one chief) had not agreed to leave the valley. They held also that the careful survey and examination of the valley provided for in the treaty should have been made at once, and claimed that it had not been made at all. Furthermore they complained that schoolmasters, blacksmiths, carpenters and farmers promised by the government in the treaty had not been sent to help them.

[238] John Owen (1818–1889) acquired the St. Mary's Mission property in the Bitter Root Valley in 1850 and built there a wooden fort which was later transformed into a more substantial adobe structure; his fort became the base for trading operations extending north to Fort Benton and Fort Dalles

career was one of interest. He seems to have lived like a prince here in the wilderness. His fine wines and luxurious appointments have been the theme of many army officers who have served in the West. Since the death of his Indian wife he has rapidly run down and is now quite a wreck.

FRIDAY, 23. Held another conference with the Flatheads at 9 A.M. and pledged the Chiefs to go with me to the Jocko Reservation.[239] Left at noon for Missoula. Crossed the Lolo Fork which was the Traveller's Rest Creek of Lewis and Clark. Spent the night at Missoula. The sky is wonderfully pure and the weather clearer than any I ever saw. The springs are the only source of the mountain streams, except the snow.

After conference with the Chiefs Looking-Glass and Eagle-Against-the-Light, in the evening visited the camp of Nez Perce warriors and witnessed a war dance.[240] Spent the night at the Missoula House.

---

and south to Fort Hall. A Jesuit, Father Lawrence Palladino, who knew him wrote: "He always had many guests at the Fort, and was famed for his hospitality to his guests and to transient travellers who were passing through the region. He was a man of very loveable, kindly and generous character, and the most influential pioneer in the country for years." He was deteriorating by the time of Garfield's visit; not long afterwards he was hospitalized, and later sent to Philadelphia to be cared for by relatives. See Seymour Dunbar and Paul C. Phillips, eds., *The Journals and Letters of Major John Owen, Pioneer of the Northwest, 1850–1871*, 2 vols. (1927).

[239] The chiefs were not committing themselves to removal but only to a visit to the reservation for inspection. "I greatly regret this detention, but I feel bound to do all in my power to save these noble Indians from the mistake they will make if they refuse. Moreover, I greatly dislike to fail in anything I undertake. It has looked as though I could not succeed—and I still fear I can not—but I will make one more good try." Garfield to his wife, from Missoula, August 23, 1872.

[240] The presence for the past two weeks of about 100 lodges of Nez Perces and Spokanes near Missoula served the interest of those clamoring for the removal of the Flatheads. Garfield visited the Nez Perces (the chiefs mentioned were of that tribe) but found no evidence of their participation in the affairs of the Flatheads except an invitation to the latter to join them on their annual buffalo hunt at the headwaters of the Missouri towards which they were now headed.

SATURDAY, 24. Our party reached the Jocko Reservation 30 miles distant about 2 o'clock P.M. It is a country of wonderful beauty. All the varieties of mountain, valley, prairie and woodland combined. In the afternoon went hunting and fishing. A few grouse, a broken rod and 5 pound trout lost off my hook were the principal events of the afternoon. The Chiefs arrived after sunset, and in the evening entertained us with a war dance accompanied by heroic recitals of the achievements of the Flatheads against their enemies the Crows, Sioux and Snakes. These customs are very effective in keeping up the pride and warlike spirit of the tribe.

SUNDAY, 25. Held a long conference with the Flathead Chiefs and after almost failing, succeeded.

MONDAY, 26. Two of the Chiefs, second and third, signed the contract, by which they agreed to remove their tribe to the Reservation when suitable buildings have been erected to receive them, they having selected sites for their dwellings and the grounds for their farms. All the money appropriated for their removal is to be paid to them and for fitting up their dwellings.[241] I am glad that they prefer to be near the Agency rather than at the Mission; it will help

[241] In return for the agreement of the Indians to remove to the reservation, Garfield pledged the government to build houses for them, give them during their first year 600 bushels of wheat, which would be ground without cost, and such vegetables as the Agency farm could spare, enclose and break up land, furnish agricultural implements, pay to the Indians as much of the $5,000 appropriated by Congress for removal as was not expended in carrying out these other provisions, and pay in ten installments the $50,000 provided for by Congress to compensate the Indians for land and improvements which they were giving up in the Bitter Root Valley. In his report Garfield indicated his belief that $50,000 was not enough for this purpose.

Garfield was sharply critical of the accomplishments of the reservation Agency over the years. As far as cultivation of the land was concerned he wrote that "one energetic farmer could alone have accomplished much more in the same length of time." After noting other deficiencies he declared: "It is a disgrace to the Government that in so beautiful and fertile a valley there should not long ago have been several hundred acres of crops, and such evidences of thrift and industry as to have attracted the Flatheads, rather than repelled them." The agreement is on pages 499–500 of Garfield's Report, Serial 1560; his quoted remarks are on page 497.

emancipate them from the undue influence of the Jesuits.[242] Soon after breakfast we started to Missoula and reached there in time for a late dinner in the afternoon; then distributed over two hundred dollars' worth of presents to the Chiefs and their associates. I think Charlot, the head Chief, will ultimately come into this arrangement.[243] Saw a letter from William Welsh, late of the Peace Com-

[242] The Flathead Agency was near the southern boundary of the Jocko Reservation; Saint Ignatius Mission was about 18 miles north of the Agency. Father Lawrence Palladino, who was in charge of the Mission, entered a strong protest against the location of the Flatheads in the area of the Agency. He argued that there was not enough good land in the area, that the Northern Pacific Railroad would probably run close to the intended settlement, and that the Flatheads, all of whom were Catholics, would be too far from the mission for regular church attendance and instruction. Garfield dealt with each of these objections in his reply. He admitted that he had noticed poor lands but declared that those in the direction of the mill and up the Jocko appeared to be very fertile and easily irrigated. The Flathead chiefs, he pointed out, had made their own selection, preferring to be near the mill. As for the railroad, he thought it as likely to go up the Lolo Fork as elsewhere, and if through the Jocko Valley, not very near the lands of the Flatheads. In any case, he reasoned, the government would be bound to protect the Indians. The religious question he admitted to be a serious one, but put forward the view that it would be best for the Jesuits to take care of the Flatheads separately and more expensive for them to do so at Fort Owen than on the reservation. One of Charlot's chief objections to removal, he said, was that he did not want his people mixed up with the others on the reservation. Both letters are in the Report of the Commissioner of Indian Affairs for 1872, Serial 1560, pp. 500–502.

[243] Although Charlot did not sign the agreement (his X does not appear on the original document) and Garfield's report makes clear that he did not do so, his name followed by an X appears on the agreement accompanying Garfield's report as published in the Report of the Commissioner of Indian Affairs for 1872. This circumstance gave rise to charges that Charlot's signature had been "forged."

Charlot and some of his followers resisted removal for nearly two decades. Charlot visited Washington in 1884 but failed to reach an understanding with the government. But the condition of his band worsened as white settlement advanced and eventually their position became untenable. In 1891 he led his people to the reservation—"Charlot's band" numbered 174 in 1892. He lived on until 1910, embittered by his experience with the white man and his government.

mission, which greatly surprised and incensed me. He says that the Indians would be justified in combining to resist removal by force.[244] He shall hear from this. Passed part of the night at Missoula.

TUESDAY, 27. Took the stage a little after two in the morning for Deer Lodge. The beautiful [Clark Fork] River has been permanently ruined by the miners, and has been for three years as muddy as the Missouri. Before the discovery of gold it was as clear and pure as any mountain stream could well be. Traces of Mullan's Road[245] are seen all along our route and a part of the way we have

[244] Dissatisfaction with the conduct of the government's relations with the Indians led in 1869 to the appointment by President Grant, under authority of Congress, of a Board of Indian Commissioners, which was to serve without pay and to exercise joint control with the Office of Indian Affairs in the Interior Department over disbursements, contracts and other Indian matters. William Welsh (1810–1878), a Philadelphia businessman and philanthropist, became chairman of the Board, which soon found that it received small cooperation from the Interior Department. Welsh resigned promptly but continued his interest in Indian affairs. The letter referred to by Garfield was written by Welsh from Philadelphia on August 13, 1872, to John Owen, who opposed the removal of the Flatheads from the Bitter Root Valley. "If the Indians cannot get their rights any other way," Welsh wrote, "they are justified in combining for defense against coercion." Garfield was annoyed by the letter since it threatened to make his task much more difficult by giving encouragement to the Indians resisting removal. He included Welsh's letter in his report, and commented thus: "I do not know on what ground Mr. Welsh bases his remarkable advice to these Indians. But were the subject left to my discretion, and were the question still open and undetermined, I should unhesitatingly say that the highest good of the Flatheads required their removal from the Bitter Root Valley." Welsh later informed Garfield that he had known nothing of his mission, and that in the letter, to which Garfield had objected, he did not refer to resistance to authority "but simply to such natural rights as are accorded to whites and blacks." He went on to say. "I rejoice at the kind feelings you are manifesting towards the Indian, for as you well know most of the frontier prospectors & speculators accord to Indians having treaties with the Government, no greater rights than to Wild Beasts." See Garfield's Report, Serial 1560, pp. 497–498, and the Garfield Papers for Welsh's letter of November 20, 1872.

[245] A military wagon road from Fort Benton to Walla Walla built and improved under the direction of Lt. John Mullan between 1859 and 1862.

travelled upon it. On the way Clagett shot seven crows in the space of five minutes. Reached Deer Lodge an hour before midnight. Steve being sober drove very slow and did not denounce Greeley anything like so fiercely as on the down journey, although he still refused to support him.

WEDNESDAY, 28. After two hours and a half of sleep at the hotel, we took the stage for Helena. While riding over the dividing line, I found that one of the express messengers was Al Graeter, a Trumbull Co. boy. Everywhere on this journey I have met men whose career in this country is a romance of itself. Reached Helena at 4 o'clock P.M. and found a large mail awaiting me. Good news from home and from Leavenworth. Took tea at Viall's in company with Swaim, Mr. and Mrs. Sanders and Mrs. Judge Wade.

THURSDAY, 29. Spent a delightful day at Helena. Accompanied by several gentlemen, we were driven at least 30 miles through the valley of the Prickly Pear. The fertility of the soil when properly irrigated is something wonderful. They showed me an acre of ground from which had been cut ninety-three bushels of wheat. We drove to the Warm Springs which are in themselves very wonderful. Took a late dinner at Col. Sanders' in company with Mr. and Mrs. Viall, Judge and Mrs. Wade and Major Swaim. A very pleasant party. In the evening visited the Chinese quarter of the city and saw something of their gambling habits. Finished a letter of instructions to Colonel Viall in regard to carrying out the contract with the Flatheads.[246]

[246] In his letter (see Garfield's Report, Serial 1560, p. 500), Garfield indicated that he had concluded "to proceed with the work in the same manner as though Charlot, the first chief, had signed the contract. I do this in the belief that when he sees the work actually going forward he will conclude to come here with the other chiefs and thus keep the tribe unbroken." Garfield had agreed that there should be built for the Indians on the reservation 60 houses or as many of the 60 as were required, the ordinary houses to be 12 by 16 feet, those of the chiefs to be twice that size. In his letter he gave detailed specifications:

The plan of the houses, for which estimates were made and examined last evening, is approved, namely, a frame 12 feet by 16 feet, boarded and tightly battened, a battened floor, and roughly ceiled on the upper joists, which shall be 8 feet above the ground-floor. The

FRIDAY, 30. Bidding our friends good by, we took the early stage
for the south, passing the dry gulch where stands the great dead
pine on which so many men were hung by the Vigilantes. The driver
told me that he predicted that the tree would not live ten days
after the first men were hung upon it. This was the driver's philosophy: "Man is the master of this world, and when his spirit goes
out, something has to go with it, and trees on which men have been
hung always die." Reached Gaffney's late at night.

SATURDAY, 31. The stock on this line have been fed only on bunch
grass nearly all summer and are beginning to show the want of
oats. The roads are getting a little heavy and we are losing time.
We concluded on this journey not to wash our faces, and thus
avoid the bad effects of the alkali dust on the skin. Our stage is
less crowded than when we came up, but the Jerkie which we took
during part of the day is unpleasantly full. Reached Pleasant Valley
for a late supper. Our appetites are wonderfully keen on this
journey. The air is a perpetual inspiration and appetizer.

September

SUNDAY, 1. Were delayed several hours because the "stock" could
not be found, it having wandered into the mountains. Made slow
progress. Reached Corbett's late at night.

MONDAY, 2. Heavy showers made the road hard for the horses and
unpleasant for us. While passing the divide from Marsh Creek to
Malad, a rattlesnake crossed our track, and this led to a long discus-

---

roof shall be of good pine shingles. The main room shall be lined
on the inside with boards at least three-quarters of an inch in thick-
ness, and the space between the outside and the inside linings shall be
filled with earth. At one end of the house shall be an adobe chimney,
and on the opposite end a matched and jointed door, a sliding-sash
window of twelve panes of 8 by 10 glass, and in the gable attic a
window of six panes.

The houses for the three chiefs shall be of the same description as
above, with a similar house added to one side as a wing, thus making
two separate communicating rooms.

sion on the origin to [of] man's hostility to the snake. A good deal of curious philosophy and much talent was developed in the party; one being a distinguished professor of medicine, and another an ex-member of Congress from Missouri. Reached Malad City in the evening. Got a good supper at Kinney's. They have dropped the "e" from the word "Malad" and the Mormons probably do not know the origin of the name of the place, which looks as sickly as the exterior of the houses, they having only dirt for their roofs.

TUESDAY, 3. It was near daybreak when we reached Corinne. We are [were] quite in doubt whether to take the western train for San Francisco and to catch a glimpse of the Pacific, or to turn our faces homeward. Finding ourselves, however, too late for the western train, and the eastern train being expected in the course of two hours, we reluctantly postponed, to a day uncertain, the pleasure of a visit to California, and taking the five o'clock train for Ogden, there secured berths in the sleeping car for the East. Out of the Echo Cañon and along the alkali plains, where here and there a flock of antelopes and a herd of prairie wolves were in sight, we swept on homeward, going to sleep a little while after we crossed Green River.

WEDNESDAY, 4. Found on board a Mr. [Mortimer James] Lawrence of the *Cleveland Herald* who had just returned from China. He had been 35 days out of reach of newspapers and was hungry for the news of what had happened in the U. S. during the interval. Good appetite and good meals and the prospect of reaching friends at home made the day pass pleasantly until 1 P.M. when we reached Cheyenne. Having nearly two hours to wait for our train to Denver, we called on Col. [James M.] Moore, Assistant Quartermaster, and visited the post. He brought us back to the station two minutes after the train had gone. We made the best of it by visiting this young Capital of Wyoming and its surroundings.

THURSDAY, 5. We took breakfast with Governor Campbell[247] of Salem, Ohio, Chief Executive of Wyoming Territory. His wife was

---

[247] John Allen Campbell (1835–1880) of Ohio, a Union officer during the Civil War, and an officer in the regular army, 1867–69, was the first governor of Wyoming Territory, 1869–75. In 1875 he received an appointment in the State Department.

an old Washington acquaintance, daughter of Judge [Joseph] Casey's. After breakfast went out to the post with Colonel Moore and amused ourselves by shooting at a mark at long range. My shots averaged the best of any of the party. Took the afternoon train for Denver, passing the young colony of Greeley, whose Chief is N. C. Meeker,[248] late a citizen of Hiram. His colony is a triumph of the co-operative principle and exhibits the success of irrigation in these plains. Reached Denver just before sundown and took supper at the hotel with Dr. [Timothy] Woodbridge of Youngstown, Ohio. Took the evening train eastward, but not being able to get a sleeping car, sat up all night.

FRIDAY, 6. Over the cheerless plains, which I think it will be very difficult to make fertile for want of water. A few buffaloes in sight, but they have been hunted until they are so wild that they keep shy of the train. These with antelopes and wolves and here and there a straggling hut near the station were the only signs of life today. Reach[ed] Salina and the borders of civilization tonight and we were able to secure a sleeping berth for Leavenworth. The prospect of rest unusually grateful.

SATURDAY, 7. The porter's cry of "Leavenworth in 20 minutes" woke us from a very sound sleep, and we had barely time to dress and wash before our train entered the Leavenworth depot. An orderly from the fort with an ambulance and four stout mules was ready to take us and our luggage and in ¾ of an hour we were taking a delightful breakfast with our wives at Major Swaim's headquarters. All had been well in our absence except Mollie, who had been sick with the chills, and she was looking thin and pale. I return greatly improved in strength, but nearly as much black and tan as the Flatheads whom I left behind.

---

[248] Nathan Cook Meeker (1817–1879) opened a store in Hiram about the time the Western Reserve Eclectic Institute was established and remained there for several years before going to work for Horace Greeley on the *Tribune*, for which he became agricultural editor. Long interested in Fourierism, he founded in 1870 the agricultural cooperative community of Greeley on the Platte River. In 1878 he became an Indian agent and was killed by Utes the following year.

SUNDAY, 8. Spent the day resting and reading my mail and reading up what the world has done since we have been gone.

MONDAY, 9. The political campaign has been waged with unparalleled bitterness and acrimony during the 30 days I have been absent. I find my own name dragged into some story which I do not understand but see only referred to in the newspapers.[249] From the

[249] On September 4, 1872, Charles Anderson Dana broke the news of the Credit Mobilier scandal by publishing documents related to it in his *New York Sun*. One of the documents listed a number of congressmen, including Garfield, as stockholders of the corporation. From that time the press devoted a large amount of attention to the matter. The affair reached the public as a result of a suit brought by Henry S. McComb against Credit Mobilier to force the delivery of shares in the corporation which he claimed. McComb was represented by Garfield's friend, Jeremiah S. Black.

In 1867 seven directors of the Union Pacific Railway Corporation, one of whom was Congressman Oakes Ames of Massachusetts, put into operation a carefully wrought plan. They organized a construction company and secured for it the charter of The Credit Mobilier of America, a corporation chartered by the state of Pennsylvania. The railroad corporation then contracted with the construction company for the completion of the remaining 667 miles of the Union Pacific line. The profits received by the directors and their associates in this scheme were the result of the federal govenment's generous subsidy in the form of lands and loans to the railroad corporation, which it had chartered.

Fearing hostile action by Congress, the group attempted in 1867–68 to forestall it by distributing through Oakes Ames shares of Credit Mobilier stock among influential congressmen. One of those approached was Garfield.

On September 29, 1872, Jeremiah Black wrote to Garfield urging him not to attempt any defense of Ames or his ring. "You have, I believe, no idea of what it is like. It will turn out to be the most enormous fraud that has ever been perpetrated." He said he thought that Garfield ought sooner or later to give the public the explanation which he had given to Black, "& wh. nobody can doubt is the true one." Black then proceeded to recapitulate Garfield's story as he remembered it from 1870, when Black had made known to Garfield the nature of Credit Mobilier:

1. You regarded O. A. as a perfectly upright man—an example of solid integrity—had no suspicion that he had private interests to take care of as a member of Congress, much less that he was a ring-leader in any fraud.

2. He offered you some stock in Cred. Mob.—offered to sell it at par, & assured you that in his judgment it w'd be a good investment.

3. You declined at first to take it (tho you believed what he said about it) because you had not the money to pay for it; and he then offered & urged you to take it on credit, w'h you did.

4. When you made the contract you were not informed, did not believe, & had no reason to believe, that the Cred. Mob. had any connection with the Un. Pac. R. R. Co., or with anything else upon w'h Congress c'd by any possibility be called on to legislate.

5. At a subsequent time, when you proposed to adjust y'r indebtedness for the stock, Mr. A. put you off by saying that the Co. was doing very well, was making dividends w'h he w'd credit on the price of the stock.

6. At a still later time he showed you an acc't in w'h you were charged with the price of the stock at par, & credited with the dividends rec'd by him for you. This left a balance in y'r favor, w'h he then paid.

7. During all this time you were not informed & did not suspect that the Cred. Mob. was connected with the U. P. R. R. Co. or that either of those companies was committing any wrong against the U. S. or any body else.

"I think I am accurate substantially," Black went on to say. "It relieves you entirely from every imputation w'h A's statement unexplained might cast upon you. It shows that you were not the instrument of his corruption, but the victim of his deception. O. A. did undoubtedly intend to corrupt the M.C.s to whom he gave the stock."

On the question of Garfield's having agreed to take the shares of stock and of his having received a payment from Ames, the story as recalled by Black is in essential accord with testimony of Ames before the Poland Committee, which investigated the matter in 1873.

Garfield himself in a published statement and in his testimony before the Poland Committee told a different story. He declared that he had never agreed to take the stock (no one ever claimed that delivery had been made) and that when he learned from Judge Black of the nature of the Credit Mobilier scheme, he at once told Ames that he would not take the stock. He denied that he had received the $329 dividend balance (after the stock had been paid for in full from dividends) which Ames claimed to have paid him. Instead, he declared that he had borrowed $300 of Ames which he had subsequently repaid.

The Poland Committee reported that Garfield had agreed to take the stock but had never paid for it, that he had received $329 as a balance of dividends,

accounts I hear Ohio is apathetic and perhaps in danger, and I must go home and give what days I can to the Republican cause. Visited Gen'l Pope. Made several calls on friends at the Fort and at two o'clock the Major took us in the ambulance across the river to East Leavenworth, where we took the train for Kansas City and at 5 o'clock were on the sleeping car for Chicago making our way eastward. Took supper at Cameron and night closed over us amid the cornfields of central Missouri.

TUESDAY, 10. Waked near Galesburg, Illinois. Our whole journey today was a succession of rolling prairies and wonderful fields of corn. I am not surprised at the pride which Illinoisians feel in their state. Its growth is the wonder of modern civilization. Reached Chicago about 3 o'clock. Made our way with some difficulty through the crowded streets. They were full of business, industry, in its fullest exercise. At 5 o'clock we were in the sleeping car for Cleveland. When making our way around the southern point of Michigan, saw more and more evidence of the bitterness and fierceness of the

---

and that after this payment there was no communication on the subject between Garfield and Ames until the investigation began. The committee was unable to find that Garfield had "any other purpose in taking this stock than to make a profitable investment," or that his interest in Credit Mobilier had in any way affected his "official action."

One thing seems very clear: that Garfield had no knowledge of the nature of Credit Mobilier until Black enlightened him in the winter of 1869–70 and "showed him how impossible it was for a member of Congress to hold stock in it without bringing his private interests in conflict with his public duty." To Black Garfield's integrity in the whole affair depended not upon "the question whether he had made a bargain technically binding," but upon the question "whether he acted with his eyes open." If Black, Ames and the Poland Committee were correct in their view of Garfield's relation to Credit Mobilier, it is to be regretted that he did not deal more candidly with the public and with the investigating committee.

The letter of Black to Garfield, September 29, 1872, is not in the Garfield Papers. The original or a copy is preserved in the Black Papers in the Library of Congress. The quotations in the preceding paragraph are from a letter of Black to James G. Blaine, February 15, 1873, which appears in Garfield's *Review of the Transactions of the Credit Mobilier Company* (1873), p. 14.

pending campaign. Wrote a note to Colfax asking about the nature of the slander against him and me and others.[250]

WEDNESDAY, 11. At 7 o'clock this morning the odor of petroleum filled the cars and informed us we were reaching the suburbs of Cleveland. In five minutes after our train stopped at the Atlantic and Great Western depot we were on the train towards home. At Solon we were joined by Mother and Harry and Jimmy. Reached Garrettsville before 9 o'clock and at ½ past ten were at home in Hiram. All the family are reunited after 50 days' separation. Wrote letters until late at night.

THURSDAY, 12. Before entering the campaign I must make a report to the Secretary of the Interior of my mission to the Flatheads and place the contract in his hands for approval and execution. Just before starting to the cars Crete suggested that Harry was now old enough to be his father's travelling companion. I therefore took him with me and we went to Garrettsville and took the train to Niles, thence to Leetonia, where we waited two hours getting dinner and visiting the iron mills and thence to Pittsburgh, where we took [the] Baltimore sleeping car for Washington.

FRIDAY, 13. Harry and I reached Washington at one P.M. Immediately commenced to work off my correspondence. Called at the Indian Department and made arrangements to meet them tomorrow.

SATURDAY, 14. Spent four hours at the Indian Department making a report of my mission to the Flatheads. Continued working at correspondence. Saw Mr. Carstens in reference to painting walls and working up the house. Went to the Treasury Department and transacted various miscellaneous business. Harry was seriously sick in the night from overeating.

SUNDAY, 15. Attended to correspondence. Called on the Attorney General and newspaper correspondents. In the evening wrote up

MONDAY, 16. Left Washington at 7.15 P.M. by the Baltimore and my diary.

---

[250] Vice President Schuyler Colfax had, while speaker of the House, contracted to buy shares in Credit Mobilier; he insisted before the Poland Committee, however, that he had changed his mind and had not done so, and had not received any dividends. The record of Oakes Ames showed otherwise.

Potomac R.R. Reached Baltimore at 9 o'clock and after an omnibus ride of one mile reached the Northern Central depot and took a sleeping car for Pittsburgh. Harry is proving himself a good traveller. Senator Wilson, candidate for Vice President, in the train with us. Also many soldiers on their way to the great convention.[251] Wilson gave me a curious history of a political forgery in the shape of a supposed speech denouncing foreigners. First that it was delivered by Hon. John [Jeremiah?] M. Wilson of Indiana at Salem, Indiana, in 1855. Second, by Hon. Schuyler Colfax, story told in 1862. Third, by Hon. Henry Wilson at Salem, Mass. Same speech attributed to each, and made by nobody. *Crescit eundo* [It grows as it goes].

TUESDAY, 17.   After breakfasting at Altoona we passed the mountains by daylight, much to the satisfaction of Harry. At 9.45 we reached Pittsburgh and were escorted to the Monongahela House among immense throngs of soldiers and citizens. I have never seen a city more gorgeously decorated. There must be from 30,000 to 40,000 visitors here. Convention met and effected its temporary organization in the forenoon. In the afternoon Logan,[252] Wilson and I spoke in the Academy of Music. Harry and I went to Hazelwood and staid at Mr. Lewis'. Heard Isaac Errett preach in the evening. A very fine sermon.

In my speech today I tried to give voice to the spirit of our assembly. In general I don't think our soldiers' meeting ought to go into politics. But this year we have been specially assailed and our right to participate in political movements has been challenged. Hence I spoke.[253]

WEDNESDAY, 18.   At 7 A.M. took the train to Pittsburgh and at

[251] On September 17, 1872, the tenth anniversary of the battle of Antietam, a convention of Union veterans convened at Pittsburgh to endorse the Republican national candidates.

[252] John Alexander Logan (1826–1886), Illinois politician and Union general, was a Republican member of the House, 1867–71, and of the Senate, 1871–77 and 1879–86. He was prominent in veterans' affairs.

[253] At least one of Garfield's friends was critical of the speech. Professor Arthur Latham Perry of Williams wrote to him on January 17, 1873: "I did not like your speech in Pittsburgh to the soldiers. It was too inflammatory, too one-sided, emphasized slight differences—sunk the common ground on which all good citizens stand."

10 A.M. left by the Pittsburgh, Ft. Wayne and Chicago R.R. for Leetonia, where we took dinner. Spent some time with Servis and talked of taking an interest with him in a patent bolt washer. At 2 P.M. left for Niles and thence to Garrettsville, where a large Republican meeting was assembled. Spoke for two hours and then went to Hiram, reaching home at half-past ten P.M. weary and glad.

I wish I could cry quits with the public for a few months, and that each might let the other quite alone. It might weary me of such unusual silence, but tonight I would take it as balm.

THURSDAY, 19. Spent the day till midnight [middle] of the afternoon in answering letters and reading up my newspaper mail. This campaign has more mean personal elements in it than any I have ever known. The disruption of party organizations leaves the mere politician to fall back on personal scandal. The Credit Mobilier story started by the N.Y. *Sun* is one of the vilest and boldest pieces of rascality in the way of wicked journalism I have ever seen. I think this independent of the fact that my own name is so unjustly involved in the lie. At four P.M. Mr. Higley came for me and took me to Windham in the midst of a heavy shower. Took supper at his house. Spoke two hours in the Town Hall. Bad cold and hoarse. Staid over night at Dr. [F. C.] Applegate's.

FRIDAY, 20. Took train to Ravenna at 9.45 and was met at the depot by Halsey Hall and John Beatty. After dinner at Hall's, Beatty and Meharg took me to Randolph, where a great procession was already in motion to the grove. Spoke nearly two hours. Though hoarse succeeded pretty well. Answered questions of bolting Republicans. Returned to Ravenna, and after supper and Wide-Awake display, spoke an hour and a half to a large crowd in front of the Court House. Did fairly well, not so well as this P.M. The enthusiasm of the people has outrun me. I am surprised at its extent and force. I think the defections from our party have helped to increase it. Passed the night at Halsey Hall's.

SATURDAY, 21. John Meharg took me to Mantua 9 miles distant, where I got the train for Solon at 9.23 and found Crete and our two mothers and two youngest children on board. Reached Solon at little after ten and found a carriage and mounted escort of 75 men awaiting me. Went with them to Chagrin Falls. After dinner the long procession from surrounding towns moved up to a groove in the outskirts of the town and I spoke about two hours. Did quite well in spite of my hoarseness. This is nearer my birthplace than I ever made a political speech before. Went to Orange with Cousin Henry Boynton. Crete and her party came down from Solon and we spent the night at the old spot where I began life. How I would love for a few days at least to be left alone by the world, as I once was in this place. Am nearly sick.

SUNDAY, 22. Spent most of the day at Henry's. Translated and wrote out the greater part of an article from the *Revue des Deux Mondes*, entitled *"Italie a l' o[e]uvre de 1861 a 1868."* [254] At 3 P.M. Henry took us to Sister Mary's at Solon where we spent the night. I am greatly depressed by illness and at the thought of having my name dragged about at the heels of newspaper scavengers, as it is now being done in connection with the Credit Mobilier slander. While it will all come out right at last, it grieves me that strangers may think me unworthy.

MONDAY, 23. Took the 10 o'clock train to Cleveland. Visited the County Central Committee. Wrote letters making appointments for next week. Took dinner at Dr. Robison's. At 2.45 P.M. took train for Grafton where I was met by Medina Committee and driven to Litchfield, ten miles, in 45 minutes. Political meeting had adjourned till evening. At 7 P.M. I addressed for two hours a very large audience. The elements were in accord and I made the most effective speech I have yet made. Spent the night at John Sears's who was a member of the Ohio legislature in 1860–1. Continued activity of the mind seems to be as necessary to the maintenance of power as to the acquiring of it. Moths and rust will corrupt.

TUESDAY, 24. Early in the morning Mr. Sears drove me ten miles to Wellington and from there Hon. Sidney Warner[255] drove me thirty-five miles to Fairfield, Huron Co., where I spoke an hour and a half in a high wind to a quiet audience. Not a great success this time. I was choking hoarse. A committee took me ten miles to Norwalk. After ten was serenaded and spoke for 20 minutes to a thousand

---

[254] M. Marc-Monnier, *"L'Italie a L'Oeuvre de 1860 a 1868,"* *Revue des Deux Mondes*, LXXVI (Paris, 1868), 821–863.

[255] Sidney S. Warner of Lorain County served in the Ohio legislature, 1862–65.

people in the streets. A good night's rest at Norwalk. I have made several inquiries today after a school mate of twenty-five years ago —Philo Stevenson—formerly of Clarksfield, Huron Co. I can hear nothing from him. I say with Tennyson "Does my old friend remember me?"

WEDNESDAY, 25. Took the 7.30 A.M. train for Toledo. Called on [Isaac] Sherwood and talked over prospects of the campaign. After dinner took cars to Haskins, twenty-five miles south of Toledo, where I was met by a committee and driven eight miles to Bowling Green, Wood Co. Fortunately for me the weather was threatening and the audience assembled in the Court House. I spoke effectively for two hours and after tea was driven twenty-two miles to Elmore where I passed the night.

This has been a hard day, and [I] ought to have caught the ague in my long ride across the low and marshy lands of Wood County among the foul mists of the evening.

THURSDAY, 26. Took the train at 7.30 A.M. for Clyde and thence to Kenton, where I was met by a committee and band—also by the Rev. Mr. [William] Dowling, a student of mine 18 years ago. After dinner joined procession of citizens for half an hour. I then spoke two hours from the Court House steps. A great and enthusiastic meeting. My voice is mending. Took tea at Dowling's, Sutton and Lorena Young (Hiram students) there also. Great procession of Wide Awakes, horse and foot, in the evening. Gen'l Hall[256] of Maine spoke an hour and a half. He made a stirring speech. I took occasion today to expose the demagogueism of Gen. Morgan.[257] He has been pretending to be a tariff man as to wool—all this for the sheep-farmers of this county. Night at the hotel.

FRIDAY, 27. In the forenoon joined several members of the Kenton Board of Education and visited the Union School which is under charge of Sutton Young. Addressed the high school for twenty

---

[256] James A. Hall (1835–1893), Union soldier, and a collector of customs in Maine, 1866–82, was an ardent Republican who was well known as a public speaker and orator. In 1872 he made a tour of the southern states, speaking in the largest cities.

[257] George Washington Morgan, of Mt. Vernon, a Union officer, was a Democratic member of the House from Ohio, 1867–68 and 1869–73.

minutes. At 11.30 took train to Urbana. Was met by Mr. [Griffith] Ellis and other members of the Urbana committee. Drove to the fairgrounds and spent two or three hours among the crowds at the races. In the evening spoke nearly two hours in the City Hall. My throat behaves well. People not so much aroused as at other places on the trip. Greeley's recent career of speaking in Ohio, Pennsylvania, Kentucky [and] Indiana has been I think unwise on his part. It has helped us. Grant's "silence" even though it be enforced "is golden" in comparison with Greeley's garrulity. Many citizens called at my room after the meeting, among others Mr. Plants[258] of Pomeroy, Ohio, late a member of Congress, but now a preacher in the Swedenborgian church. I believe there is much good and truth in Swedenborg, but I don't believe he intended to found a sect.

SATURDAY, 28.   At five P.M. [A.M.] took the train for Xenia where I arrived at 7. Found B. F. Wade who at the age of 72 is making vigorous speeches every day. Will that be said of me 31 years hence? I weary at the thought of such a possibility. After breakfast a committee met me and drove to the Ohio Home for Soldiers' Orphans, where we visited a few minutes and then proceeded 18 miles to Wilmington, Clinton Co. Met my old friend and brother Senator, J. Q. Smith, now a candidate for Congress. After dinner spoke in the City Hall one hour and three-quarters. My throat behaves unusually well and I succeeded well in the speech. Short-hand reporter for the *Cincinnati Commercial* was there and reported me. Mr. Warwick of N.Y. is to follow me this evening. After meeting drove back to Xenia. At 8.20 took cars to Dayton and at midnight took Atlantic and Great Western sleeping car for the north. Very tired by [but] happy in the thought of reaching home and a few days' rest.

This has been a very hard week; but I think it has been fruitful in good results. Several times during the week I have had pleasant recognitions of the fact that I have not done so much hard work without making the result felt and recognized among the thoughtful men of the country.

---

[258] Tobias Avery Plants (1811–1887) was a Republican member of the House from Ohio, 1865–69, and judge of the Court of Common Pleas in Meigs County, 1873–75.

SUNDAY, 29. Reached Freedom Station from Dayton at 8 A.M. Mr. Hine took me home to Hiram. Attended church and heard a very solid sermon from B. A. Hinsdale. He is steadily growing in strength.

MONDAY, 30. Worked up my correspondence and read up the great mass of newspapers that had accumulated in my absence. Prepared an outline of a long speech on the issues of the campaign in which I followed up the history of the liberal movement and the coalition with the Democrats in connection with the Minority Report on the Ku Klux.[259]

Read up a curious chapter in Greeley's congressional history as found in the *Globe* of January 25th, 1849, but I will not use it against him in the canvass. I will do nothing to increase the spirit of personal detraction which so fearfully prevails in this campaign.[260]

October

TUESDAY, 1. Went to Cleveland by the morning train and attended the great mass meeting. Was met at the depot by Mr. Starkweather

[259] In April, 1871, Congress established a joint select committee to report on the condition of affairs in the late insurrectionary states. In its reports the committee divided along party lines. The Republican majority emphasized evidence of Klan activity, supported the Administration's southern policy and recommended the continuance of the President's authorization to suspend the privilege of the writ of habeas corpus. The Democratic minority considered Klan activity grossly exaggerated, charged Grant with maladministration in the South and condemned the suspension of the privilege of the writ of habeas corpus. The Liberal Republicans were in essential accord with the minority report. The reports are in *House Executive Documents*, 42 Cong., 2 Sess., Serial 1529.

[260] Horace Greeley was a Whig member of the House from New York for a few months in 1848–49. On January 25, 1849, he sought to amend the army appropriation bill to effect a reduction in expenditures. In arguing against an appropriation for army recruiting he declared with reference to Indian wars that "if we had no army, we should not get into these wars at all, except at a few exposed points. Our people would not be so ready to encroach upon the Indians; they would not act with the same impunity that they now do, if we had no army to back them." See *Congressional Globe*, 30 Cong., 2 Sess., pp. 370–371.

and taken to the Kennard House where I found Speaker Blaine. We called on Senator Wilson at the Weddell House. Wilson spoke on the Public Square at 2 o'clock, but the rain drove us to the rink where I spoke at ½ past three. Was reasonably successful. Great parade. Fireworks in the evening. Spent the night at Dr. Robison's, where he rubbed my neck with Wizard Oil and succeeded in working out of it the rheumatism of which I had a sharp attack this morning.

I undertook today a new line of argument and shall watch its effects on the campaign hereafter. It was a chronological statement of the history of the Greeley-Democratic Coalition.

WEDNESDAY, 2. Went by 12 o'clock A.M. train to Painesville and stopped at the Parmly House. Great crowd of people notwithstanding the rain. In the afternoon spoke two hours to a crowded audience in the Hall. In the evening spoke an hour and a half at the Opera House making a long speech. My speech of the afternoon was more successful than most I have made. Lake County is wonderfully aroused. Spent the night at the Parmly House. My first speech of today was on a higher key of intensity and force than I mean to use again. The defections from our party in this town have roused me too much.

THURSDAY, 3. Made a few calls with Mr. [William H.] Upson and at ten o'clock took a carriage with Messrs. Scofield[261] and Teachout for Madison 12 miles distant. We were escorted by a squad of Wide Awake cavalry. At two o'clock addressed a large out door meeting for an hour and three-quarters. At 6 o'clock went by rail to Willoughby, where I was met at the station by two or three hundred Wide Awakes and a great crowd of people. The College Hall which would hold about 1,500 people was crowded to its utmost capacity. After I had spoken for half an hour word came that there

---

[261] Jonathan F. Scofield, one of the editors and proprietors of the *Painesville Telegraph*, was chairman of the Republican Central Committee of Lake County. In 1873, with Garfield's support, he became postmaster at Painesville, a position he held for a number of years.

This was Garfield's first congressional election in which Lake County formed part of his district; in the redistricting he lost Mahoning County. The change relieved him from the pressures of the Mahoning iron interests.

were 500 people at the door who could not get in and who requested that I come out and address them a little while. Two hundred of them had come from Painesville. I went out and addressed them for one quarter of an hour and then returned and finished my speech in the hall. Am quite hoarse and very tired. Spent the night at Dr. Eli Clark's.

FRIDAY, 4. Took the morning train for Ashtabula where I waited an hour and then by the new railroad went to Jefferson. Took dinner at S. A. Northway's[262] and then for nearly two hours addressed a very large mass meeting in front of the Court House.

Returned in the evening train to Ashtabula and spoke for an hour and a half in the Opera House to a crowded audience, while Dr. Burrows and Hon. L. S. Sherman[263] addressed a still larger audience in the Park. When our Opera House meeting adjourned we all went down to the Park and I spoke again for twenty minutes to not less than three thousand people. About 500 Wide Awakes with torches were present. Spent the night at Henry Fassett's.

SATURDAY, 5. Took the morning train to Painesville, where I got breakfast at the Parmly House, and then went by the new narrow gauge road to Chardon. Was met at the depot by a large delegation and escorted to the village. After dinner addressed not less than 3,000 people in front of the Court House for nearly two hours. Messrs. Hathaway,[264] D. W. Canfield, and the brothers McCalmont drove with me to Parkman, 16 miles distant. After taking supper at Mrs. Darius Lyman's,[265] addressed a very enthusiastic meeting of not less than 3,500 people in the open air. Did not commence

---

[262] Stephen Asa Northway (1833–1898), Ashtabula County lawyer and political leader, was a Republican member of the House, 1893–98. In 1874 he won a number of delegates from Ashtabula County to the nominating convention in opposition to Garfield; in 1876 he withdrew his candidacy before the convention met.

[263] Laban S. Sherman, Ashtabula lawyer, member of the Ohio legislature, 1852–55, judge of the Court of Common Pleas for the 9th district, 1877–92.

[264] Isaac Newton Hathaway (b. 1827), Chardon lawyer, was a member of the Ohio legislature, 1874–75 and 1880–81.

[265] Wife of Darius Lyman of Portage County, chief of the Navigation Division of the U. S. Treasury Department.

speaking until nearly 9 o'clock. Display of artillery, fireworks, Wide Awake torches and several bands of music, and the entire audience to a supper prepared by the citizens. Hinsdale had come over from Hiram and we drove back together reaching home about an hour after midnight.

SUNDAY, 6. Attended church and rested. Am very weary and quite hoarse.

MONDAY, 7. Accompanied by Jimmy went to Garrettsville and took the morning train to Warren in the midst of a heavy rain. Was met at the station by Messrs. Austin, Morgan[266] and Taylor and went with them 12 miles to North Bristol. Toward noon the weather cleared up. After dinner at Mr. Hughes's proceeded to the grove where at 2 o'clock were assembled not less than three thousand people. Spoke for an hour and three-quarters and took a lunch at the tables prepared in the grove for the audience. Drove back to Warren and made calls in the evening. Have been consulting with our friends on the situation and spent the night at Harmon Austin's. I hope never again to be so anxious about the result of an election.

TUESDAY, 8. Took the morning train for Garrettsville and thence drove home to Hiram. Voted about noon and read and rested until towards evening. It is difficult to calculate chances of this day's work in the three great states of Ohio, Pennsylvania and Indiana. I think we shall carry, but we cannot measure the defection from our own party, and the election may be close. We may lose it. Went to Cleveland in the evening train. Mother joined me at Solon. We stopped at Dr. Boynton's. Spent until 12 o'clock at the Rink; received election returns. We have gained a great victory. Our party have had some heavy loads to carry. The presidential election is virtually ended, but I suspect this is the last presidential victory for the Republican Party.

WEDNESDAY, 9. We have carried everything before us except the governorship of Indiana. This campaign has been remarkable for its personal violence and for the uncertainties attending it. Our party ought, perhaps, not to succeed now, but the combination against us

266 Orlando Morgan, Warren businessman, was chairman of the Republican Central Committee of Trumbull County.

was so absurd and so wicked as to make our party relatively high toned and noble.

Took the morning train for the West with Mother at 8 P.M. Reached North Byron Station, Kent County, Mich., where my brother Thomas, his wife and son met us. After supper at Mrs. Thomas' near the station, drove home to my brother's in Jamestown. Brother Thomas shows the marks of his years more than I supposed.

THURSDAY, 10. Went over to my brother's farm to study the condition of his affairs. Urged him to secure a good team and agreed to give him $100 towards its purchase. Visited and renewed old memories. Towards noon walked five miles with my brother to Uncle William Boynton's.[267] Then visited Aunt Harriet Boynton[268] and took tea there. Took the five o'clock train at North Byron for the East. Reached the main line of the Lake Shore Road at Lockhart, Indiana at 10 P.M., but could get no sleeping car until we reached Toledo, two hours after midnight. This made a very hard night of it. With a good allowance of food and sleep, I hardly know yet the limits of my powers of work and endurance; but when either of these conditions fail I reach the limit very soon.

FRIDAY, 11. Reached Cleveland at 7.25 A.M. and ten minutes thereafter was on the Atlantic and Great Western train. Reached home at ten in the morning. Spent the rest of the day in working up correspondence and resting. The Coalition of Liberal Republicans and Democrats seems to have broken down the rank and file of the Democrats. They don't preserve their old discipline, but broke ranks considerably in the late fight. I think Mr. Greeley has been a positive element of weakness in the coalition. Either Groesbeck[269] or [Charles Francis] Adams would have made a much better run. His speeches in his own behalf hurt him seriously. I doubt if any President can aid himself by speaking [in] his own campaign.

[267] William Boynton (1818–1873), half-brother of Garfield's father.

[268] Harriet Wilson Boynton, widow of Garfield's father's half-brother, Jerry Boynton, who died in 1871.

[269] William Slocum Groesbeck (1815–1897), an Ohio lawyer, was a leader of the Liberal Republican movement. Dissatisfaction with Horace Greeley as the party's candidate led a small group of liberals to nominate him for the presidency in 1872.

James Mason and wife came in the evening. Spent the night at Rudolphs'.

SATURDAY, 12. Delivered a lecture in the College Chapel on the life, services and character of William H. Seward,[270] who died two days ago. There is much in the career of Mr. Seward to admire. I do not think he ever seriously harbored personal enmity. I find a great difference between him and most of the old anti-slavery leaders. He was an able defender of liberty and never rendered his advocacy offensively personal. In this he greatly differed from most of his associates.

In the afternoon went with Crete to Uncle Charles Raymond's,[271] where we visited with the four surviving members of Crete's mother's family. After tea went to Hinsdale's where we spent the evening.

SUNDAY, 13. Attended church. Hinsdale preached. In the evening I delivered an address to a large audience in the church on the Indian Question.

MONDAY, 14. Spent the day in finishing my correspondence, overhauling the library, putting my papers in order, settling bills at the stores and closing up my Hiram affairs preparatory to leaving for Washington. Sent four of our trunks to Garrettsville in the afternoon and made arrangements for an early start. Made the usual annual measurements of the children. This will be the 19th trip that my family have taken with me to Washington. Public life makes it impossible for a man to have that fixed home life so necessary to the proper training of a family. Before very long I must seriously consider the bearing of this fact upon the developement of my children.

TUESDAY, 15. Left for Garrettsville with my family, 8 strong, where we were joined by the 9th (Mrs. Humphrey from Cleveland) and took the train at 8.45 for Niles and thence to Leetonia, which we reached at 11 o'clock. After dinner we took the 2 o'clock train for Pittsburgh, which we reached at 5. After supper and waiting until 7.25, took the train and two and one-half sections of sleeping car

[270] William Henry Seward (1801–1872), governor of New York, 1838–42, U. S. senator, 1849–61, secretary of state, 1861–69.

[271] Charles Raymond married Emeline Mason (d. 1881), sister of Garfield's wife's mother; they lived in Hiram.

for Baltimore, checking our trunks through to Washington for the first time in our experience. Still we were compelled to ride about three miles in carriages to get from the Harrisburg depot to the present depot of the Baltimore and Potomac R.R. It will be many months before the tunnel under Baltimore is done so that we can connect directly from the Northern Central to Washington.

WEDNESDAY, 16. Reached Baltimore at 7 in the morning. Drove through the city about two miles and at 8.20 took the Baltimore and Potomac Road for Washington where we arrived at ten o'clock and found 6 painters in the midst of their work and the house upside down. For the fourth time sod is being put down in the yard. Took rooms at Mrs. Whittaker's diagonally opposite our house. Had the basement cleaned so that we sat down to dinner in the kitchen at four o'clock, an excellent one furnished by the joint hospitality of Messrs. Rose and Boston. Family in good condition and feeling well at the prospect of a clean house.

THURSDAY, 17. Superintended the work of the painters who are painting the interior walls and wood work of all but the basement story. Made arrangements for sodding the yard for the fourth time —all other efforts having proved failures: once from a lack of proper soil underneath, twice from poor sod and bad watering after it was down. I think my three failures have taught me how to succeed.

Already the crowd of applicants for help begin to pour in upon me. No class of men need a reform in our civil service so much as members of Congress. For myself I have said for many years—and I say it now with stronger emphasis—that the most intolerable burden I have to bear is the importunate, sometimes meritorious, sometimes worthless and impertinent, seekers for executive appointments. It was a great thing that Thomas Hughes said when [he] declared in his speech at N.Y. that he could not secure the appointment of a clerk in Great Britain.

FRIDAY, 18. Continued the work of yesterday, with the addition [of] a long business visit to the Interior Department. Also looked into the method of procuring a patent in France and in England for the Stoffer nut-lock washer, and wrote to Servis in regard to it.

The rooms in the upper story of our house were finished so that the carpets and furniture may be put in tomorrow. Took Crete to Samuel Kerby's where we selected and purchased some honestly-made furniture for one room so as to put a better set in the boys' room. We hope they will appreciate it and respect the room more by reason of its better appointments. In the evening consulted with Col. Stevens, Clerk of Committee [of] Appropriations in reference to calling the Committee for Nov. 10. The estimates are not yet ready. Harry and I staid in the house over night.

SATURDAY, 19. Had the upper story cleaned out and the carpets and furniture put in place. Called on the President in the morning and had a long talk over the late elections. He compared the noise made by the Liberal Republicans to the deceptive noise made in the West by prairie wolves. He once estimated at 100 the noise made by two of them when he was an officer in Western Texas. This is the first story I have ever heard him tell by way of illustration. I hope he will be able to endure the new victory. Called on Sec'y Boutwell in reference to the estimates, and urged him to hurry them up. Called on Board of Public Works in reference to my special taxes for street and sidewalk. Got the family into the fourth story in the evening and so we at last spent a night at home. It has for the first time, of late, occurred to me that I am the head of a large family. I have always, hitherto, called it a small one.

SUNDAY, 20. We are all weary with the work and travel of the past week and have rested quietly at home, reading and sleeping. Visited Prof. Henry in the evening.

MONDAY, 21. I find myself in great need of a better knowledge of chemistry than I obtained while in college. I am engaged in trial of a case to be heard in the U. S. District Court for Northern Ohio, Oct. 29th, wherein two rival chemical paint patents are in contention. The evidence shows three leading chemists on a side, in collision with each other; and to handle the case intelligently I ought to know enough to sift and weigh the opposing views. That much I do not know. If it is possible [to] learn enough before the day of trial I will do so. I have been at the elements today and have made some progress. I went to the Capitol, Congressional Library, Law Library, and have collected much material for the work. But with my other engagements and duties the time is fearfully short. Took lunch with Gov. Cooke,[272] and talked over the political and financial affairs of the District. This city is being made beautiful by the improvements, but I fear that heavy burdens are being laid upon the tax-payers. All this will come up for consideration when the Appropriation Committee meets. A day of hard work.

TUESDAY, 22. Another day of miscellaneous work finishing correspondence and putting affairs in order before leaving for Ohio. I greatly dislike to leave home at this time, with the house unfinished and many things to be done in and around it; but two lawsuits pending in Ohio and some remaining duties in the campaign make it necessary that I go. This business of dividing life between Ohio and Washington—this moving twice a year—is very unpleasant. I fear its effect on my children will be to leave them with no settled sentiment of home. Perhaps this is a necessary incident to public life, but it is a very uncomfortable way. I wish I could now know what the effect of such a life would be on the developement of our children. If I thought it would be thoroughly bad, I should abandon public life for that reason alone.

WEDNESDAY, 23. Finished an article for the *New York Independent* on the Indian question in which I criticise the theological methods adopted for civilizing the race.[273]. Continued the kind of work

---

[272] Henry David Cooke (1825–1881), long associated in the business affairs of his brother Jay, a leading financier of the period, was the first governor of the District of Columbia, 1871–73, after it was given territorial status.

[273] William Hayes Ward, editor of the *Independent*, asked Garfield to write an article on the Indian policy of the government—"such a one as would succinctly give the facts and show up the wisdom or unwisdom of changing it. You know the *Tribune* calls it an 'utter failure.' " Ward to Garfield, September 9, 1872.

"The Indian Question" appeared in the *Independent* of October 31, 1872. Garfield here expressed the view that the Indians needed practical assistance and instruction before theology. The Jesuits, he felt, had been more successful than other missionaries because they recognized this. He indicated that President Grant's policy was to ask the churches to help to secure faithful Indian agents "rather than to come forward with their theologies." Garfield received $25 for his article.

recorded yesterday until one o'clock, when I took the train for York. Reached there at six and spent the time till midnight at Judge Black's house. With him reviewed our Phillips case and its further demands. Also our dues from the Hunter case in the Supreme Court, not yet paid. Also had a long talk with him on the political situation. It is clear to us that the Greeley movement is a blunder from beginning to end. Also reviewed the Credit Mobilier story and heard from him the history of that organization. I never meet Judge Black without feeling what power culture and genius of mind has to overcome all the roughness of partisan feeling and make a man a great and delightful friend. I am glad the Judge is elected to the [Pennsylvania] Constitutional Convention.

THURSDAY, 24. Awakened in the mountains. Found Mr. [Darius] Lyman and several other acquaintances on the train. Took a late breakfast at Pittsburgh. Reached Leetonia at 2 o'clock and Hiram at 6 o'clock. Found Father Rudolph's family well, but after my great mail was finished I felt how desolate a home is with the family away. This perhaps is the first night in fourteen years that I have ever staid at Father Rudolph's house unaccompanied by Crete. How strangely a man's life drifts out from his control! A few years ago, I could map out my months and days to my own liking. Now they have a current of their own that drives on without much reference to me or my will. I am in the grasp of forces that almost enslave me in reference to my time and movements. Perhaps this is God's mode of discipline.

FRIDAY, 25. Went to Cleveland by morning train to consider the case of the Cleveland Chemical Paint Co., which it is expected will soon come on for hearing. Spent the day with T. Burton [Thomas K. Bolton], one of the counsel, looking over the details of the case. It bristles with chemistry at every point and I now feel how fatal a thing it is for a man to neglect any branch of his college course. Chemistry is the only study in the course that I disliked and although I passed fairly well, I did not study it with the love for it that I felt for other studies. I must atone for it by working it up again. Spent the night at Dr. Robison's.

SATURDAY, 26. Continued working on the Paint Case, also attended to some correspondence and in the afternoon went to Hiram, where I worked on my letters until a late hour of the night. Anxious for news from home but received none. The political excitement seems to have died out wholly in Ohio since the October election.

There may be some danger from apathy, though I think it will affect the Democracy more than it will us. That party has not now the remarkable discipline that characterized it a few years ago. The signs are abundant that it is breaking up. If it is heavily defeated this fall, it can hardly make another national fight.

SUNDAY, 27. Attended church and listened to a very stupid sermon from a very ordinary man—a stranger. For myself, I could have spent the day more profitably in reading, writing, or resting.

MONDAY, 28. Worked on my correspondence until near noon and then went to Hinsdale's to work on our article for the census. We have agreed to prepare one, equal in length to fourteen pages of *Appleton's Encyclopedia*, for a new work to be issued by Dr. Thomas[274] of Philadelphia. Took the evening train for Solon and spent the night with Sister Mary. Am making arrangements with her to come to Washington in a day or two to be with Crete until after her approaching sickness. It is very distressing to me to be away from home at this time, but I cannot well avoid it.

TUESDAY, 29. Went to Cleveland in the morning train with Mary. Went to Dr. Boynton's and after dinner made some purchases and completed arrangements for Sister to start tomorrow for Washington. Our Paint Case will not come off at present and the Patent Marble Case in Lake County Court will be postponed until next session. Took the evening train for Cincinnati to take further part in the presidential campaign. It is difficult to arouse either party to much activity, for the Democracy are discouraged and the Republicans feel sure of success, both conditions being a cause for lethargy.

WEDNESDAY, 30. Reached Cincinnati early in the morning. Took breakfast at the Burnet House. Visited Sam Reed of the *Gazette* and looked over the most dreadful newspaper article I have ever seen. The

[274] Joseph Thomas (1811–1891), Philadelphia lexicographer, educator and physician, was associated with the preparation of a number of reference works. A breakdown in health caused his retirement before completion of the encyclopedia for which Garfield was writing. The article by Hinsdale and Garfield appeared under the heading "Census" in *Johnson's New Universal Cyclopaedia: A Scientific and Popular Treasury of Useful Knowledge*, I (1874), pp. 840–848.

pretended disclosures of Victoria C. Woodhull concerning Henry Ward Beecher, Theodore Tilton and wife, and some other persons.[275] Beecher and Tilton must speak in response to this assault. I think that Woodhull has done her worst towards destroying the Woman's Rights Movement. Went on "Change" by the invitation of President Covington[276] and made a brief speech. In the evening addressed a very small audience at Mozart Hall. Succeeded reasonably well in my speech. Took the ten o'clock train for Toledo.

THURSDAY, 31. Reached Toledo at 6 and took breakfast at the Boody House, a new hotel of surprising dimensions for a city the size of Toledo. Evidently these people have a faith in the great future for their city. At 11 o'clock took the train for Bryan, Williams County, and spent the remainder of the day and night at William Letcher's, my cousin.

November

FRIDAY, 1. Spent the day visiting with Cousin William Letcher and his brother Amos Letcher, who was Captain of the canal boat *Evening Star*, while I was driver of the same in 1850 [1848]. Also visited Cousin Charles Garfield and family. Spent some time at the court, where I found several old acquaintances among the members of the bar. Visited the artesian wells in the neighborhood of Bryan. In the evening spoke about two hours in the Hall to a very large audience; succeeded fairly well.

[275] Numerous people had known for some time of the alleged illicit relations between the Reverend Henry Ward Beecher (1813–1887), minister of Plymouth Congregational Church, Brooklyn, and the wife of his friend Theodore Tilton (1835–1907), editor of the *Independent* (until his dismissal as a result of the scandal in 1871). Full disclosure of the scandal was made by Victoria Woodhull in the November 2, 1872, issue of the sensational *Woodhull and Claflin's Weekly.* In 1874 Tilton sued Beecher for $100,000, charging him with adultery with Mrs. Tilton. After a trial of six months which attracted nationwide attention, the jury failed to agree on a verdict. Public opinion on the matter remained sharply divided.

[276] Samuel F. Covington, president of the Cincinnati Chamber of Commerce and Merchants Exchange.

SATURDAY, 2. Forty minutes after midnight, took the sleeping car for Cleveland where I made connection east on the Mahoning Road and reached Niles, Trumbull Co., at ten o'clock. Took dinner at Josiah Robbins', and at two o'clock, accompanied by Mr. Clark, attended public meeting in the large hall in the school building. After, Mr. [Alphonso] Hart and I addressed the meeting, he making the first speech and I concluding with a speech of 40 minutes. I made this as my principal point, that the election of Mr. Greeley would be a great shock to political morality in this country by offering a premium to politicians to turn traitor to their principles for the sake of office. Home at Hiram in the evening.

SUNDAY, 3. At church. Heard a very good sermon by Hinsdale. Prof. Wakefield[277] and wife visited me in the afternoon and talked over the Yellow Stone Expedition.

MONDAY, 4. Spent the day in correspondence and working up the census article with Hinsdale. At four o'clock drove to Auburn Corners (9 miles) and in the evening addressed a large meeting for two hours, thus closing up one of the most uncomfortable campaigns through which I have ever passed. To many men this campaign has been a choice of two evils and in some respects it has been so to me. The faults of the Republican Party are many and serious, but compared with the combinations against them, even their faults are virtues. Drove back and reached Hiram at half-past 11 with a sense of great relief that the campaign is ended.

TUESDAY, 5. Was the eighth voter in Hiram that cast his vote today at the presidential election. Immediately thereafter drove to Garrettsville and took the train for Cleveland. Received with my mail at the station four letters from Crete which had accumulated for me at Cleveland. The streets of Cleveland are silent and desolate. The great horse epidemic[278] has stopped the sound of wagons, ex-

[277] Edmund Burritt Wakefield (1846–1921), college professor and Disciple minister, taught for many years at Hiram College, where he first served as professor of natural science, 1871–74. Garfield's influence with Ferdinand Hayden was responsible for Wakefield's accompanying the Yellowstone expedition during the summer of 1872. Garfield expected the experience to redound to the benefit of the college.

[278] In September, 1872, a horse disease called epizootic influenza broke out in Toronto and appeared about a month later in Niagara Falls, New

cept as here and there an ox or a man trundles along. This epidemic teaches a new and startling [truth] concerning the value of the horse to modern civilization. The election is proceeding very quietly. Took the Pittsburgh train for the East at two o'clock.

WEDNESDAY, 6. As we passed Harrisburg at 5 o'clock newspapers were brought on board giving the general result of the election. Greeley cannot have carried more than eight states.[279] The Democracy would have accomplished more if they had nominated one of their own number. The defeat is something almost unparalleled in American history. Our first great anxiety now is to know whether victory will make us insolent or wise. Next to defeat the saddest thing to me is victory. I never understood the reason, but notwithstanding it is so. Reached Freedom at 8.20. I found it very difficult to get across to the Washington train. The four mules that hauled the cars were hired at $32.00 a day. Scarcely a horse was seen in the streets. Strange that the horses are so stricken at the time when the chief horseman of the nation has been so highly honored. Reached home just before noon. Gratified to return. Tired beyond measure with the work of the campaign. Almost too tired to rejoice at the victory. Especially in view of the confession made above.

THURSDAY, 7. Later returns seem to show that Mr. Greeley has carried but seven states. This reminds me of the success of my prediction in my speech of last Monday evening at Auburn, where I could count seven states for Mr. Greeley, but did not see how he could get any more. Men who leave a political party to form a new one ought to know that it is due to themselves and to the principles they advocate that they should go into the minority at least for one year until their party has attained a growth springing from the

---

York. It spread across the United States, reaching San Francisco in the spring of 1873. Thousands of horses and mules succumbed to the malady; in New York City alone it was estimated that 1,500 horses perished during the first six weeks of the prevalence of the disease there. "I left my family [in Ohio] well on Jany 21, but have not heard from them since—owing to the stoppage of the mails by reason of the epizootic," Garfield's friend Francis Servis wrote him from Montana Territory on February 14, 1873.

[279] Greeley carried only six states—Georgia, Kentucky, Maryland, Missouri, Tennessee and Texas, with 66 electoral votes. Grant received more than 55 per cent of the popular votes.

principles they advocate. The combination of Democrats and Liberal Republicans struck for victory rather than for the planting of new ideas. Spent the day in bringing up my correspondence and attended to many little odds and ends of business about the house. The interior painting has proved a success and is more economical than paper would be, provided the paint stands as well as I think it will.

FRIDAY, 8. Found that the insurance on my house will run out tomorrow and that it was inadequate in amount. I have today insured it in three companies, the Home of New York, the Phoenix of Hartford, and the Phoenix of Brooklyn. Total amount of insurance is $14,500 covering the house, furniture, wearing apparel and books. For three years insurance from —— I have paid $142.80. Delayed business, like old debts, are disposed of with difficulty. I have worked several hours on the debris and residuum of the work that has been accumulating during the summer and fall. The pressure of office-seekers has already begun. Would that something could be done so [as] to reform the civil service and so as to protect public men from this importunate pressure.

SATURDAY, 9. I visited General Sherman and spent two hours with him listening to his delightful reminiscences of his late tour through the Caucasus and other portions of the Russian Empire. I am always charmed with the vigor and heartiness of General Sherman. Talked with him about the successor of General Meade and urged the appointment of General McDowell as fitting and right. He is entitled to the place by seniority and service. I fear the old impressions of Bull Run will keep McDowell out of the place.[280] Went to the Congressional Library and ordered books for my study of the census, preparatory to writing an article for Dr. Thomas' *Cyclopedia.* Also visited General Walker[281] on Flathead business. Visited Albert Bris-

---

[280] William T. Sherman was then general of the army. Garfield's intimate friend Brigadier General Irvin McDowell was eager to succeed to the post left vacant by the death on November 6 of George Gordon Meade. Despite Garfield's fear that the memory of the first battle of Bull Run, July, 1861, in which McDowell commanded the Union forces, might defeat him, McDowell was promoted to major general and given command of the Division of the South.

[281] Francis Walker was then commissioner of Indian affairs.

bane in the evening and heard his account of his acquaintance with Fourier, of whom he is evidently a worshiper. Says Fourier was an uglier Dante.

SUNDAY, 10. Attended church and listened to a dry and sapless sermon of the most verbal and legalistic order.

MONDAY, 11. Our French girl, Charlotte Bachelard, after a service of a year and a half, leaves us for higher wages at Mr. Roessle's. We have thought so much of her that I regret to find her at last a mercenary Swiss.[282] Continued work on my report on the Flatheads, which was begun yesterday. Called at the Treasury in the afternoon and examined the condition of the estimates for appropriations for the coming session of Congress, and had a long conversation with the Secretary in regard to financial affairs. Worked off correspondence as usual. In the evening read farther in *Peregrine Pickle*. I do not quite remember the date when it was written, but I am trying the experiment of determining its date from the internal evidence of the book, its historical references and the state of the arts as exhibited in the peculiarity of speech and the like. The author's description of Commodore Trunnion's efforts to reach the church and be married are exceedingly clever.

TUESDAY, 12. Answered letters and continued work on the Indian report. Went to the Capitol and arranged to have my Committee Room put in order. Boston has suffered a calamity by fire almost as severe in proportion to her population as the loss at Chicago last year.[283] I find many words used in *Peregrine Pickle* which are now

---

[282] Charlotte Bachelard's departure was a blow to the family, and Garfield promptly addressed letters to T. E. Roessle, proprietor of the Arlington Hotel, who had engaged her, and to John Hitz, Swiss consul general in Washington. According to Roessle, Charlotte had told him Garfield had secured another in her place. Later Garfield talked with Hitz about the girl and also wrote another letter. An interview between Charlotte and Hitz is mentioned in the entry for November 20. The letters to Hitz are in Garfield's letterbook, November 11 and November —.

[283] The greatest fire in Boston's history occurred on November 9 and 10, spreading over 67 acres on which stood nearly 800 buildings filled with merchandise. Fourteen people died in the fire and damage loss was estimated at more than $75,000,000.

nearly or quite obsolete, such as "thof" for "though;" "wool" for "will;" "thingumbob" which, though recognized, is now obsolescent; "rumbo," a kind of drink, does not appear in our modern dictionaries. Pickle meets an English doctor in Paris, a shallow pretender to classical learning whom Smollett calls a mere index hunter who held the eel of science by the tail.

WEDNESDAY, 13. Continued work, as yesterday. Paid annual premium on my life insurance amounting to $149.25 on $5,000 insurance. If I live long enough I shall pay more than my heirs will get. Smollett uses the word "tipping" for "giving;" "charleton," in the sense of "conjuror;" and "canal," in the sense of "medium." He uses, also, the word "Capissens," which I do not find in the dictionary. Thus far I have found no date mentioned in the book. Professor Henry called and desired me to accompany him to Philadelphia and New York. Crete still well.

THURSDAY, 14. Went to the Capitol and consulted with Mr. [Edward] Clark, architect of the Capitol building, in regard to the progress of the pneumatic tube. I'm distressed at the delay and negligence of Brisbane in pushing his experiment. I think there is great merit in his invention, but he seems wholly inefficient in the way of execution. Continued work at my desk as yesterday. *Peregrine Pickle* becomes very weary with its endless repetitions and disagreeable intrigues. Taste in England must have been gauged on a low level if this story was popular. The author possesses great versatality of expression and smoothness of style. But unless I am greatly mistaken, he has failed in his caricature of a Welshman's broken English when he makes it like that of a Dutchman's. Thus far the incidents prove only that the date of the book is subsequent to the Charles' and James' of England.

FRIDAY, 15. Finished my report on my mission to the Flatheads. In it, I have criticised Mr. Welsh, ex-Indian Commissioner. *Peregrine Pickle* must have been written later than *Roderick Random*. Probably before Franklin's discovery of the identity of electricity and lightning, for he speaks, Volume I, page 69, of the effect of friction upon a glass tube, as if that were at the top of electrical knowledge. It was before the French "oi" was changed to "ai." It was when tiewigs and bags over the hair were worn. It was after Marlborough's wars in Flanders. It was when Bath and Tunbridge were fashionable watering places, and Vauxhall and White's Chocolate House were places of resort in London. It was while Handel was living.

SATURDAY, 16. Went to the Post Office Department on postal business. Delivered my Indian report to the Secretary of the Interior. Finished a large amount of correspondence. Wrote to Felix Brunot[284] of Pittsburgh, Chairman of the Indian Commissioners, in regard to my criticism in the *Independent* of Welsh's letter. *Peregrine Pickle* was written during the life of Princess Amelia and long after the the times of Rubens and Van Dyck. At its date, Virginia was a great tobacco raising province. This fixes it before the American Revolution but probably during the reign of George III. The plot of the story is very loosely connected. It has but little dramatic force. Its hero was a gross, brutal libertine. A long digression of more than 130 pages is made to enable "a woman of quality" to recount her own shameful intrigues. What she says is not necessary to the thread of the story, but seems to be introduced from a sheer love of nastiness.

SUNDAY, 17. At home. Hurried rapidly over to the last volume of *Peregrine Pickle*. At this date such a book would not be tolerated. This speaks well for the comparative morals of our age.

MONDAY, 18. Went to the Treasury Department. Got Mrs. Reed restored to her place and saw the Second Comptroller in regard to my mileage account as Commissioner to the Flatheads.[285] Received a letter from Dr. Thomas accepting my suggestions concerning the treatment of the topics Statistics, Census, Population and Representation in his forthcoming *Cyclopedia*. Commenced the preparation of the census article. Read with great interest the pamphlets of Sir

[284] Felix R. Brunot (1820–1898), Pittsburgh businessman and philanthropist, was president of the Board of Indian Commissioners of which William Welsh had been head for a brief period in 1869. He spent a number of summers visiting Indian tribes. See note 244.

[285] Garfield computed his mileage at 6,308 miles; the Treasury Department, using different tables, arrived at 6,001. Garfield questioned the Department's figure, and pointed out that he had not included the extra mileage which resulted from his going by way of Ft. Leavenworth to pick up Swaim. He was finally allowed $1,087.60, somewhat more than he had at first claimed.

William Petty, who wrote from 1661 to 1686 under the nom de plume of Captain John Graunt.[286] He wrote a discussion on the "Bills of Mortality" which has laid the foundation for modern vital statistics. In his dedicatory epistle of the tract of 1661 occurs this passage which seems to be the beginning of modern meteorology: "I understand yourselves are also appointed means how to measure the degrees of heat, wetness, and windiness in the several parts of his Majestie's Dominions."

TUESDAY, 19. Five members of the Appropriation Committee met at the Capitol today. Assigned to the members present the same bills as last year. Made arrangements for our winter's work.

Got additional books from the library for my census article. Read up the history of the Greek and Roman censuses and continued the work until near midnight. The Roman census seems to have been borrowed from that of Solon, established about 40 years earlier. I do not yet find any distinct account of the stopping of the practice of taking the census, though I suspect it arose from the unwillingness of kings to have the resources and the condition of their empires known to the mass of the people. That same consideration prevented the introduction of modern censuses in France and other monarchies. Today I am 41 years old and my Uncle Thomas, the only surviving Garfield of the generation next preceding me, is 71.

WEDNESDAY, 20. Stopped at Brady's[287] on my way to the Capitol and sat for a photograph for Doctor Salter.[288] Five members of the Committee met at half-past ten and took up the Indian Appropriation Bill. Continued work on it until after one o'clock and nearly

---

[286] Garfield here repeats an error of Bishop Burnet and Thomas B. Macaulay, who attributed *Some Natural and Political Observations . . . Made upon the Bills of Mortality* (1662) to Sir William Petty (1623–1687). The title page bore only the name of John Graunt, the actual author. Sir William edited a greatly improved edition of the book (1676) after the death of his friend Graunt.

[287] Mathew B. Brady (*c.* 1823–1896), famed Civil War photographer, continued his work in Washington for many years; his studio in 1872 was at 627 Pennsylvania Avenue.

[288] Francis Salter, a Washington physician, had formerly been in the Pension Office, and more recently had acted for veterans seeking pensions.

completed it. Heard Prof. Peirce[289] on some additional appropriations for the Coast Survey, and also some minor matters. In the
afternoon finished the Greek census section of my article for the
Cyclopedia. Also wrote the paragraph on the etymology of the word
"census." Called on Brisbane in the evening and discussed the
prospects of the Pneumatic Tube. Curious row resulting from an
interview between Consul General Hitz and Charlotte [Bachelard].
Late at night Crete's illness begins.

THURSDAY, 21.   By an hour after midnight Crete's labor began fully.
It continued at regular intervals until twenty minutes past five in
the morning, when she was delivered of a fine large boy, younger
than his father by 41 years and two days. I am grateful for the
safety of both mother and child.[290] Went to the Capitol and spent
five hours in hard work on the Legislative Appropriation Bill. Returned in the afternoon very tired. Continued work on the Roman
Census. Am greatly interested in Mommsen's[291] chapters on the early
constitution of Rome and the relation of the Servian census to the
reformed constitution. General Eaton,[292] Commissioner of Education,
and his brother, Col. Eaton,[293] from Memphis, called in the evening
and we had a lengthy conversation on the tendencies of our educational system. I believe that our Union schools are pushing the

[289] Benjamin Peirce (1809–1880), mathematician and astronomer, was
a professor at Harvard University and from 1867–74 also superintendent of
the U. S. Coast Survey. He was the father of Charles Sanders Peirce, who

[290] Abram (Abe) Garfield (1872–1958) had a distinguished career as a
was an assistant in the Coast Survey, 1872–84.

Cleveland architect after graduating from Williams College, 1893, and the
Massachusetts Institute of Technology, 1896. In 1925 he was appointed a
member of the Commission of Fine Arts (national). In 1897 he married
Sarah Granger Williams, who died in 1945; in 1947 he married Helen
Grannis Matthews.

[291] Theodor Mommsen, *The History of Rome*; translated by W. P. Dick-
son, 4 vols. (New Edition, N. Y., 1870).

[292] John Eaton (1829–1906), Union soldier, was head of the U. S. Bureau
of Education, 1870–86, and president of Marietta College, 1886–91.

[293] Lucien Bonaparte Eaton, Union soldier who settled in Memphis after
the war, was U. S. marshal for the Western District of Tennessee, 1870–77;
he became a very large property owner in Memphis.

young children too hard and we shall ultimately see the evil effects of this overwork.

FRIDAY, 22.   Had a hard day's work in committee on the Legislative Appropriation Bill and in the afternoon worked on the Roman census. Prepared to go to New York in the evening; lost the train by half a minute and returned wondering whether such a slip has any ominous significance, as many believe. Resumed work on the Roman census and kept at it until midnight. Many points in it are very obscure, such as the basis of the Servian census, whether it was on property generally, or on landed property exclusively. I am inclined to follow Mommsen in the latter view, although it is difficult to see how the inhabitants of a city could all be possessors of farm lands.

SATURDAY, 23.   Finished the discussion of the Roman census and am tolerably well satisfied with the result. It is more able and thorough than any I have seen in the cyclopedias. I found some valuable points in Napoleon's *Life of Caesar*,[294] but most in Mommsen's, whose work convinces me that most of our ancient history must be rewritten. Mother and Brother Joe[295] came at noon. Visited the Patent and Post Office departments in the afternoon. At 8.50 took the train for New York.

SUNDAY, 24.   Reached the Brevoort House at half-past [*sic*]. I have concluded to make this my New York hotel for the future. Met [David A.] Wells and had a long visit. At 3 o'clock P.M. went to dinner at A. T. Stewart's.[296] He is in his new house in 5th Avenue, a remarkable structure built solidly of marble. He and his wife are nearly 70. They have no children and are alone in this vast marble palace. It is difficult to see how it can seem to be a home to anybody.

MONDAY, 25.   Took breakfast with Mr. Hooper of Boston and then

---

[294] Napoleon III, *History of Julius Caesar* . . . ,2 vols. (1865).

[295] Joseph Rudolph (1841–1934), brother of Garfield's wife, attended the Western Reserve Eclectic Institute, served in the 42nd Ohio Infantry Regiment during the Civil War, and at this time was employed in the railway mail service. During Garfield's presidency he had charge of the Mentor farm.

[296] Alexander Turney Stewart (1803–1876) most famous New York merchant of his day. He was the owner of the new Niblo's Theater mentioned in the entry of November 25.

in company with Judge Hilton[297] and Mr. Wells visited Niblo's Theatre, which will be completed in a few days. The arrangements of the stage are marvels of mechanical skill.

Called on Mr. Stewart at his store at one o'clock, and had a pleasant chat in regard to his successful career in business. He told me how it began. He said, "It all results from three things, truth, ————, plodding." Mr. Stewart has never had his picture taken. Bismarck sent him his own portrait with a request for an exchange. Stewart returned a thousand dollars rather than a portrait. He is a remarkable man. Tended to various items of business, shopping, etc. At 6 o'clock took dinner at General McDowell's in company with his family and Gen'l Drum.[298] I am delighted to hear that the President has today appointed McDowell to the vacancy occasioned by the death of Meade. Took the 9 o'clock train for Washington.

TUESDAY, 26. Reached home a little before seven A.M. Read my large mail. Answered letters and at 11 o'clock went to the Committee on Appropriations. Proceeded with the Legislative Appropriation Bill, hearing the Commissioner of Internal Revenue, the Adjutant General of the Army and several other persons. It is difficult to keep the appropriations from increasing. In some departments of the government they ought to increase. But everything that grew out of the war ought to decrease. This evening's mail brought me a very remarkable letter from Ralston Skinner of Cincinnati, in which he claims to have discovered that the unit of measure employed in the construction of one of the great pyramids is the same as the British inch and was also employed in the construction of the Jewish Temple and the Tabernacle within it. The discussion is, to say the least, very curious.

WEDNESDAY, 27. Answered correspondence in the morning and at 11 o'clock met the Committee and continued work for 5 hours on the Legislative Appropriation Bill. Heard the Postmaster General, the Attorney General, the Commissioner of Patents and a number of

[297] Henry Hilton, New York lawyer and former judge, was the counsel and business advisor of Alexander T. Stewart, who left him a large legacy and whose successor he became in the great mercantile concern which Stewart had founded.

[298] Richard Coulter Drum was U. S. assistant adjutant general; he served as adjutant general, 1880–89.

other parties in regard to their estimates for appropriations. Very nearly completed the Legislative Bill. Mr. Hale of Maine reached the city and met with the Committee today. It has occurred for the first time to me that while the work of the Committee of Ways and Means looks out towards the industries of the people as the particular subject of contemplation, that of the Committee of Appropriations looks inward upon the machinery of the government and reviews in detail all its various functions. Every monied transaction of the government has usually to be brought in close review in making appropriations, and here is soonest discovered the decay or overgrowth of any part of the fabric.

THURSDAY, 28. The War for the Union has nationalized Thanksgiving. At the South it was hated as a Yankee Festival. There Christmas was in higher repute than Thanksgiving. Since the war the Executive of the U. S. has taken cognizance of the day and this day is now set apart throughout the nation by proclamation of the President. Staid quietly at home today and took with the family my Thanksgiving dinner. Crete was not able to come down stairs. Worked on the census. In the evening called on Speaker Blaine for an hour and a half. He is vigorous and intelligent, but cares a good deal more for the machinery of politics than I do. He believes the Civil Service Reform a humbug. I should favor [reform of] the Civil Service if for no other reason [than] of getting partially rid of the enormous pressure for office.

FRIDAY, 29. Completed the section of my census article relating to Sweden. Attended to correspondence, and at 12 o'clock met with the Committee on Rules at the Speaker's Room, and discussed an amendment to the rules. At 1 o'clock met with the Committee on Appropriations, finished the Legislative Bill. Had some discussion as to the action of the committee last session on the postal telegraph scheme. There is a difference of opinion among the members as to the action then taken. It gives me trouble.

At ten minutes before six this evening Horace Greeley died. The close of his career has been most sad. His great political mistake of 1872 has killed him while he was yet in full vigor of mind. He felt that his reputation was so seriously shattered and his usefulness nearly destroyed. This with the overstrain of work has killed him. Much in his life was admirable but as is true with most men of force, he was headlong, opinionated and sometimes oppressively arrogant. His death raises curious questions for the Electoral College which meets next Wednesday.[299] It is the first time I believe that a presidential candidate has died between the election of the electors and the meeting of the Electoral College.

SATURDAY, 30. Called on Judge Black at the Arlington and went with him to the Interior Department to introduce him to the Solicitor. At 11 o'clock met with the Committee and worked until after three. Finished our three bills. Closed our recess work and separated until the session of Congress next week. The members are beginning to gather in and the bustle and expectancy created by the coming session are everywhere apparent. Several gentlemen called in the evening.

December

SUNDAY, 1. Attended church, the weather fearfully cold. At 2 o'clock dined at Donn Piatt's. Called on Speaker Blaine and urged the importance of requiring an investigation into the Credit Mobilier scandal and agreed to call a Democrat to the Chair and ourselves introduce the resolution. Judge Black called in the evening and staid three hours.

MONDAY, 2. Committee met at ten o'clock and reviewed the print of the Legislative Bill and finished the Indian and Pension [bills]. Got them in readiness for introduction in the House. At 12 o'clock M. the House met with a large attendance of members. After prayer and the usual formalities of informing the President and Senate that we were ready for business, the Speaker introduced a resolution for the Credit Mobilier investigation. The President's Message was read as usual and was very long. Our three appropriations bills were introduced. The House unanimously passed a resolution noticing the death of Horace Greeley and was especially respectful of his career. Sister Mary left us for Ohio on the 5.30 P.M. train. Several persons called in the evening.

[299] The electoral votes were cast on December 4, the day of Greeley's funeral. The Democratic electors cast 3 votes for Greeley and divided the remaining 63 among four living politicians; the Greeley votes were not counted in the final tabulation.

TUESDAY, 3. Committee met at half-past ten o'clock and heard the Public Printer and his clerk concerning his own, and the estimates of the various departments. I think our change of the law last winter has wrought a beneficent reform in that branch of the public service. It holds the several executive departments responsible for their expenditures. The House set for about two hours and adjourned. In the evening attended the first lecture of Prof. Tyndall[300] on light. He was handsomely introduced by Prof. Henry, and after very pleasant preliminary remarks, proceeded to discuss all the scientific discoveries on the subject of light in their chronological order, illustrating each step by interesting and striking experiments. The audience was an unusually brilliant one, and the lecture was a very great success.

WEDNESDAY, 4. Finished that portion of my census article relating to the British census. Continued correspondence and at 11 o'clock met the Committee on Appropriations, discussed several deficiencies and ordered a partial deficiency bill. Listened to the request of the Governor of the District and the Board of Public Works for a hearing. Set tomorrow for that purpose. Several callers in the evening, Judge Black among the number. Sat until midnight over the 9th census, just out.

THURSDAY, 5. Committee met at half-past ten. Had the Board of Public Works and the Committee on the District of Columbia with us, and discussed thoroughly the work which the Board has done on the streets and avenues fronting the government property. House passed a bill for building six new sloops of war.

Attended Prof. Tyndall's second lecture on light; he discussed Newton's emission theory; showed wherein it was a failure. Discussed the work of imagination in science and then [proceeded] to the developement of the undulatory theory of light. The discussion was very clear and satisfactory and the experiments exceedingly fine. Returned from the lecture in company with Senator Schurz. Called at his room and had a long talk on his view of politics.

FRIDAY, 6. Committee on Appropriations spent the morning in discussing the estimates for appropriations for the Board of Public

---

[300] John Tyndall (1820–1893), British physicist whose work included studies of the qualities of atmospheric light, was superintendent of the Royal Institution, London.

Works. The subject is full of difficulty and whatever the decision of the Committee may be, its action will encounter a good deal of opposition and objection in the House. General [Philip S.] Post, Consul at Vienna, called on me at the Committee Room in regard to appropriations for his consulship. In the House a bill was passed abolishing the offices of assessor and assistant assessor and placed the duties of these officers upon the commisioner and the collectors. Called on Mr. Brisbane after the close of the session and discussed the prospects of the pneumatic tube.

SATURDAY, 7. Worked off correspondence. Made some additions to the census article and at 11 o'clock went with Dr. Thompson to visit the Columbia Hospital. On my return called on the President and on the Comptroller of the Currency. At 2 o'clock in the afternoon Committee on Appropriations assembled and in company with the Board of Public Works visited Georgetown and the various parts of Washington to examine the work they have done on the streets and sewers. Continued this inspection until half-past 5 o'clock in the evening. They have accomplished a vast amount during the season and have greatly bettered the condition of the city, but I fear the burdens on the poorer classes of taxpayers will be very heavy. Attended Prof. Tyndall's 3rd lecture on the polarization of light. Did not hear half the lecture and lost many points.

SUNDAY, 8. Attended church in the forenoon. In the afternoon at ½ past two called around with General [David B.] McKibbin to visit Providence Hospital. Called in the evening on Gen'l Sherman. John Hawley of Detroit visited me in the evening and we visited until after midnight.

MONDAY, 9. Committee considered a number of communications from the departments. Authorized the passage of a bill to man the new life-saving stations on the coast of Cape Cod, which during the day I introduced into the House and had passed. Also, Committee listened to a decision of the Supreme Court by Judge Story in 1830 on the title of the U. S. to the fee in the streets and public squares of this city. I am every day amazed with the steady encroachment of all the departments of the government upon the money in the Treasury. There is a constant demand everywhere. The Committee on Appropriations is the natural antagonist of all the departments in this regard. We need an expert in the employ of the Committee to examine all the accounts. House adjourned at ½ past three. In the evening attended Tyndall's lecture.

TUESDAY, 10. In Committee heard the Board of Public Works and General Babcock and before the close of the meeting Committee voted, with one dissent, to reimburse the Board of Public Works to the amount of one and one-quarter million. This will no doubt be furiously assailed in the House. In the evening attended Prof. Tyndall's 5th lecture. The last half of it was devoted to spectrum analysis and was exceedingly fine. I should have added in its proper place that in the House we took up the Indian Appropriation Bill. Mr. Sargent made a speech of nearly an hour and a half, setting forth in a very interesting way the leading facts concerning our Indian policy. We made good progress with the bill. Got nearly half through.

WEDNESDAY, 11. Attended correspondence in the morning. Prepared a statement of my knowledge of the Credit Mobilier case. Met the Committee at half-past 10. Heard several parties in regard to deficiencies and then went to a room in the basement of the Capitol to witness experiments on the proposed new torpedo for coast defense. Heard a full statement of the different kinds of torpedoes now in use. The leading points of this one are a secret in possession of the government engineers. Today the Indian Appropriation Bill was finished. In the evening dined at Secretary Delano's with a large number of gentlemen, Mr. Phillips,[301] the new Solicitor General, among them.

THURSDAY, 12. Committee finished the preparation of the partial deficiency bill covering about one and three-quarter millions. Heard Dr. Linderman[302] of California on the amount necessary to buy

[301] Samuel F. Phillips (1824–1903) had recently entered upon his duties as solicitor general of the United States, a position which he retained until 1885. In 1881 Garfield nominated him as judge of the Court of Claims and named William E. Chandler solicitor general. Chandler was not confirmed, Phillip's nomination as judge was withdrawn and he stayed on as solicitor general.

[302] Henry Richard Linderman (1825–1879), once a practicing physician, had a career in government service in the field of monetary affairs. In November, 1872, he recommended monetary changes in a report to the secretary of the treasury. He helped draft the coinage act of 1873 and on its passage was appointed first director of the Bureau of the Mint, a position he held until his death.

machinery to put into the new mint at San Francisco. Also heard Prof. Peirce in regard to deficiencies in the Coast Survey appropriation. Also Messrs. Wells[303] and Finkelnburg of Missouri on the increase for the cost of U. S. building at Saint Louis. In the House introduced Deficiency Bill and had it set immediately after the Pension Appropriation Bill; which latter bill was taken up and passed after a short speech of ten minutes made by me in explanation of the appropriations. In the evening had a long visit with Wm. M. Evarts[304] and a sketch of the trial of the *Alabama* Case before the Geneva Tribunal.

FRIDAY, 13. Committee took up and finished the Consular and Diplomatic Appropriation Bill and ordered it reported to the House. Heard Judge Kelley in favor of printing certificates of stock for the National Centennial Celebration. Congress has been drawn into this scheme unconsciously and is almost now committed to make large appropriations for that celebration. Perhaps we ought to do it, but it ought to have been done in a more open and avowed manner. The William and Mary College appropriation was taken up in the House and called up an amendment to open the College to colored people. I intended to go on with the Deficiency Appropriation Bill, but found the temper of the House ruffled and so I postponed it until Monday. John Hawley left in the evening. I dictated a large number of letters.

SATURDAY, 14. Worked up correspondence. Dictated letters until about ten o'clock. Then spent four hours among the departments on other people's business. I do not know that I have ever been much more weary of this sort of vicarious suffering than I am tonight. The great crowd of people that come upon me for one thing or another draw heavily upon my vital force and go far towards exhausting the

[303] Erastus Wells (1823–1893), Democratic member of the House from Missouri, 1869–77, 1879–81. He was president of the Missouri Railroad Company, 1859–83.

[304] William Maxwell Evarts (1818–1901), statesman and lawyer, was chief counsel for Andrew Johnson in the impeachment proceedings, counsel for the United States before the Arbitration Tribunal at Geneva, 1871–72, and counsel for the Republican party before the Electoral Commission of 1877; he defended Henry Ward Beecher in the suit brought against him by Theodore Tilton. He was U. S. attorney general, 1868–69, secretary of state, 1877–81, and senator from New York, 1885–91.

large measure of strength which I possess. Called on Mr. Blaine and Judge Black in the evening. There is something wonderful in the conversational powers of Judge Black.

SUNDAY, 15. Did not attend church. Am not at all well. We have tried a new French girl,[305] and she is likely to fail on our hands the first thing. We are nearly disgusted with La Belle Nation!

MONDAY, 16. Committee heard the Board of Health of the District of Columbia; the Texan Frontier Commissioners; Mr. Twichell[306] of Boston on the purchase of an additional lot for public buildings in that city; and several other parties. In the House at about 3 o'clock went into Committee of the Whole on the Deficiency Bill, and spoke for 35 minutes explaining the appropriation. Debate continued until half-past four, chiefly on the appropriation for improvements in the District of Columbia, when the Committee rose and the House adjourned.

TUESDAY, 17. Committee heard Mr. Clagett in regard to frauds in the Indian Service in Montana. Also gave another hearing to Mr. Twichell on the purchase of additional grounds for the Boston Post Office building. Also a report from a special committee on the reorganization of the Interior Department. Appointed several subcommittees on other matters. In the House I found that a special order had been set some weeks ago which took the day from us, and I was not able to get up the Deficiency Bill. Mr. Brooks made a speech of an hour in the way of a personal explanation of his relations to the Credit Mobilier. I propose to await the action of the Committee of Investigation before I discuss the subject in the House. Committee met at 7 o'clock in the evening. Heard the officers of the following telegraph companies: Atlantic and Pacific, Pacific and Atlantic, Franklin and Western Union. Heard also the Postmaster General and Mr. Lines. Committee adjourned a little after eleven o'clock.

WEDNESDAY, 18. After our late session last night Committee did not meet today. At 2 o'clock House went into Committee of the Whole on the Deficiency Bill. After having a limited debate during which a number of votes were taken, and by which my Committee were

[305] Claudine Charles had been secured through a New York employment agent and had been checked on by the wife of General McDowell.

[306] Ginery Twichell (1811–1883), Republican member of the House from Massachusetts, 1867–83.

sustained, at half-past three o'clock a message came in from the Senate announcing the death of Garret Davis[307] and the Committee of the Whole rose to enable the House to act on the resolutions. This brought us to an adjournment. Early in the morning the Ohio, Indiana, and Illinois two per cent bill was passed after an hour's debate. I did not know enough about the subject to vote intelligently on the matter, except that I voted for Mr. Sargent's limiting resolution. That failing, I declined to vote on the bill.[308] During the day the President sent for me to visit him at his room in the Senate. He was anxious to secure two appropriations before the holidays—Vienna Exposition and Texan Frontier Commission.[309]

THURSDAY, 19. After hearing various parties on appropriations, Committee listened to Mr. Palmer's report on the Postal Telegraph Bill, known as the Hubbard Plan. In view of the difference of opinion among the Committee, both as to the merits of the plan and as to the Committee's action last session, it was agreed that Mr. Palmer might report the bill either to be recommitted to the Committee or for consideration of the House with the understanding that it was not the unanimous report of the Committee and that some members reserved their individual right to modify or oppose the bill. I am still undecided as to what ought to be done. In the House finished the discussion of the Deficiency Bill including appropriation for improvements in the District of Columbia and with one amendment limiting the action of the Board in future, the bill passed, with all its amounts of appropriation unchanged, by a vote of 109 to 45. Also passed deficiency appropriation for the Texas Frontier Commission.

[307] Garret Davis (1801–1872), Whig member of the House from Kentucky, 1839–47, Whig and Democratic member of the U. S. Senate, 1861–72, died on September 22, 1872.

[308] The bill provided for the payment to certain states by the federal government of money due them from sales of public lands within their borders; the amount due was two percent of the sum received for the land. Sargent proposed that the amount spent by the federal government for laying out and making roads be deducted from the two percent.

[309] In May, 1872, Congress authorized the appointment of a commission to inquire into depredations by Indians and Mexicans on the frontiers of Texas.

In the evening read two speeches on the French Spoliation Claims.[310]
FRIDAY, 20. Committee met at half-past eleven and after consultation agreed to meet on Friday the 27th day of December and hold sessions the remainder of the holiday vacation, which lasts until January 6th. The House found itself without a quorum and after repeated efforts to secure it and a developement of the rule that the Speaker cannot sign a bill in the absence of a quorum, which I believe is a new decision in our parliamentary history, the House adjourned. The Deficiency Bill passed the Senate with an unimportant amendment, but the opposition through members of the House made it impossible to secure its final passage today. In the evening after working off correspondence, read up the French Spoliations until half-past 11. This subject has greatly attracted my interest, and I am inclined to oppose the claim. And though it has passed the Senate many times and the House a few times, I think we should put it to rest if possible.
SATURDAY, 21. Spent the forenoon on correspondence and the census article. Nearly finished the modern censuses of European countries. At half-past twelve took Crete out in a carriage to make preparations for Christmas. This is the first time she has been out of the house for nearly 50 days. We spent four and [a] half hours in the shops. I drove also to the Capitol and procured additional documents in the French Spoliation Claims. Read on that subject until near midnight. Our children have the epizootic, the regular horse disease, and Irvin and the baby are quite sick.
SUNDAY, 22. The cold wave that crossed the Rocky Mountains four days ago and was announced by the Signal Bureau has reached our city. At home until three o'clock, when I went to the Smithsonian and saw Prof. Hayden's Yellowstone collection. French Spoliations in the evening.

[310] During the wars of the French Revolution and Napoleon, great losses had been sustained by American owners of ships and cargoes as a result of French action. Some of the claims which resulted had been settled in accordance with a treaty with France made in 1831. Others had been assumed by the United States, but had never been settled. In 1871 Charles Sumner sponsored a bill providing for the adjustment and satisfaction of claims for spoliations committed by the French before July 31, 1801. In December, 1872, Simon Cameron made an unsuccessful effort to bring the bill to a vote. Settlements were finally made between 1885 and 1925.

MONDAY, 23. Attended to correspondence in the forenoon. Read further on the French Spoliation Claims. Visited the Treasury Department. Went to the Capitol for more books and from 2 o'clock to 5 rode with Crete getting Christmas presents for the family. At 6 o'clock took dinner at Wormley's with Gardiner Hubbard, where several topics of general interest were discussed, physical geography and postal telegraphy among the rest. I greatly dread the Postal Telegraph scheme and its effects on the government in the direction of centralizing its power. It is a great misfortune that our party is to be so strong next Congress. Better for us if we had a small majority. Worked till after midnight on French Spoliations.

TUESDAY, 24. Spent the forenoon on the census article and completed it with the exception of a few points to be obtained from the Superintendent of the Census. The article fills eighty-seven pages of manuscript and has cost me a great deal of labor. I shall send it to Dr. Thomas in a day or two. Spent three hours in the afternoon finishing shopping for Christmas and also hunting for a new cook. In the evening continued my study of the French Spoliation Claims. Read the speeches of Senators [Simon] Cameron and Vickers[311] in favor of the claims and the discussions of Senators Morton, Conkling,[312] Scott,[313] Frelinghuysen[314] and Stewart[315] on the insurance phase of the question and the supererogation of insurers to the rights of the insured. The whole question is full of difficulty, but I find very little which is new in the recent handling of the matter. I have nearly reached the conclusion that the claims have no ground to stand on and that I shall resist them in the House.

WEDNESDAY, 25. Staid at home all day and helped the children in

[311] George Vickers (1801–1879), a Democratic member of the Senate from Maryland, 1868–73.

[312] Roscoe Conkling (1829–1888), a Republican member of the House from New York, 1859–63, 1865–67, U. S. senator, 1867–81.

[313] John Scott (1824–1896), a Republican member of the Senate from Pennsylvania, 1869–75.

[314] Frederick Theodore Frelinghuysen (1817–1885), a Republican member of the Senate from New Jersey, 1866–69, 1871–77, member of the Electoral Commission, 1877, secretary of state, 1881–1885.

[315] William Morris Stewart (1827–1909), a Republican member of the Senate from Nevada, 1864–75, 1887–1905.

their Christmas sport. Read the French Spoliation Claims. I have nearly completed the examination of the very voluminous documents on the subject, embracing also the treaty for the cession of Louisiana. I think the position can be fairly maintained that between July, 1798, and the date of the Treaty of September 30th, 1800, war existed between France and the U. S. and that most of the indemnity claims went down as a consequence. This afternoon Jimmy fell on the steps and struck his mouth on the iron railing and before he got off his lips froze to it. We had much difficulty in getting him off.

THURSDAY, 26.   Continued work on French Spoliations and finished the census article. My classmate Lavalette Wilson[316] called on me today and I have induced him to stay over so that we can have a reunion here tomorrow evening of such members of the class as are in town. One of the clearest speeches I have yet found on the French Spoliations is that of Chancellor [George M.] Bibb of Kentucky, made in the Senate in 1835. It is more judicial in spirit than any I have read. Webster's last speech in 1835 has staggered me somewhat about the war question.

FRIDAY, 27.   Work on correspondence and Spoliations until near 11. Went to the Capitol and met Committee on Appropriations, and we worked four hours on the Naval Appropriation Bill. Completed it except a few points reserved for further consideration. Worked on Spoliations in the evening until 8 o'clock, when my classmates Wilson, Noble[317] and Gilfillan, the last two with their wives and the three and myself having nine children in all. Had a very pleasant supper at 9½ o'clock and spent the evening delightfully. Noble was the youngest member of our class and though a very bright boy was sent to college too early. He was as he says in the gristle and the

---

[316] Lavalette Wilson (b. 1827) graduated at Williams College in 1856 and became an educator and a civil engineer in the state of New York.

[317] Joseph Franklin Noble (1837–1922) had a career of nearly sixty years in the Presbyterian and Congregational ministries after graduating at Williams College in 1856 and at the Union Theological Seminary in 1861; he also did a large amount of editorial work. He was the son of Mason Noble, who is also mentioned in the diary, and who at this time and until his death in 1881 was pastor of the Sixth Presbyterian Church in Washington.

metaphisical studies were too heavy for him. He has grown greatly in intellect since graduation.

SATURDAY, 28. Committee met from 12 to 3. Finished the Naval Bill except a clause relating to the Naval Academy. In the afternoon worked on the French Spoliations. At five o'clock took dinner at Smalley's. Returned and prepared notes for a lecture on my trip to Montana and beginning at 9 o'clock spoke an hour to a company of about 30, in a familiar talk about the mountains, their physical characteristics and influences upon life and character among them. Crete was with me. We had a very pleasant company and they seemed to be interested in my talk. Albert Brisbane was among them and was very much interested in the general discussion that preceded the narrative and when the narrative was fully started he fell asleep.

SUNDAY, 29. With my classmates Wilson and Gilfillan went to church on 6th St. on the Island[318] and heard Frank Noble preach. He made a very able and finished sermon greatly to our delight. Nearly sick in the afternoon and evening.

MONDAY, 30. Have been nearly sick all day. Worked off a large number of letters however. Called on Mr. Sargent about noon. This afternoon took a Russian bath which was pretty severe treatment but I hope it will help throw off my cold. There is something wrong with my circulation. Many times in the night I wake with a feeling of numbness in my arms and fingers which I do not understand. I should have rested and loafed during this vacation instead of studying French Spoliations so much. In the evening played with the children. Read Tennyson's "In Memoriam" and retired at 9 o'clock.

TUESDAY, 31. Worked on correspondence and French Spoliations until towards noon, then went to the Committee on Appropriations where we heard the Sec'y of War and the Sec'y of the Navy on the increase of the number of cadets at the two academies resulting from the increase of the number of members in the House of Representatives. Committee concluded to provide for the increase in the Military Academy but not for the Naval Academy. We propose for that that

---

[318] The area, in southwest Washington, was actually an island when the old Washington Canal (Tiber Creek) and James Creek formed a continuous waterway from the Potomac to the Anacostia; the canal was filled in during the early 1870's.

the course be extended to six years, two of the years to be used at sea and four at the Academy. In the evening wrote my 19th [17th] New Year's letter to Burke. The year has been a busy one with me, full of events, and it leaves me overworked and sad, heartily wishing to be rid of public life.

1873

January

WEDNESDAY, 1. The New Year finds me not well, but overworked. Took Harry to the Executive Mansion and called on the President and on Mrs. Grant and Nellie Grant. Showed the little boy the most notic[e]able points of the New Year's Reception. Spent about four hours in making New Year's calls on the wives of Cabinet Ministers, Senators, and friends. At six o'clock took dinner with Albert Brisbane, Miss Bates, and Miss Virginia Vaughn.[1] The latter lady I knew in Columbus thirteen years ago. Donn Piatt sent around tickets for the Theatre and Crete and I went to hear *Arrah-na-Pogue* as rendered by Dion Boucicault[2] and his wife. It was very well done.

THURSDAY, 2. Dictated a large number of letters and among others one to Dr. Thomas of Philadelphia, forwarding my article on the census, which makes 88 pages. Colonel Ralph Plumb,[3] my old com-

[1] Virginia Vaughn of Cincinnati, described by Garfield in 1861 as an artist, musician, writer, and public reader of literature. In that year she was rooming at the home of William T. Bascom in Columbus, where Garfield and Jacob D. Cox also roomed. See Garfield to wife, February 17, 1861, Garfield Papers.

[2] Dion Boucicault (1820–1890), Irish-born actor and dramatist, had recently returned to the United States after an absence of ten years. His wife at this time was Agnes Robertson. *Arrah-na-Pogue* (1864) was one of his most popular plays.

[3] Ralph Plumb (1816–1903), of Ohio, served on Garfield's staff, 1861–63, as assistant quartermaster with the rank of captain. He was later brevetted lieutenant colonel and after the war moved to Illinois. He was a Republican member of the U. S. House of Representatives from Illinois, 1885–89.

panion in arms in the Sandy Valley Campaign, was here this afternoon and visited us and took dinner with us and spent the evening. I have been reading with much interest the biography of the late Mr. Seaton,[4] partner in the firm of Gales and Seaton, publishers of the debates of Congress and of the *National Intelligencer*. The book is full of sketches of Washington society, extending back to 60 years ago. Etiquette and the relative grades of social life among official persons seems to have been a very serious matter in those early days. Almost as grave as diplomacy.

FRIDAY, 3. Worked off my correspondence and at 11 o'clock went to the Capitol where the Committee met at 12 M. and went over the estimates for fortifications. After considering the items in detail and discussing some of the growths of expenditures and the direction of public service, the Committee concluded to restrict the total appropriation for fortifications and coast and harbor torpedoes to 2,000,000 of dollars. In the evening took dinner at Sec'y Robeson's in company with Mr. Belknap, Sec'y of War, and Messrs. Hooper, Scofield, Sargent, Niblack and Marshall. A pleasant company of gentlemen and an elegant dinner. The social power of Washington and its effect on public events has never been adequately understood by the majority of people. I think I have probably made a mistake in keeping up my work during the Holiday Vacation.

SATURDAY, 4. On my way to the Capitol took another electrical bath, which makes two with yesterday's, and at 12 o'clock met the Committee on Appropriations. Heard General Humphreys and Col. Casey of the Engineers on a variety of points connected with fortifications and the military service and completed the Fortification Bill. Read Mark Twain's "Great Beef Contract"[5] to the Committee. Twain is the most successful of our humorous writers in my judgment. At 7 o'clock in the evening Mrs. Garfield and I took dinner at Mrs. Dahlgren's.[6] Spent a delightful [evening]. Formed a pleasant ac-

---

[4] Josephine Seaton, *William Winston Seaton of the "National Intelligencer"* (1871).

[5] "The Facts in the Case of the Great Beef Contract" first appeared in *Galaxy Magazine*, May, 1870. It was reprinted in *Mark Twain's Memoranda* (1871).

[6] Sarah Madeleine Vinton Dahlgren (1825–1898), the widow of Rear Admiral John Adolphus Dahlgren (1809–1870) of the U. S. Navy, was a

quaintance with Wm. Page [Beach] Lawrence, the writer on international law.

SUNDAY, 5. It rained heavily all the forenoon and I did not attend church. Mr. Lawrence sent me some documents touching the French Spoliations, which I read during the day. I am gratified that this distinguished publicist holds that the Spoliation Claims are without merit. In the afternoon Gen'l McDowell called while I was out. At half-past four I went around to the Arlington and visited him. In the evening Mr. Hale,[7] our Attorney before the British Commission, called and gave me an interesting account of the proceedings of the Commission. Retired about ten o'clock, hoping to get more sleep than I usually do.

MONDAY, 6. Worked on correspondence until ten o'clock then went to the Committee where the action of the sub-committee during the late recess was ratified, and the three bills, Naval, Military Academy, and Fortifications, were ordered to be reported to the House. Also a bill for deficiency in the Judiciary Fund and another for deficiency in the English and American Commission. Nearly the whole day was consumed in the House on the Credit Mobilier business. A resolution was passed by a large majority, ordering the Committee to sit with open doors.[8] I voted for it because I would not appear unwilling to have anything with which my name is connected exempt from the fullest investigation. But I think the principle of holding committee meetings with open doors is all wrong. I have suffered great annoyance and perhaps had much unnecessary anxiety in regard to this whole business. It['s] rather however a matter of pride and perhaps I have no right to expect to get along in this stormy public life with[out] some imputations being made against me.

---

prominent Washington writer and translator. Her works include the much-read *Etiquette of Social Life in Washington* (1873).

[7] Robert Safford Hale (1822–1881) was the agent and counsel for the United States, 1871–73, before the American and British Mixed Claims Commission established in accordance with the Treaty of Washington (1871). He was a Republican member of the House from New York, 1866–67 and 1873–75.

[8] The motion instructed the House committee investigating Credit Mobilier to make public testimony already taken, and to continue without secrecy as to either "past or future proceedings." It was adopted by a vote of 130–7.

TUESDAY, 7.   Called on the President this morning and asked him to withhold the publication of the order in the case of Colonel Runkle, until the friends of the latter can present some mitigating circumstances. The Colonel has been heavily sentenced by a Court Martial for some wrong done in the Freedmen's Bureau. The President agreed to withhold it temporarily.[9] In the Committee heard the Board of Health in regard to the necessity of further appropriation. Also made some amendments to the Legislative Bill. The Naval Appropriation Bill was introduced into the House by Mr. Hale. After the morning hour went into Committee of the Whole on the Legislative Bill and completed twelve pages. Home in the evening.

WEDNESDAY, 8.   The same old story. Letters in the morning; Committee at half-past ten; House at twelve. Went nearly through the estimates for the Post Office Department. After the morning hour took up the Legislative Appropriation Bill. Pushed it steadily until one-quarter before five. Made good progress. Completed nearly thirty-five pages of the bill. Had a brisk debate as usual on the Bureau of Education. Came out of the House with a severe headache. At

[9] Benjamin Piatt Runkle, of Ohio, a nephew of Garfield's journalist friend Donn Piatt, retired from the army as a major in 1870, but continued to act as a disbursing officer for the Bureau of Refugees, Freedmen and Abandoned Lands. In 1872 he was convicted by a court-martial on charges growing out of his activities as disbursing officer and sentenced to be cashiered, imprisoned and heavily fined. President Grant remitted all the sentence except that providing for cashiering (see entry for January 16 below). In 1877 President Hayes disapproved of the conviction and sentence and revoked the order of the secretary of war of January 16, 1873, declaring that Runkle ceased to be an officer of the army from the date of the order. Runkle thereupon claimed and received pay as a retired major from 1873. When he sued for longevity pay also, the government put in a counterclaim for payments made him since 1873. The Court of Claims held that he was entitled to pay since 1877 but not to longevity pay nor pay for the period 1873–77. Both parties then appealed to the Supreme Court. The Court held that Runkle had never been legally cashiered or dismissed from the army because it did not positively and distinctly appear that the proceedings of the court-martial had ever been approved or confirmed by the President, and that Runkle was thus entitled to the pay he claimed. *Runkle v. United States* and *United States v. Runkle* (122 U. S. 543).

seven o'clock dined with Mr. MacFarland, whose guests were Senator Thurman, Representatives Cox, Kerr, Frye, and myself, David A. Wells and Ward. Had a pleasant evening.

THURSDAY, 9.   Took a Turkish Bath at half-past nine. Went to the Committee at ten, where we heard the Postmaster General and Mr. Bangs[10] for an hour on the increase of business and expense in the Post Office Department. Then heard Mr. Whiting in regard to some complications in the relations between the telegraph companies and the Signal Service Bureau. Mr. Whiting suggests that we release the Telegraph Companies belonging to the Pacific R.R. from the obligation of having half of what they do in the way of telegraphing for the Government withheld on the original charter of the road.[11] This the committee refuses to do. Dined in the evening with Governor Cox, Senator Schurz and some others.

FRIDAY, 10.   Committee on Appropriations discussed some items of the Legislative Bill and agreed to ask the House to strike out all increase of salaries that had been put in by Committee of the Whole. We must do this or else to be consistent must raise several that have not been raised. Completed the Post Office Appropriation Bill. Ordered it reported with a new section regulating the rate for carrying the mail on railroads. At 12 o'clock went by appointment to the office of the Postmaster General to be present at the opening of bids for supplying stamps for the next four years. The rate paid during the last four years was 27½ cents per thousand. The lowest bid presented today was that of the Continental Bank Note Co. of N. Y. at 14.99 cents per thousand. A remarkable reduction in the price. In the House after the morning hour went into Committee of the Whole on the Legislative Bill. After an hour's debate the increase asked for the Bureau of Education was lost by four votes.[12] Proceeded with the bill

---

[10] George S. Bangs, general superintendent of the Railway Mail Service.

[11] The Pacific Railroad Act of 1864 provided that one-half of the compensation for railroad and telegraph services rendered for the government by the companies receiving government subsidies under this act should be applied to the payment of the bonds issued by the government in aid of the construction of the railroads.

[12] The increase was to cover the cost of collecting and sending to the Vienna Exposition educational materials used in American schools—slates, books, blackboards, maps, and the like. The vote was 78–74 against the increase.

when a debate sprung up concerning the Committee of Claims which lasted until half-past four when the Committee rose and the House adjourned.

SATURDAY, 11. Committee did not meet this morning. I called at Judge Knott's [Nott's][13] at 9 o'clock and went over some of the points in regard to the Court of Claims alluded to in Boardman Smith's[14] speech of last evening. Then returned and went over other points of the appropriation with Mr. Conant[15] of the Treasury. Went to the Capitol at 11 and looked over the statute and prepared for the morning discussion. In the House after the morning hour we took up the Legislative Bill and had a long and stirring discussion on Smith's amendment.[16] At the end of an hour and a half beat him by an overwhelming majority. Finished the bill except an amendment concerning the Pacific Railroad which was sprung on it by Randall.[17]

SUNDAY, 12. Went this morning to Dr. Shedd's[18] and staid an hour in the Turkish Bath. From 113 degrees of heat to a plunge in

[13] Charles Cooper Nott (1827–1916), a judge of the U. S. Court of Claims, 1865–1905; from 1896 he was chief justice. Except for a short period he also reported the decisions of the court, 1867–1914. He married Alice, the daughter of Garfield's beloved mentor, Mark Hopkins.

[14] Horace Boardman Smith (1826–1888), a Republican member of the House from New York, 1871–75.

[15] Charles F. Conant, chief of the Warrant Bureau of the Treasury Department.

[16] The report of the Committee on Appropriations contained a clause appropriating $400,000 to pay judgments of the Court of Claims. When it came up for consideration, Smith charged that money was being paid illegally to certain Southern claimants for wartime losses, and offered an amendment designed to halt alleged irregularities. Garfield investigated the matter, found Smith to be in error, and refuted his charges. After considerable debate the amendment was lost.

[17] Samuel Jackson Randall (1828–1890), was a Democratic member of the House from Pennsylvania, 1863 to his death. He was speaker of the House, 1876–81.

The amendment prohibited the government from paying money for the "transportation of mails, troops or otherwise" to any railroad company in default for interest on United States bonds given or loaned to the company for building the railroad.

[18] William B. Shedd, a homeopathic physician who described himself as a "medical electrician," offered "Turco-Russian baths" at 903 E. St., N.W.

cold water is something of a shock. Went to Church at 11. Several
people called in the afternoon. I had a very large mail that took me
most of my spare time during the day to read. Called on Mrs. Johnson, the widow of Simeon Johnson, in the evening. I am not at all
well. I have symptoms of biliousness and the overwork which I am
daily obliged to do makes me fear that I shall permanently injure my
health, but I hardly know how to avoid it.

MONDAY, 13. Usual morning work until 10 o'clock. Then walked
down the Avenue with Crete and reached my Committee at 11. Discussed a few questions on appropriations and also the pending
amendment to the Legislative Bill and resolved to do something
towards recovering the House from its feeling of panic which the
discussion of the Credit Mobilier and the Pacific R.R. seems to have
brought upon it. In the House the day was filled with the usual Monday miscellany. The troubled condition of affairs in Louisiana came
up and absorbed attention for over two hours. I made a speech against
seizing the State authorities but in favor of a careful investigation of
the official facts furnished us by the President, and introduced a
resolution directing the Committee on the Judiciary to report the
situation to the House. This prevailed.[19] About half-past four o'clock
the House adjourned. Home in the evening.

TUESDAY, 14. Appropriation Committee did not meet this morning.
At 11 o'clock went before the Credit Mobilier Investigating Committee and made a statement of what I know concerning the Company. I am too proud to confess to any but my most intimate friends
how deeply this whole matter has grieved me. While I did nothing
in regard to it that can be construed into any act even of impropriety
much less than corruption, I have still said from the start that the
shadow of the cursed thing would cling to my name for many years.
I believe my statement was regarded as clear and conclusive. In the

---

[19] The debate developed over a motion which provided that the House
and Senate appoint a joint committee to investigate and determine whether
there existed a legal and established state government in Louisiana, where,
after the election of November, 1872, two governments emerged, each
claiming to be the legitimate one. Since the President had submitted to the
House documents on affairs in Louisiana, Garfield moved that the documents
be printed and the matter referred to the Judiciary Committee. The motion
was adopted.

House took up the Legislative Bill at one o'clock and the Committee considered it until four, when it was reported to the House and the previous question sustained. The House then adjourned. Singular incident in reference to Mr. Ames and myself, to be mentioned when the result is known.[20]

WEDNESDAY, 15. Called on Mr. Ames this morning and received his answer to my letter of yesterday, denying he made any statement criticising my testimony. Committee disposed of a large amount of business on the docket. Finished amendments to the Legislative Appropriation Bill in the House and bill passed at ten minutes before two o'clock. But few changes have been made except such as the Committee on Appropriations requested. At 2 o'clock House took up the Indian Territory Bill.[21] In the evening dined at Welcker's with Messrs. Ward, Dawes, Hawley, Frye, and several others. Gave to the press my correspondence with Ames.

THURSDAY, 16. At ten o'clock went to the President's with Mr. Shellabarger, to ask a removal of a portion of the sentence [of] Major P. B. Runkle. The President granted the request. Reached the Committee Room at half-past eleven and though there was no meeting called four of us were there. Talked over some matters relating to the Appropriations. In the House got into Committee of the Whole and Gov. Swann started the Diplomatic Bill. The rest of the day spent on the Oklahoma Bill. At the close of the day I moved to lay it on the table, which was carried by a large majority. At 6 o'clock went to the Smithsonian to attend the annual meeting of the Board of Regents. We had a very interesting meeting. Ex-President McLean

[20] Garfield had heard that morning that Oakes Ames had said that he had lent Garfield $400 and that Garfield had not only refused to pay him but was aiding his accusers in the Credit Mobilier investigation. To bring the matter to an issue, Garfield immediately sent Ames a check for $400. Ames returned Garfield's letter with a note on the back denying that he had said that Garfield had borrowed $400 or that Garfield was aiding his accusers. He added that he was returning therewith the $400 "as not belonging to me." The letter of Garfield, with Ames's endorsement, is in Garfield's letterbook for 1873. See note 249 for 1872.

[21] Known also as the Oklahoma Bill, the measure provided for the establishment of the Territory of Oklahoma and of a territorial government whose responsibilities would include better protection for Indian tribes.

[Maclean][22] of Princeton made a report on the ownership of Field's [Peale's][23] picture of Washington now held by the Smithsonian. Prof. Agassiz[24] made some interesting remarks concerning the effects of glacial action on this continent.

FRIDAY, 17.   Usual Committee meeting; several parties heard. House spent nearly all the day with bills on the Speaker's table. Dined at Mr. Hooper's with Prof. Agassiz and wife and Prof. Peirce. I know of few characters more simple and grand than Prof. Agassiz. He carries all the sweetness of childhood in his nature, with the strength and massiveness and grandeur of a very great man. He has invited me to spend a part of the Summer at Nantucket Island where he and other scientific men are to lecture to teachers. I should be glad to accept the invitation. At half-past 9 o'clock went with Crete to Speaker Blaine's reception, the first of the session. It is almost my first visit this winter, except going to dinners.

SATURDAY, 18.   At half-past ten went to the room of the Committee on Commerce, where I presided over them and a Committee of my own in joint session, while we heard a very large delegation from Philadelphia from the several civic and commercial organizations in favor of a large appropriation for the erection of walls on the Susquehanna to prevent the ice gorge. At 12 o'clock Committee on Appropriations met in their own Committee Room to hear the same gentlemen in regard to appropriations for light houses on the Delaware River. In the House the day was spent with unfinished business and private bills until after three o'clock when I moved to go into Committee of the Whole; but it was so late in the week that the

[22] John Maclean (1800–1886), president of the College of New Jersey (Princeton), 1854–68, was a regent of the Smithsonian and a member of the Executive Committee.

[23] Titian R. Peale (1799–1886), of Washington, D.C., had presented a claim for a portrait of George Washington painted by his father, Charles Wilson Peale (1741–1827), in the possession of the Smithsonian. The report by Maclean was adverse to the claim.

[24] Louis Agassiz (1807–1873), Swiss-born naturalist, one of the greatest scientists of the nineteenth century, was professor of natural history at the Lawrence Scientific School, Harvard, 1848–73. He was first appointed to the Board of Regents of the Smithsonian Institution in 1863 and served until his death.

House concluded to adjourn. So we got no other work done. At 7 o'clock went to Dr. Brodhead's[25] on Capitol Hill, where with Comptroller Tayler,[26] Senators Sherman and Hamlin and Representative Poland and a few others spent a pleasant evening.

SUNDAY, 19. Attended church with Crete and Mother and the two boys. In the afternoon spent several hours with Dr. Hayden on the prospects of the Geological Surveys. In the evening several people called, among them General Hazen, Mr. Bowman, Dr. Hayden, and also Mr. Gardner [Gardiner],[27] the topographer of Clarence King's[28] expedition. I am troubled to know what to do with the large number of exploring expeditions Congress has on hand. There should be a consolidation of all the Geological and Geographical expedition[s] in their work under one head, leaving the survey of the lakes to the Engineer Corp[s] and of the coast to the Coast Survey.

MONDAY, 20. Committee met at half-past ten and made a preliminary examination of the Senate amendments to the Indian Appropriation Bill; also prepared an amendment to the Boston Post Office Bill. In the House the whole day was exhausted with the usual Monday business, motions to suspend the rules, etc. I failed after several earnest efforts to get into Committee of the Whole on the appropriation bills. At 7 o'clock P.M. met with the Regents of the Smithsonian Institution where, after the transaction of business, we listened to a very interesting talk of Prof. Agassiz on the recent *Hassler* Expedition to South America.[29] His predictions were verified as to

[25] John M. Brodhead, second comptroller, Treasury Department.

[26] Robert W. Tayler, first comptroller, Treasury Department.

[27] James T. Gardiner (1842–1912) was chief topographer until 1873 of the U. S. Geological Survey of the Fortieth Parallel.

[28] Clarence King (1842–1901), geologist, mining engineer and administrator, had been engaged for several years in directing a survey across the Cordilleran ranges from eastern Colorado to the boundary of California. The results were published in *Report of the Geological Exploration of the Fortieth Parallel,* 7 vols. (1870–80). When the U. S. Geological Survey was established in 1879. King became its first head, resigning in 1881. See Garfield's entry for August 13, 1879.

[29] The *Hassler,* a steamship of the U. S. Coast Survey, sailed from Boston for the West Coast in December, 1871, with a number of scientists on board who engaged in scientific investigation and the collection of specimens. The

the supposition that sea dredging would bring up animals similar to those of the fossil periods, because they live under great pressure and with but little light, as do the animals of the fossil period. He found numerous evidences of glacial action sweeping from southward to northward, all along South America.

TUESDAY, 21. Committee met a little before 11 o'clock and blocked out the work on the Miscellaneous Appropriation Bill. Assigned a portion of it to Sub-Committees and considered other portions. In the House after the morning hour the day was spent in discussing Shellabarger's bill to revive our drooping commerce. Mr. S. made a long and able speech in his usual severely solemn style. Dined in the evening with Mr. Ward, Prof. Agassiz, Prof. Henry, Messrs. Hale, Hooper and Allison[30] and a member of the British Legation. A very pleasant company.

WEDNESDAY, 22. Committee met at half-past ten and finished the consideration of the Senate amendments to the Indian Appropriation Bill, several of which were important. In the House most of the day was uselessly spent on Shellabarger's bill to revive commerce. Introduced and carried through a bill to pay deficiencies in the British and American Claims Commission. Today Mr. Ames went before the Poland Committee and testified directly contrary to his former statement and to the testimony of other gentlemen, myself among the number.[31] He is evidently determined to drag down as many men with him as possible. How far he will be successful it

---

objects of Agassiz and his group were to collect zoological specimens and to learn the boundaries of the different faunae, particularly along the coast from the Straits of Magellan to California.

[30] William Boyd Allison (1829–1908), a Republican member of the House from Iowa, 1863–71; U. S. senator, 1873 to his death.

[31] In a statement presented on December 17, 1872, to the House committee investigating Credit Mobilier, Oakes Ames said that he had agreed to get ten shares of Credit Mobilier stock for Garfield but that Garfield had never paid for them nor received them. When questioned he said that he did not think that Garfield had received any dividends, and added, "He says he did not. My own recollection is not very clear." On January 22, 1873, his recollection clarified by some memoranda he had found, he testified that he had paid Garfield $329. According to Ames he had sold bonds, which were Garfield's share of a bonus given to stockholders, for $776, and had received a dividend of $600 on the stock. From this $1,376 he had deducted $1,000 in payment

remains to be seen. But in the present condition of the public mind, he will probably succeed in throwing a cloud over the good name of many people. He seems to me as bad a man as can well be.

THURSDAY, 23. At ten o'clock went to the President's with Senator Sherman and several members of the Ohio Delegation to request the appointment of Edwin Coles [Cowles] of Cleveland to the Diplomatic Service. From there went to my Committee and heard Montgomery Blair[32] on a claim pending before the Committee. Also, heard Mr. Mullett on the appropriations for the public buildings. In the House went into Committee of the Whole and finished the Consular and Diplomatic Bill. Also took up the Naval Appropriation Bill and went over 25 of its 27 pages. Took dinner at 7 at Mr. Shepherd's with a party of about 25 Senators, Representatives and citizens of Washington.

FRIDAY, 24. Committee met at half-past ten and heard Col. Benét of the Ordnance Dep't on the appropriations for arsenals and armories. Concluded to appropriate liberally for three, Springfield on the Atlantic Coast, Rock Island in the Mississippi Valley, and Benecia in California. Agreed to drop all the rest from the bill and appropriate $50,000 as a general fund to take care of them. In the House finished the discussion of the Naval Appropriation Bill and passed it. Mr. Ames has gone from bad to worse in his testimony today contradicting the statements of Colfax, Kelley and others and is seemingly determined to smutch everybody before he is broken.

SATURDAY, 25. Worked up correspondence in the morning. In the House, private bills being in order, we did but little general legislation. I made another ineffectual attempt to get the Deficiency Bill through, which was in relation to the expenses of the U. S. Courts. But the Democrats objected to it, because, among the expenses, was the cost of enforcing the amendments to the Constitution. In the evening called on MacFarland of N.Y. At 8 o'clock went to Mr. Wilson's to the celebration of the anniversary of the birth of Robert Burns. Several speeches were made and several Scottish songs were

---

for the stock and $47 in interest. This left $329, which he turned over to Garfield. "That," said Ames, "is all the transaction between us. I did not deliver him any stock before or since."

[32] Montgomery Blair (1813–1883), lawyer, was postmaster general in Lincoln's cabinet.

sung. I spoke for a short time, tracing the relation between the Welsh and the Scottish races, branches of the Celtic race and the characteristics of the two as shown in their resistance to Rome and in the general spirit of the people. Blaine and Bingham also made speeches. In these days of tempests and obloquy, the thought of Scotland and Burns, of literature and song, comes to me like the breath of summer sunshine. Home at 11.

SUNDAY, 26. Took a Turkish bath at 10 o'clock and spent the day at home. Worked up case 131 on the Docket of the Supreme Court,[33] on which I am to make an argument in a short time. The case is an interesting one in the law points involved but I am doubtful whether it can be successful before the court. Towards evening went with Crete to see a girl that she had partially engaged as a cook. Then made a call on Mr. and Mrs. Riddle. Continue[d] work on the case until 11 o'clock in the evening.

MONDAY, 27. Committee heard two or three parties on questions of appropriations and then went through and passed upon the estimates for the Light House service as reported to the Committee by Hale. In the House was the usual Monday legislative wash-day and but little was accomplished save the abolition of the Franking Privilege. It was done in a spirit of demagogueism, but it was a good thing to do. In reference to the Credit Mobilier Involvements I have passed through many phases of feeling and suffering but tonight I settle down in the conclusion that a true life and solid character, which I venture to assert is mine, cannot be destroyed by this thing.

TUESDAY, 28. In Committee heard Mr. Myers[34] of Philadelphia in regard to the Post Office at that place; also heard Mr. Clark, Architect of the Capitol, on Appropriations for the Capitol Building and grounds. In the House took up the Indian Appropriation Bill and acted on the forty-odd Senate amendments thereto, which took up two hours, and at half-past three o'clock the death of Mr. Strong[35]

[33] *Burke v. Smith* (83 U. S. 390), a case involving the New Albany and Sandusky City Railway Company, an insolvent corporation, on appeal from the U. S. Circuit Court of Indiana. Garfield was a lawyer for the appellants.

[34] Leonard Myers (1827–1905), a Republican member of the House from Pensylvania, 1869–75.

[35] Julius Levi Strong (1828–1872), a Republican member of the House, 1869 to his death on September 7, 1872.

of Connecticut was announced. The Credit Mobilier Investigation still dragging. Stevenson's attempt to involve Blaine in impropriety for holding stock in an Iowa R.R. Co. seems to have exploded. A general condition of distrust and suspicion prevails in the House and among the press.

WEDNESDAY, 29. In Committee considered and settled the appropriations for life saving stations for the Revenue Marine Service; also for most of the public buildings under control of the Treasury Department. Several difficult questions about the limit of expenditure on public buildings came up for consideration. It seems to be of but little use to fix any limit, as they are quite sure to make their calculations so as to transcend them. In the House the day was spent on the Colorado Bill,[36] and on a question of privilege about a witness who refused to testify before the Wilson Committee.[37] At half-past six dined at Mr. Mullett's with a large Company of gentlemen. At ten attended the President's reception. Another cold wave has struck us and we are now having one of the coldest nights of the season.

THURSDAY, 30. Heard several persons on items for appropriations. Spent most of the morning with the Public Printer examining the

[36] The measure provided for the admission of Colorado as a state. Its opponents, including Garfield, succeeded in tabling the bill, their chief criticism being that Colorado's population was too small to warrant statehood.

[37] Testimony had disclosed that in 1864, while Congress was considering an act which provided for federal aid in the construction of a transcontinental railroad, Thomas Clark Durant, vice president of the Union Pacific Railroad Company, brought to Washington money and bonds belonging to the railroad and delivered the bonds, valued at between $100,000 and $150,000, to Joseph B. Stewart, a Washington attorney. Stewart in some way disposed of the bonds and received for his services $30,000. As a witness before the Wilson Committee investigating Credit Mobilier, he stated that no bonds had been turned over to any member of Congress or person connected with the Executive Department of the government. But he refused to say to whom he had given bonds, despite warnings from committee members that he had no legal right to withhold such information from the committee. Stewart was charged with contempt of the House and arrested. In an address to the House he denied the charge, standing upon his rights as a citizen and upon his duty as a lawyer to keep secret certain transactions between him and his clients. He was held as a prisoner until February 28, when the House released him.

estimates for printing for the next fiscal year. We are endeavoring to distribute the amount of printing to the several departments so as to limit the expenses in that direction. In the House nearly the whole day was devoted to a question of privilege; to the question whether Mr. Stewart, an attorney here, should be compelled to answer before Wilson's Credit Mobilier Committee touching matters received by him in confidence as an attorney. Stewart made a speech of an hour. He was committed for contempt. We succeeded in getting the Appropriation Bill for fortifications passed before the House adjourned. Dined in the evening at S. P. Brown's,[38] with a large number of Senators, Members and citizens.

FRIDAY, 31. In Committee settled the estimates for the public printing and the distribution of the amount to be printed for the several departments. Heard the Commissioner of Agriculture and passed a deficiency for him. Heard the Botanical Gardener and agreed upon appropriations for his garden. In the House the day was spent mainly on private bills. Dined in the evening at Speaker Blaine's with Mrs. Blaine, Gail Hamilton (Miss Dodge)[39] and Messrs. Allison and Palmer. Gail Hamilton is very brilliant in conversation. This Winter would be a delightful one in spite of all its hard work, but for the ugly shadow of the Credit Mobilier, which throws a gloom over every social circle.

February

SATURDAY, 1. Committee did not meet this morning. Went to the Treasury Department and Post Office on business. Among other things talked with the Sec'y of the Treasury on some points in the Legislative Appropriation Bill. In the House the day was spent

[38] Samuel P. Brown, Washington businessman and member of the Board of Public Works of the District of Columbia; he lived at Mt. Pleasant, which he had founded.

[39] Mary Abigail Dodge (1833–1896), author and editor whose pseudonym was Gail Hamilton, moved to Washington from Massachusetts in 1871. Among her many books were *Woman's Worth and Worthlessness* (1872). She was an opponent of woman suffrage. She was a cousin of the wife of James G. Blaine, whose biography she published in 1895.

mainly on private bills. Had an interview with President [Andrew D.] White of Cornell University and several other gentlemen connected with the Agricultural Colleges. We discussed the Senate Bill which dedicates the proceeds of the public lands to the extent of 500,000 acres for each state for the use of the agricultural colleges. I do not believe in a college to educate men for the profession of farming. A liberal education almost always draws men away from farming. But schools of science in general technology are valuable. I am in some doubt what ought to be done with this bill. They desire me to take charge of it in the House. At 8.50 took the train for Philadelphia.

SUNDAY, 2. Reached Philadelphia about three o'clock, but slept in the sleeping car until 7. Took breakfast at the Continental Restaurant, and at 10 called on Judge Black at his boarding house in Cypress Street and spent the day and evening with him. He has been quite ill and telegraphed for me yesterday. Went carefully over the ground of the Credit Mobilier and found his remembrance of my conversation with him in 1870 was substantially the same as my own. Also talked with him on the general condition of public affairs; the state of distrust in which the public mind is thrown by the course of recent events. It is exceedingly cold here, indeed much colder than I have ever known it before this Winter. At half-past 11 P.M. took the train for Washington.

MONDAY, 3. In Committee heard Prof. Peirce on the items of the Coast Survey, and adopted all his estimates except the item of $50,000 for the Geodetic Survey on the continent to connect the two series of coast surveys. We reserve that item to consider in connection with the surveys of the Engineer Dep't. Acted also on the items for surveys for the public lands of the West. Heard General Humphreys and Lieut. Wheeler[40] on the military service in the West. Heard also a delegation of ladies in reference to the appropriation for the Soldiers' Orphan Asylum in this city. In the House secured the passage of the bill appropriating for a deficiency in the expenses of the British and American Claims Commission, with a Senate amendment appropriating one-half million dollars for the

[40] George M. Wheeler, of the Army Corps of Engineers, was in charge of military and topographical surveys west of the hundredth meridian.

N. Y. Postoffice Building. Mondays in the House are becoming a nuisance.

TUESDAY, 4. In Committee heard Horatio Seymour[41] and Mr. Wines[42] in favor of an appropriation for the Prison Discipline Society. Also Mr. Hinckley[43] of the Philadelphia and Wilmington R.R. and the P.M. General in regard to new routes for the transportation of mails. Took up the Army Appropriation Bill and nearly finished its items. In the House carried the conference report on the Indian Appropriation Bill and late in the afternoon carried the preliminary motions for going into committee on the P. O. Appropriation Bill, but it was so late the House adjourned before anything was done. Our appropriation bills are getting into close quarters and there is much danger that we shall fail in getting them through by the 4th of March. The Democrats seem determined to have an extra session if possible to take partisan advantage of the panic resulting from investigating committees.

WEDNESDAY, 5. Committee heard Colonel Benét on the Ordnance appropriations; also, Sec'y Boutwell on Senate amendments to the Legislative Bill affecting his department; also a speech of Horace F. Clark, President of the U. P. R. R. on the Senate legislation touching the interest of that road. I am satisfied that Congress is making a senseless raid on railroads growing out of the feeling of panic that now prevails here. In the House after the morning hour got into Committee of the Whole on the Post Office Appropriation Bill and did a pretty full day's work on it. Held the Committee until near five o'clock when Boutwell [Butler] took occasion to make an assault on me as brutal as his nature was capable of and this statement is superlative of its strength. Dined in the evening.

THURSDAY, 6. A heavy morning's work was accomplished in the Committee. We finished the Army Bill after hearing further from the Ordnance Dep't. Heard Dr. Ingalls [Nichols] on the appro-

[41] Horatio Seymour, whose interest in penal reform stemmed from his years as governor of New York, was president of the Prison Reform Congress which met in Baltimore in January, 1873.

[42] Frederick Howard Wines (1838–1912), social reformer, was secretary of the Illinois State Board of Charities, 1869–92, 1896–98.

[43] Isaac Hinckley, president of the Philadelphia, Wilmington & Baltimore Railroad Company.

priations for the Deaf Mute College and for Prof. Hayden's survey. Heard a deputation of Editors and Publishers in regard to rates of printing used in the Public Printing Office. Also heard Mr. Schell of N. Y. and Mr. Sheldon of La., the first in regard to the Pacific R.R. and the second in reference to a Marine Hospital at New Orleans. Consider[ed] several other items. In the House after the morning hour fought through the P. O. Appropriation Bill and passed it at 5 o'clock, the Committee carrying every point. Dined at 7 o'clock at Sec'y Fish's with a large number of Senators and Representatives. At 10 o'clock went to Delano's and attended his reception.

FRIDAY, 7. In Committee finished the Army Bill and made good progress on the Sundry Civil Bill. Heard Mr. Burchard in regard to land office in Illinois. Heard General Babcock at length on estimates for appropriations for public buildings and grounds in Washington and fixed the Army appropriations, largely reducing the estimates. Settled the vexed question of the Geodetic Survey of the Interior in favor of the Coast Survey but at a reduced figure.[44] In the House after the morning hour we took up the appropriations for the Military Academy which occupied the rest of the day, but it passed with only two amendments at 5 o'clock. At home in the evening. Richard Hawley, Jr. dined with us.

SATURDAY, 8. Took a Russian Bath and then went to the Committee where we began a little after eleven o'clock to work incessantly until three. Nearly finished the Sundry Civil Bill passing on the appropriations for the Navy Yards and a large number of miscellaneous matters. In the House the day was devoted to private bills, mainly to the reports of the Committee on Claims. Toward evening the Committee on Commerce reported back the River and Harbor Appropriation Bill and proposed to refer it directly to the Committee of the Whole, without a previous reference to the Committee on Appropriations. This I resisted and after some debate the bill

[44] Benjamin Peirce, chief of the U. S. Coast Survey, had informed Garfield that a primary geodetic survey cost less than five dollars per square mile while a topographical survey cost more than eighty dollars per square mile. The Sundry Civil Bill as enacted alloted $36,000 "for extending the triangulation of the coast survey, so as to form a geodetic connection between the Atlantic and Pacific coasts of the United States and assisting in the State surveys, including compensation of civilians engaged in the work."

was withdrawn. Several gentlemen called in the evening. At 8 o'clock went with Crete in company with Mrs. Dahlgren to the Literary Reunion at Horatio King's.[45]

SUNDAY, 9. Attended Church and heard a very fair sermon on "Patience." In the evening dined with Judge Black and Mr. Thompson[46] at Welcker's. The Credit Mobilier Investigation is drawing to a close and Ames expects to return to the City tomorrow. I am anxious to present the testimony of Judge Black with regard to my relation to the affairs. But the condition of the public mind is so wrought up that it is hardly possible for any one to be heard with fairness until [unless] his testimony still whets the appetite for scandal. Judge Black feels very confident that nothing in the case will ultimately injure me, but I doubt if he sees all the forces that are now at work to injure and defame. Did some further work on the railroad case and though I consider it a close and doubtful one, yet the main point, the obligation of subscribers to pay in good faith their subscription, made before the organization of the corporation, seems to me clear, from all the cases I have examined. Several persons called in the evening, among others Prof. Baird in regard to his appropriation for food fishes.

MONDAY, 10. In Committee reviewed the print of the Miscellaneous Bill and added a number of new items. Heard Professor Powell in regard to explorations in Colorado, and also heard Mr. Starkweather[47] in favor of an appropriation for the New London Naval Station. Committee concluded to throw out both New London and League Island. Committee order[ed] the bill reported to the House. Read to the Committee a confidential letter from Mr. Shellabarger, alleging that the appropriation for preserving clothing in the Quartermaster's Department was a swindle. Committee agreed to send for the Sec'y of War and the Quartermaster General tomorrow morning. In the House the day was spent in the usual rough ways incident to Monday's work. A great deal was attempted in

[45] Horatio King (1811–1897), a lawyer and former postmaster general (1861), was a prominent figure in Washington life for many years. The Saturday Evening Literary Club met at his home.

[46] John McCandless Thompson (1829–1903), a Pennsylvania lawyer, was a Republican member of the House, 1874–75, 1877–79.

[47] Henry Howard Starkweather (1826–1876) was a Republican member of the House from Connecticut, 1867 to his death.

the way [of] suspending the rules but little was accomplished. Oakes Ames has returned with his memorandum books, but no intelligence has yet transpired of what new revelations he has to make.

TUESDAY, 11. In Committee reconsidered appropriations for League Island and New London and allowed a quarter of a million for League Island and five hundred thousand for New London. Heard the Quartermaster General and other officers of his department in regard to the appropriation for the preservation of clothing in answer to an allegation that the process was a swindle—allowed the appropriation. Finished several items in the Sundry Civil Bill. In the House introduced the bill and set it for tomorrow. After the morning hour, got into Committee of the Whole on the Army Appropriation Bill and after an hour's general debate it took but 30 minutes to finish the bill in committee and pass it in the House. Evening session at half-past seven on Claims. Mr. Ames has finished his exhibits of memoranda and Colfax has put in testimony sustaining his own statement.

WEDNESDAY, 12. In Committee heard the Board of Public Works in regard to appropriations for next year but declined to move in the matter as the subject has already been referred to the Committee on the Judiciary. At 11 o'clock Horace F. Clark, President of the Pacific R.R. and J. Hughly [Hubley] Ashton, Counsel of the U. S. against the Road, were heard by the Committee in regard to the Senate amendment touching the road. Just before the Committee adjourned Gen'l Butler came in and asked an appropriation of $40,000 to enlarge the Hall of the House by removing the South Lobby and the Speaker's Room. At one o'clock the Senate and House met in Joint Convention to count the votes for President and Vice President. The work continued until eight o'clock in the evening. This work is one of the most delicate and dangerous in all the machinery of the Government. Whenever it is in progress the country treads on the verge of anarchy and revolution. Neither our Constitution or laws provide any safeguard against trouble.

THURSDAY, 13. Committee considered a number of items for the different bills and heard several parties in regard to appropriations. In the House after the morning hour the day was devoted exclusively to reports of the Committee on Commerce. I, however, made a statement as to the condition of the appropriation bills and carried a motion to meet at 11 o'clock after this week. Attended a meeting of the Board of Regents of the Smithsonian Institution at 7 o'clock. A number of interesting [subjects] were discussed. Prof. Henry not being well the Board met in his parlor. The contributions of money and specimens of a scientific character that are now coming into the Institution are rapidly increasing its possessions.

FRIDAY, 14. In Committee considered the Senate amendments to the Legislative Appropriation Bill and acted on all but the last three. Also considered some miscellaneous subjects before the Committee. In the House got into Committee of the Whole [on the Sundry Civil Appropriation Bill] soon after the reading of the Journal and though we had but an hour and a half and the first reading of the bill was not dispensed, objections on the Democratic side being made, we finished the first reading and also finished eight pages of the second reading. At 2 o'clock the House took up the question of distributing the *Alabama* awards and spent the remainder of the day on it.

SATURDAY, 15. In Committee considered a number of miscellaneous items to be added [to] the Sundry Civil Bill and the Legislative Bill. Heard Mr. Starkweather in regard to an appropriatiou for the Naval Station at New London and agreed to put on $50,000 in the bill. In the House most of the day was spent on Butler's bill for distributing the *Alabama* awards and the bill passed. I voted against it believing it was an unjust distribution of the award and not in the spirit of international law nor honorable to the Gov't.[48] In the evening dined with Ben Holladay of California and about twenty other gentlemen, Senators and members, among them Senators Conkling and Ramsey[49] and Representatives Beck, Banks and Kellogg.[50] It was a very elaborate and brilliant dinner.

SUNDAY, 16. One of the dreariest days I have ever known. It com-

---

[48] Garfield was actually paired with John Lynch of Maine, and during the roll call he said that Lynch, if present, would have voted for the bill, and he (Garfield) against it.

[49] Alexander Ramsey (1815–1903), Whig member of the House from Pennsylvania, 1843–47; territorial governor of Minnesota, 1849–53; governor of Minnesota, 1860–63; Republican senator from Minnesota, 1863–75; secretary of war, 1879–81.

[50] Stephen Wright Kellogg (1822–1904) was a Republican member of the House from Connecticut, 1869–73.

menced to rain at six in the morning and for seven or eight hours the City was a vast river of slush. At ten o'clock took a Turkish bath. Did not attend church but spent most of the day in reading the testimony in the Credit Mobilier Investigation. In the evening called at Speaker Blaine's and at Mr. Phillips'. Several gent[lemen] called on me before I went out.

MONDAY, 17. Committee met at ten and considered a number of miscellaneous matters for the Sundry Civil Bill and for the Deficiency Bill. Heard Mr. Clapp, the Public Printer, in favor of the deficiency for the current year. Piatt returned from Philadelphia with a letter from Judge Black addressed to the Speaker on the subject of the Investigation.[51] In the House the day was spent in the usual miscellany of suspension of rules and the like. Voted for the Agricultural College Bill with some misgivings as to the wisdom of the measure. In the evening Senator W. F. Sanders[52] of Montana called and spent two hours with me. Sheldon and his wife and several other friends called in the evening. Wrote letters until a late hour.

TUESDAY, 18. In Committee heard Messrs. —— and Ashton, Counsel for the U.S., and Mr. Wilson, Chairman of the Credit Mobilier Committee No. 2,[53] on the Senate amendment in regard to the Pacific R. R. Co. This consumed the entire hour so that we transacted no other business, except to hear Gen'l Chipman and General Babcock and a delegation of the citizens of Washington in favor of rebuilding a bridge across the branch of the Potomac. In the House went into Committee of the Whole and made progress of about ten pages on the Sundry Civil Bill, when the Committee arose and listened to the report of Mr. Poland in regard to Credit Mobilier No. 1. The report produced a profound sensation and was listened to with silence and painful interest. It recommended expulsion in the cases of Ames and Brooks and found no cause of action against other members of the House. I am not satisfied with some of the statements of the Committee in reference to my case; but with Ames's

---

[51] See note 249 for 1872.

[52] Wilbur Fiske Sanders was a member of the House of Representatives of the Territory of Montana at this time.

[53] Two select committees of the House were appointed as a result of the Credit Mobilier scandal. The first, headed by Luke Poland of Vermont, investigated the alleged bribery of members of the House. The second, headed by Jeremiah M. Wilson of Indiana, ranged more widely.

memorandum and testimony before them, they probably thought they were doing right.[54] After the report was finished and a little discussion in regard to it, a day—next Tuesday—was fixed for hearing. Went again into Committee of the Whole and got over four pages of the bill. House adjourned at half-past four.

WEDNESDAY, 19. In Committee finished the contested points on the Senate amendments to the Legislative Appropriation Bill and ordered them reported to the House. In the House went into Committee of the Whole and made considerable progress on the Sundry Civil Bill, until one o'clock, when the Committee rose and allowed the bill for printing the Congressional Debates to be considered. A little after one o'clock the President sent for me to call on him at his room in the Senate and wish[es] us to bring up for action the bill in regard to our fisheries. It seems to be necessary to act on it immediately in order to keep the national faith with England.

THURSDAY, 20. In Committee ran over the estimates for the Deficiency Bill and distributed different parts of it to several members. Committee agreed to sit this evening at half-past seven to complete the bill. In the House made considerable progress on the Sundry Civil Bill, reaching the 34th page. A stormy uncomfortable spirit pervaded the House and an attempt was made to start an impeachment against Colfax. Committee met at half-past 7 and worked nearly three hours on the Deficiency Bill. Heard officials from the Treasury, War, and Interior Departments.

FRIDAY, 21. In Committee considered additional amendments to the Deficiency Bill and got it nearly ready for introduction. In the House at 2 o'clock got into Committee on the Sundry Civil Bill and held them to the work until 6, when the bill was nearly finished. Asked the Committee to rise to enable me to suspend the rules and put the bill and amendments into the House for action. But the House was so thin that I did not press the motion. In the evening worked up correspondence and made some calls.

SATURDAY, 22. At home until 10 A.M. In Committee finished several miscellaneous appropriation estimates for the Deficiency Bill. In the House finished the bill itself, after a debate of an hour and more than two hours voting. At half-past 5 went to the President's Dinner.

[54] The Poland Committee accepted as true the statement made by Oakes Ames on January 22 with respect to his dealings with Garfield. For his testimony on that date see note 31.

Crete had assisted Mrs. Grant at her afternoon reception. Had a pleasant dinner with the family and a few friends. At 10 o'clock went to Mrs. Dahlgren's Reception and thence home.

SUNDAY, 23. At home nearly all day. Read up the Report of the Credit Mobilier Committee and prepared materials for a speech in case I found it necessary to make one. Called on several gents in the evening.

MONDAY, 24. In Committee the proof sheets of the Deficiency Bill were before us and several corrections and additions were made. In the House Poland's Report came up at 12 o'clock and at the same hour the New Albany R. R. Case came up in the Supreme Court. Kerr[55] and I went over and asked that it be passed over informally. Mr. Burke[56] of Cleveland came before the day was over and I dined with him and his wife at the Ebbitt House and then went back to the House until near eleven. Twelve speeches have been made during the day and evening. Walked home with Scofield of Pa. and got to bed after one o'clock in the morning.

TUESDAY, 25. Committee met for a few moments to hear the P. M. General in regard to appropriations for postage in the several departments during the next year. Debate was again resumed in the House on the expulsion of Ames and Brooks. Recess at five. Took dinner at the Ebbitt House with Mr. and Mrs. Burke and talked over our case in the Supreme Court. House met at half-past seven in the evening. Galleries were thronged. Butler made a very able speech against jurisdiction and also made a very adroit defence of Mr. Ames more brilliant than solid.[57] Debate continued until one o'clock. It has been very able and in the main reasonably fair. I am waiting to see whether I am attacked before I determine whether I will speak. The finding of the Committee leaves my case in a very unsatisfactory and unjust form, but I doubt whether this is the time to correct it.

WEDNESDAY, 26. The whole day in the House was consumed in

[55] Michael C. Kerr, member of the House from Indiana, was counsel for the appellees in *Burke v. Smith*.

[56] Stevenson Burke, a member of the Cleveland law firm of Estep and Burke, was one of the appellants in the case mentioned in this entry (see note 33). See also entry for February 27. The appeal was lost.

[57] The text of Butler's speech appears under the date February 26, 1873, in the *Congressional Globe*, 42 Cong., 3 Sess., Part III, Appendix, 176–182.

debates on the Credit Mobilier. Though a spirit of excitement and some panic prevailed, the minds of the members of the House throughout the debate on the whole has been calm and fair, with the exception here and there an ebullition of personal feeling. The evening session during which several speeches were made and an arrangement was entered into to consider the previous question pending at 11 o'clock tomorrow, was very interesting. I have taken no part in the general debate and shall only speak in case I am assailed.

THURSDAY, 27. The R. R. Case No. 131 was set for 11 o'clock this morning, but the vote on the expulsion of Ames and Brooks was set for the same hour and I could not leave the House. Mr. Burke argued the case alone on our side. The question of the jurisdiction of the House over the offences of its members committed before their election was not brought to a fair test. The preamble recited that "Whereas, Serious doubts were entertained of the jurisdiction." Some voted against this because they had no doubts on the jurisdiction, but being opposed to it, others because they had doubts on the question of jurisdiction. Brooks and Ames were censured. The attempt to censure Kelley and Hooper broke down and the Committee was discharged from the whole subject.

FRIDAY, 28. Soon after the meeting of the House went into Committee of the Whole on the Legislative Appropriation Bill and spent nearly the whole day in debating it. I opposed the amendment for an increase of the salaries of members, although I think if a reasonable increase of salaries generally were made and the increase fairly adjusted among the different officers of the Gov't it would be a good measure. An amendment was carried in Committee to make the salaries of members $6,500. I succeeded in fighting off the Morrill amendment, which tends to strangle the independence of the Courts.

March

SATURDAY, 1. Finished the Legislative Appropriation Bill and took up the Deficiency Bill of 40 or 50 pages, continued its discussion during the day and evening and finished it up at one o'clock Sunday morning. This is the last of the bills that have passed the House for the first time. I am very much worn out with work and want of rest. Hinsdale and wife and daughter and Wakefield and Swaim came this afternoon.

SUNDAY, 2.   As Chairman of the Conference Committee on the Legislative Bill I sat with Butler and Randall of the House, and [Lot M.] Morrill, Carpenter and Bayard[58] of the Senate from ten o'clock this morning until nearly 6 in the evening settling the points of differences between the two houses. It was a very hard day's work. Committee agreed to increase members' salaries to $7,500. This will make great trouble and I am in doubt what I ought to do. If I decline to sign the bill I abandon its management to Butler who knows but little of its details and would run the risk of an extra session. If I sign the report I shoulder a part of the responsibility of the increase of salaries.[59]

MONDAY, 3.   House met at 9 o'clock, before 11 the Conference Report on the Sundry Civil Bill was adopted. I declined to go on the Conference though I had charge of the Bill, for I had to go on the conference on the Legislative Bill. At 2 o'clock I brought in my report and at the end of an hour after some debate it passed by eight majority.[60] An evening session was held at 11 o'clock. The

[58] Thomas Francis Bayard (1828–1898) was a Democratic senator from Delaware, 1869–85; secretary of state, 1885–89; ambassador to Great Britain, 1893–97.

[59] The bill which came from the Conference Committee and was enacted into law provided for an increase in the salaries of congressmen from $5,000 to $7,500, retroactive to March 4, 1871, the beginning of the current Congress. Even though Garfield had opposed the increase on a number of occasions, his decision to support the conference report brought him more criticism in his district than any other act of his political career. To soften the criticism, he refused to take the extra pay for the session just ended, covering back into the Treasury the sum of $4,548. In justification for his final action in supporting the bill he argued that as chairman of the Appropriations Commitee it was his responsibility to get passed a measure of such importance (containing as it did a multitude of items not related to salaries), the failure of which would necessitate a special session of Congress. So violent was public reaction to the "Salary Grab" that at the beginning of the next session of Congress, legislators vied with each other in introducing bills to repeal the salary increase; congressional salaries were returned to the former level.

[60] The report of the Conference Commitee was adopted by a vote of 102–96.

Deficiency Bill came over from the Senate. I had it referred to a Conference Committee and with Sargent and [William E.] Niblack met the Senate Conferees at midnight and at half-past one reported it to the House and it passed, thus clearing the decks of the House and finishing our last appropriation bill ten hours before the close of the Session. Reached home at half-past three o'clock very tired.

TUESDAY, 4. House met at half-past nine. Finished up a number of minor matters of legislation. At half-past 11 I made a brief statement by way of personal explanation in regard to the Credit Mobilier Investigation protesting against the special finding of the Committee in my case and giving notice that I should address the public on the subject. At 12 o'clock Congress expired. Went to the Senate and witnessed the dissolution of the old Congress, the Inauguration of the Vice President, the swearing in of the new Senators and then adjourned to the East Portico of the Capitol to see the Chief Justice administer the oath to the President-elect and to see the latter read his inaugural speech. About fifteen thousand people were present. Out of the bitter cold away from the crowd I reached home late in the afternoon. I retired early and slept long and hard.

WEDNESDAY, 5. Slept until a late hour and woke still tired with the strain of the session. Worked up correspondence in the forenoon. Visited Donn Piatt's with Major Swaim. Made a few calls in the afternoon and evening and visited with friends who are stopping here until a late hour at night. The day has been cold and uncomfortable without, but the City is full of people who linger on the debris of the Inauguration Ceremonies.

THURSDAY, 6. Worked up my correspondence in the forenoon. Then went to the Capitol, overhauled my desk and settled a number of minor matters. In the afternoon made good progress in answering my accumulation of letters. After[wards] went with Crete and Mr. and Mrs. Hinsdale and Major Swaim and called for an hour on Mr. [Charles] Sumner. Had a very pleasant visit. He showed us his rarities in the way of books and pictures which he brought from Europe last fall. Mr. Sumner's health is very much shattered and though he is just now improving I fear he will never fully recover. In the evening called on several persons. Finished some work at my desk and got to bed a few minutes after midnight.

FRIDAY, 7. Worked up correspondence. Also wrote a brief on Testimony in relation to the Credit Mobilier. Did some work in the Departments. Went shopping with Crete and at half-past five took the train for Baltimore on the way to Cleveland in company with Swaim. I go to Cleveland to argue the Paint case in the U. S. Circuit Court. It will be hard work to tone myself up to sufficient energy for this work, after the weariness of this long session. We got a sleeping car at Baltimore and were soundly asleep before the train reached Harrisburg.

SATURDAY, 8. Reached Pittsburgh at ten o'clock, an hour behind time. After breakfast at the Hotel parted with Swaim, who took the Pan Handle Route and I went to Leetonia. Wrote several letters and worked on the Paint Case until three o'clock when I took the train for Niles and thence westward for Cleveland. Harmon Austin with Mr. Morgan rode with me to Leavittsburg. A great storm is raging among the people concerning the increase of salaries, especially that which pays the increase to the 42d Congress. Called on Judge Fisher[61] at the Kennard House to consult over our case. Spent the night at Dr. Robison's.

SUNDAY, 9. Went to East Cleveland and called on Dr. Streator, attended church there and took dinner at Streator's after church. Back to Dr. Robison's in the evening. Furious snow storm set in just at night and several inches of snow fell. Called on Mr. Coles [Cowles] in the evening.

MONDAY, 10. After breakfast at Dr. Robison's, went to the Kennard House and took a room and worked during the day and until midnight on the Paint Case, preparatory to its argument tomorrow. The case is full of difficulties and the testimony is very voluminous and conflicting. The chemical experts who have given testimony in this case are at loggerheads with each other, and it is difficult to see how science can be tortured at the hands of its defenders in such a manner. On looking over the whole field I am satisfied that the rival parties ought to settle and unite their forces, rather than be fighting.

TUESDAY, 11. Continued work on the case until 11 o'clock when Judge Fisher and I went to the Court Room and Judge Emmons[62]

[61] Samuel Sparks Fisher (1832–1874), of Cincinnati, a prominent patent lawyer, a counsel in the paint case for the Cleveland Chemical Paint Company. He was U. S. commissioner of patents, 1869–71.

[62] Halmer H. Emmons, judge of the Sixth U. S. Circuit Court, 1870–77.

not having arrived we consulted with Mr. [George F.] Harding of Philadelphia and the other counsel for the complainants and found that there were hopes of a settlement between our clients. Fisher and I on the assembling of the Court at 2 o'clock filed a supplementary answer and the other side asked for a continuance of the case until the next term. We met later in the afternoon to arrange terms of settlement but did not succeed. Burke arrived from Washington. The Doctor and I called at Mr. Benedict's[63] and stated to

WEDNESDAY, 12. Spent the day with Fisher and the other counsel him the circumstances of my vote on the Salary Bill.

in discussing terms of settlement and found that there was too much feeling between the parties to adjust the matter at once. Mr. Harding seems to have a contingent interest in his clients' case and this seems to disincline him to a settlement. Personally I would prefer to try the case, but I am satisfied that it is best for both parties to settle. Called at the *Leader* office in the evening. Spent the evening and night at Dr. Robison's with Burke. My vote on the Salary Bill will probably do me much damage in the district, but the *Herald* and *Leader* are publishing strong articles in my defence.

THURSDAY, 13. Completed arrangements with counsel on the other side to hold back our answer for ten days. Still in hopes of a settlement. Called at Dr. Boynton's on the West Side. Purchased Riddle's *Bart Ridgeley*, a story of Northern Ohio. Took a lunch with Dr. Robison at his packing-house and at 1.55 took the Pittsburgh train for Washington. At Ravenna Halsey Hall came on board and accompanied me as far as Alliance. He is a true earnest friend. Read Riddle's book with great interest until I reached Wheeling, where, finding no sleeping car for the East, I spent the night at the Saint James House.

FRIDAY, 14. Took the Eastern train at six o'clock and spent a long weary day on the road except the time occupied in finishing *Bart Ridgeley*. The book is a minutely local sketch of life in the woods of Ohio and is exceedingly well done, though I think the hero of the story is very frankly egotistical. I however like the book very

[63] George A. Benedict, Cleveland lawyer, city official, postmaster and journalist, became one of the editors and proprietors of the *Cleveland Herald and Gazette* in the early 1850's and served as editor for over a decade prior to his death in 1876.

much and none the less because it is evidently biographical in its character. Took dinner at Cumberland and at 11 o'clock reached Washington with a bad cold and retired. Found the children getting better of their whooping-cough.

SATURDAY, 15. At home today reading my mail and answering letters. I am suffering from a very severe cold and from the overwork of the last two weeks. A large amount of neglected business is lying on my hands for adjustment. I have made some progress on it. I find that the storm over the increase of salaries is blowing more fiercely than ever. The increase itself would not have excited so much indignation had it not been made retroactive in its application to members of Congress.

SUNDAY, 16. My cold has led to a worse cough than I have had for many years. I am really suffering from this unusual malady. It is a cold gusty day and I staid at home. Crete finished *Bart Ridgeley* and enjoyed it very much. I re-read with her some of the later portions. Also read up some copies of the *Nation* that have lain neglected during the closing weeks of the session. Mr. Hubbard called a little while in the afternoon and talked over the project for spending the Summer at Nantucket. Played with the children in the evening and made some efforts to get acquainted with them after my Winter's neglect of them.

MONDAY, 17. Worked on correspondence until half-past ten o'clock, then called at the President's, the Att'y General's and the P. O. Dep't, then went to the Capitol. I found that the President had appointed Mrs. Carey[64] Postmaster at Ashtabula Village on the recommendation of Senator Stewart, her brother. I am a good deal troubled about this matter, not knowing how it may be received by the people. The Ravenna Post Office question is also up again. Home in the evening half sick with a cold and cough.

TUESDAY, 18. Worked on correspondence until half-past eleven

---

[64] There were objections in Ashtabula to the appointment of Mrs. L. A. Carey, sister of Senator William Morris Stewart of Nevada. To protect Garfield from unjust criticism, President Grant wrote him a letter telling him that he had made the appointment during Garfield's absence from Washington. Although the Senate confirmed the nomination promptly, Mrs. Carey resigned in April; the President then appointed Joseph F. Sexton as her successor.

o'clock; then went to the President's in reference to the Ravenna P. O. While there saw the members of the Cabinet sworn in by Judge Cartter. Then went to Dr. Shedd's and took a Russian bath. Attended the children's dancing school with Crete, Harry, and Jimmy at Marini's Hall. In the evening made several calls and nearly sick. The baby is very sick with the whooping cough and we are made exceedingly anxious for his safety.

WEDNESDAY, 19. Awoke with a very severe cold. Threatened with pneumonia. Staid in doors nearly all day reading and writing a little. I am now experiencing for the first time, in a marked way, the injustice with which an excited people will treat a Representative. Since the adjournment of Congress they have come to find how indignant they are at the increase of salaries of Senators and Members, and instead of noting the fact that I opposed it at every stage until the final passage of the appropriation bill containing it, which I felt it to be my duty to support in order to save an extra session, they blame me for that vote as though I had been for the increase all the time. At home in the evening, retired early.

THURSDAY, 20. Worked on correspondence and also went over the history of the legislation in regard to the increase of salaries to answer the questions and criticisms of some constituents on the subject. A great storm is being made over that increase in Ohio and the fact that I voted finally on the Appropriation Bill that contained it, although I voted every time against the increase itself, is being used savagely against me throughout the country. I went to the Capitol during the day and requested the confirmation of Mr. [Winfield S.] Krake as Postmaster at Ravenna. It rained heavily almost all the afternoon and evening.

FRIDAY, 21. At home nearly all day bringing up correspondence and completing history of the salary amendment to the Legislative Appropriation Bill. The displeasure of the public is frequently as unjust as its applause. I have many times been praised far beyond my deserts and for what I did not deserve. Now I am being blamed for what is not blameworthy and for what I have not done. Perhaps it is a necessary part of human experience to try both sides. But for the Credit Mobilier matter I would not continue in public service another day. But I am not willing to appear to be driven from it by mere clamor.

SATURDAY, 22. Worked up correspondence until ten in the morning, then spent several hours with Judge Black listening to a case in which he wishes my help and also in talking over the Credit Mobilier. Finished a full statement of the history of the salary increase in the two Houses of Congress and forwarded it to Harmon Austin, accompanied by a long letter. Commenced to read Thackeray's *Henry Esmond*, a story of Queen Anne's time, involving much that is of historic interest to the Colonial Period of this country.

SUNDAY, 23. Attended Church and afterwards made some calls. Several persons called here during my absence. The first brightness that Spring has brought appears on the earth and in the air today. Senator Hart called in the evening and spent two hours. Mr. Smalley also came in. He sails for Europe in two weeks to write up the Vienna Exposition for the *New York Tribune*. I greatly wish I could go. The breadth of the sea would give comfortable distance between politics and me. But I suppose I cannot go.

MONDAY, 24. Spent most of the day in making out a table showing the analysis of the six votes by Ayes and Noes in the House, on the salary question. I have a real attack of rheumatism in my shoulders which is very painful and nearly disables me. This is one of the signs of getting old and a painful one it is. After all it appears that the astrologers were not all wrong in supposing that some influence on humanity was exercised by extraordinary conjunctions of the planets. It appears that more planets are now and are to be in sight of the earth than ever before for many centuries, and their effect upon the light and heat of our planet are being curiously studied. That may account for our wretched Winter and possibly for the mental upheavals among men.

TUESDAY, 25. Called at several of the Departments on business. Saw Secretary Robeson in reference to Commander Weaver's[65] assignment at the Navy Yard. Also called at the Treasury Department. A

[65] Aaron W. Weaver (d. 1919) was appointed to the U. S. Naval Academy from Ohio, graduating in 1854. He retired as rear admiral in 1893. Garfield's friend Frank Mason of the *Cleveland Leader*, a nephew of Weaver, wrote to Garfield in behalf of his uncle. As a result of Garfield's help, the secretary of the navy gave Commander Weaver permission to continue at the Navy Yard until July 1, and later transferred him to the Nitre Depot at Malden, Massachusetts.

day of hard work on my correspondence. In the evening dined at Speaker Blaine's with Senators Allison and Pool.[66] A pleasant party. Reached home before eleven, finished first volume of Thackeray's *Esmond*. It is a powerful sketch of life a century and a half ago.

WEDNESDAY, 26. Am feeling very wretchedly today with rheumatism in the shoulder. Got off a large number of letters. In the afternoon went with Mr. Noble to start the case of the 6th Presbyterian Church against the Baltimore and Potomac Road.[67] I drew [do] it as a friendly act and not for fee. I drew up the warrant for a Justice to sign, ordering the Marshal to summon the jury to meet on the tenth of April and value the damages done to the church by the laying of the tracks. Went to Dr. Shedd's and took an Electric Bath for my rheumatism and experienced much relief.

THURSDAY, 27. This morning the telegraphic Dispatches bring word that the Trumbull County Convention, which met at Warren yesterday to nominate a delegate to the Ohio Constitutional Convention, passed a vote of censure upon me for my vote on the Appropriation Bill containing the retroactive salary clause and requesting me to resign. I would be glad to be relieved of the odious burdens of public life, but the Convention has acted under the influence of passion and wholly misunderstands my conduct in the case. I spent most of the day in preparing lists of the voters on the salary clause showing the part that each took. Gilfillan and Thorp called in the evening.

[66] John Pool (1826–1884), a senator from North Carolina, 1868–73, and an attorney in Washington, 1873 to his death.

[67] The building of a station on Sixth Street by the Baltimore and Potomac Railroad Company and the laying of tracks along the street from Virginia Avenue to the station had adversely affected the Sixth Street Presbyterian Church, of which Mason Noble, the father of Garfield's Williams classmate, Frank, was pastor. Having failed to get a settlement from the railroad, the church took the matter to court. A jury awarded the church $11,500 in damages. When this award was confirmed by the Supreme Court of the District of Columbia, the railroad appealed to the U. S. Supreme Court, which affirmed the judgment on December 6, 1875. See *Baltimore and Potomac Railroad Co. v. The Trustees of the Sixth Presbyterian Church* (91 U. S. 127).

FRIDAY, 28. Spent a considerable share of the day at the Capitol. Finished up some odds and ends of business. In the evening had an unusually large mail and answered a number of letters. The *Cleveland Leader* comes to hand with an article joining in the general hue and cry against me on the salary bill. It is difficult to see where this storm of passion will end. The *Cincinnati Times and Chronicle* of the 25th has a more false and unjust article against me on the subject than any other I have yet seen.

SATURDAY, 29. In the morning called on the President and delivered the memorial in regard to the Ravenna Post Office. Had a conversation with the President in regard to the Salary Bill. He said if the bill had not passed he would have been compelled four years hence to draw at least $25,000 out of his private property to enable him to leave town. Went to the Capitol, then came home and prepared an answer to the further criticisms on the salary question. Letters from the District received this evening seem to indicate that I ought to be there and I have telegraphed to Mr. Austin that I will come if he thinks necessary.

SUNDAY, 30. Worked all day in preparing for the press a documentary history of the Salary Clause. I also wrote a reply to a late article in the *Cincinnati Times and Chronicle*. I do not yet receive the resolutions of the Warren Convention. They can hardly be so unmanly as not to send them to me. After eight in the evening received a dispatch from Mr. Austin telling me to delay starting from [for] Ohio until I hear further. I am glad of this. About eight o'clock was taken with a severe pain in the femur bone, either neuralgic or sciatic, I cannot tell which. I suffered severely for several hours.

MONDAY, 31. Nearly finished the preparation for printing of the pamphlet on the Salary Question. Part of it has been set up in type and I have read the proofs. In the morning called at the Secretary of State's office and found that he had gone to New York. Called on Bancroft Davis, the Ass't Secretary, in regard to the appointment of Honorary Commissioners to the Vienna Exposition. The Cincinnati papers continue their assaults with unabated fury. It is evident that they have more interest in breaking me down in the future politics of Ohio than in denouncing the salary bill. I doubt if the *Cincinnati Times and Chronicle* will publish my last letter.

April

TUESDAY, 1. Worked off about twenty letters and went to the Post Office Department and adjusted ten or a dozen questions of Post Offices and Post Roads. This evening brought me a large number of letters from friends in the district showing the character of the great excitement there over the salary question. It appears to be a kind of epidemic which has seized the people and no one can foretell its result. Spent the evening at Mr. Semken's[68] with Professor Marix[69] and Mr. Latta. This is the first evening for many weeks that I have not spent in hard work.

WEDNESDAY, 2. The letters still come pouring in on the salary question. The Ashtabula Convention has carried through a vote of censure. Hinsdale writes me a long letter saying I must come home and fight the battle there. Harmon Austin thinks I had better not come yet. Halsey Hall says come and so it goes. Colonel Piatt sent for me to look over an attack on Credit Mobilier which he thinks Job Stevenson has made on me in the *Cincinnati Commercial*, and to which Piatt is writing a response.[70] There does not seem to

[68] Probably F. A. Simkins, an Ohio man who, as a result of Garfield's help, was a clerk in the office of the comptroller of the currency. He was very grateful to Garfield and sometimes rendered him clerical assistance.

[69] Henry Marix, a clerk in the State Department.

[70] A long article, "The Inside Works of the Credit Mobilier Swindle and Some Other Scandals," appeared in the *Commercial* on March 31. The portion relating to Garfield was uncomplimentary. Having referred to the fact that some of the independent papers had treated Garfield "with distinguished consideration" with reference to the scandal, it added: "Even Donn Piatt, the most bilious of all those who accumulate bile at the hideous wrongs that were perpetrated by wicked congressmen, found his liver in excellent working order when he looked on Garfield and beheld him that he was good, and many people marveled thereat." It attributed Piatt's support to his involvement with a firm which supplied to the government a process for preserving army clothing, and which was thus dependent on Garfield's Appropriations Committee. Piatt's long reply, which included a vigorous defense of Garfield, appeared on April 5. Job Stevenson, in a letter to Garfield, April 7, 1873, denied that he had had anything to do with the article, and said that he thought that it did Garfield injustice.

be in me as much fight as formerly and of all things that I loathe and detest it is a contest in relation to myself. I can fight battles for others, but to fight men for disliking me for disapproving of my course hurts my pride and my self-love more than anything I have been called upon to meet.

THURSDAY, 3. Concluded to make up a pamphlet on the Salary Bill without any special personal defense, reserving that for a letter in answer to the Warren Resolutions, if they ever come. I went to the *Globe* office and arranged for cutting down the pamphlet to 12 pages. It appears that on Saturday last the Ashtabula Convention also passed a vote of censure, although Mr. Howells says it was done in disregard of the demands for the Ayes and Noes and was really not the action of the Convention. This will doubtless bring the same result from Lake County where I am less known. Every word in defense seems only to fan the fiery flame.

FRIDAY, 4. At work with correspondence. Today Harry has had the most singular illness I have ever known. He awoke feeling dizzy and remained in bed until near nine o'clock, when his knowledge of past events utterly disappeared. He had simply the possession of his outer senses, but nothing more. He knew none of the family. His legs were entirely paralized. Two doctors consulted over him nearly two hours. Tried a blister to his back. He continued sick but without fever until two o'clock when his mind wholly returned, but his legs did not regain their usefulness and he went to sleep at seven o'clock in the evening.

SATURDAY, 5. At six o'clock this morning Harry awoke to all appearances perfectly well, with no symptoms whatever of his trouble yesterday. The doctor supposed that he had received some blow on the head or spine, but we now see no evidence that his illness arose from that cause. It possibly may have been from a derangement of the stomach. Received from the printer the record which I had prepared of the Congressional proceedings on the Salary Bill. I am now preparing a letter to my Constituents on the subject of their censure of my vote. Whether I shall survive the storms and breakers of this Winter remains to be seen. The spirit of detraction has become epidemic, but I hope the reaction will set in soon.

SUNDAY, 6. Attended church and afterwards made further progress on the letter to my constituents. It is difficult to make it sufficiently short for a newspaper article. I am still debating whether I will let them know that I have refused the back pay. My pride says no, and the implication that I have drawn it argues the other way. In the evening called on Colonel Piatt, and had a long visit. He is a strange man, develops a strong and firm friendship mingled with a recklessness about his friends that is sometimes amazing. He has written a letter to the *Cincinnati Commercial* in answer to the late attack on him and me in reference to the Credit Mobilier.

MONDAY, 7. Spent the most of the day in finishing a letter to my Constituents on the salary question. It seems as though I should never be able to end this subject. I am making some little improvements in the grounds about my house. Putting up cedar posts for clotheslines, also planting and training vines about the doors and walls. In the evening went with General Mussey to the house of the Rev. Mr. Noble to get the materials together for trying the case of the Sixth Presbyterian Church and the Baltimore and Potomac R. R. for damages. Have concluded to stay here until Thursday and try the case for the jury and then I think I shall go to Ohio.

TUESDAY, 8. Attended to my correspondence in the morning. Spent the balance of the day on my letter on the salary question. It is wonderful what an excitement this matter has created. The children are improving rapidly. Endeavored to find my note given to Wm. Shields for lot added to my grounds corner 13th and I St. but did not succeed. Was informed by Downman and Weaver of 7th St. that they had transferred it to one Bradley, but on calling at his place of business I found he had never owned it.

WEDNESDAY, 9. Occupied a considerable portion of the day on my letter to my constituents. Dictated a few letters, in relation to my votes on the Salary Clause, to intimate friends. Have concluded to visit Judge Black at York, Pa., in order that I may confer with him in regard to the present condition of affairs and receive the benefit of his valuable advice. I have felt more anxiety to leave public life and give my whole attention to my family, for the last few weeks, than ever before.

THURSDAY, 10. After attending correspondence, went to the 6th St. Presbyterian Church at 10 o'clock to try the case of damages done to it by the Baltimore and Potomac R. R. This trial lasted until half-past five o'clock. Messrs. [Daniel] Clarke and [Samuel T.]

Phillips spoke for the Railroad Co. General Mussey was with me; he opened and I closed the argument. I feel very well satisfied with our presentation of the case. We think the Church will get a $10,000 verdict. This case held on so late that I could not get away on the train this evening as I expected and so I staid over. In the evening called on the Sergeant-at-Arms and did some other business.

FRIDAY, 11. Left Washington at 8.40 A.M. and reached Baltimore only to find that no train left on the Northern Central until 1.15 P.M. Went to Barnum's and wrote letters, and then went to Guy's and got a terrapin stew.[71] At 3.40 P.M. reached York, where Mrs. Black and her daughter were waiting to take me to Brockie. Spent a delightful evening and night with the Judge in his new house. He is a glorious man; full of ideas and of power. We discussed a new phase of Negro nature. He says they do not preserve their traditions, religion, or language, but always conform to what they find. They make bad mortar for a national structure.

SATURDAY, 12. Spent the whole day with Judge Black and Chauncey and his son. The range of conversation was wide and varied. Towards evening I read the Judge my memoranda on Credit Mobilier. He says he will come into the discussion by and by and back me up. Out of the dreary stormy night, into a very dark and troubled future, I took the train for Pittsburgh, and in half an hour was asleep with troubled dreams of broken idols and thunder clouds.

SUNDAY, 13. Reached Pittsburgh at 9 A.M. After breakfast wrote letters and read until one P.M. when I took the train for Leetonia, where I arrived at 4.20 P.M. Dinner at Hotel then livery to Warren 28 miles, fearfully muddy, and reached Harmon Austin's 11.30 P.M., cold, tired, and with more external discomforts than I ever before felt since I have been in political life. But I will try the elements, and whatever betide will try to make the result a matter of education to my own spirit.

MONDAY, 14. Spent the day at Warren, visiting with several friends, among them Kinsman, Perkins,[72] Morgan, Hutchins and T. E[J]. McLain. Went over the points of my letter with them and discussed

[71] Guy's Monument House, a Baltimore hotel.

[72] Henry B. Perkins (b. 1824), a leading Republican of Warren, was president of the First National Bank. He was a member of the Ohio Senate, 1880–83. His residence was reputed to be the finest in Warren.

the situation on the salary question. E. B. Taylor has broken out in open abuse of me, on account of the Ravenna P. O. In his case I am contrained to say (to my Journal only) Oh gratitude! "Where are the charms that sages have seen in thy face." Went to Hiram in the evening and spent the night at Burke's.

TUESDAY, 15. Came down to Father Rudolph's and lighted the fire in the old room where my books and papers are, and began to work. Life here, at my old desk, is as though I had turned a leaf down, on the 5th Nov. and had not opened the book since. "But another book was opened," in another place and the whole world have been reading, wildly, angrily, and falsely. It is cold dismal weather, and the task before me is more dismal still. But for the sake of the truth, and of those who love me, I am bound to do to and demand for myself—Justice.

WEDNESDAY, 16. Worked on my letter to the District rewriting a large part of it, and adding at Burke's suggestion more personal matter, referring to my past work. I find this town, in which and for which I have done so many years of hard and poorly requited work, is in a state of angry ferment, with worlds of mean slings about me for the salary vote. Perhaps Sidney Smith was right when he said, "Gratitude is a lively appreciation of benefits expected." But here is discipline for my soul—perhaps for the people of Hiram.

THURSDAY, 17. Finished revision of letter and made two copies, one for Ritezel[73] of the *Warren Chronicle*, the other for Halsey Hall of Ravenna. At three P.M. went to Freedom, and took the train to Ravenna. Was most cordially received by Halsey and his father and by other friends. Put the letter into the printer's hands. Visited several friends in the evening, and looked over the field of trouble. Spent the night at Hall's retiring two hours after midnight.

FRIDAY, 18. Letter got into print and proof read by noon, when I took train to Cleveland, having written letters to each of the leading papers of the District, enclosing proof slips of letter. Went to *Herald* office and arranged for printing a supplement for several papers

[73] William Ritezel (1828–1902), a Warren newspaperman from 1854 until his death, was editor of the *Western Reserve Chronicle*, a weekly, and of the *Warren Daily Chronicle*. He was described as one of the "able counselors and active leaders" of the Republican party in Trumbull County. He was a member of the Ohio House of Representatives, 1868–71.

in the District, giving [a] copy of my pamphlet from the *Globe*. Saw Reed[74] of Ashtabula, and found him ready to hear the facts on the salary question. He takes the supplements. Spent the night at Dr. Robison's. Distressed at hearing no news from Crete. I have written her six times. *Beatissima feminarum* [Most blessed of women].

SATURDAY, 19. Spent the day in arranging for the supplement for Warren, Jefferson, and Painesville papers, and in finding out the state of the Paint Case, which I think we shall succeed in settling without further litigation. This is the birthday of the best woman I have ever known. I wrote her a long letter, and thanked her for being born and for being my wife. Went to Hiram in the evening. Walked up from Jeddo and found a letter from Crete. All well at home. I have set the battle in array in the District, and we shall see how it will go.

SUNDAY, 20. Wrote letters; read Hare's *Rome*,[75] and at eleven attended church and heard a good sermon by Burke, suggested by a sentence which I read to him from Crete's letter. After meeting I went to Burke's, with Alvah Udall, to dinner. Visited till half-past four then came down to the desk. Church in the evening, and books and letters till a late hour.

MONDAY, 21. This is the date of my letter to the District.[76] I wonder what my boys will think of it twenty years hence. I wonder what I will, if I am alive. Perhaps all this trouble may look very small and be laughed over. Perhaps not. For it may mark the decline and fall of my political power. Let either fate befall I shall hope to make culture and sweetness out of it. I now take up my other woe, the Credit Mobilier. When and where to publish it is the question with me. I must wait until the salary storm is somewhat abated. Called on my old classmate, Symonds Ryder, who is dying of consumption. He can last but a short time.

TUESDAY, 22. The ground was covered with snow this morning, and

---

[74] James Reed (1812–1889), editor and proprietor of the *Ashtabula Telegraph*, 1856–89. It was said of him that he "was ever a staunch and reliable Republican."

[75] Augustus J. C. Hare, *Walks in Rome* (1871).

[76] "To the Republican Voters of the Nineteenth District," Hiram, April 21, 1873.

the raw dreary day has dragged itself along, with nothing to relieve it but the work I have on hand, and the mail which brought me a letter from Crete. At eleven I went to the College and attended a recitation on the Constitution of the U. S. Teaching is a noble work which pays as it goes—pays in young fresh gratitude, not of the Sidney Smith kind. I think the reaction has set in on the salary question, but how fast and how far it will go, remains to be seen. Received my first letter from each of my two boys, Harry and Jimmy.

WEDNESDAY, 23. Worked on correspondence and official business which has steadily increased on me each year since the peace. Played croquet with the Reverend Clayton Smith and family, part of the forenoon. Received a large mail, which brings new evidences of a better state of feeling. I can see a change coming over the spirit of this town, and I think the more thoughtful and intelligent part of the people will settle down to a right view of the case by and by. A good letter appears in the *Geauga Republican*. It is evidently written by Hon. A. G. Riddle, for it bears the marks of *Bart Ridgeley's* style.

THURSDAY, 24. Wrote a large number of letters and nearly caught up with my correspondence. The mail brought me several district papers containing my letter. The editors thus far treat it kind, some enthusiastically. At four P.M. attended a lecture of Burke's on figurative language, as used in the Bible. Took tea at his house and spent the evening there, till 8 P.M. Joe [Rudolph] came home this evening. Worked up letters and wrote for my journal. Read in Hare's *Rome* until half an hour before midnight. I long to revisit the "City of the Soul." "When, Goodwin, when?"

FRIDAY, 25. As near as I can sum up the situation in the District on the salary question there are the following classes:

1. My enemies, who are so for any and all reasons. They make all they can out of it, *per fas et nefas* [through right and wrong].

2. The narrow mean men to whom a dollar is the chief unit of life, and who think that no bill is important enough to be saved, if increase of salaries were on it. Most of these would be permanently alienated.

3. The nervous excitable friends who think an attack ruins a public man, and think any thing is a mistake which makes a clamor. These will in the main come back when the storm subsides.

4. Those who thought the vote was wrong, but hoped I could show reasonable cause for casting it. These have come back.

5. Those who believed in me in spite of appearances, and said all the time, he'll come out right. They are fightingly right and never went away.

I did good work today on the Credit Mobilier article.

SATURDAY, 26. Worked into good shape the Chapter which I wrote in the rough last night on Credit Mobilier. Answered many letters. The mail brought me no letters from Crete. This makes me home-sick. At half-past three went to Hinsdale's, and played croquet till the rain came on. Took tea at his house and stayed there until 8 P.M. The rest of the evening wrote and read Hare's *Rome*. It is a dreary evening—cold and rainy without and the shadows of the external world project themselves inward. How will all this turmoil appear to me ten years hence? *Ad quem finum? J'ai beaucoup d'ennui parce que la plus bonne femme de tout le monde n'est pas avec moi a cette heure* [To what end? I am very bored because the best woman in the whole world is not with me now].

SUNDAY, 27. Heard a good sermon from Burke in the forenoon. He and Mary came here to dinner, and in the afternoon I went with Burke into the woods and caught a breath of the spring which begins to live again after the long winter. Read and wrote until evening, when I listened to another good sermon from Burke. After church read *Walks in Rome* till a late hour, and reveled in the palace of the Caesars and the temples of the forum. Rome grows upon me at every new contemplation of her history. I greatly desire to see her again.

MONDAY, 28. Wrote letters and studied until 2½ P.M. when I went to Burke's and he and I, Thayer and Mrs. Robbins played croquet, when we took tea with Frank Smith and Sarah Lyman (née Rudolph).[77] After tea I sat with Burke till after nine P.M. hearing a case of difficulty between two college boys, and aiding in its settle-ment. It recalls my old work here and brings back my old love for school work. A letter from Crete today discusses the difficulty of handling our stormy boys. It is a greater problem than Credit Mobilier. I am homesick to be with them all.

[77] Both Frances Smith and Sarah Rudolph Lyman were former students at Hiram.

TUESDAY, 29. Spent most of the day in doing two things; answering letters and writing a review of that part of Ames's Testimony which pretends to detail our conversation and give his interpretation to some figures I made in his room. Also wrote a short article for the *Christian Standard*[78] on the Disciple dogma of "Thus saith the Lord," in express precept or approved precedent. In the evening went to the College with Hinsdale, and made a short address to the Sophomore Class on the occasion of their organization as a class society. Teaching young people came back to me as an old pleasure which I greatly relish. *Walks in Rome* the remainder of the evening. This book makes me long to see Rome again.

WEDNESDAY, 30. Took the morning train to Solon and walk[ed] along and upon the worst Solon roads I have seen for many years. Found Hetty [Hitty] there and had a good family visit. How true and sweet and anxiously regardful for me, these dear sisters are. Each blow that falls upon me they feel, as though it fell upon them. Hunted for an hour in the beech and maple woods. Visited Stephen for an hour. Held the plow a little. Took the six P.M. train for Hiram. Walked up from Jeddo, reaching Father Rudolph's at nine. Retired early and read *Rome* till sleep wooed and won me.

May

THURSDAY, 1. Wrote letters and put my affairs in readiness for leaving for Washington tomorrow morning. Made some preparations to address the class of 1873 this P.M. At 2 P.M. attended the exercises of Class Day in the College, which consisted of Music, Class Biography, a Poem and an Oration and the planting of the class tree in the campus. After which I made an address of half an hour in the chapel on the monumental significance of the tree to the life of the

[78] Garfield was a member of a group which in 1866 chartered the Christian Publishing Association for the purpose of publishing a religious weekly. *The Christian Standard* first appeared in Cleveland in April with Isaac Errett as editor. At first the paper was not a financial success and in 1868 the stockholders turned over the property to its editor, who in 1869 moved it to Cincinnati under new arrangements. Within ten years it was the leading Disciple journal.

class. Ford came and visited me. The salary storm is abating. In the evening attended class supper and responded briefly to a toast. Ford spent the night with me at Rudolph's.

FRIDAY, 2. Went to Cleveland on the morning train. Transacted some business in the City. Took dinner with Mrs. Robison and Hezzie, the Doctor being away. Took the two o'clock train for Wheeling. Read *Walks in Rome* by the way. The day began in sunshine but ended in a dreary rain. Reached Wheeling at 10 P.M. and found it best to wait till morning. After I had retired the Editor of the *Intelligencer*, hearing that I was at the McLure, called on me, and I gave him a welcome from my bed. He was formerly a Washington correspondent. After he left I read Watterson's address on Journalism,[79] which profession is now in its Goth-Vandal period, as I think.

SATURDAY, 3. Was awaked an hour too soon, and without having had sufficient sleep, took the train at 5.50 for the East. Lunch at Benwood. Twenty miles before we reached Grafton we came upon an engine wrecked for [by] a falling rock from the hill side, and lay in the rain nearly seven hours before we could get on. Read Adams' eulogy on Seward and was greatly delighted with it.[80] Crossed Taggart's [Tygart] River in a dugout and got dinner at a log cabin. Returned and finished first volume of *Walks in Rome*. I am thinking of making an address at Hudson College on the new aspects of Politics, the fight with corporations. Reached Grafton at five where I waited in the dreary hotel, wrote and slept until eleven o'clock, when I took the Eastern Express.

SUNDAY, 4. Passed a very uncomfortable night, not sleeping much. It rained all night. Took breakfast at Martinsburgh, and spent the time till noon reading *Walks in Rome*. Finished the first volume. At half-past twelve took the train at Washington Junction and a few minutes after two reached home. Found all the dear ones well. Lizzie and the children had gone to the cars to meet me; but missed me by a few minutes. Harry has his first long pants, the kind of

[79] An address entitled "The American Newspaper" which Henry Watterson (1840–1921), noted journalist, had just delivered at a meeting of the Indiana Press Association in Indianapolis.

[80] *The Address of Charles Francis Adams of Massachusetts, on the Life, Character and Services of William H. Seward, Delivered by Invitation of the Legislature of the State of New York, in Albany, April 18, 1873* (1873).

garb he is henceforth to wear through life. All such changes are peculiarly sad to me. It is delightful to get home once more. The spring is starting in, in earnest, here. Several friends called during the day and evening, Mr. Riddle among them.

MONDAY, 5. Finished reading my accumulated paper mail. Answered a large number of letters. Made some calls. Cleaned the decks as nearly as I could for resuming work on my Credit Mobilier paper. Evidences are not wanting of the tendency towards a disorganization of the political parties of the day. If I can get the time I think I will deliver an address at the Hudson College Commencement on the next conflict in American Politics, namely: the fight against corporations. It is a difficult and somewhat perilous theme to handle, but it is one that must come before long.

TUESDAY, 6. Answered letters and worked as usual. News came by the afternoon paper that Mr. Ames had been stricken with paralysis and is probably dying. This embarrasses me in view of the fact that my criticisms of his testimony may be taken unkindly in case of his death. All proper charity should be shown to the dead, but the grave even ought not to shield positive wrong to the living. I shall prune the article of all bitterness and keep it within the limits of judicial statements so far as I can.

WEDNESDAY, 7. Called at the Interior and Post Office Departments. Learned that Chief Justice Chase had been stricken with paralysis at ten o'clock this morning, in N.Y. The effects of the last ten years of excitement has done much to break down the health and lives of public men. There was much in the character of Mr. Chase that I have always admired. He has been my friend for many years and I have never abandoned him during his hours of adversity and unpopularity. Ames is still living. The *Nation* has a good article on my letter to the District. Messrs. Mussey and Spencer called in the evening. Had a long talk with Henry [Spencer] on his social and domestic difficulties. The Woman's Rights Doctrines have broken up the peace of his family.

THURSDAY, 8. Worked on correspondence and Credit Mobilier paper. General burst of appreciative eulogy appears in the papers on the life and character of Mr. Chase. It is hard that a man should be treated with so much wicked abuse as Chase has suffered during many years of his life, and have all credit at last with the confession that they were lying about him when they have spoken evil of him. Perhaps they will now overdo the praise as they have before overdone the blame. I shall always remember with pleasure the six weeks spent as his guest, in the Fall and Winter of 1863 during the Fitz John Porter Court Martial.[81] I there saw the embryo of the National Banking System as it was developing itself in his mind.

FRIDAY, 9. Nearly completed the main argument on the Credit Mobilier review, but have not yet summed up the points. Arranged for sending it to the printer, who hopes to have it in type tomorrow. Just now news comes that Ames is dead. I shall write a few words of preface referring to the fact. Donn Piatt and I took the 9 o'clock P.M. train for N. Y. to attend the funeral of Mr. Chase. Found on board the principle officers of the Government here, except the President, and had some interesting conversation on public question[s]. In conversation with Mr. Mullett he tells me that Mr. Dymond,[82] late Private Secretary of Secretary Seward, remembers distinctly to have copied Seward's first draft of the dispatch to the British Government on the *Trent* Affair, which was bel[l]igerent in its tone and refused to give up Mason and Slidell, that it was sent to Mr. Lincoln and returned interlined in his handwriting, the tone materially changed and the hostile tone taken out and that Seward was greatly vexed by Lincoln's act. This seems to be in conflict with Mr. Adams' statement of the case in his late oration.

SATURDAY, 10. Reached the Brevoort House at 7. After breakfast made some calls. Attended the funeral of Mr. Chase at Dr. Tyng's[83] church. The concourse was very great. The class of men who attended the funeral illustrate the tastes and characteristics of the Chief Justice. After the Episcopal Burial Service was performed, Dr. John Hall, who was our shipmate on crossing the ocean in July 1867, delivered the funeral address. It was very appropriate and at times eloquent. Perhaps this is the first time in history that the funeral service of the Chief Justice of any nation was preached by a foreigner who had never seen the country of the deceased until 6 years before.

[81] See note 170 for 1872.

[82] Probably Theodore W. Diamond, who was for many years a clerk in the State Department.

[83] Stephen Higginson Tyng (1800–1885), rector of St. George's Episcopal Church, was one of the most celebrated clergymen of his day.

After his funeral spent two hours with Whitelaw Reid[84] at his room. We have drifted apart a good way still without losing our friendship. Called on Mr. and Mrs. Fish in [on] 17th St. Had a pleasant visit; the Secr'y showed me photograph copies of Seward's first draft of the letter of instructions to Mr. Adams before he went to Saint James, with Lincoln's erasures and additions made on the 21st of May 1861. It shows that Lincoln was a master on that subject and gives me a new view of his acquaintance with affairs at that time. Dined at General McDowell's with his family and Whitelaw Reid. Came to Washington with the funeral party and the body of the Chief Justice on the 9 o'clock train. Had a long talk with Secretary Fish concerning the early genius of Palmer[85] the sculptor. Fish seems to have been his Maecenas. Got General Mc-Dowell and Piatt together and did something to reconcile them. Had further talk with Reid on the salary question. Also renewed my acquaintance with Hiram Barney.[86] I met him first at Mr. Chase's table.

SUNDAY, 11. Reached Washington at 6.30 in a heavy rain. We followed the body of the Chief Justice to the Supreme Court room, and then I came home. Spent the day mostly indoors. Finished the second volume of Hare's works on Rome, a most delightful and valuable book. Notwithstanding it has rained nearly all day, the

[84] Whitelaw Reid (1837–1912), editor of the *New York Tribune*, 1873–1905, Republican candidate for vice president, 1892, ambassador to Great Britain, 1905–12, was a longtime friend of Garfield. Born in Xenia, Ohio, he was a journalist during the Civil War. In 1868 he published in two volumes *Ohio in the War*. During the campaign of 1880 he was a strong editorial supporter of Garfield and his intimate correspondent, particularly on New York affairs. Had he wished the appointment, Garfield would have made him minister to Germany. There are numerous letters from Reid in the Garfield Papers, especially for the years 1880–81.

[85] Erastus Dow Palmer (1817–1904), whose works included *White Captive*, which was often compared with Powers' *Greek Slave*, and a bronze statue of Robert R. Livingston, which was commissioned by the state of New York, and placed in the Capitol in Washington in 1874. Palmer was abroad during 1873.

[86] Hiram H. Barney (1804–1879), principal of the first public high school in Cincinnati, state commissioner of common schools, 1854–57, and professor of didactics in the City Normal School of Cincinnati from 1869.

sun came out brightly towards evening and gave us a beautiful May sunset. Gen'l McDowell called in the evening and spent several hours. I never arise from a visit with him without increased feelings of respect and veneration for him. The tendencies to idleness which show themselves in most army officers seems never to have afflicted him. His mind is clear, correct and full of resources. He gave me an interesting history of sugar manufacture in Cuba, also some suggestions working in his mind towards an invention for getting sacharine matter out of the cane. From his statement it is clear that the tariff on sugar should be reclassified.

MONDAY, 12. Worked up correspondence and the Journal and attended some matters about the house and yard until 11 o'clock. Took Crete, Mother and Lizzie to the Capitol to attend the funeral of Chief Justice Chase in the Senate Chamber. There were present the President and Cabinet and foreign legations, a considerable number of Senators and Representatives and a great congregation of lesser officials and citizens of Washington. Tiffany[87] of the Metropolitan Church preached the sermon. At the conclusion of the services we drove through the Smithsonian, Agricultural and Monumental grounds and several other portions of the City. Returned home at three. Called in the evening at Welcker's on General McDowell and Whitelaw Reid. After returning home read proof of my article on the Credit Mobilier, as far it has gone.

TUESDAY, 13. Today finished my article on the Credit Mobilier and also wrote the prefatory note alluding to the death of Mr. Ames. While it embarrasses me to publish this review just now, though on the whole I should be more embarrassed not to do so, and I think my preface will explain the ground of my action. Mr. Boynton and General Muzzey [Mussey] called in the evening, also, Att'y General Hill. I have about concluded to give up the trip to Saint Louis.[88] Called at the Pension Office today to see what time the excursion should start from Saint Louis. Hal and Jim had the com-

[87] O. H. Tiffany, pastor of the Metropolitan Methodist Episcopal Church in Washington, the church of Chase and President Grant.

[88] Garfield had been invited to a "Congressional Convention" originated primarily for the purpose of gaining the favor of congressmen for large appropriations to improve the navigation of the Mississippi. It was held in St. Louis, May 13–15.

pany of our little neighbor Jennie Young and it gives me my first experience in being the father of "young folks" who have a society of their own.

WEDNESDAY, 14. Read proof sheets of my first part Credit Mobilier Review and worked on correspondence until one o'clock when I took a drive through several of the interesting suburbs of the City with Mr. Boynton. The City has grown wonderfully since I first saw it, and I shall be glad if it turns out that the improvements are not being over done. I am afraid they are undertaking too much and that the pressure of taxation will fall too heavily upon the citizens. Several people called in the evening. I have great respect for the ideas of Major L'Enfant, the Engineer who laid out the original plan of Washington City. It must have required no small power of imagination to see the future city in the wild woods of his day.

THURSDAY, 15. At work in the usual way. I find many delicate and difficult questions arising in the course of my discussion of the Credit Mobilier. It is related to so many men, some good, some very bad, and then the principal person whom I criticise is now dead. Finished the article, however, for better, or for worse, and shall commit it to its fate, at the hands of the public. Went to the P. O. Dep't on business for friends and constituents. Got Lizzie a place for June 8th in the Topographical Bureau of the Post Office Department. In the Evening Miss [Mary E.] Perkins and Miss McCall took dinner with us. They are the teachers, respectively of Jimmie and Harry, and I am glad to talk of late methods, and see how the teaching world has been going since I left it. Capt. Weaver of the Navy called in the evening. I have accepted the Hudson College invitation to deliver an address before the College July 2.

FRIDAY, 16. Finished the final revision of my review of the Credit Mobilier, and at noon took it to the printer's. At 3 P.M. went with Crete to Mrs. Dahlgren's to meet Mrs. Almira Lincoln Phelps of Baltimore. She is a venerable and amiable old lady about 75 years old, and seeing her recalls my school days at Chester, when I studied her Botany and made an Herbarium on the Linnaean system. There were present at Mrs. Dahlgren's many cultivated men and women, among them, Donn Piatt, Mrs. Freyer and Miss Boyle.[89] The latter

[89] Esmeralda Boyle (b. 1840), a Washington poet whose works included *Thistle-down* (1871). She also contributed a weekly letter on society in America to Donn Piatt's paper, the *Washington Capital*.

is beautiful, and has published two volumes of poems, which give much promise of future achievements. Late in the evening reviewed most delightfully with Crete the memories of Chester days, and other *festas dies*. I see no reason why wedded life and years should be a bar to re-wooing.

SATURDAY, 17. At ten o'clock went to Gen. Mussey's office on 4½ St. and at 11 went to the U.S. Supreme Court of the District to move for the ratification of the award of the jury in our Sixth Presbyterian Church case *vs.* the Baltimore and Potomac R. R. I was admitted to the Court, on motion of Gen. Mussey; but after the Court had delivered an opinion in an appeal in a murder case, they adjourned. I then went to the Capitol, transacted some business, visited the glorious old Library, as usual when I am there, and returned home to a good dinner and a lovely May evening—though on my way home, I stopped at the Att'y Gen'l's office, and got a copy of the bill about to be filed against the Pacific R. R., the Credit Mobilier, and other spoliators of the Pacific Road, and of the U. S. In the evening read the life of Gregory the Great. He was a man of marvellous power.

SUNDAY, 18. This has been a golden day, and better than weather or any external condition, is the fact that my soul is emerging from the shadows which the late winter of scandal and outrage has thrown upon me. I have carefully gone through two defenses of myself, one in reference to the salary amendment, and the other the Credit Mobilier. I have now said my say, and shall leave the result to the logic of the facts, and shall try to resume the course of study and work from which I have been so sadly diverted. After church and early dinner I took all the family, (except Harry who was visited [visiting] at Mr. Dungan's)[90] in an open carriage, and drove to Crystal Springs [Silver Spring], the old country seat of the Blairs, and thence to Brightwood, and back by and through the grounds of the Soldiers' Home. Washington is becoming one of the finest cities in our country, and I know of none that has so near it and in all directions so many beautiful suburban country retreats. Had an interesting visit with A. Brisbane in the evening. He is a genius.

[90] William Dungan, a neighbor of the Garfields in Washington.

MONDAY, 19.   Took the revise of the final print of my Credit Mobilier
Review to the printers. It makes a pamphlet of 28 pages including
title-page and waste. When [Went] from Public Printing House to
the Patent Office and attended to a number of Department matters.
Thence to the Navy Dep't, then the Executive Mansion and finally
to the Treasury. Have put in train the preparation of materials for
a magazine article on the appropriations of the late session of
Congress. After dinner Rose (brother of George) came, and wrote
letters for me until after ten o'clock. A hundred copies of my
Credit Mobilier Review[91] came, and I have sent off a few copies
accompanied by letters. Have also recommended the appointment of
Eugene Huntington Sedgebeer[92] of Painesville to a naval cadetship.
He is a stranger to me, but is well recommended. In the evening
took Crete and Mother to the Franklin School concert, and staid
till half-past nine. My letters today give evidence of more storm
and abuse on the salary question. "Let them rave," as Tennyson says.
TUESDAY, 20.   Wrote several letters and enclosed copies of my Credit
Mobilier review. About half-past nine o'clock, Mr. Daniels of this
City came and retained me in a suit brought against him by a Mr.
Driggs of New York.[93] After hearing his statement, I agreed to help
Gen. Payne in the case for $500, and one-quarter of the amount
that may be awarded to Daniels by the Court. Went to Gen. Payne's
office on Louisiana Avenue and look[ed] over the papers in the

[91] *Review of the Transactions of the Credit Mobilier Company and an Examination of that Portion of the Testimony Taken by the Committee of Investigation and Reported to the House of Representatives at the Last Session
of the Forty-second Congress Which Relates to Mr. Garfield* (1873).

[92] Young Sedgebeer, the son of Joseph Sedgebeer, a prominent citizen of
Painesville, withdrew from the entrance examination for the Naval Academy.

[93] Joseph Daniels, a Washington lawyer, had represented Seth Driggs of
New York City in connection with claims of Driggs presented to the Vene-
zuela Claims Commission. The two men had fallen out, and Driggs was
now attempting to recover from Daniels money and certificates which he
claimed that Daniels was unlawfully retaining. John Driggs, the nephew of
the plaintiff, was also involved in the case, as were the heirs of John Clark.
Garfield was brought in to assist James G. Payne, a Washington attorney
representing Daniels. The case of *Driggs v. Daniels* was fought in the courts
of the District of Columbia.

case. Suggested the amendment of our cross-bill, which was done. In the evening dined with Albert Brisbane, and heard him talk of Fourier, and the social philosophy. B. is a wonderful man, full of genius and eccentricity. Much that he says of social philosophy comes within the circle of my own experience. The philosophy of marriage is a study worthy the highest intellect and is full of the most spiritual thought we can reach. I hope Brisbane will come down to the earth and finish his tube.

WEDNESDAY, 21. It is a dreary, drizzly day, and my spirits partake of the general depression of the atmosphere. I am trying to prepare an address for Hudson College, July 2, on some of the future issues of American politics, and particularly the management of corporations. I am not [now?] in doubt whether I can seize the salient points of the subject and present them to a company of young men, so as to make them feel an interest in them. But first let me see if I can get a full understanding of the theme. Went to the Departments and transacted some odds and ends of business. Also to the Library of Congress, and got some books for my address. I have also agreed to deliver an address at the Commencement at Willoughby, June 25, 1873.

I wish the political forces would let me alone this season, that I might get some culture out of the six months to come. *Sed Deo aliter visum* [But it is otherwise decreed by God].

THURSDAY, 22. The Ohio Republican State Convention yesterday passed resolutions against Credit Mobilier and the salary bill, and the tone of proceedings indicated a desire to slap me in the face, while pretending not to do it. It remains to be seen, whether the men inside Ohio politics are going to dispose of life and honor as they please. Whatever they may assume to do, they have never had my honor put in their keeping, and I don't intend they shall. I went to the Court to argue a motion in the Daniels-Driggs case, but found the Circuit Court did not meet today. Went to the Capitol and arranged for the distribution of some documents, so as to clear the decks before the franking privilege expires next month.

Read Fourier on monopoly, agiotage, and joint-stock corporations. His writing of 1808 sounds like prophecy fulfilled. Corporations had hardly made a scratch on the surface of society at that date.

FRIDAY, 23. Went to the Supreme Court of the District and made and argued a motion to file a cross bill in the case of *Daniels v. Driggs*. The motion was allowed. Also carried our motion before the court in banc to have the jury award in the case of the Sixth Presbyterian Church tried before the full bench. During the evening worked up correspondence, and read for my address before the College Societies. I find that somebody in Warren, probably Judge Sutliff,[94] has been making a fresh assault on me on the salary question. A long, stupid, malignant article of four colum[n]s appeared in the *Chronicle*. I wrote to Harmon Austin suggesting some points in answer. I sometimes think I have made a mistake in answering anybody's criticisms, but it seemed on this occasion to be necessary. I have never seen any sufficient reason why I should be singled out as the only one among congressmen who have been pursued in this manner, unless it be that I am in the way of some people who have schemes of their own.

SATURDAY, 24. Went with Crete and Harry and Jimmy to Mt. Vernon on the steamer *Arrow*. The boys had a good day of it, and we a pleasant one, although the weather was very hot. I read the leading speeches of the St. Louis Convention, and also read some in Charles Francis Adams', Jr., book on railroads.[95] In the evening Colonel Don Pardee, of New Orleans, came from Annapolis, where he is a visitor to the Academy. Had a long and pleasant conversation with Colonel Pardee reviewing old memories and discussing the condition of affairs in New Orleans, where he is a prominent Judge of one of the leading courts. Our reconstruction in Louisiana is manifestly a failure, and I fear we shall be compelled to take military control of that state.

Congress was greatly at fault not to have taken action on the affairs of that wretched state, at the last session. Perhaps Judge Black's view of the want of "set" in the Negro character may have

[94] Milton Sutliff (1806–1878), a Warren lawyer, was a justice of the Ohio Supreme Court, 1858–63. He was a Republican until 1872, when he accepted the Democratic and Liberal Republican nominations as candidate for Congress in opposition to Garfield, who defeated him by a vote of 19,189 to 8,254. Garfield regularly polled a smaller percentage of the votes of Trumbull County than he did elsewhere in his district.

[95] Charles Francis Adams, *Chapters of Erie and Other Essays* (1871).

something in it, and that they will be found untempered mortar in the national temple.

SUNDAY, 25. Soon after breakfast went with Judge Pardee to call on Senator West, and from there with West, made a call on Senator Pool, who is organizing a national workingmen's association, with branch societies in each city. I think it means a new party, based on the labor question. From Senator Pool's we drove through the public grounds, returning home to an early dinner. In the evening Mr. Brisbane called and gave us a talk on his social philosophy, particularly his doctrine of the currency. He believes in a sort of automatic system of exchange of currency into bonds, and bonds into currency, at the will of the holder, discarding gold and silver as a worn-out barbarism. Brisbane is as impractical as possible, but very brilliant. He wants to convert me to his theory of the currency, and have me take charge of what he calls the "great movement." Says Butler will do it if I don't. An ideal standard of value may come some day but in this matter of fact world we must have something tangible as the basis of our currency.

MONDAY, 26. Pardee left us at six o'clock in the morning. The mail brought my first response from the district to my review of the Credit Mobilier. Mr. Howells speaks in the highest terms of it. At eleven o'clock went to the court, and after consultation with counsel and with the judges, fixed tomorrow morning for the trial of the Sixth Presbyterian Church case against the Baltimore and Potomac Railroad. Then went to the law library and consulted authorities, and got ready for trial. Then called at the Treasury on Department business. On returning home at ½ past three, Professor Baird, Commissioner of Fisheries, calling, took me with him to the Virginia end of the Long Bridge to see the shad-hatching establishment lately set up there. At dinner I explained to the boys the processes by which eggs are obtained and shad are hatched. In the evening several gentlemen called, among them Hill, my classmate, who stayed until near eleven o'clock. He tells me that the *Springfield* [*Republican*] has a long article on my Credit Mobilier review, and on the whole, a favorable one.

TUESDAY, 27. Went to the Treasury, Post Office and Interior Departments on business. At eleven o'clock took up the trial of the case of the Sixth Presbyterian Church against the Baltimore and Potomac

Railroad. The other side moved to send the case to the District Court. After two hours' argument, their motion was overruled. They then moved to quash our inquisition as improper in form. Filed exceptions and demurrers. The cause continued until near four o'clock, when I concluded my speech in response to Mr. Phillips. I think we won the case, although, of course, not sure. After working off a considerable number of letters and finishing up some other business, I took Mother and Mollie and went to the 8 o'clock train on the Baltimore and Potomac for Baltimore. At ten o'clock we were in the Northern Central sleeping car for Pittsburgh on our way to Ohio. My family is now so large that it is convenient to divide it into two brigades. This is the first time I have moved them in detachments from a sense of their numerousness. I am very much tired out with the work of the last few days and particularly of this day.

WEDNESDAY, 28. Awoke near Altoona, where we took breakfast. I feel a sense of fatherly pride in having little Mollie sit beside me at the Hotel table, as my sweet little protected companion. The developement of her child life is a delightful study to me, and on this trip I am doing something to form her acquaintance. It is a pity that I have so little time to devote to my children. I can see the effect of my attentions to Mollie even on this trip. We reached Pittsburgh too late to make the connection at Leetonia, and so went to Cleveland by the Cleveland & Pittsburgh R. R. We reached the City at 7½ P.M. and stopped at Dr. Robison's. He and I called on Mr. Cowles in the evening and had a pleasant visit. Talked on the relation of the state to Railroads. I tried my theme for the Hudson address on Mr. Cowles's mind to test the question of its interest to others.

THURSDAY, 29. At seven A.M. took Mother and Mollie to the Mahoning Depot and put them on the cars for Solon. Then went to the Union Depot and took the 7.20 train for Painesville. Went to the Court room and found that the Rudolph-Sweeney case had been again postponed. After looking over the principal depositions with Burrows, I was driven to Little Mountain by Mr. King and looked through the cottages there with a view of taking one for my family during the hot weather. It is a delightful place. Saw Bisbee of Chester whom I have not seen for 15 years. We then drove to Mentor to look at the site of the P. O. and of the place where some of the citizens want it. The fight about it is a tempest in a teapot. Took tea with Hon. Geo. Steele, who took me to the station. Went to Cleveland on the six-twenty train and spent the night at Dr. Robison's after calling on Mr. Terrill and getting propositions in reference to a cottage at Little Mountain.

FRIDAY, 30. Spent the forenoon in making calls and looking over the newspapers. Harry Jones came to the Doctor's for dinner and we had a meeting of the "Quintinkle"—a pleasant reunion defined by Jones as "the place where we unwind." At 2 P.M. drove to the Cemetery, and saw at a distance the Decoration Ceremony. It is a beautiful custom but will not last many years I think. Took the Dummy train[96] to Newburgh with Jones, and called at Browning's to get a cook for Crete. Played four games of croquet and was then driven to the Mahoning train and went to Solon. Walked to Sister Mary's and found Mother, Mollie and the rest well. The dear little girl was glad to see me and slept with me for the first time I believe. On all hands the evidences of advancing years accumulates. I am in middle life. My sisters and brother are beyond it. Mother venerable and feeble, with weight of years. Life runs now—it formerly crept slowly.

SATURDAY, 31. Went to the Center to find a girl in case the Browning girl fails us. Took the 8 A.M. train to Garrettsville and reached Hiram at ten. Spent the *solidam diem* [entire day] in reading and writing letters, visiting Burke and the friends and making arrangements for the coming of the family. Mother Rudolph gave me some letters that Crete wrote her from Chester 24 years ago. Worked among my books on the Hudson address. Read some from Galton's *Hereditary Genius*.[97] Martha[98] drove me to Garrettsville where I took the four P.M. train East. Burke went with me as far as Warren. I went thence to Leetonia. After supper took livery to Columbiana Station and there read Herbert Spencer on R. Roads until the mid-

[96] A train pulled by a locomotive having condensing engines, and thus no noise of escaping steam.

[97] Francis Galton, *Hereditary Genius: An Inquiry into Its Laws and Consequences* (1869).

[98] Martha (Lane) Rudolph was the widow of Lucretia Garfield's brother John (1835–1862). She and her children lived in Hiram.

night train came, when I took the Pacific Express for the East and was soon asleep bound for the dear ones at Washington. Surely life runs impelled by the new forces of our time.

June

SUNDAY, 1. Awoke in the mountains and got breakfast at Altoona. I found on reaching Harrisburg that I could not get a train for Baltimore before 11 o'clock at night and so kept on to Philadelphia. Read several articles from Herbert Spencer—one on the Railway and another on the Bank Act. On reaching Philadelphia went to 1111 Girard St. and took a Turkish bath which seemed to be bad for me for it induced headache and other unpleasant feelings. After getting dinner at the Continental Restaurant read and wrote until ten o'clock. Commenced reading Bagehot's *Physics and Politics*.[99] Took the train for Washington.

MONDAY, 2. Reached home at 6 o'clock in the morning very tired and nearly sick. A large accumulation of letters and papers. Spent most of the day in reading and answering letters. In the afternoon went to the Capitol and got some books from the library. The English reviews and magazines are now very full of the subject of railways. At 8 o'clock in the evening Mrs. Dahlgren called and by previous arrangement we went with her to call on the President and Mrs. Grant. They were sitting on the South Balcony of the White House with a number of friends and we had a very pleasant visit of an hour, although I was nearly sick and was glad to get home and into bed.

TUESDAY, 3. Awoke this morning feeling very unwell. I have a sharp attack of the dysentary and am feeling a muscular soreness all over my body as if I had a very severe cold. Nevertheless worked off a large number of letters and read several magazine articles in reference to railways. In preparing my address for Hudson, I am embarrassed with the amount and richness of material rather than for the want of it. Several persons called during the day, but I was too ill to do much visiting or to go out. Towards evening I was taken with a turn of vomiting and went to bed miserably ill.

WEDNESDAY, 4. Passed a very uncomfortable night; part of the time

[99] Walter Bagehot, *Physics and Politics* (1873).

I was really ill. Towards noon I was able to get up and dictate a large number of letters and do some reading. Attended Harry's examination at the Franklin School Building. Harry did very well; though I think he is like me in this, that he does better under pressure than on ordinary occasions. Some of the nervous boys did not do themselves justice. I am persuaded that our public schools are overworking their scholars. I saw many signs of nervous exhaustion among the little fellows in Miss McMahon's class. Perhaps this is a part of the overstrain of which Galton speaks in his book on *Hereditary Genius*, where he says our civilization is too much for the stamina of the race.

THURSDAY, 5. Better, but still sick with the dysentary. Worked up correspondence and resumed the preparation of my Military History for the War Department, which I began more than a year ago and was compelled to lay aside. I find a number of interesting points in the history of my Sandy Valley Campaign that had nearly passed from my memory. I should have been less successful in that campaign if I had had more experience. I should have run less risk, and, probably, produced less results. In the afternoon attended the Examination of Miss Perkins' School. Jimmy received a diploma for excellence and scholarship. His work during the season in school has been a fine success.

FRIDAY, 6. Finished the history of my military services. It makes about forty pages of manuscript. Still unwell but at three o'clock drove to the Treasury Department and thence to the War Department and delivered to the Adjutant General my sketch and also the blank books, records, and official papers relating to my Sandy Valley Campaign. In the evening my classmates Hill and Gilfillan called and spent some time. At half-past eight Crete and I joined Mrs. Dahlgren, and visited General and Mrs. Sherman at their residence on I St. Met General and Mrs. Morgan L. Smith,[100] whom I have not seen since the Winter of 1866. At that time they consulted me as a lawyer on the validity of a divorce which had just been granted to General Smith in a New York Court, but the validity of which was disputed by his former wife. Home at 11 o'clock. The heats of the Washington Summer are beginning to be felt.

SATURDAY, 7. Worked up correspondence and brought up my ac-

[100] Morgan L. Smith (1821–1874), who had distinguished himself as a Union officer, was a Washington businessman.

counts to the first of June. Went to the P. O. Department and got a place for Lizzie. Also, transacted some business at the Interior Department, and at the Congressional Library. Overhauled my book list after I returned home, and did some reading on my Hudson address. In the evening Major Brown drove me out into the country to A. R. Shepherd's place where we remained until nearly eleven o'clock, Judge Cartter, Dr. Bliss, and several other gentlemen being there. Rolled ten pins and had a pleasant time. I am somewhat better this evening.

SUNDAY, 8. Continued reading up for my Hudson address. Dictated a portion of it to be sent on to Hiram after I get there. Nearly finished the letters on hand and closed up a number of miscellaneous matters, preparatory to leaving for home tomorrow with the family. Still unwell not having recovered from my dysentery. In the evening Crete and I called at Mr. Duggan's [Dungan's], also at Mr. Riddle's and Don Piatt's and Gilfillan's, to make our parting call on these friends. On many accounts Washington is a desirable place of residence. Crete finds herself liking it better than ever before and having quite a homelike feeling.

MONDAY, 9. The day was very full of miscellaneous work in preparing to get away to Ohio with my family. I made several trips to the Departments and one to the Capitol, to close up my business. Made out a bag of books and documents for use during vacation. Collected materials for a magazine article on the appropriations of the late Congress. Dictated to Rose the opening part of it. Answered nearly all the unanswered letters, and set the house in order generally. At 5.35 P.M. we (the family and Mary McGrath)[101] took the train on the Baltimore and Potomac R. R. and at 8.50 we were on the sleeping car at Baltimore for Pittsburgh. My little folks are becoming good travelers.

TUESDAY, 10. Reached Pittsburgh at 9 A.M. and got breakfast at the Union Hotel. In an hour we took the Pittsburgh & Ft. Wayne R. R. for Leetonia where we waited until three P.M. and there took the train for Garrettsville via Niles. Reached Father Rudolph's at 7 P.M. wet, tired and happy. During the trip I have read Isaac

[101] A young woman employed as a nursemaid in the Garfield household for a number of years.

Errett's address at the Wooster Missionary Society, and have done some work on my own addresses soon to be made. The change from Washington to Hiram brings its great compensation of coolness and gives special delight to the children. It rained heavily in the evening and night.

WEDNESDAY, 11. Spent most of the day in answering an enormous mail, which had accumulated since I left. In this I feel the loss of Rose. I shall also miss the Library of Congress. Every condition of life has its debit and credit account. In the evening went to President Hinsdale's with Mr. Udall to arrange the business for the approaching meeting of the Board of Trustees. The College is more and more directly grappling with the fates in the struggle for existence. The elements are quick and active, and the contest is being rapidly narrowed down to well-defined limits. I am not sanguine as to the result. It is harder for an institution as for a man, to "roost" high than low.

THURSDAY, 12. Cleared the decks for work and commenced my article on Appropriations for *The Republic.* The cool vital air of this hill braces me up and I work easily and with pleasure. Wrote nine legal cap pages and got ready for the statistics of the late session. I am surprised that so little has ever been said or written on the philosophy of appropriations. I believe my speech of Jan. 26th, 1872, was the first of its kind in Congress. I get a visit out of Burke each day and it helps us both. Griffith,[102] a student, came to get help on the Postal Telegraph Question.

FRIDAY, 13. Plunged in figures nearly all day. Made progress of about seven pages and in the afternoon, added a little croquet with Burke. The Treasury Accounts have been kept in the most artificial manner. It is extremely difficult to put the expenditures of one year in a shape to be compared with those of other years. I am greatly annoyed at the non-arrival of my bag of books, for part of my statistics are in it. The hired girl question to [is] again confronting us. I took the evening train for Newburgh to see if I could get the girl at Josiah Browning's, as they are about to leave for California. Failed and returned to Solon, and spent the night at Sister Mary's. The Burnett girl partially arranged for there, has probably failed us.

[102] James Henry Griffith, a member of the class of 1873, Hiram College.

Spent a pleasant evening but regretted that Mother and Mollie were absent, in Orange.

SATURDAY, 14. Took an early breakfast and went to the village in search of a girl. Sister Mary went with me to Mr. Deedy's, but we failed. Mary succeeded in getting a Miss Kennely to help us one week for five dollars and her travelling expenses. This is the tragic question of domestic life—how to get needed service and how to render it without a loss of caste. Went to Hiram on the 8 A.M. train. My books came and I resumed work successfully. Many letters are coming to me in reference to the Credit Mobilier. That entanglement which I regard as far more serious than the salary question, seems not to be so serious as the latter in the popular mind. The jealousy of the people towards their public men is perhaps salutary but it is frequently cruel. I sometimes think that the average man has but a small comprehension of the things around him. Yet he is fiercely certain in his opinion of all things.

SUNDAY, 15. Made further progress on my magazine article, but found renewed difficulties from the unscientific groupings of the public accounts. Attended church in the forenoon and heard a good sermon from Burke on children, and their relation to the economy of life. I can see that his studies have led him to increased Latinism. He seems to prefer a long ponderous word of Latin origin, rather than one short crisp Saxon word. This is a tendency which gives him solidity, but impairs his popular force. This century, as Marsh says, in his lectures on the English Language,[103] is growing more Saxon than the 18th century was. Crete and I had a long and delightful stroll in the old woods. We are younger in some ways than ever before. This last thought is perhaps one of the sweet delusions of middle life. The day has been a perfect amethyst.

MONDAY, 16. Rose early and went at the article, with good health and keen enjoyment. At 10 A.M. the Solon girl came to help us a week which pushes off the tragic question for seven days. By five o'clock I had completed my article of thirty legal cap pages and was pretty well satisfied with it. This last fact makes me fear it is not a success. Burke came late in the day and we went over the College Accounts. In the evening worked up some of my letters, which the magazine article

[103] George Perkins Marsh, *Lectures on the English Language* (1860).

has pushed over. Father and Mother Rudolph came in and talked over the question of Joseph's approaching marriage and the disposition they ought to make of their property. I advise a will which will give Joseph the property after they are gone but not before. I ask as Crete's portion the cradle in which she was rocked, and no more. The sweet air has made me well again, and so are Crete and the little ones.

TUESDAY, 17. Finished my article on Appropriations for *The Republic*. It covers 30 pages of legal cap, and will make about ten pages of the magazine. It is out of the ordinary range of political articles, and I hope is of the higher and better sort. I must now turn to my Hudson address. But Commencement is to intervene and I can do but little till that is over. I have collected a great mass of materials for my address, but the subject is a difficult one, both on account of the political danger of the theme and the literary danger that it cannot be made interesting to such an audience as I shall have at Hudson. Harmon Austin and several other friends came today. Spent the evening in visiting and talking over the political situation in the District.

WEDNESDAY, 18. At ten o'clock the Board of Trustees met in the Reading Room of the College and had a long session, during which the condition of the College was fully examined. The Board was last year increased to twenty-four members and some new and vigorous materials were added. At one o'clock several of the members took dinner with us, among them Dr. Streator and George A. Baker.[104] The Board continued its session till late in the afternoon. In the evening the Sophomore class had a public performance under the tent. Every such occasion brings to my mind the conviction that I am drifting away from youth and its sentiments.

THURSDAY, 19. The Board reassembled at 8.30 A.M. and completed its work. Fifteen hundred dollars were raised among the members to meet the College expenses. I gave one hundrd and fifty dollars, which was more than I could really afford, but it seemed necessary. At half-past nine attended the Commencement. The exercises were good, but there was a tone of censoriousness running through many

[104] George A. Baker, head of the Cleveland Lightning Rod Works, was a Hiram trustee, 1872–84; he endowed a chair of mathematics and astronomy at the college.

of the speeches, which was hardly becoming in young men. Hon. A. G. Riddle made the address in the P.M., and he and his daughter Hattie were our guests. A dozen political friends called on me in the P.M. and held a conference on the situation in the District.

FRIDAY, 20. Had a delightful visit with Mr. Riddle, on literature, politics and life. At eleven went to the College and attended the Alumni Society. Mr. Riddle was elected an honorary member. I introduced him in a brief speech and he responded handsomely. In the cool of the evening Riddle and his daughter left us and I resumed work on the Hudson address, but was too much worn out with the work of the last three days to accomplish much. The life and vitality of young people presses with a kind of exhausting effect upon us who have worn off its first bloom.

SATURDAY, 21. Got to work in earnest today, and finished about ten pages including the introduction and the first section of the theme itself. I have become confirmed in my method of work. I must substantially finish as I go. Some men write with great rapidity and then rewrite with care, revising and changing. The first is the creative spirit the second the critical. This method has some advantages, and perhaps among other things it gives more continuity to the composition. But I run the two processes together. I cannot well write a new sentence till I am satisfied myself with the last. This makes me a slow worker for it requires many erasures and changes to keep the proper proportions of the article.

SUNDAY, 22. Attended church and heard a good sermon from Burke. He is steadily growing in intellectual strength. I wish he were also growing in the elegancies and graces of speech. I feared he has carried his contempt of shams too far. After church I continued work on my Hudson address. I frequent[ly] come to a place where I work three or four hours before I can advance half a page. I sometimes think no one will ever appreciate the work put into a page.

MONDAY, 23. This day was essentially a repetition of Saturday last, varied only by writing some letters. Some pleasure and much drudgery in my day's work.

TUESDAY, 24. Turned aside from the Hudson address to prepare notes for an extempore address to be delivered at Willoughby College day after tomorrow. Chose for theme "culture, and its relation to success." This brings me back to my old school and teaching days and I am quite at home in it. Culture is from the Latin *Cultus,* or *Coltus,* the cutting part of a plough, whence our word "colter." The work of culture is well typified by the tearing up of the sod and bringing the soil into play. Success too is a getting down into a thing, *sub cedare,* to go under it, and lift it from below. But worth is better than success.

  Tis not in mortals to command success,
  But we'll do more, Sempronius, we'll deserve it.

WEDNESDAY, 25. Burke went with me to Cleveland and we spent part of the day in the Library looking up some facts for my two addresses. Every day I miss Spofford[105] and our great Library of Congress. Went to Carson's and ordered a summer suit. Olive coat and waist coat and dark pants. Price $49.50. Took dinner at Dr. Robison's and at four o'clock took the train to Willoughby. Dr. E. G. Clark met us at the depot and we went to his house. In the evening spoke one hour to a full house and satisfied myself fairly well. Near the close quoted Tennyson's "Bugle Song" to illustrate the permanence of culture. Spent the night at Dr. Clark's.

THURSDAY, 26. After spending the morning in chat, and walking along the banks of the Chagrin, we took the 9½ A.M. train for Cleveland. Took dinner at Dr. Robison's. Went to the bookstore where I bought James Fitzjames Stephen's work on Liberty, Equality and Fraternity.[106] A bold' discussion of some new political and social questions. Reached home in the evening and found a large mail and could not get at my Hudson address because of epistolary impediments. I feel the need of rest, or what is better, a change of work.

FRIDAY, 27. Put in a good day's work in undertaking as a part of the address to answer the criticisms made on the democratic principle by Lord Macaulay in his letter of 1857 to H. S. Randall.[107] I don't think

[105] Ainsworth Rand Spofford (1825–1908), was associated with the Library of Congress from 1861 until his death; he was head librarian, 1864–97. He was renowned for his vast knowledge.

[106] James Fitzjames Stephen, *Liberty, Equality, Fraternity* (1873).

[107] Thomas Babington Macaulay (1800–1859), English historian, wrote on May 23, 1857, a long letter to Henry S. Randall, whose biography of Thomas Jefferson in three volumes was published in 1858. In it he said: "I have long been convinced that institutions purely democratic must, sooner or later, destroy liberty, or civilization, or both." He predicted that democracy in the United States would, in the twentieth century, as population grew and

much better of Mr. Jefferson than he does, but I do [not] agree to the validity of his objections. Perhaps the mass of the people may not be fitted to control and manage a government, but if they have no voice in it they may be more dangerous to society than if they take part in its management. The letter is a very strong one and will bear much study.

SATURDAY, 28. Spent two hours in working off Congressional Documents before the frank expires[108] and then resumed work. Had Robertson[109] here to copy a portion of my manuscript. Entered upon the discussion of the railway problem. I desire to do full justice to the value of the new force of the steam locomotive. I ask what the U. S. has done for it and what it has done for the U. S. I shall then inquire what it has done and is doing to the U. S. and to our form of Government. Are our institutions strong enough to handle this new force?

SUNDAY, 29. I wanted to go to Aurora today to attend the yearly meeting of Disciples of Portage but was unable to get a team. I do not feel well enough to work much. I was rather in a critical than a producing mood and so went carefully over the pages already written. I am pretty well pleased with it, as far as it has gone. The three points of danger, viz: foreign complications, territorial extension and universal suffrage, I think are well done. About the railway question I feel more anxiety, for I can do but little with remedies, and must content myself with stating the question.

MONDAY, 30. Today the franking privilege expires (it was to me more a burden than a privilege) after a checkered life of 84 years. In many ways its abolition will work changes, social and political. I sent off a few more documents and letters—the last a document, the

---

economic conditions worsened, produce either dictatorship or ruin. "Thinking thus," he wrote, "of course, I cannot reckon Jefferson among the benefactors of mankind." See "What Did Macaulay Say About America?" in *Bulletin of the New York Public Library*, July, 1925, pp. 459–481.

108 Under the new law, which was to go into effect on July 1, congressmen would no longer enjoy the privilege of sending or receiving free mail.

109 George Andrew Robertson, a member of the class of 1874, Hiram College, became a well known newspaperman, associated during his career with a number of Cleveland papers.

compendium of the 9th Census, and a letter returning fifty cents sent as postage by S. S. Barrett of Amboy, Ohio. The best results I expect are the disappearance of the abuse of the frank, and if we may hope for it, a reduction in the amount of useless public documents. Made good progress on the Railway paragraph of my address, which I fear grows too long.

July

TUESDAY, 1.   Put in a good three-quarters of a day's work, less one hour devoted to a bore, worse than the one who met Horace in the Via Sacra. I tried to quell him by silence, by restlessness, by looking wistfully at my manuscript, but like all his genus he was a pachyderm. A ten-penny nail would not find the raw, for he has none. At last he left me reluctantly, apologizing for the brevity of his visit. At five P.M. Burke and his wife, Crete and I drove to Aurora [and] stopped at Reuben Cannon's,[110] where a large company of friends greeted us, and we visited until near midnight. At two o'clock we were awakened by the collision of two thunder storms. The conflict was wonderfully fine and a splendid rain followed.

WEDNESDAY, 2.   Rose early and wrote five pages nearly finishing the address. At nine we started for Hudson which we reached in a heavy shower. Stopped at ex-President Hitchcock's, who is very ill of a fever. The tent was abandoned and Commencement was held in the College chapel. At the conclusion of the exercises, joined in the Alumni Dinner. At two P.M. went on the stand and wrote the 72d, the last page, whilst the band was playing. Then read one hour and a quarter to a large audience.[111] It is very hard for me to read an address, but I think it was successful. After a political interview with Gov. Noyes, started for home, supping at Lauren Hinsdale's,[112] and reaching home at eleven P.M.

[110] Reuben Cannon, of Aurora, a political supporter of Garfield, was a member of the Ohio House of Representatives, 1868–71.

[111] "The Future of the Republic: its Dangers and its Hopes," in Burke A. Hinsdale, ed., *The Works of James Abram Garfield*, II, 46–69.

[112] Laurence Hinsdale (1831–1876), a cousin of Burke A. Hinsdale.

THURSDAY, 3. Spent the day in making preparations for an address at Ravenna tomorrow. I take for my theme the era of the Revolution, the origin and results of its ideas. At five P.M. Capt. Rudolph took me in his carriage en route to Ravenna, but we were caught by a shower in Freedom, and stopped for the night at Henry Thayer's, where we had a good old fashioned visit conversing on everything that came into our minds. Not much time for thinking of tomorrow's address. Old Prob don't promise well.

FRIDAY, 4. Finished the journey to Ravenna at an early hour and stopped at Halsey Hall's. Visited several friends and after a noon lunch went to the public square, where about three thousand people were assembled. The band played twenty minutes, the chaplain prayed twenty-five minutes more. The Declaration was read. I spoke twenty-five minutes and the rain came and dispersed us. My address for [was] a fair torso, though hardly an Elgin marble. At 3 P.M. several friends met me at Hall's to discuss the political situation, which they think is good. In the evening called at Mr. Williams'[113] and at Darsie's.[114] Night at Hall's.

SATURDAY, 5. At 8 A.M. took train to Cleveland, where I looked for a girl [to] help without success. Took dinner at Dr. Robison's and came home on the evening train. I have not [now] completed my public engagements for the present. I have had no rest since the adjournment of Congress. Since that date I have written what would make a duodecimo volume of 250 pages. The tire of months is in me and I must take some rest. But the girl question presses for solution. No rest till then, and is there then? Perhaps we must look to China for a solution of it.

SUNDAY, 6. This morning I slept, slept, slept, and was still sleepy. Went to church where, Burke having surrendered the pulpit to another for the day, I was tortured by the feeblest little preach[er] it has been my misfortune to hear for many months. It is a fraud on the community, and a wrong to the young man. I presume he is the victim of a foolishly fond mother and the still more foolish zeal of

[113] Isaac Williams, a merchant and farmer, was a close friend and active political supporter of Garfield. At this time he was a member of the Republican Central Committee of Portage County.

[114] George H. Darsie, pastor of the Disciple Church in Ravenna, 1871–76.

Christian friends who think that the only conclusive evidence of piety is an attempt to preach. The sermon was not a landscape, not even so diversified as a prairie. It was a flat foggy bog, in which the preacher was too feeble even to flounder.

MONDAY, 7. Determined to loaf and rest, and so helped turn the washing machine and hang out clothes. Commenced to read the Epistles of Pliny the younger; not so much for their ability as for the pictures I hope to find in them of Roman life, in an age past the prime of Roman greatness and virtue, but yet before she had consciously lost her strength. Joe comes home this evening and brings a request from Ravenna that I write out my address. This will prolong my work but I think I will do it.

TUESDAY, 8. Spent a good share of the day in writing out the Ravenna address. It was better than I thought. We are so apt to judge things by their close that I had associated my speech with the storm that stopped it. Wrote nineteen small pages and read more in Pliny. Burke comes down here or I go to him every day and we run over the little nothings, or the middle sized somethings that come in our way. Took Joe to Garrettsville and visited Lodge No. 246 F.A.M.[115] in the evening.

WEDNESDAY, 9. Went to Burke's and read three chapters of his manuscript of a book on the evolution of the church. He proposes to apply the doctrine of evolution to ec[c]lesiastical history and to the growth of Theology. I think his book will be a success.[116] In the afternoon made further progress in my address and a book of Pliny. I am delighted with much in it, although he is conceited, vain and artificial. It seems like the writings of Addison's time, in its precise

---

[115] Garfield was a member of the Free and Accepted Masons during the last two decades of his life. He was initiated in 1861 into Magnolia Lodge, No. 20, Columbus. In 1864 he was raised in Columbus Lodge, No. 30. In 1865 he affiliated with Garrettsville Lodge, No. 246. In 1869 he became a charter member of Pentalpha Lodge, No. 23, Washington, D. C., thereby ending his membership in the Garrettsville Lodge.

[116] In 1878 Hinsdale published *The Jewish-Christian Church: A Monograph*; in his forward he noted that the chapters making up the book were originally written as parts of a much more ambitious work, which had been brought to a standstill several years before. In 1879 he published *The Ecclesiastical Tradition*.

and artificial spirit. Why have his epistles lived? But I am glad they have survived.

THURSDAY, 10.   Finished the Ravenna address in a reasonably satisfactory manner. Wrote some letters and finished the third book of Pliny. His letter (XVII) to Gallus in the second book is a charming description of his villa near Ostia, his Laurentinum. The description is too vague for a draughtsman, but while I was finishing the address Crete drew a sketch of the villa, and on the whole I think a very successful one. If I had time I would study the distribution of wealth among the Romans. The rich men must have been few in number, but very rich. I don't know how else there were such numbers of villas.

FRIDAY, 11.   Ravenna address got off in the morning train, and at ten the stage brought us a young girl. If she does well, it is well. The address has left my letters behind and the day was spent in bringing up this journal in pencil for Rose to copy and in Pliny's letters with some of my own far less entertaining. Burke spent an hour with me in chat. Prof. Wakefield called. Crete got a little time to sit with me in the Library part of the afternoon. And is the rest coming now? And if it does, won't it be laborious, or at least tiresome to manage? And now Pliny, art resting—or is the togated [togaed] life of the unseen world as busy as yours, late of Rome and Comum?

SATURDAY, 12.   I have today felt an unusual desire to sleep. Slept two hours after breakfast and was still very dull and sleepy. Wrote letters; made a swing for the children, and in doing so found I am a less agile climber than formerly. Read more in Pliny. Epistle 19, book IV, is a better picture of conjugal love than often appears among the ancients. In the late afternoon took Crete, Mollie and Irvin to Garrettsville. Home at seven and a half, when Mr. and Mrs. Cole of Garrettsville were awaiting us. Had a long visit—*inter alia de rebus publicis* [among other things on public affairs]. I stumbled by happy accident upon a passage in Lucretius' *De Rerum Natura*, Lib. I-63 which shows the oppression of religion, in any attempt to study nature. The same old case of Theology vs. Science, still pending in the courts of the human mind.

SUNDAY, 13.   Slept more and still am not rested. Attended church and heard a fair sermon from Burke. But he was tired too. In the afternoon Crete and I went to the old home on the hill, and spent a few hours with Burke and his wife. We four strolled in the woods in the old grass walks, which my feet have known these twenty years. I can see that my old friends the trees are growing old, but less rapidly than I. Burke has a passion for trees, knows their names and species, but does not know much about plants. Large objects and groups attract him, as oxen and the Constitution did Webster. The day was still and voiceless. Nature may sometimes reflect our own moods, but she seems wholly unsympathetic. She seems to say "I care for nothing; all shall go."

MONDAY, 14. Still feeling unwell, due partly to the reaction from overwork and partly to the imprudence of wearing an undershirt in which I had bathed [in] the Cuyahoga, with the boys, a few days ago. The little fellows are in the period when swimming seems to be about the highest good in life. Went to Burke's and listened to a few chapters of the book in which he is discussing the evolution of the church—its ecclesiastical polity and its theology, applying the modern doctrine of evolution to his subject. It forms a fine framework on which to arrange his facts, and will lead to the discovery of new relations of old facts.

TUESDAY, 15. Am better today, though not yet valid, as the Latins would say. Made some progress on my accumulated correspondence. Also read up newspapers and magazines on which I had fallen behind during the preparation of late addresses. Spent most of the afternoon in revising my Hudson speech for the press. I think it will be well to publish it, although my discussion of the railway problem will probably elicit some adverse criticism. I have risked an attack on the Dartmouth College Case. I believe I have struck some new and valuable lines of thought in the discussion of corporations.

WEDNESDAY, 16. Went to Cleveland with Burke and consulted with Marvin[117] and Baker to arrange Baker's bequest to Hiram College, by which he endows a chair with $1,000 per annum during his life, and gives a legacy of $10,000 at his death. Visited Carrie Ransom's studio and saw her fine picture of General Thomas at Chickamauga.

---

[117] Andrew J. Marvin, a Cleveland lawyer, was a member of the Board of Trustees of Hiram College, 1872–99.

In the evening several friends from Trumbull, Portage, Geauga, and Ashtabula counties met at my room at the Weddell and discussed the political situation of the 19th District. It was a fine example of that noble and unselfish friendship. There were present H. R. W. Hall, J. C. Beatty, S. P. Wolcott,[118] Harmon Austin, A. House,[119] W. C. Howells, Geo. H. Ford,[120] J. R. Conrad[121] and R. R[P]. Cannon. Spent the night at the Weddell.

THURSDAY, 17. Came home on the morning train. At Solon Jimmy and Sister Mary came on the train and went home with me. At Garrettsville got a croquet set for the children, and the rest of us. Letters again in the usual way. At one o'clock went to the College and heard a recitation of a vacation [class]. It was the speech of Colgocus and Agricola's reply. The hour brought by [back] fresh and happy memories of my work in the old building fifteen years ago. I now for the first time link Tacitus in association with Pliny the younger. In the evening played croquet with Burke, Crete and Martha. Visited much with Sister Mary.

FRIDAY, 18. Determined to publish a pamphlet edition of fifteen hundred copies of my address at Hudson, and set about a careful revision of it all and a re-writing of some parts. I find much pleasure in the work, more than I usually experience in revising. I find it neccessary to handle my quotations from Fourier very carefully. There is so much in his *Théorie des Quatre Mouvements et des Destinées Générales* that I cannot endorse nor indeed quite understand, that I may by quoting a part be suspected of following him. Received a

118 Simon Perkins Wolcott, a lawyer of Kent, Portage County, was a student of Garfield at the Eclectic. He was a member of the Ohio Senate, 1882–85.

119 Alonzo A. House, a businessman of Bristol, Trumbull County, was a member of the Board of Trustees of Hiram College, 1882–1900.

120 George H. Ford, a lawyer and banker of Burton, Geauga County, was the son of Seabury Ford (1801–1855), who was governor of Ohio, 1849–50. He was a member of the Ohio House of Representatives, 1872–75, and of the Ohio Senate, 1884–89. His brother, Robert Neil Ford, was associated with him in banking.

121 Joseph R. Conrad, a businessman of Atwater, Portage County, was a member of the Ohio House, 1872–73. In 1872 he offered to support Garfield for the senatorship.

letter from my classmate Captain Rockwell[122] of Fort Yuma, asking me to transact some delicate law business pertaining to his wife's estate in Baltimore. I will do it, if I find it feasible to undertake it.

SATURDAY, 19. Finished my revision of the Hudson address. In order however to send it to the printer's by the Evening Express, I have hurried the final revision too much. In one respect I should have studied the relation between its parts, maintained the proper perspective, if I may so use that word. Mother has been overhauling her old letters, and has found some from me as early as 1849. Indeed she has found the first one I ever wrote. She has some curious treasures in that way. I see that I had a very early passion for statistics. In the evening took Harry and Sister Mary to the cars, en route to Solon. Stopped at Dr. [E. B.] Lee's and played croquet an hour. Read Fourier in the evening. He was a man of immense grasp, but a dreamer.

SUNDAY, 20. Attended Church. As the Pastor was absent they had a social meeting, and at its close a business meeting at which the financial affairs of the church were discussed. This illustrates the power of long continued habit. For many years Father Ryder's influence dominated the Church and he fixed the habit of individual thrift and of raising but little money for church purposes. The result is that with

---

[122]Almon Ferdinand Rockwell (1835–1903) graduated with Garfield at Williams and studied medicine in Philadelphia, where in 1858 he received an M.D. degree. He practiced in Lockport and Oswego, New York until the Civil War. In 1861 he joined the staff of General Don Carlos Buell and participated in major campaigns in the West. He became an officer in the regular army and during most of the decade after the war served at various Western posts in the Quartermaster Department. He was transferred to Washington in 1874 and thereafter was often with Garfield, who in 1881 appointed him superintendent of Public Buildings and Grounds. In 1862 Rockwell married Henrietta Kerr Hunter. They became the parents of a son Don and a daughter Lulu who were friendly with the Garfield children. Henrietta and her sister Isabel Hunter Card had an interest in property in Baltimore which was partly owned by the Wells Brothers, who also owned adjoining property. Colonel Brewer was an elderly man who acted as agent for the Rockwell and Card interest. The Wells Brothers refused to contribute to the repair of the jointly owned property. Garfield, believing that the property would grow in value, advised Rockwell to buy the interest of the Wells Brothers.

one of the best preachers in the whole body the church totally neglects salaries and makes faces in its attempts to raise even what it pays.

MONDAY, 21. Answered a number of letters and read further in Pliny. I am greatly surprised that the Plinys have been so much neglected by classical students. He is but rarely mentioned in literature and yet we are indebted to him for many striking and interesting facts of Roman life in the first century of the Christian Era. He was very vain and had an intense passion for P. Perhaps no more than Cicero, his greater countryman. If I had the time, I would try to write a book on the distribution of wealth among the Romans. It must be that the enormous wealth of a small class left the multitude extremely poor. I would be glad to know what was the character of a distribution that produced such results.

TUESDAY, 22. Wrote a large number of letters and nearly caught up with my correspondence. Read further in Pliny; also brought up my neglected readings of the *Nation*. In the afternoon W. J. Ford came from Burton with his carriage and in the evening drove me home. Stopped at the house of my friend, the Honorable G. H. Ford, where a large company of his relatives and friends were assembled and where a very pleasant evening was passed. The stiffness of old Presbyterianism is rapidly giving way. Members of that Church young and old danced with great fun and enjoyment and evidently without scandal, a thing which could hardly have occurred twenty years ago.

WEDNESDAY, 23. Three carriage loads of the Fords with relatives and friends visited Punderson's Pond about three miles from Burton, taking along a little yacht. The pond is celebrated in connection with Mr. Bart Ridgeley. We sailed on the lake, swam in the lake, fired at a mark and played like boys generally. Returned to the old Ford Mansion for dinner at five. In the evening listened to an address in the Town Hall by Homer Woodward. Spent the night as before at G. H. Ford's.

THURSDAY, 24. Crete and Jimmy arrived at 8 o'clock and I met them at W. J. Ford's at breakfast. Played croquet until eleven o'clock, when we all attended the family picnic in the groves of the Fair Grounds. After dinner toasts were read, responses made, and antiquarian articles illustrating the early settlement of the town were exhibited. In conclusion I responded to a toast to the country, succeeding rather well. Together with several friends took tea at George H. Ford's and enjoyed a delightful drive to Hiram arriving home at nine in the evening.

FRIDAY, 25.   Took the morning train at Garrettsville for the East and at Girard caught the train on the new road from Ashtabula to Pittsburgh and reached New Castle, Pa. at noon. Burke met me at the Station and drove me to T. W. Phillips' where he and his wife were guests. Played croquet in the early part of the afternoon and at four o'clock went to Charles Phillips' on the other side of the town, where two other games of croquet were played and where we also took tea. The afternoon was spent pleasantly and we returned to Thomas Phillips' for the night.

SATURDAY, 26.   I am adding to my play days, the first I have enjoyed for nearly a year. Today was mainly devoted to croquet, some discussion of politics, theology and business intervened, but croquet was the main item in the bill of fair [fare]. Pennsylvania is becoming more and more a grim and dirty money making state. It will be necessary for me to tone up my affection for her to prevent losing it altogether. It rained powerfully in the evening.

SUNDAY, 27.   Attended the Sunday School in the morning where I made a short speech and listened to a powerful sermon from Burke in the forenoon and also another in the evening. He is growing steadily in strength and I feel sure that every increment of growth brings less rather than more of public attraction to his style. His mind is theological in its cast and deals with general principles. He should be more specific, more patriarchal. Very heavy rain in the evening.

MONDAY, 28.   At nine o'clock Burke and Mrs. Hinsdale left for Medina County, after playing a game of croquet. Thomas Phillips and I took the noon train, he for Rochester and I for Pittsburgh. Waited at the latter place until 6.40 during which time I finished the reading of Mr. Riddle's lectures on the law and lawyers, and on the philosophy of political parties.[123] There is much of value in this volume but on the whole I do not esteem it so highly as I do *Bart Ridgeley*. There is a good deal of intuitive power in Mr. Riddle's mind, and his mind acts quite free of the trammels which ordinarily

---

[123] Albert Gallatin Riddle, *Law Students and Lawyers, the Philosophy of Political Parties and Other Subjects: Eight Lectures Delivered before the Law Department of Howard University* (1873).

limit mental operations. He thinks that a political party will not die so long as it shows capacity to receive new ideas. Took the 6.40 P.M. train for the East.

TUESDAY, 29. Waked just before the train reached Baltimore and soon we entered the new tunnel which passes under the City and we were enabled to pass directly through without change of cars. This is the first time I have been able to avoid the delay and discomfort of the Baltimore omnibuses. Reach[ed] Washington at 8.50 and went directly to Welcker's, where I got breakfast and a bath. Call[ed] at 1227 I St. and found the house closed and being without a door key, I went to the Capitol and spent some time in the Library of Congress. Found the house open at four and Lizzie in it. Every thing going on well. After dinner at Wormley's Senator Sumner called on me and we drove for two hours and a half. Had a delightful conversation on books, men and things. He sketched an outline of his late European tour.[124]

WEDNESDAY, 30. Wrote letters, visited several of the Departments and transacted considerable business. I wish to preserve some of the points of Mr. Sumner's conversation of last evening, viz.: The grounds of his leaving home including discussions with Longfellow and other friends. Earl Granville's telegram inviting him to dine with him in London.[125] He called on Lady [Mrs.] Grote[126] and she gave him that portion of her husband's manuscript relating to the death of Socrates. His dinner with Lady Stanley and her husband the Dean of Westminster.[127] The tears of Lady S. at meeting him in the memory of her brother Sir Edward [Frederick] Bruce.[128] The visit of two days to the Chateaux. The etiquette with which he was received by the

[124] Charles Sumner made his last visit to Europe, September 3–November 26, 1872.

[125] Granville George Levesen-Gower (1815–1891), second Earl Granville, was British foreign secretary, 1870–74 and 1880–85.

[126] Harriet Lewin Grote (1792–1878), widow of George Grote (1794–1871), author of *The History of Greece*, 12 vols. (1846–56). Her own publications included *The Personal Life of George Grote* (1873).

[127] Arthur Penrhyn Stanley (1815–1881), dean of Westminster, 1864–81.

[128] Sir Frederick William Adolphus Bruce (1814–1867) died in Boston while British minister to the United States, 1864–67. He and the wife of Dean Stanley were the children of the seventh Earl of Elgin.

Duke of Devonshire.[129] His visit to Paris including his dinner with President Thiers[130] and their discussion of art. Thiers thought Michael Angelo by far the greatest artist, but was not ready to name the greatest work of art.

THURSDAY, 31.   Visited several of the Departments and transacted a considerable amount of business besides. Made arrangements with Mr. Carstens for painting several rooms of my house; also, made a contract with Bright to cut a window in the east wall of the Library and to put a grate in Mother's room. The day has been excessively hot and I shall be excessively glad to get back to the North.

August

FRIDAY, 1.   Took the nine A.M. train for Baltimore and reached the Mount Vernon Hotel at 11 A.M. Took a carriage and went to Fell's Point to look after the Rockwell and Card interest in the Kerr Estate. Called on several parties including Col. Brewer and the Wells Bros. Worked on the business until five P.M. when, having done all that could be done, returned to the hotel and took dinner. Translated several pages from the Latin of Sheaffer's Life of Pliny the Younger[131] and took the 8.40 P.M. train for the West en route for home. The day has been excessively hot, followed by rain in the evening.

SATURDAY, 2.   Reached Pittsburgh at 8.40 A.M. After breakfast took the train for Leetonia and spent the four hours of waiting in translating eight pages of *Vita Plinii*, and writing it out. It is pleasant to find that I have not lost my Latin, but that it readily comes back to me on call. The life I am translating is written with that thoroughness of detail that characterizes German scholarship. Nearly every statement is supported by reference to Pliny's Works. Took the three o'clock P.M. train for Garrettsville. Found Joe on the train and reached home at 6½ P.M.

---

[129] William Cavendish (1808–1891), seventh Duke of Devonshire, was known for his work in advancing British science and industry.

[130] Louis Adolphe Thiers (1797–1877), French statesman and historian, was president of the Third Republic, 1871–73.

[131] Probably Gottfried Heinrich Schaefer, whose edition of Pliny's works appeared in 1805.

SUNDAY, 3. Find myself quite unwell from the heat and overwork of the week. It is rarely that I stay at home from church, but I did so today. I do not always go because I prefer to for my own sake, but because I think a man should maintain the habit partly for his own sake and partly for the sake of others. Read further in the life of Pliny and commenced Cicero's *De Senectute*. The weather and difficulty of finding sufficient help make us conclude to break up for a few weeks and go to the Little Mountain, if I can get a cottage there.[132]

MONDAY, 4. Went to Cleveland and transacted some business and made arrangements with R. P. Wade[133] to rent a cottage at the Little Mountain and to go there near the end of this week or at the beginning of next. Visited Dr. Robison and took dinner with him. Went to the Printer's and read the proof of a portion of my Hudson address, the publication of which has already been unreasonably delayed by the printers, Nevins Bros. Spent the night at Dr. Robison's. In the evening Mr. Cowles came, and we visited until a late hour. He is a man of good abilities and of much information. Played a few games of chess with him and Dr. Robison.

[132] Garfield rented the "handsomely furnished" cottage of Amasa Stone, Jr., of Cleveland, for $3.75 a day (with coal oil and the services of chambermaids and lamp man included in this charge). Meals in the Club dining room were $1.75 a day for adults and $1 for children.

Little Mountain is a standstone formation about six miles from Lake Erie, in the northwest corner of Chardon, Geauga County. On its top is an irregular high tableland, half a mile wide, with precipitous rocky margins around much of it. It was largely covered with pine, oak and chestnut trees. The Mountain House was built there during the 1830's. During the 1850's D. W. Stocking of Chardon built a house and cottages. A new chapter in the history of Little Mountain opened when wealthy Clevelanders got control of it, "and converted it into a remote suburb of Cleveland." Stocking sold the Club House to the Little Mountain Club in 1872.

[133] Randall Palmer Wade (1835–1876), son of Jeptha Homer Wade (1811–1890), was associated with his father in business and was also secretary and treasurer of the Little Mountain Club. The elder Wade was one of Cleveland's wealthiest businessmen. Although the foundation of his fortune was the telegraph (he was the first president of Western Union), he became involved in many enterprises, including banking. His home and that of his son on Euclid Avenue were showplaces.

TUESDAY, 5. Went home in the morning train. Wrote letters and read Cicero. The discussion of old age is very clever and adroit but hardly sound. No doubt there are compensations for the loss of youth and its impulses, but most of them come from experience and not from old age. If we could have youth and with it the experience which old age brings, perhaps we should see that Cicero's argument is wholly sound. I feel the need of the German Language and I am tempted to undertake its acquisition. What I learned of it in college has nearly evaporated. The stores of German scholarship ought to be open to a man who wishes a liberal and broad culture. I am not too old to master it, but perhaps too busy. We shall see.

WEDNESDAY, 6. I took up Prof. Baird's [Blair's][134] book on the ancient pronunciation of language and read about half of it. The attempt has been made in a really scientific spirit to ascertain how the Romans sounded their letters, and I think it will be ascertained with approximate accuracy. It is clear to my mind for example, that the Latin C was always read like K. The argument against it is mainly founded on the alleged absurdity of saying Kikero, but that sounds odd to us only from habit and from its similarity in sound to our word "Kick," which of course has no force as an argument. The German pronunciation Tscetscero is better than our English method, but still is indefensible.

THURSDAY, 7. Nearly finished the book on the Latin pronunciation. It is evident that great attention was paid to euphony, and nicety of pronunciation by the Latins. I am inclined to think that the age of purism is the age past the grip and originality of a people—when they have time for such niceties. They have but little time for such delicacies when they are busy with strong thinking. Read several chapters in [De] Senectute. The answer of Themistocles to the citizen of Seriphos, was good, viz.: "True I should not have been enobled had I been a citizen of your town. But even if you had been an Athenian, you would have gained no prominence at all." The spirit of the joke is a part of human nature.

FRIDAY, 8. Crete and I went to Garrettsville and took the morning train to Youngstown to see a girl, but on reaching there found she

[134] Walter Blair, *Latin Pronunciation: An Inquiry into the Proper Sounds of the Latin Language during the Classical Period* (1873).

had already hired to Miller Rany. We sat about the Depot for an hour, and I finished the book on Latin Pronunciation. They seem to have settled the ancient sounds pretty well except in reference to the dipthongs. We returned to Garrettsville at 2 P.M. and drove up to Uncle Charles Raymond's and spent the afternoon with a large company of friends. Played croquet and visited until evening, when Crete and I went to Ozias Allyn's and purchased butter for now and next winter. Reached home late in the evening, after a pleasant drive. We found Nellie Rockwell and her boy at Father Rudolph's and had a good visit.

SATURDAY, 9. Spent the day visiting, writing and reading [De] *Senectute*. I have now read half of the work and have found no passage which I have not been able to construe satisfactorily, without the aid of a lexicon. I regret that I have not equally well kept up my Greek. Though the Greek is easier of construction than the Latin, it is not so easily remembered. Perhaps, however, this may arise from the fact that we have more practice in Latin, because it so frequently appears in our general and professional literature. In the evening played croquet at Mr. Stanhope's with Mr. and Mrs. Stanhope,[135] Mr. and Mrs. Hank[136] and others, and took tea with them all. I am having more rest than at any other time since last summer.

SUNDAY, 10. Attended church and listened to a sermon from Rev. Mr. Taylor of Pa. He said many good things but it was of the dissertation style and filled with a kind of pietism which is disagreeable and is not productive of spiritual muscle. The motive of getting to heaven is in reality as selfish as the desire to get money or fame. The old motto of *Esse quam videri* [To be rather than to seem] might profitably be changed to *Esse quam possidere* [To be rather than to have]. Why not? What we are, what we become is of vastly more consequence than what we get or attain objectively. Read Cicero and visited with Nellie. The day went out in a drizzle.

MONDAY, 11. Took the whole family—wife, five children, and Mary McGrath to Garrettsville, and thence to Cleveland. Stopped at Dr.

[135] R. Stanhope, a Hiram farmer, was a member of the Board of Trustees of Hiram College, 1879–82.
[136] Richard M. Hank, a Hiram businessman, was a member of the Board of Trustees of Hiram College, 1872–80, and treasurer of the board, 1868–76.

Robison's and took dinner. Read the final proof of my Hudson address. Went shopping with Crete, and at 4 P.M. took the train to Mentor and stage thence to Little Mountain, where we arrived in time for tea, and established ourselves in the cottage of Mr. Stone, where we hope to have a little rest from the cares of politics and to give Crete and her hired girl a rest from the heavy tasks of housekeeping without sufficient help. The Cleveland Club has pleasantly arranged their part of the Mountain for comfort and rest.

TUESDAY, 12. Spent most of the day in the little affairs of arranging the cottage for the comfort of our family during our stay here. Pushed [*De*] *Senectute* and found a passage which I don't quite get the construction of. A cold drizzly rain came on which makes the Mountain too cool and wet for comfort. A delegation of citizens from New Lyme followed me here to push the Post Office fight now raging in that town. It really seems that the smaller an office is, the more feeling there is in the adjustment of it. Everybody comprehends a little, and not many a great one.

WEDNESDAY, 13. Made some further arrangements for the comfort of the cottage and to get ourselves settled. In the afternoon attended a burlesque Woman's Rights Convention. Conducted by Mrs. Hale of Cleveland, assisted by Mrs. Bates and others. The ladies showed a good deal of brilliant wit and ability in their speeches. They dragooned me into a speech which was rather a difficult thing to do under the circumstances. The day was fine and the attendance large, both houses, the Club and the Lake View, contributing to swell the audience. Rest and recreation are so nearly strangers to me that they are specially welcome and will be prized for a short time.

THURSDAY, 14. A cold drizzling rain made the day gloomy and uncomfortable. The cottage was damp and I spent most of the day in getting and putting up a stove. I found in the loft of the barn an old stove with the hearth and one leg broken and in getting it in order experienced some of the feelings expressed by the Danbury News man.[137] It is remarkable how much comfort there is in a wretched old stove when it is the best you can get. This would not be tolerated

[137] James Montgomery Bailey (1841–1894), humorist associated with the *Danbury* (Connecticut) *News* and known as the Danbury News Man, published two books in 1873, *Life in Danbury* and *The Danbury News Man's Almanac.*

in any farm house on the Reserve, but tonight we are all proud of it. The children think there was never a nicer stove. The soft rain and the external gloom make the interior comfort of the cottage more marked. Relativity is the great gauge of life.

FRIDAY, 15. This mountain is the abrupt termination of the rocky ridge that divides the waters of the Lakes from those of the Gulf. It stands out like a precipitous headland seven hundred and fifty feet above the lake. It does not seem to be an upheaval. I can see no evidence of direct volcanic action in its formation. It is a conglomerate of sandstone and quartz pebbles, the latter evidently smoothed and rounded by the wash of a prehistoric ocean and the present strata in which they are embedded were formed in [a] later geologic period. The caves and isolated cliffs are evidently the effect of water, and the breaking off of crags undermined by the waves. In some places the effects appear to a casual observer as the effect of volcanic action. But I think they are not.

SATURDAY, 16. This day has been an improvement on its predecessors and I have had an opportunity still further to revive my old love for Geology. The lengthy fissures and deep caves I have visited today, still further confirm me in the belief that this ridge is water born. The great ocean must have receded and left this as an enlarging island, beaten and honeycombed by the waves. The ridge extends through Thompson and Nelson where it presents quite the same appearance, and thence exhibits itself in Hiram in the somewhat modified condition, more sand and less quartz, but recovers its normal features in Twinsburgh, Kent, Cuyahoga Falls, and Akron. It was probably the glacial ocean of which Agassiz speaks, which covered this continent at the time this ridge was formed. Agassiz thinks that the lakes were a string of stranded glaciers which ploughed their beds in the soft rock of the uprising continent. What a lonely stretch of dateless ages rises to our view, as we think of this picture.

SUNDAY, 17. Dr. Streator and I took a horse and buggy and drove to Mentor where we attended the Disciple meeting and heard a good sermon by C. B. Lockwood of Cleveland. Such a sermon is not often heard from a layman, nor even from a professional clergyman. His theme was the Lord's Prayer, as read by the light of Swedenborg's strong and clear intellect. After meeting we went to old brother Thomas Clapp's and took dinner, and had a good visit. It was a fine and healthful awakening of old memories. We then called at Henry Clapp's but found Eliza too ill to see us. Drove back to the Mountain in the gray of the evening. It is due to a man's life and soul that he stand by his past as long as he can reasonably approve it. And for this reason as well as others I am glad to stand by the old memories of the Disciples.

MONDAY, 18. A model Post Office row at New Lyme, Ashtabula County, has been following me for several weeks. Letters, petitions and, finally, delegations for and against the Centre and the south part of the town have vexed my soul, with the smallness of the material out of which men can get up a fight. Even large-minded sensible men get stirred up, after a ridiculously small fight has got fairly started. It requires some patience to listen to the small details of such a quarrel, but there is a certain psysological [psychological] interest, with which I study the parties to this strife and the motives by which they are moved. I have had several long sessions with the belligerants since I came to the Mountain and for the reason given above really enjoyed it. Still it did not lessen my distress at the smallness of human nature.

TUESDAY, 19. Went with Dr. Streator to various points in Mentor, where he was looking for a farm for his nephew. This gave me a fine opportunity to study the growth of real estate in this delightful farming country and what is far better the trip has added another ring of growth to the very dear and solid friendship that I find growing up between us. He is a man of quiet and gentle demeanor, of great native warmth of heart with a large generous mind, cultivated and rendered self-contained and prudent by much knowledge of life and especially of its hard business side. Experience has hardened the pulp of his nature into the solid and substantial material of character. We stopped in the evening at J. C. Hodges' and talked of old times and war and we sung "John Brown" and the "Battle Hymn" together.

WEDNESDAY, 20. Another delightful day with Dr. Streator, among the farms of Lake County. He told me the story of his early life, which is full of pathos and tenderness guided by a bold and manly spirit. Such a man deserves the eminent success which I am glad to know the Doctor has achieved. In the morning read Stephen's remarkable book *Liberty, Equality and Fraternity*. The author attacks some of the commonly received opinions in regard to these three topics. He makes a powerful attack on Mill's doctrine of Liberty. He seems to belong to the Carlyle school—the worshippers of force—who think the mass of mankind are asses and need the strong curb and hand of a master. There may be more truth in this view than we Republicans are willing to admit.

THURSDAY, 21. Stephen raises a very rational doubt in reference to the separation of Church and State. He says that the prevailing notion that the State should keep hands off in reference to religion, means not so much a tribute to liberty, as a confession of public skepticism or at least indifference to the questions of religion. He says that if the truths of religion were really believed and felt to be vital to the highest good of men and nations, governments would legislate for them, would fight for them and against their antagonists as they now do against political error. Every page of his book challenges thought and sets the tides of reflection in flow. But I am resting now, not thinking closely.

FRIDAY, 22. In answer to a call from Harmon Austin, I went to Warren, via Cleveland, dining at Dr. Robison's, and arrived at Austin's house in the evening. The knot of enemies that have been assailing me in Trumbull County have resolved that no one shall be nominated to any office in that county without first declaring himself my enemy. In the evening I consulted with friends and advised them to resist this impudent and unjust demand and fight on the proffered issue. The enemy is resolved to utilize all the clamor that is now raging against Congress, and make it tell on my future. I think they can be beaten in this new Trumbull County move, if my friends offer a bold front and no compromise. After a late session with friends staid at Austin's over night.

SATURDAY, 23. Accepted the invitation of A. House of Bristol to accompany a Sunday School Excursion to Ashtabula. Twenty-one cars were filled at Girard, Niles, and other places along the line of the new Ashtabula, Youngstown and Pittsburgh Railroad, and with this company I went over the line for the first time. We had a very pleasant picnic and stroll along the piers and the lake shore. It was delightful to watch the emotions of those who had never seen the lake before. It is sad to think how many sensations can never again come, such as first impressions of things that become passé. I formed some very pleasant acquaintance and felt the public pulse through the wrists of the picnic. Took evening Express for Painesville and then by carriage to Little Mountain at 7 P.M. where I found Dr. Robison and wife as Dr. Streator's guests, D. P. Rhodes and several other Cleveland gentlemen. New rules.

SUNDAY, 24. The rain prevented us from going to Church at Mentor. The Episcopal service was read in the Club hall by Prof. Sanford[138] of Cleveland. At the Sunday School Dr. R. and I spoke. The members of the two clubs united and made a pleasant and effective school. The power of a little child over men and women is one of the great forces of the world. In the afternoon the sun came out and the two doctors' families and mine went rambling in the woods. The Mountain is rich in ferns, mosses and lichens, and some fine varieties were gathered. Besides the pines that crown the summit, there is what I have never before seen, an abundance of Chestnut Oak, a species whose bark and leaves very closely resembling [resemble] the chestnut, but yet it is a sturdy tough oak. Dr. R. called my attention to it. In the evening we visited at Dr. Streator's cottage and had a very pleasant time. Dr. R. is a faithful friend and so is Dr. S.

MONDAY, 25. After breakfast Dr. Streator's family and part of mine took the hack for Kirtland and after a pleasant ride along the Chagrin River, visited the Mormon Temple. I never think of that strange people without a mixture of admiration and contempt. Admiration for the boldness of the attempt they made in the world of ideas and actions, and contempt for what appears to be the hollow shams and deceptions by which they carried out their objects. In looking at this deserted temple, I can not repress a feeling of regret at the monument of failure they left. Yet they deserve a grander failure than this. Their origin was curiously connected with the early history of the Disciples. Indeed the theological doctrines of the two are almost identical in every thing except in reference to spiritual gifts and polygamy. Sidney Rigdon[139] must have stamped his own ideas very

---

[138] Solomon N. Sanford was principal of the Cleveland Female Seminary, a position he had held since the spring of 1858. In 1867 he sailed with Mark Twain to the Holy Land as a member of the party whose experiences are recorded in *The Innocents Abroad* (1869).

[139] Sidney Rigdon (1793–1876), who had been a Baptist preacher, was introduced to Campbellite ideas by Adamson Bentley, whose daughter he married. After acting a number of years with the Disciples, he embraced

strongly upon the movement. Returned to the Mountain in the afternoon and spent the remainder of the day in recreation and loafing. This must be my last day with the Streators here. The acquaintance has been very pleasant.

TUESDAY, 26. Took the morning train for Cleveland, taking with me a part of Dr. Streator's family. After transacting some business, took the afternoon train for Ravenna, and then took the Atlantic & Great Western R. R. for Wadsworth, where General Don A. Pardee, Capt. Pardee and Capt. Henry[140] met me, and we drove in the night and rain to the house of Capt. Pardee, where we had a pleasant visit preparatory to the Reunion of the 42d O.V.I. to be held at Medina tomorrow. The group of friends gathered at Pardee's house tonight has passed through remarkable changes during the last twelve years. In 1861 Don was a young lawyer in Medina, Geo. K. Pardee and Chas. E. Henry were my students in Hiram, I a teacher and State Senator. We were all looking out upon the opening war with the apprehensions and hopes of young men looking into [the] dreadful unknown, the like of which may never again be seen in

---

Mormonism in 1830, and became a close associate of Joseph Smith. In 1832 Smith and Rigdon were tarred and feathered in Hiram, where Mormonism had made great progress and had aroused much excitement. Many on the Western Reserve believed that Rigdon had written at least a part of the Book of Mormon. After the death of Smith, he broke with the Western Mormons and for a time led an Eastern group.

140 Charles E. Henry (1835–1906) of Geauga County was one of Garfield's most devoted friends. He attended the Eclectic during Garfield's principalship, and joined the 42d Ohio Infantry Regiment when it was organized. In the army he attained the rank of first lieutenant, although in later life he was always known as "Captain" Henry. In 1869 Garfield secured for him an appointment as railway mail agent, and four years later a much more lucrative position as special agent of the Post Office Department. His travels in connection with this position made it possible for him to act as confidential reporter and agent for Garfield. He was at Columbus in January, 1880, when Garfield was elected senator, and at the Republican National Convention in Chicago the following spring. In 1881 Garfield appointed him U. S. Marshal of the District of Columbia, a position from which Arthur removed him in 1882. There are many letters from him in the Garfield Papers. He is the subject of an excellent biography, *Captain Henry of Geauga, a Family Chronicle* (1942), by his son Frederick A. Henry.

this Republic. Tonight we are men in middle life, to whom the first sensations of manhood have become things of the past and to whom its activities have become living realities. Spent the night here. WEDNESDAY, 27. Two carriages took Mrs. Pardee, Capt. G. K. Pardee, Gen'l D. A. Pardee, Capt. Henry and me to Medina. We stopped at the Hotel where many of our comrades were assembled. At ten A.M. the Regiment assembled and organized for business. At 11 we met on the public square where we were welcomed by the Hon. H. G. Blake,[141] to whom I responded. Then reassembled in the Hall and enjoyed a fine reunion of over two hundred members of the 42d O.V.I. I know of no organization of soldiers in which there is so much cordial comradeship and so little ill feeling, as in our old regiment. We had a good dinner at the hotel, and in the evening the young people of Medina gave the regiment a ball at the Hall. Sat up until a late hour with Sheldon, Pardee and Henry and had a pleasant reunion and visit. Hotel over night.

THURSDAY, 28. Took the morning train to Cleveland, where I met Crete and our two oldest boys. Did some shopping and examined Nevins and [Brother's] print of my Hudson address. It is the worst piece of work that I have ever had done. So bad that I refused to accept it and they have agreed to [re]print eight pages on which are the greatest number of provoking blunders. It was an attempt on my part to get a job done more cheaply than at Fairbanks', an attempt I shall never repeat. We took the four P.M. train for Mentor, and thence by stage reached the Club House on the Mountain in time for tea. The ride was delightful, and the coolness of the Mountain was most grateful after the heat and dust of the day in the city and in the cars.

FRIDAY, 29. After working up correspondence Crete and I went down to Mentor and visited Henry Clapp and his family, who resided in Hiram many years when I was at the head of the Institute. Eliza Glasier, née Clapp, is at her father's, and is broken down by overwork. She was very bright and ambitious, and after losing her husband, and passing through the wide realm of grief, turned to work teaching, and in three years by over work broke down her nervous

---

[141] Harrison Blake, a member of the Medina law firm of Blake & Woodward, had been in both the Ohio House and Senate during the 1840's.

system and is an almost helpless invalid. It was delightful, not-[wit]hstanding the sadness of it, to review the school work of fifteen and eighteen years ago and see what manner of people we were in those days.

About sunset Crete and I returned to the Mountain—along the sandy roads and among the beautiful farms of this lake coast.

SATURDAY, 30. Our future as a family is more than usually uncertain. What the next year of politics will bring is most problematical. We have sold our little home in Hiram and cannot conveniently stay at Father Rudolph's next summer. I have therefore bought a share in this Club for $400.00 and have contracted for the building of a cottage for $625, so that we can come from Washington next July and spend the Summer and early Autumn here. If I stay in Congress this arrangement will be convenient. If I do not I hope to settle in Cleveland at the law, and still the Club will be of use in the hot weather. It is a very good place for children and much of our immediate future must be devoted to them. Listened to the music and songs at the Hall in the evening.

SUNDAY, 31. I intended to go down to Mentor to meeting but there were no teams to be had, and I could not go. An Episcopal minister happened [to be here], who read the Service of his church, and preached a stupid, but fortunately short sermon. We then had Sunday School and I spoke a short time to the school and the young people. Then a party of us took a delightful walk across the Western side of the Mountain to a cliff called the Temple. The view is quiet but charming and the mosses are finer than any I have seen here. The party were Mrs. Wade, Mrs. Bates, two or three other ladies and Crete and I. Poor Mrs. Wade is quite an invalid and the walk was too much for her. This life of ours has been something like life on ship-board so far as its isolation and freedom are concerned.

September

MONDAY, 1. Got a horse and buggy and with Crete drove to Painesville and stopped at A. L. Tinker's.[142] On my arrival found that

---

[142] A. L. Tinker, a Painesville lawyer; his wife was the sister of Garfield's friend Wallace J. Ford.

there was a County Convention in session. I was embarrassed by the fact, for it has been my desire to keep wholly aloof from county politics. The Convention appointed a Committee to wait on me and invite me to address the Convention. I did so and spoke half an hour. It seemed to be well received by the convention. In the afternoon Mr. and Mrs. Tinker took us to Fairport harbor where we met a Mr. Garfield who is in charge of the Government repairs at that place. Returned to Painesville about sunset, and after tea, drove in the edge of the evening back to the Mountain, stopping by the way at J. C. Hodges' and singing "John Brown" and Co. It has been a delightful day.

TUESDAY, 2. Today we spent most of the time in preparations for leaving the Mountain tomorrow morning. We made and received calls from our Mountain friends, settled the bills and during the day received a telegram from Mr. Pierce of Hiram that he would come for us with his big wagon. On the whole our stay has been very healthful for the children. The children with whom they have associated are not rough and nasty in talk as most of those who have had no tight rein held upon them. In this respect I think we have been fortunate. For ourselves we have rested and have formed some very pleasant acquaintances. We were forced to go to the Mountain because we could not get a hired girl. In the evening I called on Mr. Ferris, who lives on the side of the Mountain. He is a man of culture but stubborn and eccentric.

WEDNESDAY, 3. At 7 A.M. Mr. Pierce came and at ten A.M. we bade good-by to the Mountain. The great spring wagon held our three trunks and a box. We passed down the West slope and turned Northward on the Chardon road, passing through Chardon and reaching Wallace Ford's at Burton by one o'clock P.M. in a heavy rain storm. There met Mother who had just arrived on a visit. Remained there until 5 P.M. when the rain ceased and we left for Hiram. The storm began again and it rained heavily until we reach[ed] home at 8 P.M. thoroughly drenched.

THURSDAY, 4. Took the morning train at Garrettsville for Baconsburgh, where Professor E. B. Wakefield met me and drove me to Green, Trumbull Co., where the Second Ohio Cavalry was holding its Reunion in the grove. About a thousand people had assembled and I addressed soldiers and citizens. At the conclusion of the address a picnic dinner was given in the grove. I then went home with Wakefield to supper and in the evening an impromptu soldiers' meeting was held in the church, and I spoke about an hour. Several of the soldiers spoke and we had an excellent meeting. Spent the night at Wakefield's.

FRIDAY, 5. Wakefield drove me to Baconsburgh. He [We] stopped at Aaron Davis' and took dinner. After dinner called on the Reverend Mr. [D. P.] Thayer at Baconsburgh Village and at one o'clock took the train for the West and reached home in the afternoon. Found a very large mail awaiting me, which kept me busy most of the evening, to read.

SATURDAY, 6. Spent the day in answering letters and bringing up my work which has been much neglected during my absence at the Mountain. My visit to Green I think was [a] very successful one. The meetings [speeches] were well received especially that of the evening, in both of which not a word was said about politics. I am satisfied that a great many prejudices were removed. I had never before visited Green and found the people very pleasant and intelligent. Visited Burke in the afternoon and on the whole made the day an effective one in clearing my docket of back work.

SUNDAY, 7. Attended Church and had a good sermon in the morning from Burke. It is rarely that I have passed a month with so little intellectual work as during the time since I went to the Mountain. But I needed the rest and the restoration of fibre which the month gave me. I dread the coming campaign. It is difficult to [for] me to behave with decency and dignity in view of the entanglements connected with the matter. I shall take Napoleon's rule of doing too little rather than too much, or rather his rule was when in doubt do nothing. I am not sufficiently in doubt to take that course, but shall lean in that direction.

MONDAY, 8. Took the morning train for the East and reached New Castle at noon. Thomas W. Phillips met me at the cars and took me to his house. After dinner we went to the Court House and found that the Oil City vs. Phillips Bros. [case] was about to be called. It was reached just before the close of the day. I was admitted to the bar of this county and had a consultation with the New Castle lawyers and Mr. [Barnet W.] Lacy, Att'y from Philadelphia, who represents the Brooke and Barrington interest. Played croquet in the evening at Charles Phillips', with Isaac, Charles and Thomas. Spent the night at Thomas'.

TUESDAY, 9. Court met at nine o'clock and our case was called. After several preliminary motions had been made, the other side asked for a continuance, and the case was set for special term the first week in November. It is the most singular case I have known. It was tried on its merits by a bill in equity and passed a final judgement in the Supreme Court; but execution was delayed until our opponents gave bonds securing us against the double payment of the judgment, or until the suit in Lawrence County shall be determined; which was then understood to be a suit to determine whether the Richardson Bros. were parties or not. But the suit has now assumed more formidable proportions, and includes the merits of the whole case and it really proposes to try over the issue already determined in the Supreme Court. Took tea at Thomas Phillips' and played croquet in the evening. Spent the night at Thomas'.

WEDNESDAY, 10. Thomas and I started in a double carriage for the Oil Regions of Butler County. We reached Centerville for a late dinner and then drove on through the rough broken country and reached the little oil village called Modoc towards sundown. It revives my old memories of the upper oil country in 1865. Spent the night in the upper story of Capt. Jack's store. I suppose this town was named Modoc because Mr. Jack, known as "Capt. Jack," is one of its chief business men.[143]

THURSDAY, 11. After breakfast we visited several wells in the vicinity of Modoc and then drove several miles to the Northeast. Visited the various developements in the neighborhood and finally the Gas Well, which for several weeks has been pouring out a volume of gas sufficient to light the City of Pittsburgh. This oil developement is more remarkable than anything I have ever seen. There are over a hundred wells in operation covering a territory about six miles in length and about two and [a] half miles wide. The wells average a depth of two hundred (?) feet and all of them flowing. The oil product is so great that the price has fallen to about eighty-five cents

[143] Captain Jack (1837?–1873), a Modoc Indian sub-chief, led part of his people in the Modoc War, 1872–73, in resistance to the government's efforts to force them to return to the Klamath Reservation. He was captured on June 1, 1873, and hanged on October 3.

per barrel. The old system of barreling and wagoning oil has passed away and it [is] now forced through pipes to the railroad eighteen miles distant, and to Parker's (?) Landing on the Allegheny 15 miles distant. In the evening we drove back towards New Castle as far as Centerville where we passed the night after partaking of an excellent supper at the hotel.

FRIDAY, 12. This hotel is the best specimen of the real old country tavern I think I have seen for many a year. We had an excellent breakfast and everything substantial and well cooked. Drove to New Castle reaching there about eleven o'clock. After taking dinner at Thomas Phillips' he and I and Mr. Agnew went to Isaac Phillips' and spent the afternoon playing croquet. We continued the game until nearly 8 o'clock in the evening, closing the last game by lamp light. Returned to Thomas Phillips' and spent the night.

SATURDAY, 13. Took the nine o'clock train for Warren accompanied by —— Phillips and his wife. We reached Warren at 11 o'clock; stopped at Harmon Austin's until after dinner, when we took the one o'clock train for Garrettsville where Mr. Ford's team met us and took us to Hiram. We reached there about four o'clock P.M. where a large mail awaited me. Spent nearly the whole evening in reading it and in bringing up the other accumulated business. Made several appointments for the campaign.

SUNDAY, 14. Attended church and listened as usual to a good solid sermon from Burke. Spent the afternoon and evening in gathering materials for my address on Tuesday next, before the Pioneer Association at Burton. I am suffering from a severe cold and do not feel fit for very hard work. I am surprised to find what rich material opens up before me in regard to the Pioneer History of this Western Reserve. It is a great shame that we have no carefully prepared history of it. The men are fast dying who saw the greatness of its growth.

MONDAY, 15. Spent nearly the whole day in working up notes for the address. The plan of my speech is: First. The Romantic period of discovery on this continent. Second. The struggle of different nations for its possession. Third. The causes which gave the Northwest territory to the U. S. Fourth. The origin and settlement of the Western Reserve. At 4 o'clock P.M. Mr. Hoadley came and took

Mother Garfield and Mother Rudolph and myself to Burton. We arrived in the evening and spent the night with Wallace [Ford] and Mary. Had a very pleasant evening. Late at night made some further preparations for the address.

TUESDAY, 16. At eleven o'clock about three thousand people had assembled on the fair grounds at Burton, and at 12 they had a very pleasant picnic. Shortly after dinner the County Historical Pioneer Society was organized and a large number of interesting relics of the early settlements were displayed. Several speeches were made by pioneer settlers and at two o'clock I commenced the delivery of my address which occupied something over an hour.[144] The address was mainly statistical but I believe the details were new to most of my hearers, and I think I succeeded in raising a good deal of interest in the subject of our pioneer history. Father Rudolph and Jimmy had driven down from Hiram in the morning and at three o'clock at the conclusion of my address Jimmy and I started for home reaching Hiram at five o'clock where I found Crete ready to go with me to the train. We reached Garrettsville at 6 and taking the train for Cleveland reached Dr. Robison's house at half-past seven to meet with the Quintinkle. Isaac Reed [Errett], Harrison Jones, Dr. Streator and wife, Dr. Robison and wife, and Crete and I were the members present. After an elegant supper we brought up the records of the Society and initiated Crete and Mrs. Streator, and we all signed the Constitution.

WEDNESDAY, 17. At 9 o'clock in the morning Harry Jones and Crete and I went to Newburgh to attend the funeral of my cousin Abram Garfield. We went to Uncle Thomas' house where his children and a large number of relatives were assembled. Abram died at Saratoga and his body has been brought here for burial. He was a man of fine business ability and had made a great success as the manager of hotels. The funeral sermon was preached by the Rev. Mr. Curtis of the Presbyterian Church assisted by Jones. Abram was buried at Lake View Cemetery in East Cleveland. After the funeral we returned by way of Cleveland and spent the night at Dr. Robison's.

THURSDAY, 18. Took the morning train for Hiram and reached home at ten o'clock. Spent the day in bringing up my correspondence and

[144] See *Pioneer and General History of Geauga County* (1880), pp. 9–21.

arranging appointments for the Campaign. I have taken a case for the Territory of Montana which I must argue in the Supreme Court, and between now and the first of October must write a brief and have it printed for the use of the Court. It is a case that involves the doctrine of the appointing power of the Executive Officer to fill a vacancy occurring in vacation, where no express provision is made in the organic law. I shall probably need to go to Washington to get the records in the case.[145]

FRIDAY, 19. Spent the day in working up correspondence and in making preparations for an agricultural address to be delivered at Edinburgh, Portage Co. tomorrow. The farmer's movement is growing to be a formidable one, but like most organizations impelled by the wrath of its founders, the grangers, as it was in some portions of the country, seem to have no well founded knowledge of the real evils of which they complain. They are assailing railroads when they should assail the legislation out of which railroads have become what they are. Sent to Garrettsville in the evening for livery team for use tomorrow.

SATURDAY, 20. After an early breakfast Jimmy and I started for Ravenna, where we arrived at nine o'clock. At ten o'clock in company with Halsey Hall, E. P. Brainerd, J. Meharg and S. Stimson[146] of Marietta, we drove to Edinburgh, stopping at the house of Isaac Williams for dinner, and then went to the Grove near the centre of the town and there, after music by the Ravenna Band, I addressed an audience of about three thousand. I spoke nearly an hour and a half and discussed this question: The American Farmer of the

---

[145] Garfield took the case at the request of his friend Governor B. F. Potts of Montana Territory. William Rodgers, who had been appointed territorial auditor by the legislature and later elected by the people, refused to surrender his office to James Fisk, who had been appointed by Potts when the legislature was not in session. Fisk brought action in the district court of the Territory and won his case. Although the Supreme Court of the Territory denied the power of the governor to make recess appointments, it upheld the lower court in respect to Rodgers. Rodgers then appealed to the U. S. Supreme Court. Garfield represented the Territory before the Supreme Court, which issued a mandate to effect the ouster of Rodgers, but did not go into the question of the governor's appointing power.

[146] Probably Rodney Metcalf Stimson, a member of the Ohio Senate, 1870–73, who had been editor of the *Marietta Register*, 1862–72.

Future; what manner of man he will be? what manner of wife and family will he have? what kind of home will he have? I discussed this question in the light of the influences now at work upon the avocation of the farmer. I succeeded more to my satisfaction than I usually do. Drove back to Hiram in the afternoon. Called by way of Mr. Curtis' in Charlestown.

SUNDAY, 21. Took the morning train at Garrettsville on the Atlantic and Great Western Road to Elmira, N.Y. On the way read a considerable portion of Castelar's *Old Rome and New Italy*,[147] a book of rare eloquence written by an orator and statesman of more than ordinary power. His discussion and history of the Catacombs of Rome give me a new view of the meaning of those remarkable works. I look with a kind of sadness upon the efforts of Castelar to introduce republican institutions in Spain. I fear the intelligence of that country is not up to the level of the republican idea. Reached Elmira at ten P.M. where I met General S. C. Boynton[148] and spent the night at the American House.

MONDAY, 22. Took the six o'clock train on the Northern Central Road passing through Williamsport to Harrisburg, a road which I have never travelled before. We arrived in time for dinner and stopped at the Arlington. Read still further in Castelar during the day's journey and also spent some time in conversation with General Boynton on the political situation. I dread this campaign more than any I have engaged in for many years.

TUESDAY, 23. Spent the day in business at the several departments and in getting the materials for the Montana case in the Supreme Court. Secured the appointment of Capt. Charles E. Henry as Special Agent of the P. O. Dep't. The business of a Member of Congress must have more than quadrupled during the last twenty years. I cannot be away from home a week without finding a large mass

[147] Emilio Castelar, *Old Rome and New Italy*, translated by Mrs. Arthur Arnold (1873).

[148] Sylvanus C. Boynton, a New York lawyer. In 1881 it was said that he spent the winters in Washington, where he lobbied and gambled, and the summers in Saratoga, where he had a card room. Shortly before the election of 1880 he wrote to Garfield that he, his son, a student in Columbia Law College, and two of his colored servants would vote for him. See Garfield's references to him in the entries for March 9, 1875, March 22, 1876, and June 16, 1878.

of department business accumulated which needs immediate attention. Every year brings me more frequently to Washington during vacation to meet the growing demands of my position. Answered letters and worked on the various matters above until towards evening, when I took the train for Ohio, going by the way of the Baltimore and Potomac Road.

WEDNESDAY, 24. A day on the cars is getting to be a dreary business. It is surprising, when I reflect upon it, how many thousands of miles I have travelled about the world during the last fifteen years; and thus far without any accident to train or passenger. I have had some premonitions of failure of eyesight. Should that occur, it will make railway travelling unendurable. Thus far I have been enabled to read and have really accomplished a good deal in that way while travelling on a railroad. Should my eyes even partially break down this resource will fail me. Reached home by way of Pittsburgh and Leetonia in the evening.

THURSDAY, 25. Spent the day in reading my mail and attending to business that had accumulated in my absence; also in working up the materials for discussion in the campaign. It is my impression that the State Central Committee and those working with them as managers of this campaign desire to ignore me as far as they can in its management. They wish to retain my friendship, secure my contributions to the expenses of the campaign and when it is over take whatever glory comes from it. It is a suicidal policy on their part. They will disgust some Republicans and probably lose positive strength.

FRIDAY, 26. Wrote a large number of letters. Worked up my back correspondence and also wrote an opinion to Judge Servis of Montana on a question which his Court is to pass upon very soon, namely, whether the Territory of Montana has the right to enact a law depriving an alien of the right of holding the soil. I hold that they have no such right. I also began the preparation of the brief on the Montana case. I worked up the history of the case and made the statement preliminary to the argument. I wrote out one branch of the argument. The question turns on the right of the Governor to fill a vacancy in vacation as an incident to his authority as the Executive of the Territory.

SATURDAY, 27. Completed about two-thirds of my brief and answer.

Worked on the ever recurring correspondence. This business of reading and answering mail is becoming a heavy portion of my daily
life. Captain Henry came to see me, and consulted about his new
appointment. We also discussed the successorship to his Route
Agency and I concluded to nominate Capt. J[asper] S. Ross, an
old Hiram student and an officer of Company A. 42d Reg't. It is a
matter of gratification that while I have recommended a great many
persons to office, I believe none except Frank Boston[149] has proved
unworthy. I have been particularly successful in appointments to the
Postal Service. The daughter of my cousin Henry was here this
afternoon and I reviewed her in geometry. It is a great pleasure to
me to go over the old textbooks. They come back fresh and pleasantly
to my mind.

SUNDAY, 28. Attended church as usual hearing a good sermon
by Burke. The season is further advanced than usual and we are
in the midst of that wonderful foliage for which Northern Ohio
is so remarkable. I heard a few days since from a gentleman who
had just returned from Europe that this coloring of foliage is
peculiar to American forests. It does not appear in Europe. If this
statement be true, I wonder what may be the cause of it. I suspect
that the vital forces both vegetable and animal (?) of our agriculture
is more active in the new world than the old.

MONDAY, 29. At work in the old way, made some advance on my
brief and also worked up further correspondence. In connection
with what I said yesterday of the difference between the active and
vital forces in Europe and America, it is clear to my mind that the
vital and atmospheric influences of this continent are working a
marked change in the physical and mental characteristics of our
people. We are growing more lean and nervous than our English
cousin. The typical American is not so rotund and hearty a person
as he was in the days of the Revolution. The pictures at the Capitol

[149] Garfield had secured Boston a job as watchman in the Bureau of Engraving. He was transferred and then discharged. He thereupon forged a
letter purportedly from Garfield to the captain of the watch asking for
Boston's reappointment. "Please reappoint him on the watch at once and
arrange it so he can be off to do some work at my house during the day as
to look after my Horses also," the letter read in part. Boston was not reinstated.

show a much more English looking set of faces than those of modern Americans. Take Washington and his Generals, the scene of the Declaration of Independence, the members of the early congresses, they will average a much fuller type of face than the Americans of today. I wish I knew who invented the picture of the typical Brother Jonathan. It is in striking contrast to that of John Bull, and yet the two strikingly represent the effect of the influences in the two countries.

TUESDAY, 30. Evan Phillips, of Portage County, Ohio, came tonight to take me to Paris. Phillips drove me this morning by way of Windham to Paris. We stopped at a house just east of the "corner," where we took dinner. At one o'clock a fair audience assembled in an orchard near the school-house, where, after music by the Ravenna Band, I spoke for nearly two hours on the issues of the campaign. My line of discussion was this; first, the origin and growth of political parties, the reasons why they originate and grow; second, the reasons why they die, illustrated by the history of the Democratic and Republican parties; third, the present duty of the two political parties, showing that this is a campaign of personalities, with principles very little discussed. I then discussed some of the leading charges that are being made against the Republican Party, Credit Mobilier, salaries, etc. and also discussed the panic resulting from the failure of Jay Cooke, showing what the panic would have been if we had had the old system of banks in States. I think the speech was very well received. Drove to Libby Phillips' where I took tea. Played a couple of games of croquet and then Mr. Phillips Senior drove [me] to Deerfield, ten miles from Paris, where I stopped at the house of N. L. Wann.[150] Spoke in the evening to a crowded house.

October

WEDNESDAY, 1. This morning Mr. Wann drove me to Randolph eight miles from Deerfield. Stopped at the house of Mr. Brainerd where several gentlemen met me and we went down to the grove

---

[150] Postmaster at Deerfield.

where I spoke to a fair audience. The *Cincinnati Commercial* sent a short-hand writer to report my speech. I spoke nearly two hours after which Mr. Isaac Williams drove me to Edinburgh. We stopped for tea at the house of Mr. Adams, about two miles from Edinburgh. After tea went to the "Centre" where a large audience was waiting me in the Town Hall. Spoke an hour and three-quarters and then drove with Halsey Hall and John Beatty to Ravenna. Spent the night at Halsey Hall's.

THURSDAY, 2. Took the train for Cleveland, stopped off at the Euclid Street Station and went to James Mason's where I expected to meet Crete. She had not arrived and I went down town and soon found her. Spent the day there in shopping and transacting several items of business. Took dinner at Dr. Robison's. Spent the afternoon at the Northern Ohio Fair where I saw nearly forty thousand people and met a large number of friends. Returned in the evening to James Mason's where we took tea and spent the night.

FRIDAY, 3. Took the morning train on the Atlantic and Great Western Road to Windham and Dr. [Applegate?] met me and drove me to his house. Played croquet until four o'clock in the evening when J. S. Smith came for me and took me to his house in Braceville where I met O. K. Wolcott and his wife and where we took tea. Went to a house in the centre of the town and addressed an audience on the topics of the day. A brass band were in attendance. Returned to Smith's and spent the night.

SATURDAY, 4. Took the train to Warren where Harmon Austin met me. Went to his house to dinner; towards evening he drove me eight miles to Baconsburgh, where I addressed a large audience in the Disciple Church. Several malignant salary men were present, who put a number of questions personal to myself and reflecting on the Republican Party. I spoke two hours and a quarter and made a very full and careful statement of the history of the salary legislation and particularly of the salary increase of the third of March last. This, I think, is the most successful speech I have made, so far as it relates to me personally. Drove back to Warren with Mr. Austin and spent the night at his house.

SUNDAY, 5. Got a livery team and drove home to Hiram, by way of Southington and Nelson, eighteen miles. The day was raw and stormy but I was anxious to get home and rest a little from the weariness of the campaign. Found a large mass of letters awaiting me and worked on them until a late hour in the evening. Requests for speeches are coming in more numerously than I can attend to, for the campaign. If it had begun somewhat earlier I could have done more satisfactory work in the district; but there is remarkable apathy everywhere in this part of Ohio, in reference to politics. I fear we shall not get out the full vote, but my meetings are better attended than ever before in this part of the state.

MONDAY, 6. Left at nine o'clock for Warren, driving by way of Garrettsville, Windham and Braceville. It rained heavily during part of the journey and at one time hailed. Reached Warren a little before noon, and went to Judge Kinsman's where I took dinner. I visited with him until three o'clock, when Harmon Austin took me to his flagstone quarry, three miles northeast of Warren, and examined the curious geological formations of the quarry; and then we drove to Mecca ten miles from Warren and stopped at the house of Squire Palmer[151] a mile north of the Centre. After tea went to the Methodist Church at the Corners and addressed a large audience. Spent the night at Squire Palmer's.

TUESDAY, 7. Started for Warren. Stopped a short time at the old Oil Diggings, where I made an investment in oil territory in 1861 [1860]. Reached Warren in time for the ten o'clock train, which I took for Cleveland. It was belated, however, and I did not reach the City until four o'clock. Took the Lake Shore train to Willoughby and stopped at the house of Dr. Clark, B. J. Loomis of the *Cincinnati Commercial* joining me. At half-past seven addressed a large audience in the College Hall on the political issues of the hour. Senator Updegraff,[152] Hon. George W. Steele and J. F. Scofield also addressed the meeting, and after its conclusion, I rode with them to Painesville and staid at the Cowles House that night.

WEDNESDAY, 8. Took the morning train on the narrow gage road to

---

151 N. W. Palmer, a justice of the peace once described as one of the township's "most substantial farmers," was active in the Republican politics of Garfield's district.

152 Jonathan Taylor Updegraff (1822–1882), a Republican of Mt. Pleasant, Columbiana County, was a member of the Ohio Senate, 1872–73, and a member of the U. S. House of Representatives, 1879 to his death.

Chardon, where I was met by Messrs. Converse,[153] Ford and Hathaway who drove me to Thompson Centre, ten miles. Not less than five thousand people were assembled on the Fair Grounds and after dinner I made an agricultural speech of an hour and a half and saw a great many friends. Drove back to Chardon in the afternoon and after tea at the Burnett House addressed a large audience in the Court House for an hour and a half. During my speech Senator Updegraff came and at its conclusion Governor Noyes spoke for an hour. Spent the night with the Governor and Senator at the Burnett House.

THURSDAY, 9. Took the seven o'clock train on the narrow gage for Painesville. Stopped at the Stockwell House. Went to the Court House at nine o'clock to attend the suit of *Sweeney vs. Rudolph and Garfield*. This is the first case in my life in which I have ever been sued and here I am only sued as a security on a note of Brother Joe's for a patent right which proved entirely worthless and he declined to pay it on the ground of want of consideration. The jury was summoned and the trial proceeded. The testimony which was mainly by affidavit was nearly all got in by the close of the day. Case can be finished tomorrow.

FRIDAY, 10. Continued in attendance upon the case until noon. Testimony was got in at an early hour. Mr. Estep[154] made the opening speech on our side and was followed by Mr. Sweeney[155] on the opposite side. Further action in the case will be had during the afternoon. At one o'clock took the train for Cleveland. Stopped an hour at the *Herald* office and finished my brief in the Montana case, the first two-thirds of which is already in print. I gave the manuscript of the remainder to the printer with directions that fifteen copies should be forwarded to the Supreme Court at Washington. Took the five o'clock train for Ravenna, went to Halsey Hall's and at half-past seven addressed a large audience in the

---

[153] Julius O. Converse (b. 1834), Chardon editor and friend and political supporter of Garfield, bought the *Jeffersonian Democrat* in 1859; he changed the name to the *Geauga Democrat* in 1866 and in 1872 to the *Geauga Republican*. There are many letters from him in the Garfield Papers.

[154] Ephraim James Estep, Cleveland lawyer, partner of Stevenson Burke; in 1875 Garfield contemplated joining this firm.

[155] E. J. Sweeney, a Painesville lawyer.

Opera House, speaking nearly two hours going quite fully over the political topics. I discussed the panic more elaborately than hitherto. I think there is an unreasoning spirit of alarm in the minds of many business men which is leading them to lock up their currency, and which, unless it subsides, will lead to an extended disaster in other branches of business than railroad building. Spent the night at Halsey Hall's.

SATURDAY, 11. Visited in the forenoon at Frederick Williams' [156] with his family and played croquet at Reverend Mr. Darsie's. Towards evening took the train for Kent. Took supper at S. P. Wolcott's, who was an old student of mine and is a warm friend. Addressed a large audience for two hours and a half and discussed the principles of the Prohibition party at great length. At the close of the meeting rode to Aurora with C. R. Harmon. The distance was eight miles and the night was chilly; we reached his house a little before midnight, where I spent the remainder of the night.

SUNDAY, 12. A cold dreary morning. Attended the Presbyterian Church and heard an excellent sermon on the sins of that particular congregation. It was a brave discussion of the actual state of affairs in that church. When that meeting ended, I went across the street to the Disciples Church where the meeting had not yet ended and where I met a number of old friends and acquaintances. They were about to begin their Sunday School and at their request I spoke a little while. On our return found that Harry and his Cousin Lewis had come for me with a carriage, and with them I drove to Hiram arriving after dark. Very cold and dreary. The past week has been a hurried one. I am glad the campaign is so near over.

MONDAY, 13. Spent the day in answering letters and visiting our Cousin Henry Boynton and wife, who came about noon. They left

---

[156] Frederick Williams (1799–1888), of Ravenna, who, according to Burke A. Hinsdale, "was farmer, county officer, elder of the local church, public minister of religion, promoter of good works, lover of good men, and hospitable householder." He was a founder of the Eclectic and for many years a member of the Board of Trustees. He was the father of three daughters, one of whom (Sophia) married Garfield's good friend, Charles Henry, and of a son, Frederick Augustus, who served as an officer in Garfield's regiment in the Sandy Valley campaign and died of typhoid fever a few months later in 1862.

before evening. An hour before sunset, accompanied by Crete, started for Auburn nine miles off, where I generally have made the closing speech of the campaign. Stopped at the house of Widow Burnett.[157] A large audience had assembled in the new Town Hall, and I spoke for two hours. Several interruptions and questions which I thought were satisfactorily answered. At the close of the meeting, I was waited upon by Committee of gentlemen from Chagrin Falls who invited me to an oyster supper, given as they said to testify their friendship and confidence. At the conclusion of the supper Crete and I left for Hiram, reaching it one hour after midnight.

TUESDAY, 14. Went up to the Town Hall and cast my vote, being the ninth man who voted. Went to Garrettsville and took the nine o'clock train for Washington. The election will be a doubtful one. I do not suppose we shall carry the legislature for the reason that we should have lost it last year even with our successful struggle for the Presidency because Hamilton County went against us and that turned the scale of the Legislature. I have above indicated my opinion of the management of the campaign and this leads me to believe that the state ticket will be in great doubt. Passed a weary dreary day on the cars going to sleep at night among the mountains of Penn.

WEDNESDAY, 15. Awoke in Baltimore train too late for the connection with Washington. Went to Guy's Restaurant and took breakfast, then went across to the Washington Depot of the Baltimore Road and taking the train reached Washington at half-past ten. Went directly to the Capitol and found that the Montana Case had been reached the night before and dismissed on motion of General Mussey, which he did at my request made by telegraph in case the briefs did not arrive. Went into the House Committee Room on Territories [and] changed my shirt. Then went to the old law library and worked until the meeting of the Supreme Court. Got the case reinstated on the Docket and argued it. They gave me a decree in open court. I found that I could not ask any special decree in reference to any one point, unless our side had made an assignment of error on that point. I therefore took a general affirmation

---

[157] Lucina, widow of Jonathan Burnett, a prominent Disciple in Auburn, who died in 1859.

of the decree of the court below. Went to the house [on] I St. [and] found Mr. Rose; transacted a considerable amount of business in the departments and spent the night at Mr. Gilfillan's. Lizzie being away from home and my having no key.

THURSDAY, 16. Spent the morning in correspondence and in tending to affairs about the house, I St. At 12 o'clock went to the Supreme Court and asked for the immediate issuance of the mandate in the Montana Case, which was granted. Then went to the several departments and accomplished what business I could during the day. Came back to the house and wrote several letters and made arrangements for putting down the carpets and getting the house in order. Also consulted with Mr. Carstens in regard to suitable colors for carpets in the different rooms where it is necessary to get new ones. Took the nine o'clock train for N. Y. and went to bed on the sleeping car as I have done so frequently during the last month.

FRIDAY, 17. Reached the Brevoort House early in the morning and found a number of friends and acquaintances. Among them Senator Allison and wife. At ten o'clock took breakfast with the Editor of the N. Y. *World*[158] and an English gentleman named Mitford who had long been in the employ of the diplomatic service at Japan. Spent most of the day at Stewart's in examining, selecting and purchasing carpets for our house in Washington. Found David A. Wells and had a visit with him. Called on ex-Secretary McCulloch,[159] corner of Broad and Wall St. He appears very much broken by the financial disasters which have overtaken him in connection with Jay Cooke. He fears the London House of Jay Cooke and McCulloch will suffer severely before the panic has spent itself.

SATURDAY, 18. Spent a considerable portion of the day in visiting friends and chief among my friends the books in the book stores. Made no purchases except Hamerton's *Intellectual Life*.[160] Called

[158] Manton Marble (1834–1917) owned and edited the *New York World*, 1862–76.

[159] Hugh McCulloch (1807–1895), comptroller of the currency, 1863–65, secretary of the treasury, 1865–69 and 1884–85. At this time he was a member of the London banking house of Jay Cooke, McCulloch & Company, which survived the panic although its American affiliate, Jay Cooke & Company, failed. The London concern was shortly reorganized as McCulloch & Company.

[160] Philip Gilbert Hamerton, *The Intellectual Life* (1873).

on Mr. Orton, Mr. Gay, the Editor of the *Evening Post*,[161] and several gentlemen whose opinions on the financial condition were likely to be valuable. Dined at the Brevoort House at five o'clock and at six o'clock in company with Senator Allison and his wife went to the Erie R. R. Depot and took the train for the West.

SUNDAY, 19. Awoke near Hornellsville, N. Y., where we took breakfast. At that point I separated from the Allisons, they going by way of Niagara Falls and I West by Salamanca and Cleveland. A cold dreary day, with little to relieve it by the blank monotonous scenery of railway travel. Towards evening met a gentleman who resides in upper Louisiana who gave me a doleful account of the situation of affairs in that state. Reached Garrettsville at six in the evening, and driving through the rain reached Hiram at seven o'clock, tired of the week's work and glad to get home.

MONDAY, 20. Read and answered a large number of letters and staid in doors while a heavy snow storm was raging without. It seems as though the year had ran ahead of itself, and that the winter had come before the ending of summer. Hinsdale is away and Hiram is quite dreary. There is much feeling I find over the election. We have lost the Legislature and the Governor, although all the other Republicans on the state ticket are elected. I sum up the causes of the election thus. First. The apathy which generally follows the Presidential Election. Second. The management of the campaign wherein a few men tried to take all the glory of it and ride into power by ignoring their comrades. The first cause brought a low vote. The second cause produced great scratching and final defeat of the state ticket.

TUESDAY, 21. Snow storm at intervals during the day. Read and wrote letters and read one hundred pages of Hamerton's *Intellectual Life*. It is an exceedingly clever book. I find in it the tracks of many of my thoughts. The author thinks bravely and writes clearly. In the afternoon Crete, Harry, Mollie, the Baby and I took the hack for Garrettsville, where we waited for the western train until nearly nine o'clock. Then went to Solon arriving too late to go down to Sister Mary's and spent the night at the hotel.

WEDNESDAY, 22. Drove down to Sister Mary's and spent the day in

---

[161] Sydney Howard Gay (1814–1888) was a member of the editorial staff of the *Evening Post*, 1872–74.

visiting there and at Sister Hitty's. In the afternoon Mr. Palmer took Mother, Crete, two of the children and myself to Orange where we visited Cousin Henry Boynton and his family and after a late tea had a long and pleasant visit. My birthplace within a hundred rods of this place is now a cultivated field with no sign of the old habitation left excepting the orchard. Spent the night at Cousin Henry's.

THURSDAY, 23. Most of the day was cold, rainy and uncomfortable. We spent the time in visiting with Henry's family and Doctor's [Silas Boynton's] until the middle of the afternoon, when he took us back to Solon to Sister Mary's. It rained heavily before we reached there. The newspapers still indicate increased stringency in the money market with the probability of further failures in consequence of the general locking up of the currency. If the panic proceeds further it will be the most senseless and stupid that I have ever witnessed in our financial history. There is absolutely no excuse for it, and yet if people lose believe [belief] in the soundness of our affairs, there is no help for it.

FRIDAY, 24. Yesterday and today I have looked carefully over the affairs of Sister Mary and her husband. They have struggled on for nearly thirty years. They have a farm of twenty-five acres, worth probably twenty-five hundred dollars and they have over fifteen hundred dollars on which they are paying interest and are unable to go forward a single step, each year being a struggle for existence and for keeping down interest. I have resolved to help them out if possible and have determined to advance them fifteen hundred dollars and take a portion of the farm at a price largely above its real value to secure me in part as I am not able to give them that much money. If I can raise the sum named I shall do so to save them from losing it all. We took the four o'clock train at Hiram [*sic*] and at Solon Mother and the children joined us. Mr. [Omar] Stocking met us at Garrettsville with his large wagon and took us to Hiram.

SATURDAY, 25. Crete and I took the morning train to Cleveland where we did some shopping and I paid some bills; took dinner at Dr. Robison's in company with Dr. Streator. We discussed the financial situation pretty fully. The tradespeople think that more currency is needed to save the country from collapse. I do not.

If we had more it would be locked up just as the present amount now is. Worked off an unusually large accumulation of letters and in reading some further chapters in Hamerton's *Intellectual Life*. Hinsdale has returned home and has had a remarkably delightful time. In the evening talked over some of the serious issues of life. The Cincinnati newspapers are making a savage assault, charging me with the loss of the election and demanding that I shall not be appointed on the Committee on Appropriations. It remains to be seen how far the reckless assaults of public journals can go in ruining public men. I am not sure but a friend of mine is right who says that the greatest danger this country has now to confront is the corrupt and reckless press.

SUNDAY, 26. Attended meeting and listened to a discourse from Burke, probably the last I shall hear from him in many months. At his request I have agreed to deliver a lecture on the Pioneer History of the Western Reserve and he announced from the pulpit that the lecture would be given in the College Chapel on Tuesday next.

MONDAY, 27. Resumed the work of clearing up correspondence and putting my affairs in order for taking the family to Washington. Settled bills, packed boxes, and cleared up the debris of the summer and read a little from Hamerton.

I have come to dread these continual changes of home, from Washington to Hiram. Middle life, and specially scholarly life, needs regular habits, and regular places where books and papers may always be found, and when one gets himself adjusted, he dislikes to break up and start afresh. I fear also that these constant changes may unfit me for steady continuous life in one place— which feeling of unrest would ill become an old man. This is probably the first time I have used the words "old man" as applied to myself in the near future. But if I live ten years longer I shall be in the near neighborhood of old age. I must resume my reading of *De Senectute*.

TUESDAY, 28. Crete and I took the morning train for Niles to see Miss Redfield and engage her to go with us to Washington. Took the eleven o'clock train for Warren. Staid at Mr. Austin's and visited there until one o'clock. Took the train to Garrettsville, driving by the Freedom Road to Mr. Ozias Allyn's, where we paid for two hundred and sixteen pounds of butter which he has been putting down for us. Rode home amidst the snow storm. Took tea in the evening at Mr. James Young's and at half-past seven o'clock delivered a lecture to a large audience in the College Chapel on the Pioneer History of the Reserve. The lecture was quite successful. At its conclusion the President of the College suggested the organization of a Pioneer Historical Society here in Hiram. A committee was appointed to report a plan for organization.

WEDNESDAY, 29. This was a busy day in settling up odds and ends of our Hiram life and preparing for leaving tomorrow. My family has become a large and expensive organization. Every year adds expense to each child, and I must seriously confront the question of supplies for our annual expenses. Did I not have so many people that I felt it necessary to help, the task would be easier. I received a letter from my brother Thomas today asking for help to pay for his team. I have given him outright over thirteen hundred dollars in the last six years and supposed I had got him on solid foundation. It is simply impossible for me to do justice to myself and help him now. I almost fear that there is a lack of proper effort on the part of himself or his family to help themselves. Worked until midnight in putting our affairs in order.

THURSDAY, 30. At eight o'clock, after bidding good-by to lumber wagons that took us and our effects to Garrettsville, Mother, Crete, One Hired Girl and five children, with another Hired Girl that met us at Niles, took the train eastward. Nine people and eight trunks composed the party. Took lunch at Leetonia and supper at Pittsburgh. Had two and [a] half sections of sleeping car from Pittsburgh eastward. Went to sleep as usual on this trip among the mountains of Pennsylvania. My eldest boy Harry has travelled over the distance between Hiram and Washington twenty times, Jimmy sixteen and the rest of them in proportion. I must have travelled it at least fifty times. It grows monotonous and weary.

FRIDAY, 31. We awoke near Baltimore and for the first time the family went under Baltimore rather than through it as heretofore. We reached Washington about nine o'clock and at half-past nine landed home. The carpets new and old were down and the house in excellent order and much as we hoped to see it. The journey as a whole has been much less fatiguing than usual. I am glad to find that I was fairly successful in selecting carpets for several of our rooms. I knew just enough of the aesthetics of color and form to be troubled about the purchase, but not enough to act with confidence in my own judgment. The purchase was therefore a little bit of education in art.

The family seem delighted to get home and I should be but for the reflection that I must go away almost immediately.

November

SATURDAY, 1 Crete and I called on Mrs. Barnard[162] and found that the girl and the expense I have already paid, twenty-five dollars, is a complete and utter failure so that we will not have her begin. This is a new chapter repeating the old tragedy of the kitchen. Spent the day in putting the Library of the house to rights, but giving a large share of it in the discussion of what is to me the most difficult question I have ever confronted, namely, what I shall do with my children in the matter of education. I believe that the mind naturally hungers and thirsts for knowledge. I cannot doubt that something is wrong with our system of education which has made both my boys hate the sight of a school book. They are bright, active, unusually full of animal spirits, and yet they hate books. I believe the cause is in the system of our public schools and I am thinking about running the risk of putting them in kindergarten schools, where they spend much less time in study than now, though it is a fearful thing to experiment with any other life than one's own. I am greatly perplexed over the question.

SUNDAY, 2. Attended church in the forenoon and evening. The Church was informed of the resignation of Bartholomew the Pastor, to take effect at the end of the month. This is well for the Church. He was a business man, a good man to look after the members,

---

[162] H. M. Barnard, a woman journalist in Washington. In 1873, at the time of the furor over the salary increase for congressmen, she prepared an article on the salary amendment to the appropriation bill. In 1874 under the name of H. M. Barnard and Company she was engaged in preparing and sending out newsletters from Washington to country papers. Over the years she wrote to Garfield occasionally from various places. Her connection with the servant girl episode is not known.

but a most inefficient preacher. Elder Bradley preached a fine discourse on the story of Jacob and Esau and the lesson of it. Spent most of the afternoon and evening in bringing up back work and getting ready to leave as I must do this evening for New Castle, Penn., to try the Phillips case, which is set for tomorrow. Took the ten o'clock train on the Baltimore and Potomac Road and went away most unwillingly from the family with a dreary night of railroad life before me.

MONDAY, 3. Change of time on the Pennsylvania and Ohio Road. Was delayed so that I did not reach Pittsburgh until about two o'clock. Waited there until four o'clock when I took the Ashtabula, Youngstown and Pittsburgh Road for New Castle. At Lawrence Junction Lizzie took the train for Warren and I went by another to New Castle where I arrived at seven o'clock. Thomas W. Phillips' carriage met me and I drove to his house. The case of Brooke, Barrington and Phillips Bros. was called today and the jury empanelled though not sworn. Everything is ready to proceed with this trial tomorrow. Spent the night at the Phillipses'.

TUESDAY, 4. At nine o'clock the jury was sworn and the trial proceeded with the examination of witnesses concerning matters which occurred nine years ago. The case is a very curious one. It has gone to final judgment in an action in equity in the Supreme Court but the decree has been suspended to await the determination of this suit. Worked until twelve, resumed at two, and worked until six. Plaintiff's testimony not yet got in. Attended the party at Isaac N. Phillips' in the evening. Went thence to J[W]. W[J]. Ford's where I spent the night.

WEDNESDAY, 5. This forenoon testimony of the plaintiff was all got in and Mr. Kurtz, my associate counsel, made a brief statement to the jury of our side of the case. We then commenced putting in our testimony, which is in large share documentary. We set up record of proceedings in the Supreme Court in order to plead as a bar to this trial. Proceedings here are according to the forms of common law. The feigned issues and other legal fictions are all in vogue here. In Ohio the Code has swept that away. Staid at Thomas Phillips' in the evening.

THURSDAY, 6. Got all our testimony in at noon. In the afternoon Mr. Dana, counsel for the Plaintiff, made his opening speech which occupied nearly an hour. He was followed by Mr. Kurtz who spoke about an hour on our side. I then began my argument and spoke for about an hour until the Court adjourned for the evening. The two main topics of my speech today were, first, the legal relation of this suit to the equity suit in the Supreme Court; second, the rule of damages that should apply to this case if any damages be allowed. After the adjournment of the Court went to Charles N. Phillips' and took tea with a large number of friends. Went to Thomas' and spent the night.

FRIDAY, 7. Continued my speech at the opening of the Court at ten o'clock and spoke about an hour and a half on three points, viz., First, if this Court can try this case, it must go into all the merits of the case and try it without regard to the other trial. Second, we have not broken our contract, but the plaintiff did break it. They cannot therefore recover damages. Third, the only thing they can recover from us is pay for services rendered. The rule of *quantum meruit* [as much as he deserved] must be applied. I satisfied myself fairly on my address to the Court and the jury. Mr. Dana followed in a speech of an hour and a half. At the conclusion of Mr. Dana's speech, the Judge occupied an hour and a half in delivering his charge to the jury and the case was submitted to them a little before six o'clock. Returned to Thomas' to spend the night. I should have mentioned in the proper place that Charles, Thomas, and Reverend Mr. Crogin and myself had a game of croquet.

SATURDAY, 8. On the assembling of the Court the verdict of the jury was delivered and the previous finding read in open court. They gave the plaintiffs thirty thousand dollars. This is thirty-two thousand dollars less than the decree of the Supreme Court. I shall be curious to know what they will do with the two decrees. Took the ten o'clock train for Sharon and thence at half-past eleven took the train to Warren where Harmon Austin met me and we spent several hours at Judge Kinsman's with Messrs. Perkins and Morgan discussing the financial and political situation. At five o'clock took the train for Garrettsville and from there was taken home in a rain storm. Spent the night at Hinsdale's.

SUNDAY, 9. After breakfast and a visit with Hinsdale went to Father Rudolph's where I staid until meeting. Joe came home a few moments after I reached the house. Attended meeting and had a good discourse as usual from Burke. Straightened up my documents and desk and gathered up my papers and completed the odds and ends of arrangements for leaving for the Winter. In the evening Joe and I drove to Garrettsville and took the six o'clock train for Cleveland. Snowed heavily during our journey. Arrived at Cleveland at seven-forty and took the street cars to 494 Case Avenue where I spent the night with Mr. and Mrs. Rhodes. They are very comfortably situated in a nice house and I almost envy their quiet and freedom from the noise and tumult of public life.

MONDAY, 10. Went down to the City and visited several parties on business. Made arrangements concluding the purchase of part of Larabee's farm. Took dinner at Dr. Robison's. In the afternoon visited the *Leader* Office, Pension Office, and also had a visit with Capt. Henry. After tea Dr. Robison took me to the Cleveland Club, where about twenty prominent citizens were assembled, H. B. Payne,[163] Amasa[164] and A. B. Stone,[165] Mr. Younglove[166] and Senator Bingham.[167] They asked me to discuss the financial situation and suggest what relief could be had from Congress.

TUESDAY, 11. Took the morning train to Ravenna and stopped at

163 Henry B. Payne (1810–1896), of Cleveland, one of Ohio's leading businessmen and Democrats, was a member of the U. S. House of Representatives, 1875–77, and of the Senate, 1885–91. It was charged that his election to the Senate was bought by his son, Oliver H. Payne, treasurer of the Standard Oil Company. He has been described (*Dictionary of American Biography*, Vol. 14, pp. 325–326) as appearing "more like a minister than the shrewd, active man of affairs that he was, a director in twenty corporations and a politician devoted to the interests of business." He was a member of the Electoral Commission of 1877. Frances Payne Bolton, who has been a Republican member of the House from Ohio since 1940, is his niece.

164 Amasa Stone (1818–1883), one of Cleveland's most prominent businessmen, with railroad, banking and manufacturing interests.

165 Andros B. Stone, brother of Amasa, was president of the Cleveland Rolling Mill Company. In 1872 he had helped found the Union Steel Screw Company.

166 Moses C. Younglove, president of the Younglove Agricultural Iron Company, and of Younglove, Massey & Company, proprietors of the Cleveland Agricultural Works.

167 William Bingham, Cuyahoga County, was a member of the Ohio Senate, 1868–69, 1872–73.

Halsey Hall's with whom I dined. Several friends called and consulted on the political situation. After spending three or four hours in Ravenna, I telegraphed to Crete on this the fifteenth anniversary of our marriage and took the train at half-past two for Pittsburgh, arriving there a little before eight o'clock. Found Senator Morton on the Washington sleeping car, with whom I had a long interview on the political and financial situation. Went to bed at ten o'clock and dreamed down the mountains, while I was thus making my sixteenth [sixth] journey to Washington since the adjournment of Congress in March last.

WEDNESDAY, 12. Reached Washington at half-past ten making the journey from Ravenna in less than twenty hours. Spent six hours in reading the mails which had accumulated since I left home ten days ago. I hope I am now here for the Winter, and I look on the coming session as the most troublesome and uncertain of any that I [have] ever seen at this distance from it. The great financial panic which has swept and is still sweeping over the country will be the most difficult element to handle. There will be a babel of opinions and remedies laid before the public, with great uncertainty as to the outcome. Everything has tended to saturate the public mind with suspicion and unfaith and no man is wise enough to see the plain path through the entanglements. It is a bad time to be in public life.

THURSDAY, 13. Found a note last evening from Judge Swayne requesting me to call. Did so this morning and had a long conversation with him in regard to the Chief Justiceship. It appears that President Grant two years ago indicated his intention to appoint Judge Swayne to this position when a vacancy should occur. It now appears that within the last two weeks he has changed his purpose and is likely to appoint Senator Conkling. On some grounds a man acquainted with politics is better fitted for the Headship of the Supreme Court, than a mere lawyer. But I fear Senator Conkling is not of the judicial mind although he is able and if he would forego all political ambitions would make an able Chief Justice. Were I the President, I think I would appoint Mr. Evarts. Visited the Kindergarten and considered the question of continuing my children in that school. I think I shall leave them there for the Winter and try the experiments. My faith in our public schools is steadily diminishing. The course of study is unnatural and the children are too overcrowded for solid healthy growth and that ought to be the chief business of children and study must not interfere with it too much. Called at Mr. Payne's and consulted on our case *Daniels vs. Driggs.* Went to the Capitol and transacted some business. In the evening visited Mr. and Mrs. Smalley and the Sumners on 11th Street and discussed the piano question.

FRIDAY, 14. The large mails begin to come in as usual on the approach of the session. It took me nearly three hours to dispose of this morning's mail. E. V. Smalley came and spent two hours in talking of his season in Europe and the political and financial situation. He went to Europe this Spring full of the passion of travelling but he has come home thoroughly satisfied. He does not desire to go abroad again. Called at the Post Office and Patent Office on business. Thorp,[168] the artist, called in the evening, and we had a long talk on his struggles and successes as an artist and also on his earnest efforts to serve his friends in the political field. He brings quite full intelligence of the situation in Ashtabula County. Before retiring read a few chapters in Hamerton's [book] on the influences of aristocracy and democracy on intellectual life. I note here what General Sherman tells me, that with the same examiners and the same tests, the cadets at West Point do not average as good scholarship as they did in 1836. How does this agree with our belief in the superiority of our public schools?

SATURDAY, 15. After working some time with the correspondents I called again on Judge Swayne and reviewed the situation in regard to the Chief Justiceship. Then went to the Post Office Department on business. Called on the Att'y General in reference to the pardon of Freeman of Parkman, now in the Ohio Penitentiary for robbing the mail. Had a long talk with the Att'y General in regard to the Chief Justiceship. It appears that a few weeks ago the President so far changed his purpose as to conclude that he would find a

---

[168] Freeman Thorp (1844–1922), portrait painter, photographer and politician, of Geneva, Ohio. He represented Ashtabula County in the legislature, 1878–79 and 1880–85. During the 1870's he spent a good deal of time in Washington engaged in photography and portrait painting. His studio was the Thorp's Gallery on the roof of the Capitol to which Garfield refers in the entry for February 13, 1872; President Grant sat for his portrait there. Several of Thorp's portraits hang in the Capitol.

Chief Justice outside of the Supreme Bench and it appears that he had nearly made up his mind on Conkling. But this plan was attended with peculiar difficulty. The appointment of Conkling is found likely to result in the appointment of a Democratic senator from N. Y., and I think the President's mind has now returned to the plan of appointment from the Supreme Bench and the appointment of Bristow[169] of Kentucky to fill the vacancy that is made. It is therefore possible that Judge Swayne may yet be appointed. Sent to the library for books concerning the discovery and settlement of the great West with which I have to write out my Burton speech of June 16th.

SUNDAY, 16.   Attended Church at the Shiloh Baptist Church on Massachusetts Avenue, where the Disciples are temporarily meeting while their house is being repaired. After dinner Judge Swayne called on me and we went carefully over the situation as referred to in the Journal of yesterday. He gave me all his intelligence on the subject and I will do what I can to assist him. I should have called on the President yesterday, but he was away in New Jersey. In the evening read Parkman's delightful book of the *Discovery of the Great West*.[170] I am greatly delighted with the character and achievements of LaSalle. I have met few characters in history of equal courage and endurance. I find myself suffering considerable distress in my stomach which appears to be indigestion and yet it may be the old bent-in breast bone brought on by my college studies. I have eaten but a very little today in order to find whether it is indigestion. Spent an hour at the Naval Observatory examining the great refracting telescope just completed.

MONDAY, 17.   Spent the day in reading Parkman's Histories. I find them intensely interesting. In the forenoon Judge Swayne called and gave me some new points in reference to the Chief Justiceship.

---

[169] Benjamin Helm Bristow (1832–1896) was the first solicitor general of the United States, 1870–72. He was engaged in private law practice, 1872–74. In the latter year he became secretary of the treasury and served until 1876 when he lost the favor of the President. His tenure in the Treasury was notable for the uncovering and prosecution of the Whiskey Ring. From 1878 until the end of his life he practiced law in New York City.

[170] Francis Parkman, *The Discovery of the Great West* (1869). From 1879 the work bore the title *LaSalle and the Discovery of the Great West*.

In the evening I called at the Executive mansion. The President was taking a nap and I would not have him wakened. He has just returned from New Jersey, where he had been to church with his Mother yesterday. The *Tribune* of this morning has a letter from a correspondent detailed [detailing] a view of my opinions in which something is said that will doubtless be construed unpleasantly and contrary to my meaning.[171] I dread the newspaper talk that will doubtless be opened up on public men this Winter. It is one of the features of public life that has lately had a rank overgrowth.

It rained and snowed dismally this evening, and I read Parkman with increasing delight. I have often thought I would love to do some historical work. It would gratify my love for discovery and thorough work.

Tuesday, 18. At half-past ten called on the President and spent an hour and a half with him alone. He talked very frankly on the subject of his message, the first pencil notes of which he was just drafting as I entered his room. He [His] discussion of the financial situation shows more study and reflection than I have known him to give any other document; though I fear he will recommend something that amounts to an inflation of the currency. He talked very freely concerning the Chief Justiceship and expressed the views mentioned on Saturday last. I think he is in doubt what to do.

---

[171] In the interview Garfield had expressed himself freely on the congressional outlook and the panic. He foresaw an unpleasant and probably unprofitable session, with angry debates on proposed remedies for the depression, many of which would be "impracticable, crude, and even absurd." With 150 new members it was difficult to foresee. "The old members," Garfield said, "will come back with their opinions considerably changed by their nine months' vacation. Their minds are like a fleece of wool that have been left out in the rain—they are saturated and dripping with the accumulations of public sentiment that have fallen on them." He looked forward to a flood of financial measures, most of them visionary and valueless. The greatest danger, he thought, was that an inflationary greenback bill would be rushed through at the beginning of the session. He described the panic as "senseless and idiotic." He expressed the opinion that although the collapse of railroad speculation could not have been avoided there was no need of the panic spreading beyond that. He took the view that the people had transferred their disgust with the political scandals to business and concluded that the country was to have another crash like that of 1837.

I told him the appointment of Judge Swayne would be gratifying to the bar and congressional delegation from Ohio, and I thought it would be more gratifying to the members of the bench than the appointment of an outsider. In the evening called on Judge Swayne and consulted on the situation in regard to the Chief Justiceship. I think the appointment clearly rests between him and Conkling. Mr. Knox,[172] Comptroller of the Currency, called in the evening and read to me a considerable portion of the forthcoming report and asked my assistance and suggestions.

WEDNESDAY, 19. Today completed my forty-second year; twice twenty-one. Fifteen [Fourteen] years of my life have been devoted to the public service without an intermission, even of a day. I was elected to the Ohio Senate in October, 1859. That service lapped on to my military life six months. My military service ran nine months into my first congressional term. So I really have had sixteen [fifteen] years of public service in the last fifteen [fourteen] years. Spent the forenoon shopping with Crete. In the afternoon worked on correspondence and the Burton speech. Several gentlemen called in the evening, among them Alex Sands[173] of Cincinnati, Hon. Geo. Steele of Painesville, Donn Piatt and wife.

THURSDAY, 20. Went with Crete to the Georgetown market and arranged for getting our beef and some other supplies there. It is one of the outrages that this city has put upon its inhabitants that they are charged from twenty to thirty cents per pound for beef, the same they charged at the close of the war, while they themselves are buying it, the hind quarters dressed and delivered at their market, at nine cents per pound. Beef has not been in fact so cheap for many years as it is now. They are making not less than three hundred per cent on the cost of fat cattle. We find that at Georgetown we can get the best cut of beef for 15 cents per pound. Returned at noon and worked on the Burton address. The study of this portion has become exceedingly interesting to me especially as told in Parkman's Histories.

FRIDAY, 21. Our little Abram is one year old today. Worked on the address until near noon. Called on General Mussey and read the

[172] John Jay Knox (1828–1892), deputy comptroller of the currency, 1867–72; comptroller, 1872–84.

[173] Alexander Sands of the *Cincinnati Times and Chronicle*.

proof and manuscript of our brief on the 6th St. Presbyterian Church. The case has been carried to the Supreme Court and we are asking to have it dismissed for want of Jurisdiction. General Mussey wrote the brief. Spent the evening in reading. I find much difficulty to get at the details of the transactions connected with the Treaty of Peace between the U. S. and Great Britain in 1783.

SATURDAY, 22. Went to the Capitol and transacted some business. While there listened to the rumors concerning the organization of the House and its Committees. I visited the library and examined the old British maps of North America from the earliest period down to the date of the Revolution. Dictated a large number of letters and continued work on the Burton speech. Have finished the romantic period and also the relation of the French to the Treaty of 1763 between England and France [in regard] to the ownership of the land. Albert Brisbane took dinner with us and instructed Crete in his theory of cooking oysters and he therefore took charge of these two dishes. He strains out all the liquor from the oysters, cooking them in their own natural juice for three-quarters of an hour. This makes them exceedingly tender and is a surprise to us. After dinner spent the evening in listening to Brisbane's theory of socialism and life. Mr. and Mrs. Spencer and George W. Steele called in the evening and the latter staid until a late hour.

SUNDAY, 23. Attended church and did not listen much to the sermon. The feeling is growing upon me that preaching of the ordinary sort is rapidly losing its power over the minds of men. There is some truth in what Brisbane says on this subject. That the religion of Jesus, like all religions, is divided into three parts: its worship; its aspirations; and its theology. In its aspirations to take hold of the sentiments and the everlasting principles of morality and wickedness it is eternal and unchangeable, but in its forms of worship and its intellectual doctrines and theology, it is perishable and must pass away. It is clear to my mind, that the theological and formal part of Christianity has in great measure lost its power over the minds of men. But the life and Christianity of Christ are to me as precious and perfect as ever. In the afternoon and evening and until midnight read, with a delight I have rarely felt for any book, the *Autobiography* [1873] of John Stuart Mill. It is amazing to contemplate the amount of work he accomplished while yet a mere boy. I cannot believe he is right in saying that he was not above the average of boys in natural powers. William Orton of N. Y. called and had a long conversation concerning public affairs. MONDAY, 24. Went on with the Burton speech and finished the third part, that relating to the acquisition of the Northwest by the U. S. through the conquest of George Rogers Clark. Was sent for this morning by Judge Swayne to consult in regard to the question of the Chief Justiceship. It has been tendered to Roscoe Conkling and he has declined it. It is very rare that a man forty-four years of age puts aside so tempting a prize. It reminds me of the refusal of the Younger Pitt, in his early youth, to accept a place in the Cabinet, saying that he declined any but the first place. Perhaps this is Conkling's reason. On my return from Swayne's I found a note from Judge Black and called on him at the Ebbitt House and from there drove to the State Department and went over the ground of the Cuban question[174] with Bancroft Davis.[175] After dinner a succession of visitors kept me in the sitting room until ten o'clock. Among them were Donn Piatt, Judge James,[176] Congress-

---

[174] Since 1868 an insurrection against Spain had been in progress in Cuba. On October 31, 1873, a Spanish man-of-war captured on the high seas the *Virginius*, a filibustering ship of American registry fraudulently obtained. The ship was taken to Santiago and within two weeks Spanish authorities had executed as pirates 37 crew members (several of whom were from the United States) and 16 passengers. The affair caused much feeling in the United States. On December 16, the Spanish turned the vessel over to the United States (it was sunk in a storm off Cape Fear on its way to New York); they also paid an indemnity for the families of the Americans executed. When the illegal registry of the *Virginius* became known, the United States withdrew an earlier demand for a Spanish salute to the American flag. It also obligated itself to take proceedings against the *Virginius* and any persons who appeared to have violated American laws in connection with it.

[175] John Chandler Bancroft Davis (1822–1907), assistant secretary of state, 1869–71 and 1873–74; agent of the United States before the Geneva Court of Arbitration on the *Alabama* Claims, 1871; U. S. minister to Germany, 1874–77; judge, U. S. Court of Claims, 1878–82.

[176] Charles P. James (1818–1899), who had once been judge of the Superior Court of Cincinnati, came to Washington to practice law in 1864; he was associate justice of the Supreme Court of the District of Columbia, 1879–92.

man Banning and the artist Thorp. Read Mill's *Autobiography* for an hour before retiring.

TUESDAY, 25. Entered upon the fourth part of my Burton speech, namely, the discussion of the claims of the various states and the Indian tribes to the Northwest territory. Visited the Post Office and the Patent Office on business for my constituents and friends and on my return wrote a number of letters. In the evening Mr. Sands of Cincinnati and George W. Steele of [Painesville] called on me and visited for some time. The alleged conspiracy to break down the old members of Congress in regard to their old places on Committees, seems itself to be broken down. I keep entirely aloof from the contest. Such seems to me the course that self-respect dictates.

WEDNESDAY, 26. Went with my colleague Mr. Woodworth to the War Department and introduced him to Secretary Belknap; also transacted some business there. Found in one of the Secretary's rooms a portrait of George Richard [Rogers] Clark, which was obtained and placed there by Secretary Floyd.[177] It is a most remarkable portrait indicating a singular combination of strength and color, a very tall and dome-like brow almost unnaturally developed in the upper portion. I am glad to have seen the picture of this wonderful man. Nearly completed the fourth topic of my Burton speech. Made an arrangement with the Postmaster General for transferring Brother Joe to the Cleveland and Columbus Road and appointing Mr. [James] Ellis of Hiram on the Lake Shore in his place. Finished the remarkable autobiography of John Stuart Mill this evening. No book I have read for many years has so deeply interested me.

THURSDAY, 27. I spent this day of National Thanksgiving in the delightful enjoyment of my books and in taking the usual Thanksgiving dinner of turkey with my family. In the afternoon and evening read up the history of Saint Clair's defeat and General Wayne's subsequent campaign over the Indians of the North West under the masterly instructions of General Washington. Wrote a portion of that part of my Burton speech relating to the settlement of the Western Reserve. Six of my colleagues called in the evening

[177] John Buchanan Floyd (1806–1863) was governor of Virginia, 1849–52, and secretary of war, 1857–60.

for a visit and to arrange for the caucus of our delegation to nominate officers of the House.

FRIDAY, 28. Worked on the Burton speech and did some Department business. A large number of people called during the day. At eight o'clock in the evening eight of my colleagues came here and held a caucus until ten o'clock in regard to nominating an Ohio candidate for some of the offices of the House. We had a long and earnest discussion with some little feeling in behalf of the candidates. The delegation is composed mainly of new men. There are only two men returned who have been members before, Bundy[178] and Lawrence.[179] At the close of the caucus Crete gave the Delegation a collation and on the whole they had a very pleasant time.

SATURDAY, 29. Made but little progress on my Burton speech. Made several calls and received many. At two o'clock the caucus assembled, twelve members being present, the thirteenth member, Lawrence, being absent. After some discussion it was decided to present Capt. Lee[180] as a candidate for Postmaster. After I left the room the remainder of the delegation resolved to send a committee to Mr. Blaine telling him that Ohio had heard with regret the proposition of the newspapers to remove me from the Committee on Appropriations and express[ed] a desire that it should not be done. It was a generous and unanimous action of the delegation. In the evening attended the general caucus in the Hall of the House of Representatives. At the conclusion of the nominations Coburn[181] introduced a resolution to divide the work of the ap-

---

[178] Hezekiah Sanford Bundy (1817–1895) was a Republican member of the House from Ohio, 1865–67, 1873–75, and 1893–95.

[179] William Lawrence (1819–1899) was a Republican member of the House from Ohio, 1865–71, 1873–77, and first comptroller of the U. S. Treasury, 1880–85.

[180] Alfred E. Lee, a veteran of the Civil War, was on the editorial staff of the *Ohio State Journal*; he was a member of the Ohio House, 1868–69.

[181] John Coburn (1825–1908), was a Republican member of the House from Indiana, 1867–75. In 1863, as colonel of the 33rd Indiana Infantry Regiment he led a reconnaissance put in motion by the first operational directive written by Garfield as Rosecrans' chief of staff. In this action he was disastrously defeated at Thompson's Station, Tennessee (March 4–5), and he and over 1,150 of his men were captured.

propriations into five or six different committees. This was not well received and the caucus adjourned. Walked to Willard's with Judge Scofield and had a long conversation on personal and political matters.

SUNDAY, 30. Had several calls in the morning, among them General Walker and Mr. Hubbard of Mass. Attended Church and heard the closing sermon of Mr. Bartholomew, who leaves his charge after today. A series of resolutions complimenting him on his work here was passed in which the matter of praise was so far overdone that the leaders could not vote for the resolution. It requires a man of more than ordinary stamp to take defeat manfully. In the evening called on Mr. Dawes and several other gentlemen. Mr. Blaine is having under consideration the proposition to change the chairmanships of several of the leading committees, in a sort of compromise spirit in hopes of pleasing both parties. What he will do I can hardly say. But he will make the great mistake of his life if he does not stand by all his old comrades and friends. What I will do in the event he changes my committee I will hold in reserve until developements are made.

December

MONDAY, 1. After dictating a number of letters in the morning called at the Printing Bureau of the Treasury Department and secured employment for Mrs. Robinson, the widow of one of the Disciples of this place. Rode with Senator Sargent in his carriage to the Capitol. After the usual meeting and greeting of old friends, the House was called to order by the Clerk, the roll was called and Mr. Blaine was elected and the officers chosen. After some debate concerning the administration of the oath to members whose rights to seats were questioned, came the drawing of seats. I was unfortunate being below the middle of the list. I had to choose a seat next the outside row. In the Thirty-Eighth Congress I drew the first choice. After debate on the subject of swearing in some members whose seats were contested the House adjourned. In the evening a caucus was held of [on] the subject of back pay. Spoke in favor of the repeal. Home at half-past ten o'clock.

TUESDAY, 2. Having heard from Mr. Scofield that the Speaker thought it strange I did not call on him, went around to his house this morning, but found he had left for the Capitol. Went as Chairman of the Committee of three with Judge Hoar[182] and Mr. Cox to meet the Joint Committee composed of Senators Anthony [and] Thurman to wait on the President and inform him that the two Houses of Congress were organized and ready to receive any communication he desired to send. He informed us that he should immediately send in his message and also inform[ed] us that he should send in to the Senate three important nominations, Williams,[183] as Chief Justice, Bristow of Kentucky as Attorney General and Shepherd as Governor of the District of Columbia. Returned to the House and after the reading of the Message concluded the discussion of the Louisiana case—Sypher[184] and Sheldon sworn in. The President has bestowed more labor on this message than any other that he has ever written. There are some crudities in his financial discussions but on the whole it is a pretty good message. Capt. Henry left for Ohio on the seven o'clock train. Made several calls in the evening.

WEDNESDAY, 3. After working at correspondence and so forth until eleven o'clock went to the Post Office Department and secured the

[182] Ebenezer Rockwood Hoar (1816–1895), a Massachusetts lawyer, was judge of the Court of Common Pleas, 1849–55, and of the State Supreme Court, 1859–69; U. S. attorney general, 1869–70; Republican member of the House, 1873–75. His brother, George Frisbie Hoar (1826–1904) was a Republican member of the House from Massachusetts, 1869–77, and of the Senate, 1877–1904.

[183] George H. Williams (1820–1910), chief justice of Oregon Territory, 1853–57; Republican member of the U. S. Senate from Oregon, 1865–71; U. S. attorney general, 1871–75. His appointment to the U. S. Supreme Court aroused so much opposition that he asked the President to withdraw the nomination.

[184] When the House convened on December 1, only two of the six representatives to which Louisiana was entitled presented unchallenged certificates of election. On the next day, however, the House voted to seat Jacob Hale Sypher (1837–1905) and Lionel A. Sheldon on the ground that they had *"prima facie* evidence of the right to seats." Immediately after the vote both men were sworn in. Sypher was a Republican member of the House, 1868–69, 1870–75.

appointment of Jason Streator as Postmaster at Hiram. The House was busy today in election cases and did but little else. Was introduced to the Earl of Westbury [Rosebery][185] who seems to be a very bright young Englishman, though not perfect in his grammar. Had a very interesting visit with Alexander H. Stephens,[186] who though feeble in body, is still mentally bright and vigorous. He informed me that he had read one of my speeches of a few years since with great pleasure and gave me a higher compliment upon its force and merits than I have received in a long time from anybody. Several gentlemen called in the evening and Crete and I also made several calls.

THURSDAY, 4. Worked on correspondence until half-past ten o'clock when I took Crete to Louisiana Avenue, to a Commissioner of Deeds for the State of Ohio and completed a deed to Sister Mary for six and one-half acres of land in Solon. Then went to the Post Office Department on business. Thence to the House where I spent the day. At last a Select Committee was appointed to take into consideration the repeal of the Salary Bill and then we witnessed the humiliating spectacle of twenty-five different members rushing in with a bill to repeal the salary clause when everybody knew that one was enough. Of course this was done merely to exhibit to the public eye an appearance of zeal. Dined at Welcker's with the Earl of Rosebery, at a dinner given by Ward. There were present Senators Conkling, Anthony, Bayard, Representatives Hale of N. Y., Frye and myself, Secretaries Robeson and Attorney General Williams. A very pleasant party. The Earl of Rosebery has read my Hudson address and spoke very highly of it. He astonished me by saying that all modern governments are tending to Republicanism and must ultimately reach it.

FRIDAY, 5. Worked off correspondence in the morning. At ten o'clock went to the State Department to consult with the Secretary in regard to our Cuban complications. It is still feared that Spain may

[185] Archibald Philip Primrose (1847–1929), fifth Earl of Rosebery, British foreign secretary, 1886 and 1892–94, prime minister, 1894–95.

[186] Alexander Hamilton Stephens (1812–1883), vice president of the Confederate States of America, 1861–65, was a member of the U. S. House of Representatives from Georgia, 1843–59, 1873–82. In 1882 he was elected governor of Georgia and served until his death.

not be able to carry out her promises in reference to the *Virginius*, in consequence of the feeble hold she has on the Cuban Government. Went to the House at twelve. But little was done up to two o'clock, when the Speaker announced the standing committees, for the 43rd Congress. After all the noise and gossip on this subject, Blaine has done the manly thing in standing by the old leaders of the House. The so-called Credit Mobilier Congressmen occupy all the old places. I am Chairman of the Committee on Appropriations and member of the Committee on Rules. After the announcement of the Committees the House adjourned. Ten years ago today I took my seat as a member of the 38th Congress.[187] I can hardly make myself believe that I have been here in active service for ten years. Then I was the youngest member in each branch of Congress, and had been so for sometime. Now there are many younger than I. Home in the evening working up correspondence and reading the papers.

SATURDAY, 6. Worked on correspondence and wrote a preface to the Burton speech addressed to the Corresponding Secretary of The [Historical and] Pioneer Society of Geauga County. Then went to several of the Departments. Got an appointment for the widow of Mr. Robinson of Indiana, late a leader of the Disciples Church of this place. Called on the Sec'y of the Navy and with him went over the financial situation in the Navy Department in reference to its preparations for possible war with Spain. In the evening dined at Sec'y Robeson's. Present, the Secretary and wife, Senators Anthony, Bayard and Sargent, Admiral Rodgers,[188] Mr. Frye of Maine and myself. We had a very pleasant dinner and the conversation took a very wide range. We must immediately confront the Cuban Question in the House, which will probably come up in the form of a deficiency bill, for the general appropriations for the current year will be exhausted before the end of this month. This bill will bring up the whole subject and will doubtless lead to an animated discussion.

[187] The 38th Congress convened on Monday, December 7, 1863.
[188] Christopher Raymond Perry Rodgers (1819–1892), chief of the Bureau of Yards and Docks, 1871–74, superintendent of the Naval Academy, 1874–78, commander in chief of the Pacific squadron, 1878–80. He was a commodore at the time of this entry, becoming rear admiral in June, 1874.

SUNDAY, 7. Attended church and listened, only a little, to a very rambling and declamatory sermon, from a Mr. Roys of Wheeling. In the afternoon read Hamerton on Intellectual Life. In the evening dined at Wormley's with Mr. Gardiner Hubbard, Messrs. Dawes, Phelps,[189] David A. Wells and Samuel H. Scudder.[190] Scudder was in College with me and graduated in the Class of 1857. In his sophomore year he became interested in Entomology and has pursued it constantly and with great success since. He has directed his energies specially to the study of moths and butterflies and is about bringing out a work which it is supposed will be the most complete and original contribution to that branch of natural history that has yet been made. There is to my mind great beauty in a life thus devoted to science. Among the anecdotes of the evening was one told by Mr. Dawes in relation to Thad Stevens.[191] He expostulated with President Lincoln against the appointment of Cameron as Sec'y of War, and intimated rather broadly that Cameron was dishonest. Lincoln says, "You mean to intimate that Cameron would steal?" "Well," said Stevens, "I do not think he would steal a hot stove." This was too good to keep and Lincoln told Cameron of it. Cameron called on Stevens and complained bitterly of his attack and Stevens promised to take back what he had said. He then called on Lincoln and said, "I have come up to take back what I said about Cameron. I am inclined to think I was wrong in saying he would not steal a hot stove."

MONDAY, 8. After dictating some letters and bringing up the journal,

[189] William Walter Phelps (1839–1894) was a Republican member of the House from New Jersey, 1873–75, 1883–89, a delegate to the Republican national conventions of 1880 and 1884, and minister to Austria-Hungary, 1881–82.

[190] Samuel H. Scudder (1873–1911), of Massachusetts, distinguished entomologist, published his greatest work, *The Butterflies of the Eastern United States and Canada, with Special Reference to New England,* in three volumes, 1888–89. He was the brother of Horace Elisha Scudder (1838–1902), editor and author.

[191] Thaddeus Stevens (1792–1868), of Pennsylvania, a Whig member of the U. S. House of Representatives, 1849–53, and a Republican member of the House, 1859 to his death.

went to the Pension Office to transact some business and thence to the Capitol where the Committee on Appropriations met at eleven and organized by electing the old clerk and messenger. The old members of the Committee besides myself are Hale and Marshall, but on the whole it is a stronger committee than that of the last Congress. We talked over the general subject of appropriations somewhat and towards the close of the hour Secretary Robeson came and laid before us a letter asking for five millions extraordinary appropriations in consequence of the prospects of war with Spain. We agreed to give him a hearing tomorrow morning at half-past ten o'clock. Not much was accomplished in the House. The Committee reported a bill in regard to the Increase of Salaries, to repeal the law of March 3d, but lost the favorable opportunity for passing it by delaying too long. They have agreed to open the general debate which I fear will be a long and useless performance. At half-past five dined with William Orton, David A. Wells and Ward and discussed a number of public questions. Home at eight P.M., worked on correspondence, etc.

TUESDAY, 9. Correspondence in the morning. Committee met at half-past ten. Secretary Robeson laid before us in detail the facts concerning the extraordinary expenditures of the Navy Department to meet the Cuban troubles. He is able to bring into immediate service but twenty-two sloops of war and eight monitors carrying in all about four hundred and seventeen guns. This I fear is not a match for the available Spanish fleet in case of collision. I was directed to prepare a bill to lay before the Committee for there [their] action tomorrow morning. The time of the House was consumed today, after the morning hour, with a spicy and violent personal debate on the salary question, which will be as damaging as it will be unprofitable. Lawrence of Ohio, and Cox of N. Y. suffered severely in the fight. In the evening Crete and I attended a reception given by Judge Swaim [Swayne] to Governor Noyes and Lady. At ten o'clock went for a few moments to the reception of Fernando Wood.[192] The merriment over the debate of yesterday [today] is very general.

[192] Fernando Wood (1812–1881) was a Democratic member of the House from New York, 1841–43, 1863–65, and 1867 to his death.

WEDNESDAY, 10. After the usual morning work, correspondence, journal, etc., went to the Committee and laid before [it] the draft of the bill which I made yesterday to meet the extraordinary expenses of the Navy Department in the Cuban troubles. We concluded to leave off all reference to the number of men to be enlisted in the Navy and also the extra million asked for by the Secretary for unexpected emergency. It is proper enough to reimburse the Department for expenses already made, allowing the future to develop its necessities, before we provide for them. Governor Shepherd came before the Committee to ask an appropriation for the Board of Public Works. I feel a good deal in doubt about the propriety of granting his request. The usual pressure of debate, proceeding from the close of the morning hour to the end of the day, was continued. Attended correspondence, and at eight o'clock in the evening went to the Ohio Sociable at General Sherman's.

THURSDAY, 11. Drove to Georgetown immediately after breakfast and looked at a horse I am thinking of buying for a saddle horse. My friends say I must ride on horseback or have some sort of exercise to regulate my digestion. The horse is a noble fellow, but I fear his price is beyond my reach. After dictating some letters walked to the Capitol and met with the Committee on Appropriations for half an hour. The House continued the discussion of the Salary Bill with a revival of the scenes of day before yesterday. Mr. Cox of New York suffered nearly as much from it [the] debate as Lawrence did two days ago. Alexander H. Stephens of Georgia, reduced almost to a skeleton, lifted to his feet by friends and supporting himself on his crutches and wearing a black cap and gloves, made a remarkable speech on the subject of salaries.[193] I have never seen so much intellectual power exhibited from so fragile and feeble a form. During his speech, which made a great impression on the House, the Speaker sent to me suggesting I reply. I did so with some effect I think but not satisfactory to my-

[193] Stephens not only defended the increase of congressional salaries on moral ground, but argued that it was politically expedient to attract the most capable men into government service. He also took occasion to say that the repeal of the franking privilege "was the greatest error of legislation of last session."

self.[194] In the evening revised my notes of the speech. Dictated some letters and at nine o'clock went with the Committee on Appropriations to witness the operations of the Automatic Telegraph, near Willard's Hotel on Pennsylvania Avenue.

FRIDAY, 12. After working off some correspondence, went to the State Department to talk over the Cuban question so that I might understand its bearings when my appropriation bill comes up, for the discussion may come then though I shall try to ward it off to a later period. I am strongly impressed with the opinion that the *Virginius* carried a counterfeit flag and fraudulent papers; that she was no doubt wholly owned and controlled by the Cuban insurgents. If this be true we must acknowledge it to Spain in the face of the world. The first three hours of the House was consumed in discussing the voting on the Salary Bill. The subject was recommitted to the Committee to bring in a bill reaching other than congressional salaries also. At three o'clock I called up the four million bill for the Navy Department and made a statement of the general grounds on which the appropriations were asked. After an hour and a half's debate the bill was passed. In the evening took the children to the theatre to hear Joe Jefferson[195] in *The Heir at Law* and *Lend Me Five Shillings*. The first piece was somewhat above the comprehension of the little ones. I think it would have been better for them to have been taken to see *Rip Van Winkle.* But the farce they liked very much. Jefferson is simply wonderful in his humor.

SATURDAY, 13. Worked on correspondence until half-past ten o'clock when I made a call on the President, in company with several Ohio

[194] In his reply Garfield complimented Stephens' speech but stated that in a world where worth is usually not measured by moral and intellectual standards, men must act on a sense of duty, as did Union soldiers who fought for little pay to save the country. He said that able men were entering the government, presented arguments against the salary increase, and urged its repeal.

[195] Joseph Jefferson (1829–1905), probably the most beloved American actor of his day, first enacted the title role in Dion Boucicault's version of *Rip Van Winkle* in London in 1865; during the following generation he played the part on innumerable occasions and was always identified with it in the public mind.

gentlemen, to ask his favorable consideration of Mr. Coles [Cowles] of Cleveland, Ohio, for a foreign appointment. After that went to Georgetown to look at a horse which I am thinking of buying. Rode back into the city. He is a very good horse but they ask $350.00 for him, which is more than I am willing to pay. Called at Wormley's to see the Mr. Hutson [Rutson][196] of England who has been introduced to me by E. L. Godkin, editor of the *Nation*. In the afternoon finished my Burton speech, and forwarded it to the editor of the *Geauga County Republican* for publication. Several friends called in the evening. Had engaged to dine in the evening with Mr. Hutson [Rutson], but did not feel well enough. I find it necessary to be exceedingly careful of my digestion. I seem to be threatened with neuralgic dyspepsia. I have been able to stand all the work that has come to me chiefly because I have had the power of sleeping well and eating. If these two forces fail me I shall break down. I need to be specially careful.

SUNDAY, 14. In the morning, after reading the mail, read up some particulars concerning the capture of the *Virginius*. Also received a letter from Mr. Haywood [Hayward][197] of Conneaut, enclosing a letter from one of the victims of the *Virginius* slaughter. An Englishman, by the name of Baynard,[198] who has sailed on the Lake here for two years, was shot. The letter was written two hours before he met his death and is a very manly and touching statement of the facts. Attended church and listened to a passable sermon by a Virginian. Wrote a few letters and made some calls in company

[196] Albert Osliff Rutson (1836–1890), fellow of Magdalen College, Oxford, was private secretary to British Home Secretary Henry Austin Bruce (later Baron Aberdare), 1868–73.

[197] Samuel Hayward, president of the Conneaut Mutual Loan Association, also enclosed a portrait of Baynard. Garfield brought the letter and portrait to the attention of the secretary of state and also promised to see that the letter went to the British minister to enable him to inform Baynard's friends in England of his death. Garfield to Hayward, letterbook, December 16, 1873. A partly illegible copy of Baynard's letter is also in Garfield's letterbook.

[198] William Baynard, single, age 37, was first mate of the *Virginius*; he is listed in a State Department document as among those executed. He is also recorded as being from the United States.

with Mr. Parsons of Cleveland. Gave my children a lecture on the story of the capture of the *Virginius* and the subsequent negotiations with Spain. Several gentlemen called in the evening, among them Senator Morrill, Mr. Dawes and my colleague Foster.[199] I must make some move for a thorough retrenchment in our expenses. My dear and admired friend Prof. Agassiz died today in Boston—died I fear of overwork. He warned me three years ago against overwork; and said he was living in daily dread of break-down in consequence of having overtaxed his strength. Many memories of pleasant intercourse socially, and at the meeting of the Board of Regents, come back to me, now that he is gone.

MONDAY, 15. Committee met at half-past ten, and I laid before [it] my views of our duty in the way of cutting down estimates and appropriations. I distributed the appropriation bills, giving the Indian Bill to a committee of three and distributing all the other bills, except the three which the Chairman usually takes. I also drafted a resolution, which, after a few modifications, was unanimously adopted, requesting the President to cause the estimates to be revised. After the adjournment of the Committee, a committee of two members of the Committee of Ways and Means came to me to confer about a similar resolution which that Committee had passed. It was finally agreed that I should introduce mine and the two Committees should work together. In the House after the morning hour Mr. Dawes opened the discussion and I introduced my resolution and a lively discussion followed, resulting in the passage of the resolution by an overwhelming majority. There are three courses before us; to cut down expenditures, increase taxes, or supply the deficit by loans or Treasury notes. The last, which is inflation, is the worst thing that can be done. In the evening worked off correspondence, corrected the notes of my speech in the House today. At half-past nine o'clock went with the Committtee on Appropriations and the Senate Committee on Post Office[s], the Postmaster General and Vice President of the Automatic Telegraph Co. to witness the operation of that system. After the slips had been prepared in the office, the President's Message consisting of 11,000 words was sent in 22½ minutes.

[199] Charles Foster (1828–1904), was a Republican member of the House, 1871–79, governor of Ohio, 1880–84, and secretary of the treasury, 1891–93.

TUESDAY, 16. Correspondence in the morning. At ten o'clock went to the office of General J. G. Payne to consult on the case of *Daniels vs. Driggs*. Then called at the City Hall to look after my interest in the estate of Uriah Hutchins deceased. Committee met me at 11 o'clock. Postmaster General came by appointment and laid before us some estimates of deficiencies. We spent an hour with him on that and on the general estimates for his department. In the House after a long debate a bill was passed repealing the Bankrupt law,[200] then the salary question came up and the session held on until six o'clock. The discussion and the votes ranging through the gamut of the demagogue's song until at last the retroactive reduction was accomplished on motion of Mr. Kasson[201] of Iowa. In the evening at eight o'clock went to the Speaker's to meet the Committee on Rules.

WEDNESDAY, 17. In accordance with the directions of Dr. Pope,[202] I this morning engaged a saddle horse for a month and after reading my mail and working up more correspondence rode for an hour and then went to the Supreme Court of the District to argue a motion; but after waiting until near twelve it was postponed until Friday morning. Committee on Appropriations did not meet. House spent all day, until nine o'clock at night, on the Salary Bill. After a series of motions, and speeches, and votes, and a very exciting session, a bill was passed, fixing the congressional salary at $6,000, and leaving all other salaries as they were. I am not satisfied with the case as it stands and fear it will not give satisfaction in view of the clamor that has been raging on the subject.

THURSDAY, 18. Committee met at ten o'clock and thirty minutes. They authorized me to report back the extraordinary Naval Ap-

[200] The Bankrupt Law of 1867 established a uniform system of bankruptcy throughout the United States, but with the panic of 1873 causing numerous financial embarrassments, congressmen decided that the law was too severe and voted for repeal, 219–44.

[201] John Adam Kasson (1822–1910), a Republican member of the House from Iowa, 1863–67, 1873–77, 1881–84; minister to Austria-Hungary, 1877–81, and to Germany, 1884–85.

[202] Gustavus W. Pope, a physician who lived on I Street near Garfield's home.

propriation Bill concur[r]ing in the Senate Amendment. Also, reported an appropriation for paying the reporters of the *Congressional Record*. We also discussed several plans for cutting down the appropriations for the coming year. In the House nearly two hours were spent in personal explanation which result[ed] in a heavy attack on Judge Hale of N. Y. for drawing salary in two capacities.[203] Got my two appropriation bills through. The salary debate has been productive of but little good and has done much harm. Dined with Mr. Ward and at 8 o'clock went to Senator Thurman's for a social gathering of the Ohio Delegation. Had a very pleasant time, remaining until a late hour. I see that the newspapers are as noisy as ever over the action of the House on the Salary Bill. The bill is not what it ought to be. It should extend beyond members of Congress. But whatever we may do newspaper clamor cannot be satisfied. The press is fast becoming intolerable in its arrogance and recklessness.

FRIDAY, 19. At half-past nine took a horseback ride, as I did also yesterday morning. At half-past ten went to the office of General Payne, where we consulted with our client Daniels in regards to the motion before the Supreme Court of the District. At 11 went to the Court and asked the postponement of the motion until the 7th of January, which was granted. Also, asked that the whole affidavit on which the motion is based should be sent up to Court.

---

[203] In the summer of 1871 Robert Safford Hale of New York was appointed agent and counsel of the United States before the American and British Mixed Commission provided for by the Treaty of Washington. In the fall of 1872 he was elected to the House. To enable him to remain at his work before the Commission, Congress passed an act authorizing the President to continue to employ Hale until he took the oath of office. Hale stayed on as counsel until the last of November, 1873. Thus, from March 4, 1873, he drew a salary as counsel at the rate of $10,000 per year, and a salary as a congressman at the rate of $7,500 per year. The attack on Hale, made by Benjamin F. Butler, Charles A. Eldredge, and Jeremiah M. Wilson, grew out of Hale's speech of December 16 in which he urged repeal of the salary increase, arguing that $7,500 a year was too large a salary for a congressman, and that the increase had not been accomplished "by square, manly, honest legislation."

Rode to the House with General Butler, who is opposing counsel. The day was spent on private bills and in debating the Civil Service [Rights] Bill. Several gentlemen called. Among others Senator Jones[204] and Frank Hutchins[205] of Warren, Ohio. The Senate has concurred with the House resolution for adjournment and Congress today adjourned to meet on the 5th day of January next. Called a meeting of the Committee on Appropriations after adjournment and agreed to assemble one week from next Tuesday. Also appointed a sub-committee to go to Boston and investigate the purchase of a lot adjoining the Post Office.[206] I appointed Mr. Hale, Tyner[207] and Hancock[208] a sub-committee, but the Committee requested me to go with Hale and Hancock, which I shall probably do. Mr. Gilfillan and wife and Mr. Rose and wife took dinner with us. Attended a

[204] Lucian Curtis Jones, of Warren, law partner of Ezra Booth Taylor, was a member of the Ohio Senate, 1872–74.

[205] Francis Edwin Hutchins, Warren lawyer. A friend of William McKinley, he became special assistant to the attorney general in 1898.

[206] The United States had begun construction of a post office and sub-treasury building in Boston in 1869. In March, 1873, Congress had appropriated funds for the purchase of land for an extension of the building. Having failed to come to terms with the owners, the government went to court in a test case. Meanwhile the land was steadily increasing in value as a result in part of the great fire of 1872. The court held that the value should be that of the date of the verdict (October, 1873), a considerably higher value than when proceedings were begun. Garfield's group, a subcommittee of the Committee on Appropriations, went to Boston to examine the land and to take testimony concerning it. As a result of its trip, the subcommittee recommended that no additional appropriations be made for the purchase of the land. Later, after further litigation, the land was obtained, and the building completed in 1885. Called by Bill Nye "an inconvenient stone quarry," it was a monument of the reign of A. B. Mullett as supervising architect of the Treasury.

[207] James Noble Tyner (1826–1904) was a Republican member of the House, 1869–75. His long career in the Post Office Department included service as second assistant postmaster general, 1875–76, postmaster general, 1876–77, and first assistant postmaster general, 1877 to his resignation on October 29, 1881.

[208] John Hancock (1824–1893) was a Democratic member of the House from Texas, 1871–77, 1883–85.

meeting of the Smithsonian Regents at seven o'clock in the evening. After eight years of service my term as Regent expires next Wednesday. This has been the most pleasant duty of my official life. I made a speech on the character of Prof. Agassiz.[209]

SATURDAY, 20.   Saturday worked on correspondence until half-past ten when I took my hour on horseback. Called at the National Hotel to see Mr. Hancock in regard to our trip to Boston. Worked on correspondence until two o'clock. Then went to the War Department on business. Made some calls with Crete at Willard's. Among others called on Mr. and Mrs. Sheppard [Shepard][210] of N. Y. Mrs. Shepard is a sister of Larkin Mead, the sculptor, and also the sister [of] Will Howells' wife. Then went shopping with Crete until dinner time. In the evening read a large mail and worked up odds and ends of business until a late hour. The newspaper press seems to have combined to set the public mind against Congress and indeed against the whole administration. It is clear to my mind that this course if persisted in will before long break down and destroy the Republican Party. The press is passing through a very dangerous and reckless phase of its career. It will find its power destroyed and repudiated by this very public opinion which it now seeks to inflame against others.

SUNDAY, 21.   After my morning ride went to church and listened to a sermon from Mr. Cutler of Va., a vehement revivalist, who thinks to drive people into the church by sharp logic. There was more sense in a few sentences of B. K. Smith of Indianapolis giving the exegesis of the first verses of 3d Chapter of Galatians— showing that the passage referred to the celebration of the Lord's Supper. After church I read nearly half of Mr. Riddle's new book, *The Portrait*. It is a powerfully written and attractive story. Its scene is laid in the Valley of the Cuyahoga River. At six o'clock

[209] In a brief talk Garfield eulogized both Salmon P. Chase and Louis Agassiz. See *Annual Report of the Board of Regents of the Smithsonian Institution* for 1873, pp. 148–151.

[210] Augustus D. Shepard was at this time treasurer of the National Bank-Note Company of New York City. He married Joanna Elizabeth Mead (1824–1914); her sister, Elinor Gertrude Mead (1837–1910) married William Dean Howells in 1862.

dined at Secretary Fish's with George Pierepont [Judge Pierrepont][211] of New York and Senator Howe and other guests. We had a very pleasant visit in which many of the phases of public life were discussed, particularly the tone and tendency of the public press. Governor Fish declares that the Metropolitan Press is almost wholly venal and this is {I} incline to believe. On my return read *The Portrait* until a late hour.

MONDAY, 22.   After working until eleven o'clock on correspondence I took my hour's gallop and then went out with Crete to get the Christmas presents for the children; also, made several calls. At 5 o'clock P.M. attended the Kindergarten Exhibition where our three children took a part and behaved very creditably. I feel some satisfaction in the experiment we have tried with them but am still uncertain whether it is wise to give them up wholly to this scheme of study. At any rate the experiment is a temporary one and I am not committed to it beyond this trial. Worked until a late hour getting my affairs in readiness to leave for Boston tomorrow. I greatly dislike to go and leave the family during the Holidays.

TUESDAY, 23.   At eight o'clock took the train in company with Hale of Maine, and [Francis H.] Smith, the shorthand reporter for Committees of the House, and spent an uncomfortable day in travelling to New York through a snow storm. A return of the piles added to my other maladies makes the trip specially undesirable. The car was very much crowded, Nilsson[212] and her opera troop being on board. Reached New York at 6, went to the Windsor Hotel for dinner. At eight o'clock took the sleeping car for Boston and left in the midst of a snow storm. During the day I have read several of the official reports; among others the report of the Supervising Architect and also I have read up the papers in relation to the Boston Post Office.

WEDNESDAY, 24.   Reach[ed] Boston at six o'clock. Mr. Ordway,

211 Edwards Pierrepont (1817–1892), New York lawyer and former judge, was U. S. attorney general, 1875–76, and minister to Great Britain, 1876–77. In 1873 he was appointed minister to Russia but declined. He was often referred to as Judge Pierrepont. Garfield's secretary apparently misunderstood Garfield's dictation and wrote "George" for "Judge."

212 Christine Nilsson (1843–1921), Swedish operatic soprano, was on tour in the United States, 1873–74.

Sergeant-at-Arms of the House, met us at the train, took us to the Revere House where a room was in readiness for us. The Postmaster at Boston, Mr. [William L.] Burt, gave us a breakfast, at which were present the Hon. Ginery Twitchell, Judge Russell,[213] Clerk of the Port of Boston, and several other Gentlemen. At 12 o'clock we went to the City Hall to take the testimony of the Street Commissioners and also the City Assessor, as to the value of the property in the Post Office Square and in the adjoining Squares. Continued in this work until four o'clock in the afternoon. We were then driven to several portions of the burnt district and examined the work of rebuilding. At five o'clock dined with the Hon. Mr. Pierce,[214] late Mayor of Boston, now a member of Congress. There were present the Mayor, the Hon. Samuel Hooper, Vice President Wilson and many other gents. Spent the night at the Parker House.

THURSDAY, 25. I find that New England has at last surrendered to the seductions of Merry Christmas. In the early Puritan days this holiday was looked upon as a compromise with the "Scarlet Lady." Today the City is as loyal to Christmas as the Pope. Hale is nearly sick with cold. And I staid indoors all day to read up the testimony before the Massachusetts Court in regard to the condemnation of the land for the Post Office. The subject is a tangled and difficult one and I am supposed to take the Court lawyers who oppose the Government at their word and hold that the U. S. has not taken the land at all. Snow has been falling steadily all day and a sturdy New England winter is about us. Judge Loughridge[215] came this morning to join the Committee in its work. Frye of Maine is also with us. Hale and I called during the day on Thomas Gaffield and had a very pleasant visit. He is an alderman and has long been in City politics, but still pushes his studies in photography and glass.

FRIDAY, 26. At ten o'clock went to the U. S. Court Room where a

---

[213] Thomas Russell (1825–1887), formerly a judge of the Superior Court of Massachusetts, was collector of the port of Boston, 1867–74.

[214] Henry Lillie Pierce (1825–1896) was mayor of Boston in 1873 and 1878, and a Republican member of the U. S. House of Representatives, December 1, 1873 to March 4, 1877.

[215] William Loughridge (1827–1889) was a Republican member of the House from Iowa, 1867–71, 1873–75.

large number of citizens interested in the property about the Post Office had assembled [and] several lawyers who had been engaged in the case before the Court. Some twenty witnesses were examined and their testimony taken in regard to the value of the property. We listened also to arguments on the merits of the case by Messrs. Shattuck, Somerby, Welsh [Welch] and several others.[216] Adjourned at four o'clock. At half-past five we dined with Mr. Shattuck at the Somerset Club in company with Richard H. Dana,[217] George [Judge?] Gray,[218] and several other gentlemen of prominence in Boston. At the close I drove out to Cambridge to visit my friend W. J[D]. Howells, where I found his sister Annie, his wife, and his mother[-in-law], Mrs. Mead. Also the poet Longfellow. We spent a delightful evening in this charming circle and after a supper left at ten o'clock in the midst of a snow storm for Boston. Spent the night at the Revere House.

SATURDAY, 27. Visited the old South Church now occupied by the Post Office. Also went carefully through the new post office building now approaching completion. Also visited the Custom House, Faneuil Hall, State House and other points of interest and at half-past two dined at the Parker House, as the guest of the Commercial Club, an organization consisting of sixty leading merchants and business men of Boston. Hon. Alexander H. Rice,[219] formerly a member of Congress, presided. In response to their call I addressed the members of the Club for about fifteen minutes in regard to the Post Office question, the Bankrupt Bill and the Currency. Richard

216 The records of the subcommittee indicate that Shattuck and Welch represented owners of some of the land which the government wished to acquire, and that Somerby was counsel for the government. These men were probably George Otis Shattuck, Gustavus A. Somerby and Charles A. Welch, local lawyers.

217 Richard H. Dana (1815–1882), a Boston lawyer, author of *Two Years before the Mast* (1840).

218 Probably Horace Gray (1828–1902), associate justice, Massachusetts Supreme Judicial Court, 1864–73, chief justice, 1873–81, associate justice of the U. S. Supreme Court, 1881–1902. Garfield's secretary presumably misunderstood the dictation, and wrote "George" for "Judge."

219 Alexander Hamilton Rice (1818–1895) was a Republican member of the House from Massachusetts, 1859–67; governor of Massachusetts, 1876–78.

H. Dana, Mr. Mudge,[220] Judge Russell, Judge Loughridge and several others spoke. Returned to the Revere House at eight o'clock took the sleeping car for N. Y. in company with General Burt, Postmaster at Boston. Our work here has been difficult but I believe we have done all that it was possible to accomplish for the time we had.

SUNDAY, 28. Reached N. Y. at half-past six o'clock. Found nearly a foot of snow on the ground. Went to the Fifth Avenue Hotel and took breakfast after which I drove to 16 Gramercy Park and stopped with the Honorable Clarkson N. Potter, member of Congress. With him I attended Grace Church, at which his brother[221] officiates and who was assisted by his brother, the President of Union College.[222] After we returned from church General McDowell called on me and informed me that he had promised I should dine with A. T. Stewart. Went around the [to] General McDowell's and spent an hour and at half-past three o'clock went to Mr. A. T. Stewart's residence on the corner of Fifth Avenue and Thirty-fourth St., where I met Mr. Sherman,[223] David A. Wells, Mr. Jones[224] and one or two other gentlemen. After some discussion of the financial situation and a visit to Mr. Stewart's picture gallery, took an elegant dinner and at seven General McDowell and I returned to Mr. Potter's. At half-past eight left for the Washington train. Found General Burt on the Jersey side of the city and took the sleeping car for Washington.

MONDAY, 29. Reached home at half-past six o'clock in the morning. Weather very clear and cold. My journey has been in some respects a pleasant one, but somewhat wearying. Glad to meet the family again. After [breakfast] finished reading the mail which had accumulated in my absence. Spent fully six hours before I had

[220] Enoch Redington Mudge (1812–1881), prominent Boston business-man, was sales agent for several New England cotton and woolen mills.

[221] Henry Codman Potter (1835–1908) was minister of Grace Episcopal Church, New York, 1868–83.

[222] Eliphalet Nott Potter (1836–1901), an Episcopal minister, was president of Union College, 1871–84.

[223] Probably Thomas G. Shearman.

[224] Probably George Jones (1811–1891), publisher of the *New York Times*.

concluded the reading of it. Brought up my journal and dictated a large number of letters, which kept me until a late hour. Feel a good deal tired out as the result of the week's work.

TUESDAY, 30. In the morning worked on correspondence. At ten o'clock went shopping with Crete and a little before twelve met a portion of the Committee on Appropriations and spent an hour or two in a general discussion of our work. Then spent two hours in the Library looking over new arrivals of English books and magazines. Returned and continued work on correspondence until dinner. In the evening a delegation from the Board of Health called on me in reference to appropriations for their work. Several other people called in the evening. Read and wrote until a late hour.

WEDNESDAY, 31. After dictating a few letters took up the case of *Driggs vs. Daniels* and read carefully and analyzed the numerous papers in the case. If I had not engaged in this case I would decline to have anything further to do with it for I seriously doubt whether our client has a good case. This is the first instance in my practice as a lawyer when I have come to such a conclusion in regard to my client; for I have usually declined to accept any case where I believed the right was not on my side. I shall, however, do the best I can, but shall set up no claim that I do not think well-founded. Resumed my morning gallop; transacted some business on the way. Sat up with Crete to watch and watched the old year out. Years ago, the death of the old year was an event that called forth much more sentiment than I can now feel. Still there is a subdued solemnity that always comes over me as the year closes. But the years go so swiftly now, they are so full of events, that I cannot tide over them as I once did; and then I am less introspective than formerly. I still cling to Tennyson and as the Holidays come, the "ring out wild bells to the wild sky" comes back to me with its charms and its memories. I close this volume which records the stormiest year of my life. The old vim of my early years has gone. Then I thought how I looked forward to the time when I should have achieved something worthy of remembrance. I looked forward to such achievements as belonging to a period of sunshine and honor and peace. I have not achieved much but I have climbed to the heighth where the wind blows furiously and cold. I now look back to the peace and quiet of other years with a sadness that hardly becomes a man of forty-two years. I can do but little to direct my life. The very pressure of my surroundings determines my pathway. It is too late to retire; the battle is set and must go on. The year 1873, has, like myself suffered some hard knocks and abuses and passes into oblivion scarred and bruised and not greatly regretted. Old but rough friend and yet fellow sufferer, farewell.

1874

January

I am not a little surprised at myself, that I have been able to continue uninterrupted a journal during the last three years. I presume I should not have done this but for the help of Mr. Rose. A man keeps a promise to another better than to himself, and I have in some sort felt under obligation to Rose to keep up this journal, otherwise I think it would have fallen like my former attempts. I shall try to continue it during the New Year.

THURSDAY, 1. I am not well this morning and the year comes in blank and damp. I continued work on the Daniels papers until eleven o'clock when I dressed and joined my college classmate, Hill, Assistant Att'y General of the U. S., in making New Year's calls. We called on the President and witnessed the usual pageant of New Year's morning at the White House. After that we spent the remainder of the day until six in the evening in making about sixty calls. Mrs. Monroe assisted Crete in receiving her calls which amounted to about sixty during the day and in the evening. Made a few calls on my neighbors in the evening and spent an hour or two at A. G. Riddle's, talking of his new book *The Portrait*, which I think is a very successful [one]. Thus ended the first lesson of 1874.

FRIDAY, 2. Even one day away from my desk brings overwork as the penalty. Spent the forenoon until eleven o'clock bringing up work, and at eleven took my morning galop, and during it visited [Francis H.] Smith, the House Reporter. Made arrangements for getting the report of our Boston examination out. Continued work on correspondence; also commenced an article for the newspapers on Riddle's new book *The Portrait*. At five o'clock, went to the office of Mr. Daniels and consulted with him and Mr. Payne in regard to [the] Daniels case in the Supreme Court of the District. At eight o'clock the Sub-committee on Appropriations, Judge Hale, Loughridge and myself, met here and considered the Boston Post Office question. Agreed on the general plan of the Report, which I am to prepare. Sub-committee adjourned at eleven o'clock. I continued to read my mail until midnight.

SATURDAY, 3. Worked on correspondence until 11 o'clock, when I took my horse-back ride bringing up at the Capitol at a meeting of the Committee on Appropriations at 12 o'clock. Had a nearly full Committee. Took up the Army Bill and worked on it very satisfactorily for four hours. We shall be able to succeed in making a large reduction, perhaps three millions. Went to the old [law?] library and obtained some authorities in reference to the Daniels Case. In the evening dictated to the House Reporter portion of the Report of the Sub-committee on the Boston Post Office.

SUNDAY, 4. Took my galop, going to Washington Heights, overlooking Rock Creek. Then, at Church, listened to an able sermon from B. K. Smith, of Ohio. John Q. Smith called on me in the forenoon, and took dinner with us. Had a pleasant visit. Several others called in the evening. I called on Speaker Blaine at nine o'clock in reference to legislative work of tomorrow morning.

MONDAY, 5. Worked on correspondence and on the Boston Post Office Report until one-quarter before ten. Horseback riding until Mr. Bangs called and spent an hour in discussing with me the propriety of putting on an exclusive train for mails between New York and Chicago; consolidating the various mail cars in one train and running it from thirty-five to forty miles an hour, making the entire distance between those two cities in twenty-four hours. Intelligence should travel faster than merchandize. I like the plan.

TUESDAY, 6. Worked on correspondence and finished report on the Boston Post Office. Mr. Olcott did not send saddle horse, so I had no galop this morning. Met the Committee on Appropriations at half-past ten, the Secretary of the Navy present. We worked on the Naval Appropriation Bill for four hours. Finished it about half-past two. Cut down the estimates about three millions, making the total sixteen millions. Later in the day I called the Sub-committee on the Boston Post Office together and read them my report of over thirty pages of manuscript, which they approved and signed. Elliott of South Carolina, a colored member, made a very effective speech in reply to Stevens [Stephens] and the other members opposed to the Civil Rights Bill.[1] Near the close of the session Hale got in the Naval Bill and set its hearing for next Thursday. The friends of large expenditures at the Navy Yards combined to prevent the early discussion of the bill; but we beat them. I presented the report of our Boston sub-committee and had it printed and recommitted. Worked in the evening on the Daniels law case.

WEDNESDAY, 7. Worked on correspondence until one-quarter past ten o'clock, when I took a short horse-back ride, and at half-past ten went to the office of General Payne, on Louisiana Avenue, and held a consultation preparatory to going into Court at eleven on the Daniels Case. Found that Judge Wylie[2] was sick and the case had to go over. I then went to the Capitol and worked about an hour on the appropriations for my Legislative Appropriation Bill. The House recommitted the Civil Service [Rights] Bill after a long speech from Butler,[3] and not much else was accomplished. In the evening read several of the latest British magazines, and wrote a long letter to Burke in regard to John Stuart Mill. Mr. and Mrs. Riddle called and spent an hour and a half.

THURSDAY, 8. Worked on correspondence until ten o'clock, when I went shopping with Crete a little while. Reached the Committee Room at half-past ten, when we took up Fortification Bill and heard Gen'l Humphreys and Colonel Casey on the various items and particularly on the discussion relating to the use of torpedoes for defence of our harbor. Committee continued its consideration of the bill until near one o'clock when we completed it, having reduced the appropriations down to $994,000, about half the corresponding

[1] Alexander Stephens of Georgia had spoken against the bill on January 5, but the speech of Robert Brown Elliott (1842–1884), Republican member of the House from South Carolina, 1871–74, was mostly a reply to James B. Beck of Kentucky, who had spoken against the bill on December 19, 1873.

[2] Andrew Wylie (1814–1905), associate justice of the Supreme Court of the District of Columbia, 1863–85.

[3] In an eloquent and witty speech, frequently interrupted by laughter and applause, Butler argued powerfully for civil rights legislation.

appropriation for last year and a reduction of nearly three millions on the estimates. After the morning hour we met in Committee of the Whole on the Naval Appropriation Bill and continued the discussion until five in the afternoon, when the Committee rose, and the House adjourned. Several gentlemen called in the evening. I assisted Miss May[s] a little in putting the boys through their lessons. Then worked on correspondence and the Journal and on appropriation estimates for the rest of the evening. During the day I saw Dr. Baxter[4] and consulted him in regard to my stomach trouble. Obtained medicine from him.

FRIDAY, 9. After correspondence went to the Post Office Department and worked an hour on cases that have accumulated. Then went to my committee and had a meeting for quite an hour. In the House we did not get to work on the Naval Appropriation Bill. There seems to be an aversion to pushing the appropriation bills. Obituary speeches were made on notices of the death of James Brooks of New York and Mr. Foster[5] of Michigan. At 7 P.M. dined with Mr. Rothery[6] at his rooms on Fifteenth Street. There were present Mrs. Rothery, Miss Charlton, Sir Edward Thornton[7] and two of his legation, Senator Sumner, Judge Hoar, Speaker Blaine and myself. We had a long talk over the nomination of Caleb Cushing and the representatives present urged upon Sumner the impropriety of pushing the appointment.[8] He is fully seventy years old, has been

[4] Jedediah Hyde Baxter (1837–1890), chief medical purveyor for the U. S. army, was Garfield's physician for several years; in 1890 he became surgeon general of the United States, a position which he would probably have reached earlier had Garfield lived.

[5] Wilder De Ayr Foster (1819–1873), a Republican member of the House, 1871 to his death on September 20, 1873.

[6] Henry Cadogan Rothery (1817–1888), English maritime expert, who was in Washington to aid in the settlement of the fisheries question, as provided for in the Treaty of Washington (1871).

[7] Sir Edward Thorton (1817–1906), British minister to the United States, 1867–81.

[8] Grant's third nomination for the chief justiceship was that of Caleb Cushing of Massachusetts (1800–1879), a distinguished legal authority. Although he was completely loyal to the Union during the Civil War and rendered effective service to the Republican party and to Lincoln, Johnson,

a bitter opponent of republican ideas and is doubtless appointed as a mere "*locum tenens*." I hear that Sargent objected in Executive Session and thus prevented his confirmation today—I am proud of him for it. Attended Fish's reception.

SATURDAY, 10. Worked on correspondence until ten o'clock when I went to the Interior Department with Mr. Woodworth of the Mahoning District to aid him in securing the appointment of a young man to a position in the Patent Office. Then went to the Treasury Department with Senator Allison to aid Capt. Russell of Des Moines, Iowa, in holding his position as a Treasury Detective.[9] Took my galop and went to the Speaker's Room at the Capitol to attend a meeting of the Committee on Rules. Set for nearly two hours to act on some proposed change in the Rules. Called on the Postmaster General on my return and transacted some business. Worked on correspondence and appropriation questions in the evening until half-past seven when Crete and I went to the Opera, and heard *Fra Diavolo*.

SUNDAY, 11. Attended church and listened to a sermon from B. K. Smith. At one took my galop across the Anacostia Bridge and went two miles into the country to Ray's and saw the Carrolls. Returned at half-past three after a ride of eight miles. In the evening translated into blank verse the third ode of the first book of Horace.

MONDAY, 12. Worked on correspondence until nearly ten o'clock, when I took my morning galop. Went to the Committee Room on Appropriations at half-past ten. Committee did not get through until

---

and Grant, his nomination was assailed on the basis of his real and imagined prewar positions and statements. A letter of Cushing written to Jefferson Davis on March 20, 1861, in which he commended to Davis a Texan who had been employed as a clerk in the office of the attorney general, was discovered, and read to the Republican caucus of the Senate by Senator Sargent of California on January 14. Immediately thereafter Grant withdrew the nomination. Cushing became minister to Spain and in that capacity worked hard and successfully to prevent an armed clash over the *Virginius* Affair.

9 Garfield's action in behalf of Captain M. T. Russell was taken at the request of his longtime friend Corydon Fuller, now a resident of Des Moines. Russell, a Disciple of Christ and former officer in the 51st Indiana Infantry Regiment, which was brigaded under Garfield in 1862, was being opposed by John A. Kasson.

about eleven. Distributed a large amount of business that had accumulated on the Docket. Reported back a number of bills and memorials improperly referred to the Committee on Appropriations, and agreed to hold a session tomorrow morning to determine what we would do with the Postal Telegraph Question. In the House after the morning hour Kelley's resolution for making up the deficit in the Treasury by a loan came up and failed by a few votes of securing a two-thirds majority. Then came a resolution in favor of retrenchment rather than taxation. Then another expressing the sentiment of Congress against increasing the Public Debt and also against inflating the currency. Then went into Committee of the Whole on the Naval Bill. Spent an hour or two in general debate. I spoke about twenty minutes in response to an attack Beck made on the Appropriation Committee.[10]

TUESDAY, 13. Correspondence until half-past ten. Went shopping with Crete until eleven. I met the Committee and we discussed our order of proceedings in regard to the Postal Telegraph. Agreed to consult our various State Delegations and find out whether they were in favor of taking the subject up at all. In one week we report the results to the Committee and determine our course. In the House after the morning hour proceeded with the Naval Appropriation Bill. The bill was read the first time and the reading by sections commenced. Debate continued until three o'clock when the Committee rose. The House proceeded to consider the Senate amendment to the Congressional Salary Bill. The previous question was ordered. I demanded the Yeas and Nays and by an overwhelming vote the House concurred in that amendment, which restores all the salaries to the rates they were fixed at before the Act of Mar. 3d, 1873, except those of the President and Judges of the Supreme Court. I hope the noise on this subject will at last subside though I am by no means sure that it will. I introduce[d] a rule from the Committee on Rules, which was adopted, requiring that

---

[10] To Beck's chief complaint, which was that the committee, and in particular Garfield, had withheld pertinent information about the need for additional naval appropriations occasioned by the crisis with Spain over the *Virginius* Affair, Garfield replied that Congress had been properly and adequately informed.

all bills appropriating money or other property be referred to the
Committee of the Whole. At six o'clock dined with Gardiner Hub-
bard in company with Senators Morrill, Sherman and Mr. Dawes.
Discussed the finances.

WEDNESDAY, 14. Correspondence, horse-back, Committee on Appropriations, in the usual order. Made further progress on the Naval
Appropriation Bill. Got Committee of Conference on the bill for
paying the Congressional Reporters. The nomination of Cushing for
Chief Justice deserves to be noted. His confirmation by the Senate
was prevented last week by one brave man, Sargent of California.
Yesterday morning Sargent discussed him fully, exhibiting his Cop-
perhead record, then procured an adjournment of the caucus until
evening and during the day, following the trial got in an anonymous
letter, succeeded in discovering what will hereafter be the famous
Cushing letter to Jeff Davis of March 20th, 1861. It was among
the Rebel Archives and had just been in the President's hands.
Sargent sent to the Cabinet demanding it. Then having procured a
copy he launched it into the caucus last evening and it exploded,
carrying away Cushing and his supporters. Both Binney and Sargent [Sergeant] of Philadelphia, when they were but little more
than sixty years of age, declined the seat of Chief Justice on account
of their age.[11] Cushing sought it at seventy-three. Worked in the
evening on correspondence and appropriations.

THURSDAY, 15. Correspondence, horseback riding and committee
work brought me to the meeting of the House. The Committee
made some amendments to the Army and Navy Bill and considered a
general bill relating to the method of preparing estimates for
Congress. In the House after the morning hour, we took up the
Navy Appropriation Bill. The Committee continued its discussion
until after four o'clock, when the Committee rose and reported
the bill to the House and it was passed without the change of a cent

[11] Henry A. Wise, in his *Seven Decades of the Union* (1872)—the source
of Garfield's story—tells of President Tyler's offer of a Supreme Court
appointment to two well-known Philadelphia lawyers, first to John Sergeant
(1779–1852), and upon his refusal, to Horace Binney (1780–1875). Each
man declined the appointment because of age, but each recommended the
other, and asked that the other not be informed of the reason for his
declension.

from the amount reported by the Committee. In the evening Crete and I called on Mr. and Mrs. Sheldon, at Willard's.

FRIDAY, 16. Another wave of cold has struck us sweeping down in brought [*sic*] columns from the Rocky Mountains. Worked on correspondence but omitted the galop this morning. Went to the Treasury Department to work up materials for the Legislative Bill. I am convinced that the permanent appropriation for the expense of the National Loan is a bad thing and it should be changed to an annual appropriation. In the evening dined at Welcker's with a number of Senators and Representatives and with Orton and Prescott of the Western Union Telegraph Company. On my return finished the translation of Horace's [third?] Ode of the First Book. I believe I have made a better metrical version than Bulwer's. I understand the [that] Senator Sherman made an able speech in the Senate today in favor of specie payments. I am glad he has reached that position, at least. I remember in 1867–1868 he was on the other side,[12] and I stood almost alone in the Ohio Delegation.

SATURDAY, 17. Worked on correspondence until eleven o'clock when I went to the Court room of the District Court to argue against General Butler's motion in the Daniels Case. The Judge was ill and did not appear. After waiting two hours came home and worked at my desk until two o'clock when I went with Mother and Crete to hear Janauschek[13] in a play dramatised from Dickens' *Bleak House*. Her personation of Lady Dedlock was very powerful and

---

[12] During the years 1866–68, John Sherman—he was a member of the Senate Committee on Finance, of which he became chairman in 1867—opposed Secretary of the Treasury Hugh McCulloch's policies which called for a contraction of the currency. Sherman not only feared that contraction would cause a sharp and damaging slump in prices, but deferred to public opinion, in particular the opinion of Ohio inflationists. He later became an ardent supporter of resumption of specie payments, which was accomplished during his tenure as secretary of the treasury.

[13] Franziska (Fanny) Janauschek (1830–1904), born in Bohemia, came to the United States in 1867 after several years as one of Germany's leading actresses. She began her career in English in 1870 with *Mary Stuart*; she returned to Germany in 1874, but came back to the United States in 1880 and made it her home the rest of her life. In *Bleak House* she played the part of Hortense as well as that of Lady Dedlock.

effective. In the evening worked on correspondence and made several calls. Very large mail came this evening which occupied me till a late hour. I am beginning to get some glimpses of the methods of cutting down the Legislative Appropriation Bill and reforming some of the abuses in connection with the permanent appropriations.

SUNDAY, 18. At Church heard a sermon by the Rev. Mr. Culter [Cutler] of Va. Called on Judge Swaim [Swayne] in the evening. Chief Justice *redivivus* [revived]. General McDowell called on me and remained until nearly midnight.

MONDAY, 19. Worked on correspondence a little while when Harrington came to see me in regard to appropriations. Went to the Committee at half-past ten and discussed the question of covering back into the Treasury some of the appropriations of last session for public buildings. This will be a very difficult work for I shall encounter so many private interests. But I think that is the only way to give the real relief sought for. This was general wash day in the House and but little was accomplished. After the adjournment the Committee on Rules met and agreed to report some new rules. Home at a late hour and went at half-past —— to argue a case before Judge Wylie. It is very hard to keep up any law practice in connection with my work in Congress. It seems as though I am even more driven this Winter than ever before.

TUESDAY, 20. Went with Woodworth to the Atty's General's office and secured young Nessle a position as Telegraph Operator. Committee met and heard Mr. Mullett for two or three hours on the advisability of stopping work on as many of the public buildings as possible. In the House the Committee on Rules brought in an amendment to the rules in reference to a suspension of the rules by a two-thirds vote, to the effect that such motion for suspension must be seconded as in the previous question before the vote on suspension is taken. This occasioned a stormy debate kept on the whole day. Mr. Dawes and I antagonized on the subject, he claiming that it was an interference with the privileges of the minority and I insisting that it was an arrangement necessary to prevent the foolish practice of buncomb legislation on Mondays. At five o'clock the Rule was carried. In the evening we had Mr. and Mrs. Black, Col. Piatt and Banning[14]

[14] Henry B. Banning (1836–1881), of Cincinnati, Democratic member of the House, 1873–79; he was Donn Piatt's brother-in-law.

at dinner. After dinner Colonel and Mrs. Sheldon came to see us.
WEDNESDAY, 21. Correspondence in the morning. Met the Committee at half-past ten. Further discussed public buildings. I fear that
the Committee are weakening on the propositions to turn back into
the Treasury part of the appropriations for last year. The pressure
from the districts against retrenchment within their own limits is very
strong. The pressure for retrenchment everywhere else is very great.
I laid before the Committee the discovery I had made in regard to the
expenses of the National Loan and found them willing to follow me
in that. We summoned the Secretary of the Treasury to meet us tomorrow morning. After the morning hour the House took up the West
Va. election case.[15] At 3 o'clock I went to the Court of the District
of Columbia and argued a motion in the Daniels Case, against General
Butler. I am somewhat in doubt as to the result, although I think
I made some impression on the Court. Gilfillan and wife called
after I returned.

THURSDAY, 22. Committee met at half-past ten and hear[d] Secretary Richardson,[16] [and] a Treasury Clerk, in regard to the expenses
of the National Loan. The Secretary made a poor show of intellectual
force in answer to the various questions propounded by the Committee. The fact is that the method of appropriating an indefinite and
permanent sum to sustain the expenses of the national loans is wholly
indefensable. In the House the day was spent on the [West] Virginia
election case. In the evening Crete and I called on Mrs. Grant and
on Mrs. Pope, who was temporarily their guest. Also called on Mr.
and Mrs. Thurman.

FRIDAY, 23. Committee met at half-past ten and considered General
Estimates Bill; went through its sections and agreed to report it to
the House went [when] the Committee is called. West Virginia
consumed another day. At half-past six in the evening Crete and I

15 There were two contested elections in West Virginia; John James Davis
(1835–1916), a Democratic member of the House, 1871–75, *vs.* Benjamin
Wilson (1825–1901), a Democratic member of the House, 1875–83; and
John Marshall Hagans (1838–1900), a Republican member of the House,
1873–75, *vs.* Benjamin Franklin Martin (1828–1895), a Democratic member of the House, 1877–81.
16 William A. Richardson (1821–1896), of Massachusetts, assistant secretary of the treasury, 1869–73, secretary of the treasury, 1873–74, judge of
the U. S. Court of Claims, 1874–96 (chief justice from 1885).

dined at Secretary Delano's with a large party of Ohio people. At ten o'clock we attended the reception at Major Dunn's[17] on Capitol Hill. There was a very large party present, including the President, Generals Sherman and Sheridan. I am distressed at the increasing redness of Sheridan's face. I regret that I have not more time to devote [to] the better social life of Washington. While there is much in the formal ceremonial life of this city that is uncomfortable and meaningless, there is nevertheless a stratum of really valuable society that I would love to cultivate, but I am worked beyond all reason and have but little time to enjoy these pleasures.

SATURDAY, 24. My morning was wholly taken up with calls except ten or fifteen minutes devoted to answering correspondence. At eleven o'clock I went with a portion of the Committee on Appropriations to inspect the work of the Board of Public Works in this District. We rode about fifteen miles and called at Gen'l Chipman's at three o'clock and took lunch, thence came home and worked on correspondence until evening when I went with Crete and Harry to hear Sothern[18] in his character of Lord Dundreary. It is [not] difficult to see why this play is so popular. As originally produced, there were three characters in it struggling for the prominence, viz.: "The Yankee," "Buddington [Buddicombe]," and "The Lord." By degrees Sothern amplified the character of "The Lord" until it has become the leading character of the play, at least so far as acting is concerned. "The Lord" is as nearly an idiot as it is possible for a sane man to be and his very folly is made exceedingly funny.

SUNDAY, 25. Attended church. There was no preaching. Parsons of Cleveland and his son Mr. Chase[19] dined with us at two o'clock and spent the afternoon. Professor Baird called in the evening.

MONDAY, 26. Correspondence in the morning. Went to the Treasury

[17] William McKee Dunn (1814–1887), of Indiana, member of the House, 1859–63, assistant judge advocate general of the army, 1869–75, judge
[18] Edward Askew Sothern (1826–1881), English actor, magnified the advocate general, 1875–81. In 1874 he held the rank of colonel. role of Dundreary, a witless English peer in Tom Taylor's *Our American Cousin*, until it dominated the play. In Washington his son Lytton enacted the role of Buddicombe. During this engagement Sothern also played the title role in *Sam* ("Dundreary's eccentric brother") and in *Garrick* and *Dundreary Married and Settled*.
[19] Richard C. Parsons, the only son of Garfield's friend and colleague.

Department and consulted with Mr. Mullett in regard to the situation of public buildings. Met the Committee at half-past ten and heard Mr. [John] Allison, Register of the Treasury, in regard to the expenses of national loans. Prepared a resolution for introduction into the House making it in order to insert a clause in the Legislative Appropriation Bill to repeal all laws making permanent appropriations for expenses of the loans. After the morning hour introduced it into the House and carried it.[20] Also, a resolution instructing the Committee on Ways and Means to report on the feasibility of making a similar arrangement for the expenses of collecting customs duties. If I can succeed in these two measures, it will be a great help in reducing expenses for the coming year. In the evening finished my review of Riddle's new book *The Portrait* which I intend to offer to the Editor of the *Chronicle* for publication.[21]

TUESDAY, 27. Correspondence in the morning. Committee met at half-past [ten?] and discussed the Telegraph Bill and listened further to Mr. Mullett. I drafted a bill to reduce expenditures for the coming fiscal year, which the Committee authorized me to introduce and ask a recommittal to them. In the morning hour Committee on Appropriations was called, when I introduced and passed a telegraph bill providing for lines between the Capitol and the Departments. About three o'clock left the Capitol to see Mr. [George B.] McCartee and spent most of the evening with him in looking over the accounts of his Bureau of Printing and Engraving in the Treasury Department. I am every day more and more impressed with the impropriety of allowing indefinite and permanent appropriations to be made for carrying on any department of the Government.

WEDNESDAY, 28. Correspondence in the morning. Committee met at half-past ten. Heard Mr. McCartee very fully in regard to the expenses of the Bureau of Printing and Engraving. Found among other things that the Treasury were paying scandalous large prices to express companies for carrying half-printed bonds, notes, etc. In the morning hour I introduced for recommittal a bill to cut down ex-

[20] The motion also provided that "hereafter the Secretary of the Treasury shall annually submit to the House of Representatives detailed estimates of the appropriations required to defray . . . [the expenses of loans, Treasury notes, or other paper issues of the United States]."

[21] The review appeared in the Washington *Chronicle* on Sunday, February 8, p. 2.

penses for public buildings. All the interests averse to this retrenchment combined and succeeded in carrying the bill to the Committee
on Public Buildings and Grounds. The action of the House on this
subject will cost the Government at least a million dollars. I was a
good deal disheartened by this successful resistance to retrenchment.
After the morning hour the Army Appropriation Bill was taken up
and our effort at cutting down the army was denounced in a speech
by Mr. Albright[22] of Pa. I followed him making I think an effective
speech in favor of retrenchment. My classmate Knox dined with us,
and Gilfillan, another classmate, called in the evening. Worked at
my desk until near midnight.

THURSDAY, 29.   Corresponded in the morning. Committee met at half-
past ten. Heard Ass't Sec'y Sawyer,[23] also a Mr. Baker, a clerk of the
Loan Division of the Treasury, concerning the expenses of the syndicate and of persons travelling on that business. The amounts paid
are exorbitant and wholly unjustifiable and although they are paid by
the syndicate, yet the syndicate had to be paid out of the Treasury.
The Committee agreed to take up the Legislative Appropriation Bill
tomorrow morning. In the House after the morning hour debate
continued on the Army Appropriation Bill and I took some part but
not much. In the evening at eight o'clock Crete and I attended the
Burns Festival where I made an address on Burns and his poetry.
The audience was very large and the occasion a pleasant one. I drew
a parallel between the three great song writers of the world, Horace,
Beranger and Burns. All three were born in poverty. The first was
the son of a freedman and afterwards a clerk in the Imperial Treasury
at Rome. He adapted the stiff form of the language of Rome to the
lyre and was really the creator of lyric poetry. Beranger lifted the
barbarous dialect of Normandy into immortal song. Burns, in some
respects greater than the other two, saved the Scotch dialect from
decay and gave voice to the sentiments and affections of all men every
where.

FRIDAY, 30.   At half-past ten Committee met and commenced Legislative Appropriation Bill. We spent the morning in revising the
estimates for the legislative expenses of the House and the various

---

[22] Charles Albright (1830–1880) was a Republican member of the
House from Pennsylvania, 1873–75.
[23] Frederick A. Sawyer was assistant secretary of the treasury, 1873–74.

offices under it. The management of this bill is to be more than usually difficult and I fear the Committee is not as hard working a body of men as the Committee of last Congress. After dinner a carriage was sent for us from the Insane Asylum and Crete and I in company with Mr. and Mrs. Hamlin of Maine went to the Asylum to witness a dramatic performance gotten up for the amusement of the inmates of the Home, about 450 souls. After a pleasant visit with the guests, among whom were Miss Dix,[24] an elegant collation was served and we returned to the city, reaching home at quarter before eleven.

SATURDAY, 31.   Spent the forenoon on correspondence and in writing out the substance of my address at the Burns Festival. At one o'clock went to the Post Office Department, transacted some business and had a long conversation with the Postmaster General. Questioned him as to the causes of the great increase in the expenditures of his department. These are closely allied with the growth of railroads. Went to the Capitol, did some work in the Committee Room, came home bringing back a large mail and working further on correspondence. At half-past six dined at Governor Shepherd's with a large company of Senators and Members. Nesmith[25] of Oregon is one of the wittiest men I ever knew. He told a story about being invited to Joe Holt's dinner a day too soon.

February

SUNDAY, 1.   Attended church and heard a fine sermon from the Rev. Mr. Hopkins of Indiana.

MONDAY, 2.   Worked two hours in Committee on the Legislative Bill.

[24] Dorothea Lynde Dix (1802–1887), humanitarian reformer, especially known for her crusade in behalf of better treatment for the insane.

[25] James Willis Nesmith (1820–1885), an Oregon pioneer, lawyer, Indian fighter and politician, was a Democratic member of the U. S. Senate, 1861–67, and of the House, 1873–75. According to Donn Piatt's *Capital* of March 8, 1874, Nesmith's story set the table in a roar. In it he recounted at length his social error. Invited to Judge Holt's for dinner he appeared a day early as a result of a misunderstanding. Received politely by the surprised and unprepared judge and mystified by the nonappearance of other guests and dinner, he stayed for several hours before he was made aware of his mistake.

Discovered that the appropriations for horses and carriages are mainly expended on horses for the private use of the officers of the House; concluded to cut off all of these except the mail horses. It is exceedingly difficult to adjust the expenditure of money to a business basis. In the House but little was done beyond ordering an investigation of District affairs.[26] At seven o'clock P.M. dined at Sec'y Fish's with Admiral [Don José] Polo [de Bernabé] (the Spanish Minister), Caleb Cushing, Orth,[27] Bancroft Davis, General Butler, Ben Perley Poore, Sam'l Ward.

TUESDAY, 3. Committee met at ten o'clock. Heard Bancroft Davis, Ass't Sec'y of State, in regard to the appropriations for that Dep't, also Congressional Printer, also the officers in charge of the Police Force. Put in two hours of effective work on the Legislative Bill, finished two or three pages of the estimates. In the House, after the morning hour, got into Committee of the Whole on the Army Bill, closed general debate and carried the paragraphs relating to the reduction of the army to 25,000 men. As Hale said yesterday in debate, "The way of the economizer is indeed hard." But we shall do the best we can to carry our measures of reduction. In the evening worked on correspondence to a late hour, and still later studied the estimates, working until midnight. I am nearly sick with a cold and a return of my stomach troubles.

WEDNESDAY, 4. Committee met at ten o'clock and worked for nearly three hours on the Legislative Appropriation Bill. We heard officers from the Treasury and several of the Departments in regard to the appropriations and made considerable progress with the bill, though it is slow work. In the House after the morning hour we got into Committee of the Whole on the Army Appropriation Bill, on which we made good progress before the day was over although the debate on collateral subjects, railroads and others occupied much time. My appro-

26 On the motion of Jeremiah Morrow Wilson of Indiana the House agreed to the appointment of a joint committee of three senators and five representatives to investigate affairs in the District of Columbia and determine whether illegal or corrupt activities had been associated with improvements in the District.

27 Godlove Stein Orth (1817–1882), Republican member of the House from Indiana, 1863–71, 1873–75, 1879–82; U. S. minister to Austria-Hungary, 1875–76.

priation bills are very far behind as it seems almost impossible to bring the House to their consideration. Emerson E. White of Columbus dined with us and in the evening several people called. I worked until a late hour on the appropriation bills and went to bed near midnight tired and half sick. Whether I shall be able to stand the strain of this Winter remains to be seen.

THURSDAY, 5. Committee met at ten o'clock and heard Mr. Sanford[28] and other representatives of the Adams Express Company. Also Mr. Leipold[29] of the Treasury in regard to the Express contract for carrying money and other securities. We were surprised to find that the Government transported over seven hundred millions of dollars by express last year besides more than three hundred millions of unfinished bonds, etc. In the House we made good progress on the Army Appropriation Bill, and finished all the appropriations in it. The sections relating to War Claims being left unfinished. In the evening dined with Mr. Phelps of N. J. There were present Godkin of the New York *Nation*, Senator[s] Sherman and Allison, Speaker Blaine, Dawes, Hooper, Roberts,[30] Mr. Rutson, of England, and myself. The discussion was social and financial, but very pleasant.

FRIDAY, 6. Called on Dr. Baxter for more medicine as I am still unwell; then on the Corn Doctor; then at the Treasury. Committee met at ten and heard the Commissioner of Customs and the Sixth Auditor and agreed upon reduction of over a hundred clerks in the Treasury. In the House, the day was consumed on private bills. The Cincinnati Delegation called on me in regard to the new public building in that city. In the evening Mr. and Mrs. Frye, Mr. and Mrs. Robinson[31] and Mr. Foster at six o'clock dined with us and spent the evening. The evening was passed very pleasantly and all the more so because it was an enjoyable informal gathering and small enough to allow the

[28] Henry Sanford of New York City, general superintendent of the Adams Express Company.

[29] Robert Leipold, chief of the Bureau of the Independent Treasury.

[30] Ellis Henry Roberts (1827–1918), a Republican, and William Randall Roberts (1830–1897), a Democrat, both represented New York in the House, 1871–75. In all likelihood the reference here is to Ellis, who was owner and editor of the *Utica* (N.Y.) *Morning Herald*.

[31] James Wallace Robinson (1826–1898), a lawyer of Union County, Ohio, was a Republican member of the House, 1873–75.

personality of each guest to be brought into full play in the conversation. I have learned to love Mr. Frye very much.

SATURDAY, 7. Correspondence until half-past ten o'clock. Then went to the Engineer's Department to get an increase of the estimates for Ashtabula Harbor, then to the President's in reference to Ben Wade's son;[32] then to the Attorney General's in regard to the estimates for his department; then to the Committee where I sat from one o'clock until half-past five, where we heard the Commissioner of Internal Revenue, the Chief Clerk of the Treasurer's Office and a clerk from the Treasury in regard to the Independent Treasuries in various parts of the country. Finished about five pages of the book of estimates on the Legislative Bill. Attended correspondence until half-past seven when Crete and I went to Willard's and spent the evening with Mr. Sheldon and wife. There were present Senator Hamlin, Mr. and Mrs. Scofield. We had a pleasant evening.

SUNDAY, 8. Attended Church. In the forenoon worked on the estimates and Mr. Gilfillan dined with us. Read three chapters of *The Ancient City* by De Coulanges.[33]

MONDAY, 9. Committee met at ten o'clock, worked until half-past twelve on the Legislative Appropriation Bill. In the House we had the usual wash day performance for Monday. The number of bills has now gone above two thousand. This is a singular developement in the habits of the House. Certainly three times as many bills are now introduced in a month as were when I first came here. I think it indicates a ferment of opinions in the public mind. In the evening worked on correspondence and appropriations until a late hour. I am still suffering from this neuralgic dyspepsia as Dr. Baxter calls it. I think it will hardly be possible for me wholly to recover while I am so hard-worked.

TUESDAY, 10. Worked on correspondence and finished writing out my address on Agassiz delivered in the Board of Regents of the Smithsonian Institution. Committee met at ten and finished several chapters of the Legislative Bill. In the House, after the morning hour, resumed the consideration of the Army Bill and carried the last three sections successfully. They embrace a radical reform in the method

32 Benjamin Franklin Wade was seeking the appointment of his son, Henry P. of Jefferson, to a federal paymastership.
33 Numa Denis Fustel de Coulanges, *The Ancient City: A Study on the Religion, Laws and Institutions of Greece and Rome* (1874).

[of] paying claims growing out of the late war. All such claims are to be taken from the Commissary's and Quartermaster's Departments and placed in the hands of the Southern Claims Commission. The Claim Agents and their friends have fought us hard all day but were beaten.

WEDNESDAY, 11. Committee met at ten o'clock and heard the Sec'y of the Interior and the Commissioners of Patents, Indian Affairs, Education, Public Lands and Pensions. We continued work until half-past twelve and substantially finished the Department of the Interior. In the House, after the morning hour, we finished the Army Bill in Committee of the Whole, reported it to the House and passed it. The Committee carried every thing that was reported and we were able to reduce the amount over two hundred thousand dollars from the first draft of the bill. In the evening Crete and I attended the Philharmonic Concert at the Congregational Church and heard an oratorio of *The Messiah.* I am not able to understand the complications of musical composers. The repetitions to me are so frequent as to be meaningless.

THURSDAY, 12. Correspondence until half-past nine o'clock. Mr. Riddle drove me to the Capitol. Committee met at ten. Went over the War Dep't estimates. Settled several other points in the Legislative Appropriation Bill working until half-past twelve. In the House after the morning hour resumed consideration of the Fortification Bill which was finished, cutting down forty thousand in the amount and then passed the bill. The House then went into Committee on the Tax Bill and Mr. Dawes made a speech of two hours and a half. He has a singular habit of making sensational speeches and saying things injurious to the party. He made a blunder of twenty-nine millions in the amount appropriated for the current year, to which I made a response at the close of his speech. The correction very seriously interfered with a large portion of his speech.[34]

FRIDAY, 13. Committee met at ten. Heard the Attorney General on his estimates for the Department of Justice. Also the Commissioner

[34] In a speech favoring repeal of a tax on matches which yielded annual revenues of about $2,500,000, Henry L. Dawes discussed the condition of the Treasury, said the balance was alarmingly low, and urged a reduction of expenditures. Since he had placed current appropriations at $319,000,000 instead of $290,000,000, his plea for retrenchment lost much of its force when Garfield corrected him.

of Agriculture on expenses for his Department. The Postmaster General came before the Committee and asked their advice in regard to putting on a fast mail between N. Y. and Chicago to make the trip in twenty-four hours. He thinks the plan is feasible and will cost no more than the present arrangement. After the morning [hour] the House went into Committee of the Whole House on the Private Calendar and among other bills presented was one by the Indian Committee to lay the foundation for paying the ravages committed by the Modoc Indians in the late war. The bill was nearly finished when I entered the Hall. I made a brief speech against it which I believe killed it; at any rate, on my motion the enacting clause was striken out.[35] In the evening Crete and I went with Mrs. Dahlgren to the receptions of Sec'y Fish and Senator Dorsey.[36]

SATURDAY, 14. After correspondence in the morning studied for about two hours on the legislation and history of the expenses of the National Loan. At ten o'clock went to the Treasury and examined several points in the accounts of the expenditures. Met Mr. Dawes who went over the ground with me and admitted that he was in error in the debate of Thursday concerning the Sinking Fund. Called on Comptroller Tayler in regard to questions connected with the National Loan. Committee met at half-past one and sat until half-past four. Completed the section in relation to the National Loan and also several other items in the bill. I am very tired this evening. The Marquis de Chambrun[37] and Mrs. Dahlgren united in requesting me

[35] In 1872–73 certain Modoc warriors, unwilling to live on the reservation assigned to them, went on the warpath and committed depredations against citizens in southern Oregon and northern California. The House Committee on Indian Affairs investigated losses resulting from the uprising and submitted a report in which reference was made to the Modoc War. Garfield thereupon argued that if damages were paid in this instance, the House would establish the policy of paying citizens for losses suffered by the hand of a public enemy. Accordingly, citizens who had had property destroyed by the enemy in the Civil War might collect damages.

[36] Stephen Wallace Dorsey (1842–1916) was a Republican senator from Arkansas, 1873–79. His role as secretary of the Republican National Committee in the presidential campaign of 1880 and his involvement in the Star Route frauds are the subjects of diary entries in 1880 and 1881.

[37] Charles-Adolphe de Pineton (1831–1891), marquis de Chambrun, was sent as a special envoy to the United States by the French foreign minister in 1865; when the French Republic was established he was appointed legal

to write a preface to Chambrun's book which Mrs. Dahlgren has just translated.

SUNDAY, 15. Attended Church, drove to the Capitol with the children, worked on the Legislative Appropriation Bill. In the evening went to dine with Mr. Hooper, Henry Adams[38] and wife, Senator Anthony and Gen'l Butler.

MONDAY, 16. Went to the Treasury Department at ½ past nine and to the Committee Room at ten. Committee worked three hours on the Legislative Appropriation Bill, finished it and ordered it reported to the House. Also, a lot of documents consisting of testimony taken before the Committee and tabular statements relating to the bill. At the close of the day introduced a bill and report, but the House refused to make the bill a special order, desiring to bring on the financial debate on the taxation of the currency before any further work on appropriation bills. In the evening worked up correspondence, and then went with Crete and the children to the Children's Ball at Marini's Hall. The reaction of overwork is upon me this evening and I feel very tired. I have received a letter from Col. Whittlesey[39] say[ing] that they are publishing my Chardon [address] in pamphlet form as one of the documents of the Western Reserve Historical Society.

TUESDAY, 17. Correspondence in the morning and worked on statis-

---

adviser to the French legation in Washington, a position he held at the time of his death; he also engaged in law practice. He and Garfield were both members of the Washington Literary Society. The English version of his book, translated by Madeleine Vinton Dahlgren and carrying an introduction by Garfield, was published in 1874 under the title *The Executive Power in the United States; a Study of Constitutional Law.* He was also the author of other books.

[38] Henry Brooks Adams (1838–1918), writer, the grandson and great grandson of Presidents, was then living in Boston and teaching at Harvard; he moved to Washington before the end of the decade. His works include *History of the United States of America*, 9 vols. (1889–91), *The Education of Henry Adams* (1906), and *Democracy* (1880). The latter, published anonymously, is a novel dealing with life in Washington after the Civil War.

[39] Charles Whittlesey (1808–1886), soldier, geologist and writer, was president of the Western Reserve Historical Society in Cleveland from its founding in 1867 until his death. Garfield was elected a life member of this society in 1874.

tics of expenditures. Went to the Treasury Department on business and reached the Committee at half-past ten where we revised some of the estimates for the Legislative Bill and took up the Indian Bill. Made considerable progress and completed two pages of the book of estimates. During the morning in the House I took part in the discussion on the Military Prison Bill, opposing it as unwise both on its own account and on account of its expense.[40]

WEDNESDAY, 18. Called on General Babcock and at the Treasury Dep't in the morning. Went to the Committee at half-past ten o'clock; made some corrections in the Legislative Bill and continued the consideration of the Indian Bill. In the House, after the morning hour, the free delivery of public documents was discussed until the close of the day. In the evening dined at Welcker's with Messrs. Beck, Ward[41] of Chicago, Dr. McDonald and his brother, a Mr. Smith of N. Y. and Mr. [Samuel] Ward. Returned from dinner at one-quarter before eight and worked until a late hour on the preparation of my speech on expenditures.

THURSDAY, 19. Committee met at half-past ten and made good progress on the Indian Bill. In the House, after the morning hour, the discussion of making public documents free of postage was resumed and continued during the day. In the course of the debate I spoke for about ten minutes against the revival of the frank, but in favor of making exchanges of county papers free within their districts. I think it is time we should antagonize the country press and the metropolitan press. The former are the best exponents of public sentiment, the latter of city and commercial sentiment. By repealing the frank we have seriously crippled the country press.[42]

[40] The bill, an amendment to an act of 1873 authorizing a military prison at Rock Island, Illinois, provided that the prison be established instead at Fort Leavenworth. Garfield contended that no military prison was needed, and that the one proposed, which was to receive sentenced soldiers from all over the United States, would be a costly item in an extremely expensive penal system.

[41] Jasper Delos Ward (1829–1902), a Republican member of the House from Illinois, 1873–75.

[42] The bill under discussion contained a section (the only section Garfield supported) providing for the free passage in the mail of newspapers reciprocally exchanged between publishers, and of weekly newspapers to

FRIDAY, 20. Worked on statistics and correspondence until half-past ten, when the Committee met and resumed the consideration of the Indian Bill. We substantially finished the bill so far as the Book of Estimates is concerned, but we have a number of additional propositions to add to it in view of the changed condition of the Indian Service. After the morning hour the House took up the discussion of private and the District of Columbia business which finished the day. At six o'clock George Steele and wife of Painesville, Mr. Scofield, wife and daughter and my colleague Smith dined with us and spent the evening. Had a very pleasant time.

SATURDAY, 21. Worked on correspondence and statistics of expenditures until 12, when the House met and consumed most of the day in the discussion of private bills. I made some further study in the Congressional Library on the subject of former deficits such as that of 1841 and again in 1858. Mr. Dawes is not correct historically when he says the Government never has levied any increased taxes in time of peace. In the evening Crete and I took the children around to Mr. Frye's to witness private theatricals of little children there. Came home very very tired.

SUNDAY, 22. Attended church and listened to a sermon from Prof. Pickering. In the afternoon read Mrs. Dahlgren's translation of the Marquis de Chambrun's book on *The Executive Power*. At seven o'clock Crete and I took tea at Mr. Blaine's with quite a large number of people. Among them were Parke Godwin[43] and his two daughters, Mr. George Hoar and wife and Mr. [David ?] Blakeley of the *Chicago Post*.

MONDAY, 23. Worked on correspondence and statistics until half-past ten when Secretary Delano called on me and showed me the difficulties he had encountered in regard to the Indian Peace Commission.[44] I then went with him to the State Department to examine the

---

subscribers in the county wherein the papers were published. When the time for voting arrived, sponsors of the measure refused to permit voting on any single section, and the bill was defeated by two votes.

[43] Parke Godwin (1816–1904) was long associated with his father-in-law, William Cullen Bryant, on the New York *Evening Post*; for three years after Bryant's death in 1878 he was editor of the paper.

[44] The Board of Indian Commissioners composed of ten unpaid civilians, sometimes referred to as the Peace Commission, had been established in

terms of an act recently passed which I think robs the Flatheads of their payment for lands in the Bitter Root.[45] On my return found Mr. Daniels awaiting me and spent an hour with him in reference to his law suit. Then went with Crete to the Insane Asylum—spent an hour in visiting the new building called the Garfield building, which corresponds with the Dawes building erected two years ago. Several people called in the evening. I have done but little work today and ought to feel better for the rest. But my dyspepsia haunts me like a ghost and I feel apprehensive of a breakdown in my health. Several people called in the evening.

TUESDAY, 24. Committee met and put in another two hours on the Indian Appropriation Bill. I am more and more troubled with our Indian problem. The passage from barbarism to civilization is difficult. The savage is cheaper than the semi-civilized man. In the House, after the morning hour, the discussion on the restoration of the frank was resumed. Everything indicates a long dragging session. I should be glad now to compromise on the middle of June as the day of our

---

1869 to improve the administration of Indian affairs. Although the commissioners exerted themselves greatly, they lacked authority, and during the regime of Columbus Delano as secretary of the interior they felt that their recommendations were repeatedly ignored and many important matters not brought before them. In June, 1874, Felix Brunot, the chairman, and five other members of the Board resigned. The Board had met in Washington a few days before this entry.

[45] The act of June 5, 1872, providing for the removal of the Flatheads from the Bitter Root Valley to the Jocko Reservation, also provided for the opening of vacated lands for sale to settlers, and further provided that none of the land should be open under the pre-emption or homestead acts. Out of the moneys obtained from the land sales $50,000 were to be reserved and set apart for the use of the Flatheads, to be expended by the President in their behalf in sums not greater than $5,000 per year. An act of February 11, 1874 (referred to in this entry), extended the homestead act to settlers on the lands of the area; this meant that little money would be derived from land sales, and the fund for the Flatheads would not come into being. This injustice was corrected by an act of June 22, 1874, which provided for an annual appropriation of $5,000 for the Flatheads for a period of ten years in lieu of the $50,000 required to be set apart by the earlier act.

adjournment. We perhaps shall do more effective work when the House begins to be distressed at its own delay.

WEDNESDAY, 25. Committee met at half-past ten o'clock. The Sec'y of the Interior and Commissioner of Indian Affairs was [were] before us and we had quite a full hearing in reference to the Indian Problem and the relations between the Interior Department and the Board of Peace Commissioners. I begin to doubt the efficiency of that Board to accomplish much. They lack business habits. I fear they are an expensive luxury. After the morning hour the debate continued on the Franking Privilege, which looks as though the frank would be restored. I will vote for no part of the bill except that which makes the country newspapers free within their counties. Even that is not absolutely the best thing to be done. There should be a discriminating rate of postage having respect to weight and distance. Calvin Gilbert[46] and wife of Solon, Ohio, came today from Chattanooga and are stopping with us.

THURSDAY, 26. Committee met at half-past ten. Finished the Indian Bill after considerable discussion, and ordered it reported to the House. Another day was consumed in the discussion and vote on the franking privilege. On the naked question of restoring the frank there were but 49 affirmative votes. When the vote was taken on Packer's[47] bill to make the circulation of public documents and newspapers within their counties free, it was found that the vote was very close. We succeeded in beating it by about two votes—Ayes 129, Noes 131. The Grangers have made some show in this debate, in a blatant blatherskite sort of way not creditable to the representatives. In the evening work till a late hour on correspondence and appropriation.

FRIDAY, 27. Spent the morning on correspondence and attending to the Daniels suit. Committee did not meet. In the House the day was consumed on private bills. About three o'clock I went to the Treasury and worked an hour or two on the estimates relating to appropriations for the next year. At seven in the evening went to the Continental Hotel to meet with J. F. Driggs, Mr. Driggs of N. Y., Mrs. Miller and son of Baltimore, Messrs. Mussey and Daniels, to try to effect

[46] Gilbert owned a farm in Orange township near the Henry Boynton farm and the Solon township line.

[47] John Black Packer (1824–1891) was a Republican member of the House from Pennsylvania, 1869–77.

a compromise of the Daniels, Driggs and Miller suits. Did not succeed. Correspondence and finance till a late hour.

SATURDAY, 28. Spent the morning on correspondence and the people who called. Judge Black was among the number. Went to the House at twelve and staid until four. The day was spent in private bills and general debate. In the course of the day had a conference with General Mussey and Mr. Miller in regard to the pending law suit. It seems as though the proposition for compromise had broken down. In the evening worked on correspondence and at eight o'clock went to Senator Chandler's to meet the Chief Justice.[48]

March

SUNDAY, 1. I did not attend church but went to the Capitol to examine some statistics relating to my speech on the appropriations. Worked until a late hour in the evening.

MONDAY, 2. Committee met at half-past ten o'clock. Considered some miscellaneous matters and revised a number of points in the Indian Appropriation Bill. In the House the day was spent in the manner usual to Mondays. I left a little after four o'clock and spent the afternoon and evening in throwing my materials into shape for a speech. I satisfied myself better with the part of the work done during the evening than anything I have accomplished in this direction for a long time. But I worked too hard and too closely and paid for it by restlessness and sleeplessness during much of the night.

TUESDAY, 3. Worked on my speech until nearly eleven o'clock and reached the Committee a good ways behind time—a bad thing for me to do. We had three Ass't Generals before us, and the Public Printer, to consider the deficiency in the amount appropriated for printing for the Post Office Department. The exhibition for the Public Printer was very bad, the charges being very much too high. In the House

---

[48] Morrison Remick Waite (1816–1888), of Ohio, was President Grant's fourth and last nominee for the chief justiceship left vacant by the death of Chase. An able lawyer who had been an American counsel in the Geneva arbitration but was not widely known, he proved an excellent choice. He was presiding over the constitutional convention being held in Ohio when word came of his appointment. The Senate confirmed him promptly.

after some preliminary business the Transportation Bill was taken up and Mr. McCrary[49] of Iowa made a long and able speech on the power and duty of Congress to regulate railroad transportation. I see in this movement the power of the Grangers. I fear it may be communism in disguise; and yet there is much in their views of the railroad issue with which I sympathize. In the evening worked on my speech.

WEDNESDAY, 4. Committee met at half-past ten o'clock. I took up the docket and distributed a large amount of business. At twelve o'clock went to the Supreme Court Room and saw Mr. Waite sworn in as Chief Justice. The associate justices in new gowns took their seats leaving the central seat vacant. Mr. Waite sat down in the Clerk's chair. After court was opened Mr. [Daniel W.] Middleton, the Clerk, read the commission of Mr. Waite and administered the oath. The other judges in the meanwhile sitting when the new Chief Justice approached the vacant chair. The others arose and bowed to him and were seated. And Judge Field[50] next read an opinion. The simplicity of this performance impressed me very much. The Court room was crowded. There were present two college classmates of the Chief Justice, Messrs. Evarts and Pierrepont. Finding that I could not get the House into Committee of the Whole on the Appropriation Bill I came home at an early hour and worked on my speech. Dined in the evening with Messrs. Hubbard, Allison, Morrill, Hamlin, Hale and Wells.

THURSDAY, 5. Committee on Appropriations heard the First Ass't Postmaster General and Public Printer in regard to the controversy about rates for printing. Also heard Judge Pierrepont and Mr. [George S.] Scott, one of the Directors of the Pacific Mail.[51] In

[49] George Washington McCrary (1835–1890) was a Republican member of the House from Iowa, 1869–77, and secretary of war, March 12-December 11, 1877.

[50] Stephen J. Field (1816–1899), associate justice of the U. S. Supreme Court, 1864–97. He was the brother of David Dudley, Henry M. and Cyrus W., all of whom are mentioned in the diary.

[51] Edwards Pierrepont, New York lawyer, was representing the Pacific Mail Steamship Company, which was seeking the continuance of a contract with the government, the terms of which had not been met by the company; a substantial subsidy was involved. Charges of corruption on the part of the company in securing the contract were circulating.

the House there was a struggle for three hours to revive the frank but after a series of votes it was defeated. Soon after three o'clock I got the floor and went into Committee of the Whole on the Legislative Appropriation Bill. I spoke about an hour and three-quarters. So far as I went I satisfied myself very well, but the hour was so late that I abridged the latter portion of the speech more than I thought to have done. At ten o'clock the reporter's notes came to me and I sat up until two hours past midnight revising. At 2 o'clock in the morning sent the last pages to the printer.

FRIDAY, 6. After four hours of sleep I arose very tired and jaded, for I did twenty hours of work yesterday, two of them on the floor speaking. Went to the Committee at ten o'clock and we considered and finished Senate amendments to the Naval Appropriation Bill. In the House private bills occupied the day. At four o'clock went down to the Printer's on Pennsylvania Avenue making an arrangement for getting out an edition of my speech of yesterday, which covers fifteen columns of the *Congressional Record*. Home in the evening tired.

SATURDAY, 7. Worked on correspondence and revised my speech for pamphlet edition. After twelve o'clock went to the House where an attack was made upon me by Fernando Wood and Beck. Did not get there in time to hear Wood but answered Beck. The way these men have with figures reminds me of what a son of Dr. [Leonard] Bacon of Yale College is reported to have said—that he knew of nothing that lied like figures except facts. Harmon Austin and Judge Kinsman came today. They took dinner with us and will spend some days. Mr. Thorp the artist called in the evening as did several others.

SUNDAY, 8. Mr. Austin went with Crete to our church and I went with Judge Kinsman to hear Dr. Mitchell.[52]

MONDAY, 9. At half-past ten I took up the Docket and passed on a number of subjects relating to the Deficiency and Miscellaneous Bill. In the House after the morning hour the death of ex-President Fillmore was announced as having occurred this morning. Resolutions of respect were passed and a Committee of Five appointed to attend the funeral on Thursday next at Buffalo, whereupon the House adjourned. I went to the Printing Office and read proofs of my speech. We had O. L. Wolcott[53] and wife and Austin and Kinsman at dinner

52 Samuel S. Mitchell, pastor of the New York Avenue Presbyterian Church.
53 Orlo L. Wolcott, farmer and businessman of Farmington, Trumbull County, was Ohio state commissioner of railroads and telegraphs, 1872–74.

with us. Several people called afterward. At seven o'clock I dined with Mr. Rothery and wife, Chas. Kingsley[54] and his daughters [daughter], two members of the Legation and Miss Frelinghuysen. Kingsley is very bright and the evening was passed delightfully. He did not like Gladstone, yet is a liberal. Says Herbert Spencer[55] has no touch of imagination in him, that Bain[56] is utterly stupid. He likes Goldwin Smith[57] but says he is hypochondriacal.

TUESDAY, 10. In the morning called on Judge Curtis[58] at the Ebbitt

[54] Charles Kingsley (1819–1875), English writer and canon of Westminster, whose many books included *Westward Ho!* (1855) and *Hypatia* (1853), arrived in the United States for a lecture tour in January, 1874, accompanied by his daughter Rose. He gave two lectures in Washington, the first on Westminster Abbey and the second on the Norsemen and their discovery of America. He was received at the White House and on the day of the dinner described by Garfield he opened the session of the House with prayer. See Robert Bernard Martin, ed., *Charles Kingsley's American Notes: Letters from a Lecture Tour, 1874* (1958).

[55] Herbert Spencer (1820–1903), English philosopher, whose writings included *First Principles* (1862) and *The Study of Sociology* (1873).

[56] Alexander Bain (1818–1903), British philosopher important for his work in psychology and education, was the author of *Mind and Body, a Theory of Their Relation* (1873).

[57] Goldwin Smith (1823–1910), English writer on history and political and economic questions, made his home in North America from 1868. He was the first professor of English and constitutional history at Cornell and was associated with the university for many years, bequeathing it the bulk of his estate. He was an advocate of the union of Canada (where he made his home for a long period) and the United States, the first step towards which was to be a commercial union.

[58] Benjamin R. Curtis (1809–1874), of Massachusetts, associate justice of the Supreme Court, 1851–57, was one of the leading lawyers of the United States. Garfield was his assistant before the Supreme Court in the case of *W. E. Tate et al., heirs of Samuel Bond, v. The New York Life Insurance Company et al.* Bond, a resident of Tennessee who had died during the Civil War, had been insured with the New York Life Insurance Company but had paid no premiums after the beginning of the war. His heirs were now trying to collect on the policy. The Supreme Court reached no decision, dividing equally on the question, thus in effect confirming the decision of the lower court. In two similar cases before the Supreme Court in 1876, in which Garfield and Matt Carpenter appeared for the insurance company, the court held that the policies were extinguished by non-payment

House in reference to our case in the Supreme Court. Committee met at half-past ten and worked on the Military Academy Bill. At half-past one went to the Supreme Court to make the motion to advance our Insurance case. Curtis was there and made the motion.

In the House after the morning hour went into Committee of the Whole on the Legislative Appropriation Bill. Beck made his promised assault, which was an unusually weak, rambling and malignant performance. The House drifted into a general and heated debate on the Sanborn contract and at half-past four I got the floor and for about three-quarters of an hour handled him more severely than I have ever handled an opponent in debate.[59] I am satisfied that he is wicked as well as weak.

WEDNESDAY, 11. Correspondence in the morning. At ten o'clock heard of the serious illness of Senator Sumner and called at his house. His physicians pronounced his case hopeless. He is dying. Went to the Capitol and attended to Committee meeting. Worked on miscellaneous subjects. In the House after the morning hour got into Committee of the Whole on the Legislative Appropriation Bill and finished general debate, when the news came at three o'clock that Mr. Sumner was dead. Committee immediately arose and the House adjourned. Mr. Sumner was the most scholarly man in public life, the

---

but that the defendants were entitled to recover the equitable value of their policies with interest from the close of the war. *New York Life Insurance Company v. Statham et al.*, and *New York Life Insurance Company v. Seyms* (93 U. S. 24).

[59] Reference is to contracts given to John D. Sanborn under legislation known as the Moiety Act. The contracts, made in collusion with Secretary of the Treasury William A. Richardson and Representative Benjamin F. Butler, enabled Sanborn to collect, at a commission of 50 percent, overdue federal internal revenue taxes in the amount of $427,000. An investigation revealed that the Treasury Department had made little effort to do what Sanborn accomplished with little difficulty. The exposure of the fraud resulted in the resignation of Richardson and the defeat of Butler for re-election. In the debate mentioned by Garfield, Beck charged that Garfield, as chairman of the Conference Committee on the Moiety Bill, had engineered the measure through the House. Garfield argued that he had reluctantly accepted the legislation after what seemed to be ample provisions had been written into the law to protect the government.

most conspicuous figure in either House of Congress and a man whose service in the Senate dates back to the day when Clay left it. Sumner was my friend; though I have never been blind to his follies yet I have believed in him as an honest and faithful man.

THURSDAY, 12. In Committee finished the Military Academy Bill and ordered it reported to the House. The House met and adjourned so soon as the message was received from the Senate in regard to the arrangements for Mr. Sumner's funeral. I went to the Supreme Court Room and spent four hours in listening to the argument in case No. 228, the case with which my case No. 716 is to be argued. I came home at the end of the day's work exceedingly tired. In the evening with Messrs. Harmon Austin, Kinsman, Ritezel, I called on the President and Mrs. Grant and spent an hour pleasantly. Found General[s] McDowell and Pope there. McDowell came home with me and told me I was on the verge of a breakdown from overwork and impressed the same thing on Crete.

FRIDAY, 13. Worked on my argument for the Supreme Court until near noon, when I went to the House and from thence attended the funeral of Charles Sumner in the Senate. He drew a great crowd as he has done many times before. The whole ceremony was very impressive, but the prayer of Mr. Sunderland[60] was far too much of a stump speech. The remains were escorted to the railroad and the great assemblage broke up. In the evening we had a large party of Ohio friends at dinner. Company staid until a late hour. I was more rested by it than by anything that has happened for a long time.

SATURDAY, 14. Worked on correspondence until ten o'clock when Mr. Ritezel came and I went with him to the Interior Department and arranged for his making a trip to the Californian Coast to do some work for the Land Office. Then went to the Post Office Department to transact some business for the District, then went to the House and listened to a speech or two, and then went to the Library and prepared my argument for the Supreme Court. Home in the evening tired but worked until a late hour on the argument.

SUNDAY, 15. Attended church in the forenoon. In the evening called on General Schenck at Welcker's and had a long visit.

[60] Bryon Sunderland (1819–1901), pastor of the First Presbyterian Church in Washington, 1853–98, pastor emeritus, 1898–1901. He was chaplain of the Senate, 1861–64, 1873–79.

MONDAY, 16. Worked on Insurance case until 11 o'clock, when we went to the Supreme Court, where I spent the day. Court consumed an hour and a quarter in reading opinions. Then extended the time of Mr. [Charles] Sanford so that he and Tremain[61] occupied the remainder of the day. Curtis was not able to be in the Court, but hopes to be there tomorrow. Our case comes on the first thing when the Court assembles. In the evening Knox and Mrs. Rudolph, Hill, Crete and myself went to hear Sothern. We had a hearty laugh. It is remarkable how genius can add interest to so absurdly a stupid character.

TUESDAY, 17. Committee met at half-past ten and commenced the preparation of the Deficiency Bill. At twelve o'clock went to Court and listened for nearly two hours to the argument of Mr. Philip Phillips and then I occupied an hour and was followed by another hour by Judge R[B]. B[R]. Curtis of Boston. The first portion of my argument was not satisfactory to me, but in the latter half I think I made a forcible argument and during the whole I had the close and careful attention of the Court. On the whole I was not ashamed to be associated with so eminent a lawyer as Judge Curtis, although there is a judicial calmness and equipoise in his manner of handling his mind that I admire. At the conclusion of the Judge's remarks went into the House and assumed charge of the Legislative Appropriation Bill, which Starkweather had been managing for some time.

WEDNESDAY, 18. Committee met as usual. Made very good progress on Deficiency Bill. In the House after the morning hour took up the Legislative Appropriation Bill and held to work until five o'clock.[62] I have never known the House in so disagreeable a temper in regard to appropriations. All the small men jump upon all the small items and go into a spasm of small economy which suggests "Economy is often an iron vice, which pinches even the guts of little mice."

[61] Lyman Tremain (1819–1878), a Republican member of the House from New York, 1873–75.

[62] Garfield confused House action of March 18 with that of March 19. The House devoted the 18th to general debate on a bill to regulate interstate commerce—referred to by Garfield as the McCrary bill and as the Transportation Bill. On the 19th the House considered the Legislative Appropriation Bill, which opponents antagonized considerably throughout its reading.

Came home very tired. General McDowell and the Judge Advocate of the Howard Court Martial[63] called in the evening.

THURSDAY, 19. Only one member of the Committee, Judge Parker,[64] met with me, the rest were gone partly to the Sumner Funeral and partly to attend the launch[ing] of one of the Pacific Mail Company's steamships from the dockyards at Chester. However, I went over considerable of the Deficiency Bill and got it ready for the Committee when they should come. In the House the day was devoted to debate on the McCrary Transportation Bill. I spent most of the day in revising the shorthand of my argument on the Insurance Case and came home in the evening very much tired out.

FRIDAY, 20. Pounding away as usual in the Committee. The Deficiency Bill is an exceedingly difficult one this year in consequence of the spasm of economy. Finished the revision of the shorthand report of my argument in the Supreme Court and put it in the hands of the printer. The House consumed the day on private bills and an election case.[65] In the evening took Crete, Libby, Mollie and Judge Black to hear Sothern in *Garrick* and we enjoyed a real intellectual feast. I feel the need of being more familiar with Boswell's *Life of Johnson* and if I can find any time after the Session, I hope to read the work carefully.

SATURDAY, 21. Read proof sheets of my argument in the Insurance

[63] Oliver Otis Howard (1830–1909) was the subject of an inquiry by a special court created by Congress on charges related to his financial practices while commissioner of the Bureau of Refugees, Freedmen, and Abandoned Lands. Major Asa Bird Gardiner, a judge advocate of the army, was appointed judge advocate of the court. Generals Sherman and McDowell were among its members. The court convened on March 3, 1874; it gave its opinion that General Howard "has not, with knowledge and intent, violated any law of Congress, regulation of the Army, or rule of morals, and that he is 'not guilty,' upon legal, technical, or moral responsibility in any of the offenses charged."

[64] Isaac Charles Parker (1838–1896) was a Republican member of the House from Missouri, 1871–75.

[65] The contested election was over the seat for the first congressional district of Georgia and involved Morgan Rawls (1829–1906), a Democrat, who served from March 4, 1873 to March 24, 1874, and his successor, Andrew Sloan (1845–1883), a Republican, who served from March 24, 1874, to March 3, 1875.

case and worked up a number of Department matters that had been neglected for some time. The day in the House was spent mainly in finishing some bills brought over from yesterday in regard to the District of Columbia and also had an election case.

SUNDAY, 22.   Attended church and heard a sermon from Mr. Lamar of Ga., a cousin of J[L]. Q. C. Lamar of the House. After dinner went with Mother, Libbie, Mollie and Irvin to the Reform School near Bladensburg. Two members of the Committee, Packer and Loughridge, were also there.

MONDAY, 23.   Committee met and worked on the Deficiency Bill. In the House after the morning hour Dawes brought up the bill to limit the circulation of greenbacks and after several calls of the Ayes and Noes, the House determined on inflation, increasing the amount of currency to 400 millions. We were able to summon less than eighty votes in opposition. Inflation has triumphed and the House by this backward step has lost nearly all we gained in the direction of specie payments in the last seven years. I am greatly discouraged over the result. General Pope and several friends called in the evening.

TUESDAY, 24.   Spent the morning in settling the Indian Deficiencies which were among the most difficult of all the questions we have for discussion in the House. After the morning hour McCrary's Transportation Bill came up for final debate and action. After a series of votes we were brought to a third reading of the bill and on that adjourned.[66] Final vote to be taken on its passage tomorrow. Worked up correspondence in the evening and had a number of calls in regard to the Rock Creek Post Office fight going on.

WEDNESDAY, 25.   The ordinary routine of correspondence in the morning. Committee meeting at half-past ten. Appropriations until twelve and the work of the House. I think I have mistaken the time in the entry for yesterday. It was today that McCrary's bill was brought to its third reading, instead of yesterday. Would that I were in robust health and had a week's time at my command. I believe I could make an effective speech on the Currency, although I could not head off the wretched policy of inflation that is now likely to succeed.

THURSDAY, 26.   Committee met and made further progress on the

[66] An erroneous statement corrected by Garfield in the next entry.

Deficiency Bill and heard Mr. Hayden on the Geological Survey, Mr. Mullett on expenditures for Public Buildings, and heard several other parties on matters of appropriations. In the House we finished the Transportation Bill. I voted for it with some reluctance and still was anxious to raise a question as to its legislative form. I do not think the bill is quite what it ought to be, but it is better than nothing. It passed by a small majority. There then followed a struggle for the floor between myself and Mr. Maynard, he for the Banking and Currency Bill and I for Appropriations. I was beaten as I expected to be, but I felt it my duty to make a test. The House then entered upon a dreary sea of talk whose further shore no man yet sees.

In the evening Crete gave a dinner party to several friends. Ellis H. Roberts and wife and sister—Welsh people—Mr. and Mrs. Monroe, Foster of Ohio, Hale and Gardiner Hubbard of Mass. made up the party, which was a very pleasant one, and we had some excellent music from Mrs. Monroe and Libbie.

FRIDAY, 27. Committee met again as usual. We heard Prof. Hayden on his Geological Survey and Mr. Mullett on some of the deficiencies on public buildings. There were some other officers before the Committee. In the House, the Currency debate dragged its slow length along. What hope have we of a sound financial policy, when the Chairman of the Committee on Banking and Currency, after studying for four months, announces it as his conclusion that money is whatever the Government declares to be money? Really the prospect of reaching solid ground is dreary enough. At half-past four o'clock Mr. Gallaudet sent his carriage, and Mother, Libbie, Crete and I went to the Deaf Mute College and took dinner and spent the evening at Mr. Gallaudet's. We had a very pleasant time and enjoyed some very pleasant performances by the students of the college. The pantomime of Mr. Jones was exceedingly fine. It rested me not a little. Home at 9½ o'clock.

SATURDAY, 28. Worked on correspondence until eleven o'clock. Then went to the Capitol and spent some time in the Library making some preparations for a speech on the Currency. I have formed the design of arraying the authorities against inflation by quoting a number of extracts in chronological order giving the opinions of leading statesmen of the last hundred years. It will probably do but little good but it will be a protest against the folly Congress is committing.

SUNDAY, 29. Went to church and heard Mr. Lamar preach. Spent a portion of the day in studying the Currency question. At four o'clock called on the President and had a long conversation with him in regard to the currency. He has written two messages which he has not yet delivered and which I urged him to send in. The result of my conversation gives me some hope that he will veto the inflation bill. It will be difficult to do so in face of the extra issue of Treasury notes.

MONDAY, 30. Committee met at half-past ten. Put in another day's work on the Deficiency Appropriation Bill. In the House the day was consumed in the discussion of the Louisville and Portland Canal.[67] I begin to doubt whether we can pass the bill as it came from the Senate without involving the Government in law suits and other controversys growing out of the rights which Kentucky may claim in the work. At half-past six dined at Donn Piatt's with Governor Cummings of South Carolina,[68] Congressman Lamar of Mississippi and Banning of Ohio. We had a pleasant evening. Lamar is a very cultivated gentleman, has read widely and thinks profoundly. He called my attention to a letter of Agassiz published at Neufchâtel, Switzerland, in 1839, in which Agassiz certified to mesmerism as a positive and effective force. The letter is published both in French and English in the——work entitled *Facts about Mesmerism*, 1840.[69]

[67] The federal government was in the process of purchasing from the Louisville and Portland Canal Company the canal around the falls of the Ohio River at Louisville. The Senate bill provided for the payment of the bonds of the company. William A. Wheeler, chairman of the House Committee on Commerce, knowing that certain parties were suing for title to the entire property, amended the bill to delay payment until Kentucky ceded to the United States jurisdiction over the canal and relinquished to the United States its right to tax the property. The federal government did purchase the canal in 1874.

[68] South Carolina never had a governor or a lieutenant governor named Cummings.

[69] Chauncy Hare Townshend, *Facts in Mesmerism, with Reasons for a Dispassionate Inquiry into It* (London, 1840), pp. 567–571. The author visited Neufchâtel in February, 1839, to attempt to mesmerize Louis Agassiz; he was successful in his effort. In the statement Agassiz describes the experiment.

TUESDAY, 31. Correspondence in the morning and reading up some authorities on the currency, preparing if need be to make a protest against the wild scheme of inflation now pending. In the House, after the vote had been taken on the Louisville and Portland Canal, in which Wheeler's amendment passed—I voting for it for the reason that I think it is due to the U. S. that we should have a clear title before we pay out any [money] for a piece of property—debate on the Currency continued during the day in the dreariest possible way. Spent the evening until a late hour in working on the currency. It is amazing how perfectly we are repeating the experiences of other generations. I am preparing a series of extracts from the writings of Washington, Jefferson, Madison and other worthies and find how completely the best thinkers are in accord on the question.

April

WEDNESDAY, 1. Continued work on the currency and on correspondence until ten o'clock. Went to the Committee room and we worked one hour and a half longer on the Deficiency Bill. At one o'clock went to the Senate and listened with dismay and sorrow to the debate there progressing. That body has at last been swept away by the doctrines of inflation. In the House we had two good and effective speeches against it, one from Phelps of N. J. and the other from Hawley of Conn. But argument has not made much headway on the subject and I fear that argument will not undo the mischief. In the evening we had at dinner Horace Steele and wife, Loughridge of Iowa, Smith of [Ohio?], Mr. and Mrs. Smalley and Mr. and Mrs. Sumner. They spent the evening and we had a pleasant time.

THURSDAY, 2. Worked on correspondence and currency until ten o'clock when Governor Cooke called and I went with him to his office and examined the accounts of the Reform School, of which he was Treasurer. He then went with me to the Committee room and we heard the statements of the trustees of that institution. It has lost eighteen thousand dollars by the failure of Cooke and Co. Additional deficiencies are coming in daily. The War Department sent in a deficiency of nearly one and a quarter millions of dollars.

In the House the debate was continued on the currency, a good speech on the right side being made by Niles of Miss.[70] After dinner Gen'l McDowell called and spent the evening. The House met tonight but I did not feel well enough to attend. Retired at any early hour.

FRIDAY, 3. Did not sleep after six o'clock but dressed and read a disquisition of James Madison on Money, in which he undertakes to prove that paper money is not depreciated by an increase of its quantity, except from the fact that an increase of its quantity throws doubts upon its prompt redemption. This would doubtless constitute a reason for its depreciation, but I think Madison refines his discussion overmuch and misses the application of the principle of demand supply. Took Jimmy with me and walked to the Capitol, where the Committee met as usual at half-past ten and made further progress on the Deficiency Bill. The House devoted its time to private bills, interrupted by a curious little discussion on the right of the Speaker to have the control of the front seat in the members' gallery. Some members have complained to the Doorkeeper that it was undemocratic to give the Speaker a special right to any one seat. The House sustained the Speaker's right by an almost unanimous vote. I approve of the custom on its merits and because it is old. We ought to maintain it for the same reason that we keep the stationary snuff box, filled with snuff, on the Clerk's Desk. Walked home with Crete at four o'clock. Got tickets for Neilson's [Nilsson's] *Huguenots* at four dollars a chair.

SATURDAY, 4. Correspondence and currency study in the morning. At ten o'clock I went with Crete, Mother and Libbie to visit the Executive Mansion and Corcoran Art Gallery, and had a very pleasant time. In the House the day was given to private bills until Judge Kelley got the floor and delivered another of his remarkable screeds on paper money, followed by a still more reckless statement by Butler. I think I must answer some of the absurdities of these speeches and will try to get the floor during the next day's debate.

SUNDAY, 5. Went with Libbie to Saint Aloysius Church to hear the singing and watch the Easter Festivities; in the evening called on Parsons and Mr. Allison. Read on the currency a little while and retired early.

[70] Jason Niles (1814–1894) was a Republican member of the House from Mississippi, 1873–75.

MONDAY, 6. Worked on correspondence and the currency until ten, when the Committee met and continued its work on the Deficiency Bill. It seems an almost endless job to get through the multitude of items that go to make up that. Several times we have supposed ourselves nearly through, but every day brings new grist to the mill. Monday was spent in the usual miscellaneous way in the House. One Judge having been absent during the argument of our insurance cases, the eight judges were equally divided and we got no opinion from the Court on the subject. In the evening took Crete and Libbie to Ford's Opera House to hear Charlotte Cushman[71] in [the role of] Meg Merrilies. Her acting was superb. I have never seen her before and this is probably among her last engagements.

TUESDAY, 7. The ordinary story repeated. The debate went drearily on as usual, no vote being reached and none in immediate prospect. In the evening I dined with General Francis Walker, Prof. Sumner, of Yale College, and Ass't Att'y General Hill. We discussed financial and political questions and had a very pleasant evening. Prof. Sumner[72] is writing a history of American Currency, and I ran over the proof sheets. The work is a good deal of value, but I could see in it as well as in the conversation of the Professor a lack of that knowledge of the world which public life brings to a man, and yet that knowledge has some drawbacks. I studied Sumner from the standpoint I myself occupied twelve or fourteen years ago, and wondered what the rough and tumble of a decade in Congress would do to him.

WEDNESDAY, 8. Committee put in another morning's work on the Deficiency Bill and brought it to a point where we will be able to finish it tomorrow morning. The Currency was debated day and evening and will I think be closed soon. I have for several days tried to get the floor, but it has been farmed out in advance. In the

[71] Charlotte Saunders Cushman (1816–1876), American actress, was best known for her portrayal of Meg Merriles in *Guy Mannering* and Nancy Sikes in *Oliver Twist*. During the week of April 6 in Washington she also played in *Henry VIII* and *Macbeth*.

[72] William Graham Sumner (1840–1910), a professor of political and social science at Yale University, 1872–1910. *A History of American Currency* was published in 1874.

evening went with Crete and Libbie to the Opera to hear Nilsson in the *Huguenots*. There was a great deal of high art no doubt in the performance, but I have never yet been able to get much meaning out of the music of an opera. Some strains I can translate in meaning and these give great satisfaction. But mere volume of scope and sound, though it may be pleasant, is not satisfactory until one has the key to it. The National was crowded to its utmost capacity.

THURSDAY, 9. Committee substantially finished Deficiency Bill, after hearing from the Post Master General and two of his assistants concerning claims for carrying the mail in the Southern States before the War. The subject is difficult. After the morning hour debate on the Currency Bill was resumed in fifteen minute speeches, the last fifteen minutes coming to me. I spoke with some effectiveness, I believe, protesting against inflation. Lamar of Mississippi gave me a higher compliment as a thinker and speaker than I have received in a long time. At half-past three the voting began and the inflationists found their victory not so easily won as they supposed. After several votes the House adjourned without concluding. I think we have made some impression on their ranks. At seven in the evening dined with Clarkson N. Potter and there were present Chas. Kingsley and daughter; Mr. and Mrs. Rothery; Mrs. Potter, stepmother of Clarkson; Mrs. Goddard,[73] grand[d]aughter of General Cass; and Messrs. Dawes, Hoar and myself—a very pleasant party. Home at half-past nine. Revised speech and got to bed an hour after midnight.

FRIDAY, 10. We had no Committee meeting this morning. I was very much worn out with the day and night's work of yesterday. Correspondence and miscellaneous work. Went to the House at twelve where we continued voting on the various propositions of inflation until six o'clock. No conclusion was reached but it is evident that the House is bent on inflation. My speech of yesterday has been favorably commented upon by some of the best minds in the House. But I have no doubt it will do me injury in the district. I could not, however, let the occasion pass without protesting against inflation. In the evening Mr. and Mrs. Roberts and Mr.

[73] Elizabeth Cass Ledward (b. 1840) married Francis Wayland Goddard, of Providence, Rhode Island. Her mother, Matilda Frances, was a daughter of Lewis Cass.

Sutton called and visited us until half-past ten. A number of other people called during the evening. I am very, very weary.

SATURDAY, 11. Correspondence in the morning. Then went to the Post Office Department on several items of business, among others to introduce Mr. Hendry of Ashtabula with a view to getting him restored to his route agency on the Railroad. Got to the House at twelve o'clock where the day was spent in voting on the various currency amendments, until half-past five o'clock when the House adjourned without results. In the evening dined with my classmate Hill. There were present Senator Ingalls[74] and Archy Hopkins,[75] both Williams students, Prof. Sumner of Yale College and Mr. Cleveland of N. Y. The table talk was mainly on currency and financial legislation. We had a good dinner and pleasant company. At nine o'clock left the party and called on Judge Black at the Ebbitt House. Heard the report on the Chorpenning Claim.[76]

SUNDAY, 12. Attended church in the forenoon. Read Boswell's *Life of Johnson* in the afternoon. Among other things went to see [the] Sergeant-at-Arms on some matters relating to his office and personally interesting to him.

MONDAY, 13. Worked on correspondence until half-past nine when I made some calls. Went to the Treasury Department to help my colleague Danforth [Danford][77] to obtain a messengership for Dr. Ashfield. Then went to the Committee Room where I took up the Post Office Appropriation Bill and heard the Postmaster General and

[74] John James Ingalls (1833–1900), a graduate of Williams College, 1855, was a Republican senator from Kansas, 1873–91.

[75] Archibald Hopkins (1842–1926), a son of Mark Hopkins and a graduate of Williams College in 1862, was clerk of the U. S. Court of Claims, 1873–1915.

[76] George Chorpenning, a mail contractor during the 1850's, had received what he considered only a partial settlement of a large claim against the government. In 1870 Congress authorized the postmaster general to adjust the accounts; the postmaster general thereupon awarded Chorpenning a large sum, but before it was paid Congress repealed its earlier authorization. Chorpenning sued and lost in the Court of Claims (1875). The Supreme Court affirmed the judgment of the Court of Claims (94 U. S. 397).

[77] Lorenzo Danford (1829–1899), a Republican member of the House from Ohio, 1873–79, 1895–99.

his assistants on the subject of the expenses of the department. In the House the day was spent in the usual Monday way. Nothing was done of much value. Today I have suffered a new pain—a sharp pain and burning sensation in the cervical cord and in the back side of my head. A pain in the [this] quarter is alarming and bids me pause. In the evening at eight o'clock went to Speaker Blaine's, where there were 30 leading members of Congress called by the Speaker to devise some method of harmonizing opinion in reference to the Currency in order to get some bill through. All shades of opinions were represented, from Butler to Hoar. I was called upon among others to express my views and stated I believed the Senate bill could pass the House though I would not vote for it, and if passed it would close the currency struggle for the session and perhaps for this Congress. I also stated that I would vote for Free Banking if coupled with a corresponding withdrawal of greenbacks. Came home at eleven.

TUESDAY, 14. This morning brought up correspondence and finished my remarks on Chief Justice Chase to accompany those concerning Prof. Agassiz, made at the meeting of the Board of Regents. Committee met at half-past ten and resumed the consideration of the appropriations for the Postal Service. Made considerable progress and adjourned at twelve. In the House, after the morning hour, the Currency Bill was resumed and after voting most of the day, the House bill was passed. The Senate bill was taken from the table and after a parliamentary struggle of an hour, it was also passed. This launched us on the sea of inflation. I think the Senate bill has more contraction in it than the friends of it suppose. I have voted steadily against the schemes of inflation and have at least keep [kept] my record clear of all complicity with that unwise measure.

WEDNESDAY, 15. In the morning footed up my accounts, from July last to the 1st of April. At half-past nine went with Mr. Daniels to the Att'y General's to consult on advancing some causes on the Docket of the Supreme Court. Committee met at ten and continued the consideration of the appropriations for the Postal Service. At half-past one got into Committee of the Whole on the Legislative Appropriation Bill and worked until five. Made slow progress, having completed but three pages of the bill. Came home very tired and nearly sick. Hardly able to sit up. Called on Colonel Parsons. The Committee investigating the District of Columbia are attempting [to] drag in his name and mine because Parsons was the attorney in the DeGolyer patent and because I assisted him by acting in his absence from the City. It is time that we ascertain whether a member of Congress has any rights.

THURSDAY, 16. Committee met at ten o'clock and continued work on the Post Office Appropriation Bill. House met at 12 and I moved to take up the Legislative Appropriation Bill, immediately after the reading of the Journal, which was done. We gave five hours of solid work to it and made about six pages of progress. It is amazing what an amount of small talk is wasted over this bill. I have never seen such slow work in the House. The most of the time has been spent over the least important matters. But little change was made in the bill, except such as was moved by the Committee itself. In the evening worked up correspondence, played backgammon and tried to rest. These days' work are telling on me and I must husband my strength as much as possible.

FRIDAY, 17. Correspondence in the morning. Homer Mills of Nelson called on me. Walked with him to the Capitol. Committee met at ten and authorized me to report the Deficiency Appropriation Bill. Spent the rest of the morning on amendments to the Legislative Bill. In the House after the morning hour, District of Columbia business occupied the time until three o'clock, when I got into committee and worked two hours, making progress of only one page on the bill. Work is very slow. Frank Hutchins of Warren and his son Frank took dinner with us at half-past five. Crete, Lizzie [Libbie] and I called at Mr. Riddle's in the evening. Recurrence of pains in my bones and muscles. It seems to be periodic, something like chills.

SATURDAY, 18. Committee did not meet this morning. Worked on correspondence and read portion of my letter to J. W. Shuckers,[78] containing reminiscences of my stay with Salmon P. Chase during the Winter of 1862–3 when I was his guest. Went to the Doctor's in

[78] Jacob W. Shuckers, *The Life and Public Services of Salmon Portland Chase* (1874), pp. 626–627. Garfield's letter to Shuckers, dated April 20, 1874, recalls his stay with Chase during the fall of 1862.

reference to my state of health and got some medicine. Went to the House at one o'clock got into Committee of the Whole on the Appropriation Bills. After an hour and a half of debate we passed the section relating to the office of the Secretary of the Treasury.[79] Continued work until half-past four and completed about two pages of the bill. Crete and Libbie and I visited the Sumners and Smalleys and we spent a very pleasant evening there with Mr. and Mrs. White. I find in the *Star* the following by George Alfred Townsend:

> To James A. Garfield
> Thou who dids't ride on Chickamauga's day,
> All solitary down the fiery line,
> And saw the ranks of battle rusty shine,
> Where grand old Thomas held them from dismay.
> Regret not now, while meaner pageants play
> Their brief campaigns against the best of men!
> For those spent balls of scandal pass their way,
> And thou shalt see the victory again.
> Modest and faithful, though these broken lines
> Of party reel and thine own honor bleeds,
> That mole is blind which Garfield undermines,
> That dart falls short which hired malice speeds,
> That man will stay whose place the state assigns,
> And whose high mind a mighty people needs.[80]

SUNDAY, 19. Did not attend church. It was raining, dreary, and I kept to the house and rested.

MONDAY, 20. Correspondence in the morning until half-past ten. Committee continued work on the Deficiency Bill and finished it. In the House after the morning hour got into Committee of the Whole and made progress with the Legislative Bill to the extent of four pages and a half which is better than our last day's work. In the evening went with Crete and Libbie to hear Clara Louise

[79] Appropriations relating to the office of the secretary of the treasury were discussed in the next three meetings of the House.

[80] The poem was clipped from the *Washington Star*, April 18, 1874, and pasted to the bottom of the page in the diary.

Kellogg[81] in the *Bohemian Girl*. Some of the airs are very fine. The tenor had really the best voice of any of the troop, as it seemed to me. Mrs. Seguin sang the part of the Gipsy Queen.

TUESDAY, 21. Committee invited the Committee on Commerce to set with us and hear a discussion of the Pacific Mail subsidy by Mr. John Roach[82] of Chester, Pa., to determine whether we will grant it. In the House after the morning hour went into Committee of the Whole and spent more than three hours in getting through two pages of the bill. Governor Woodford,[83] the Chairman of the Committee of the Whole, is not at all an efficient presiding officer. His tones of voice are an irritation to the Committee. This circumstance makes the progress of the bill still slower than it would be. In the evening worked on correspondence and prepared a letter for J. W. Shuckers in regard to Mr. Chase to be published as a part of the Life of the late Chief Justice which he is writing.

WEDNESDAY, 22. In the morning worked on correspondence and finished Shuckers' letter. Committee met at half-past ten and finished the Post Office Appropriation Bill. We have concluded to leave the Pacific Mail Subsidy until a consultation is held between three committees—Post Office, Commerce and Appropriations. After the morning hour, resumed consideration of the Legislative Bill and made 15 pages of progress up to the time of adjournment. The President has vetoed the Currency Bill and in his message has taken ground squarely against a further depreciation of our money standard. This illustrates anew the fact that General Grant is one of the luckiest of men. For twenty years no President has had so fine an

[81] Clara Louise Kellogg (1842–1916), American dramatic soprano, organized in 1873 The English Opera Company and attempted to popularize French and Italian operas in English. During the engagement in Washington she also sang in *Fra Diavola, Il Trovatore, Maritana,* and *The Marriage of Figaro.*

[82] John Roach (1813–1887), sometimes called "the father of iron shipbuilding in America," built in 1874 the *City of Peking* and the *City of Tokio* for the Pacific Mail Steamship Company. He was a leading advocate of a strong American merchant marine.

[83] Stewart Lyndon Woodford (1835–1913) was lieutenant governor of New York, 1867–69, and a Republican member of the House, 1873–74. He was U. S. attorney for the southern district of New York, 1877–83.

opportunity to stay the current of popular delusion and mischief. He has done it manfully and against the remonstrances of many gents who are especially near to him. The veto will make much angry feeling in the West, but the more thoughtful men of all sections will rejoice. In the evening visited my colleague Foster in company with Scofield and Frye.

THURSDAY, 23. Correspondence in the morning. Committee met at ten o'clock and heard Mr. Hubbard until 12 o'clock on the Postal Telegraph. Immediately after the meeting of the House, I went to the Executive Mansion and called on the President to thank him for his noble veto message. I had a long and pleasant talk in regard to it. He said he supposed a few of his friends who had committed themselves very strongly to the Currency Bill would be permanently embittered by his veto, yet he could not help it. He had tried hard to find grounds for signing it and at one time thought he could. But the more he studied it, the more he became convinced of the dangerous character of the bill. I also talked with him in reference to appointing Scofield[84] to the vacancy on the Court of Claims. This will be done unless the Sec'y of the Treasury resigns and accepts that place. Returned to the House at two o'clock and resumed consideration of the Appropriation Bill. Worked until half-past four making fair progress. House took a recess until half-past seven, when we resumed consideration of the bill and worked until ten. Reached the forty-eighth page. Crete and Libbie went with me to the House, and staid throughout the meeting.

FRIDAY, 24. After working on correspondence, called at Colonel Piatt's; then to the Committee where the Secretary of State and the Chairman of the Committee on Foreign Affairs [appeared] and we finished the Diplomatic and Consular Appropriation Bill and ordered it reported to the House. Went to the Supreme Court to move for the admission of Judge [Joseph R.] Johnson of Canfield. Before the Court came in word was sent me that the Journal had been read in the House and I got Ass't Att'y Gen'l Hill to introduce Johnson. I went to the House and got into Committee of the Whole

[84] Garfield's congressional friend Glenni W. Scofield of Pennsylvania. As it turned out, Secretary Richardson did resign and accept a position on the court, and Scofield had to wait for his place on the court until Garfield appointed him in 1881.

and worked on until five o'clock. We finished the War Dep't which was admitted [omitted] yesterday and reached the foot of the 62nd page of the bill, when the Committee rose and the House adjourned. In the evening took the family to Ford's Theatre to hear the Vokes.[85] Performance was one of the most brilliant of its kind I have ever seen. Full of art and grotesque wit which kept the great audience in roars of laughter. We found Brother Joe at the house on our return.

SATURDAY, 25. Correspondence and the departments in the morning. At 15 minutes after 12 I got the House into Committee of the Whole on the Legislative Bill and worked steadily until half-past five, when we completed the bill and reported it to the House, where I got the previous question on the bill and amendments seconded and the main question ordered, and the vote by which it was ordered reconsidered and laid on the table so as to complete the action without further amendment in the House on Monday, or whenever it comes up next. Though the bill has been debated a long time, we have on the whole got it through in fair shape. In the evening went to Welcker's and visited Wells. Returned at nine o'clock and found Mr. and Mrs. Smalley and Mr. and Mrs. Sumner at my house and they spent the evening until a late hour. Libbie sang and played and we had a pleasant time.

SUNDAY, 26. Attended church and heard a sermon by Prof. Loos, who came home with us, took dinner and spent the day. Retired early.

MONDAY, 27. Correspondence in the morning and Committee at half-past ten. Committee considered the amendments that have been made in the Legislative Appropriation Bill in Committee of the Whole and agreed upon what ones we would insist on and on what ones we would resist. Set tomorrow morning for a hearing of the Pension Bill. As soon as the morning hour was ended in the House, a message came from the Senate in reference to the death of Mr. Sumner. Judge Hoar of Mass. made the first address; his speech was able and beautiful, but he has a bad voice—a falsetto—full of the Yankee twang. Here and there, there was a touch of

[85] A performing group known as the Vokes Family of five English brothers and sisters (Fawdon, Frederick, Jessie, Victoria, and Rosina), dancers, musicians, and actors, who specialized in farce, burlesque, and light drama.

extravagance in his delineation of Mr. Sumner, but on the whole it was good. Much the most striking speech of the day was that of Mr. Lamar of Mississippi, in which he studied Mr. Sumner from the Southern standpoint. Orth's eulogy was measured and commonplace. Rainey, the colored member, spoke well. Mr. Dawes made an important point on suggestions that [Thomas Hart] Benton made to Senator Sumner soon after the latter entered the Senate, saying to him that he came into public life too late; that the great issues had been decided, namely, national banking, tariff, and nullification. We may learn from this that each age will have its great issues and we cannot say that the greatest has past. Potter spoke briefly and well. I left when Kelley commenced. His speaking is very unpleasant to me.

TUESDAY, 28. Correspondence in the morning. Went to the Navy Department on business. Committee met at half-past ten, considered and concluded the Pension Appropriation Bill. Also heard a Bishop of the Episcopal Church on the Northern Sioux Indians. In the House, shortly after the Journal was read, took up the Legislative Appropriation Bill and spent the day in voting on it. At quarterpast five concluded the votes and the bill passed. It has been the longest struggle I have ever had on any Appropriation Bill I have had charge of. I made a speech of twenty minutes, before the voting began, in which I set forth the effects of the bill and the reforms that were embraced in it. Home in the evening. My sprained ankle is giving me a good deal of trouble. Mr. and Mrs. Henry came tonight at ten o'clock.

WEDNESDAY, 29. Worked on correspondence in the morning. Committee met at 11 o'clock and considered amendments to the Indian Appropriation Bill. After an hour spent on the bill of the Foreign Affairs Committee in relation to the citizenship, we got into Committee of the Whole on the Indian Appropriation Bill and Loughridge and Parker each made able and valuable speeches. Home in the evening.

THURSDAY, 30. Committee met at 11 o'clock this morning and considered amendments to the Indian Appropriation Bill. In the House after an hour spent on the Naturalization Bill, the Louisville and Portland Canal Bill was taken up and I made a short speech advo-

cating an amendment.[86] In the evening dined at Welcker's with
General Schenck and Senators Allison, Anthony and Stockton,[87]
Representatives Dawes and Orth, Lord Fortescue[88] and Mr. Arring-
ton,[89] Mr. Sartoris,[90] who is about to marry Nellie Grant, Mr.
Rothery, Mr. Hurlbert of the N. Y. *World* and Ben Perley Poore.
It was an elegant dinner and a very pleasant company. Reached
home at ten o'clock and after a visit with our guests retired at eleven.

May

FRIDAY, 1. [No entry]
SATURDAY, 2. Committee did not meet. I went to the House at
quarter-past eleven and spent half an hour in the Library looking
over the monthly box of books that comes from England. I get but
little time to pay my devotions to the new books and the Library;
but half an hour does something to tranquilize one's mind to making
up for the loss of being in public life. In the House the day was spent
on private bills. I left at four o'clock and went to see the Doctor
in regard to my sprained ancle. John Gould[91] of Aurora took
dinner with us and spent a portion of the evening. Very tired.

[86] Garfield resisted a move to refer the bill to the Committee on Commerce, arguing that the bill as amended was acceptable. The House passed it.

[87] John Potter Stockton (1826–1900) was a Democratic member of the
Senate from New Jersey, 1865–66, 1869–75.

[88] Dudley Francis Fortescue (1820–1909), third son of the second Earl
Fortescue; he was a member of Parliament, 1857–74.

[89] This is an error. Hugh Fortescue (1854–1932), Viscount Ebrington,
a nephew of Dudley Francis Fortescue, was in the United States in 1874
at the same time as his uncle. He became Earl Fortescue in 1905.

[90] Algernon Charles Frederick Sartoris (1851–1893), of England, married
Ellen (Nellie) Wrenshall Grant, daughter of President and Mrs. Grant,
in the East Room of the White House on May 21, 1874. His mother
was Adelaide Kemble Sartoris, a writer and opera singer and sister of
Fanny Kemble. Nellie separated from her husband some years later.

[91] John Gould was a staff correspondent for the *Cleveland Herald*; he
later became widely known as a contributor to farm journals. His father, of
the same name, also lived in Aurora.

SUNDAY, 3. Attended church and heard a sermon from Prof. Loos, who came home with us to dinner. After dinner took a drive of three hours and had a pleasant [time].

MONDAY, 4. Correspondence in the morning. Committee met at 10 o'clock, took up the Appropriations for the surveys of the Public Lands and completed them. In the House nothing was done in the appropriations; the whole day was spent in motions to suspend the rules. I regret to say that having a Speaker in the Chair who is a candidate for the Presidency makes it more difficult to get on with the public business; for the reason that he is anxious to oblige so many people that he gives the floor to all sorts of subjects rather than appropriation bills. Thus this day has been mainly wasted. I sent to the Library for Jane Austen's *Mansfield Park*, because my classmate Hill who was here last night told me that nine distinguished Englishmen being together agreed to write down on a piece of paper the name of the best novel they ever read. Six of them wrote *Mansfield Park*, and one of the six was Lord Macaulay. For that reason I determined to read the book, as I have never read any work of Mrs. [Miss] Austen's.

TUESDAY, 5. Drove with Mrs. Barnard to the Navy Department to aid her husband who is Ass't Naval Constructor at Pensacola.[92] Took Crete and the ladies to the Executive Mansion on my way. Then went to the Committee. We heard some pension agents in regard to their rates of pay. Then took up the light house estimates and acted on most of them. In the House the day was spent on the proposed appropriation for the Centennial.[93] I have been some troubled about this question, but on the whole think we ought not to incur the expense. On my motion the House took a recess until half-past seven to go on with the Indian Appropriation Bill. No quorum being present, a call of the House was held. A few of the absentees were brought before the House and being very angry they resisted all efforts to do business and wasted the time of the House until ten o'clock without doing anything.

[92] William H. Varney was assistant naval constructor at Pensacola at this time.

[93] The Centennial Bill provided for an appropriation of $3,000,000 in aid of a centennial celebration and international exhibition to be held in Philadelphia in 1876.

WEDNESDAY, 6. Correspondence in the morning. Committee met at ten o'clock and continued work on the Sundry Civil Appropriation Bill. The whole day was consumed in a discussion of the Centennial. Left the House at an early hour and went to doctor's to consult concerning my foot. Spent the evening at home. Several people called in the evening and I looked over some points in reference to the Centennial appropriation. Prepared to make a short speech tomorrow. I am satisfied that the international feature is a great mistake and will result in disaster and failure. If they change that feature of it and make it a national celebration, I shall be glad to see it go forward.

THURSDAY, 7. Committee met at ten o'clock and heard Professor Baird on the Fish Commission and on the Smithsonian. The Committee acted on those two items. The House met at eleven o'clock and soon entered upon the discussion of the Centennial. I spoke twenty minutes, taking the ground indicated in the Journal of yesterday. Mr. Dawes spoke and at two o'clock the bill was reported to the House, Hawley of Conn. making the final speech. The vote was taken and the bill defeated by over forty majority. Sympathy for the defeated led a good many members to vote for reconsidering with a view to letting them down easily, or giving them another chance. Voted on the reconsideration until five o'clock, when a motion was made to lay the bill on the table and the House adjourned. Capt. Rudolph and his wife left us this evening for Ohio. Reviewed the notes of my speech and read *Mansfield Park*.

FRIDAY, 8. Committee met at ten o'clock and heard several gents on estimates for the Sundry Civil Bill. In the House the Centennial Bill was allowed to be recommitted and the rest of the day was spent on the Private Calendar. We, however, introduced a bill so to modify the rule as to give Saturdays to the public business rather than to private. In the evening Crete and I visited [the] Sheldons at Willard's and spent a pleasant evening.

SATURDAY, 9. Committee met at 10 o'clock and heard parties in relation to estimates on the Sundry Civil Bill. In the House the day was spent on miscellaneous business and the Indian Appropriation Bill. After a long and tedious debate the House adjourned. In the evening worked on correspondence and read Jane Austen's works.

SUNDAY, 10. Attended Church and heard sermon from Mr. Loeben-gier. In the afternoon went with Professor Baird to the rooms of Professor Powell and looked at his maps and photographs taken in the Colorado Country. Spent the evening in reading *Mansfield Park.*

MONDAY, 11. Correspondence in the morning and at ten o'clock the Committee resumed work on the Miscellaneous Appropriation Bill. At eleven o'clock the House met and continued the ordinary Monday work until half-past two when I became satisfied that the Speaker was assuming too much control over legislation on Monday. I therefore interrupted the business by making the privileged motion to adjourn. This the Speaker resented angrily and some unpleasant words passed between us, but when the vote on my motion was taken it showed that the House was with me. We passed the Military Academy Bill and got through 11 pages of the Deficiency Bill. Early in the morning we had passed the River and Harbor Bill under a suspension of the rules, in order to prevent the increase of appropriations by different interests in the House. At half-past five I took the special train with Generals Sherman and McDowell, the Sec'y of War and several other gents for Harrisburg where we arrived at eleven o'clock in the evening. Spent the evening with Senator Cameron.

TUESDAY, 12. In the morning drove with Senator Cameron to his farm of seven hundred acres on the banks of the Susquehanna. It is a beautiful and well cultivated farm. At ten o'clock attended the Meeting of the Army of the Potomac and was called upon to make a short speech. Spent the afternoon at Senator Cameron's. In the evening attended a reception of Governor Hartranft.[94] At ten o'clock in the evening attended a banquet of the Army of the Potomac and responded to the toast "To the President." This was a noble gathering of the ablest soldiers of the Army of the Potomac. The antagonisms and rivalries of this army are in painful contrast with the harmony and comradeship of the Army of the Cumberland. Retired at a late hour.

WEDNESDAY, 13. A little after five took the train for Washington.

[94] John Frederick Hartranft (1830–1889), Republican governor of Pennsylvania, 1873–78.

Finished the second volume of Mrs. [Miss] Austen's *Pride and Prejudice,* reached home at eleven and got to the House at a quarter before twelve. Governor Swann failed to get up his Diplomatic Bill yesterday and the Steamboat Inspection Bill was under discussion. At 3 o'clock got into Committee on the Deficiency Bill and got through 18 pages. Came home in the evening very tired and read and answered a large mail.

THURSDAY, 14. Worked on my large mail that had accumulated all during my absence at Harrisburg. At half-past ten Mr. Gallaudet drove me to the House. The Committee took up the Choctaw Claim[95] and discussed it until half-past eleven o'clock. Did not conclude the consideration of it. After the morning hour went into Committee of the Whole on the Deficiency Bill, and after some sharp debate ran through the 13 remaining pages and ordered the bill reported to the House. Then took up the Consular and Diplomatic Bill and Gov. Swann spoke on it for an hour, when the Committee rose and passed the Deficiency Bill. We have made exceedingly good progress during this week.

FRIDAY, 15. Correspondence in the morning. Committee met at ten and heard several persons on appropriations. In the House the day was spent on private bills. One of them for the rent of the *Clara Dolsen*[96] Steamer was reported by my Committee. It passed after a long debate. In the evening took Crete and Mother and the children to Marini's Hall, to attend the exhibition of the Kindergarten School. I think the little ones are doing very well. The school now numbers nearly seventy. I am troubled to know what to do with the children next in regard to their education. They do not seem to have that hunger and thirst for knowledge that I always felt when I was a child.

[95] The Committee on Appropriations included in its bill a provision to pay the Choctaw Indians a long-standing claim. Garfield admitted that the U. S. owed the Choctaws a debt, but questioned the integrity of the claim and the propriety of acting on it until further investigation by Congress. The House supported him, 118–103.

[96] In 1862 the Union navy seized the *Clara Dolsen* and used her until spring, 1864, when she was returned to her owners. The bill mentioned by Garfield appropriated $66,150 for the relief of the owners; it passed with an amendment reducing the sum to $22,050.

SATURDAY, 16. Worked on Correspondence. Committee did not meet this morning. House met at eleven o'clock and after a struggle with the Committee on Ways and Means for the possession of the floor, we succeeded in getting into Committee of the Whole on the Consular and Diplomatic Bill. And after four hours' debate directed particularly to Mr. Orth's amendment reorganizing the consular service, the bill was finished. I then moved to take up the Post Office Appropriation Bill, which was accordingly done. The bill was read the first time, and then several paragraphs were read for final action. The Committee then rose, passed the Consular Bill and the House adjourned. Thus we have completed the Indian Bill and passed five other bills this week, which is the best week's work of the session. Dined this evening with Senator George Brown of the Canadian Dominion and a large party.

SUNDAY, 17. Attended Church and to avoid listening to a very stupid sermon, translated the Fifth Ode, Book First of Horace. After dinner rode for an hour or two with Judge Black and spent the evening with him.

MONDAY, 18. Correspondence in the morning. The Committee met at ten o'clock, though I was half an hour late in consequence of stopping at the tailor's. Continued the consideration of the Choctaw Net Proceeds Claim, which was very troublesome. I am in doubts what we ought to do in regard to it. In the House the usual Monday work until 2 o'clock, when the new rule went into operation for the first time and gave the remainder of the day to the District of Columbia.[97] Got some books from the Library relating to Jane Austen, and in the evening read her life, written by her nephew J. E. Austen-Leigh, Vicar of Bray, Berks.[98] It is astonishing how little is known of her life. In this respect, as in some others, she seems to resemble Shakespeare. Her fame seems to have been mostly posthumous. Her novels are model pictures of quiet life, and not disfigured by the scenes of most of our novels.

TUESDAY, 19. Correspondence in the morning. Committee met at half-past nine o'clock and after a long discussion concluded by one

[97] On May 8 the House adopted a rule which set aside "the third Monday of each month, after two o'clock P.M., . . . to reports from the Committee on the District of Columbia."

[98] J. E. Austen-Leigh, *A Memoir of Jane Austen* (1870).

majority to postpone the Choctaw Claim until next session. In the House the day was spent in discussing the Moiety Bill.[99] Mr. Howells came during the day and took dinner with us and spent the night.

WEDNESDAY, 20. Correspondence in the morning. Went to the War Dep't on business connected with the Appropriations Committee. Committee met at half-past nine and continued work on the Sundry Civil Bill and heard several parties before the Committee. After the reading of the Journal in the House we got into Committee of the Whole after a contest with the Committee on Ways and Means for the floor in which we were successful, and proceeded with the discussion of the Post Office Appropriation Bill with [which] occupied the day. Finished most of the bill and adjourned at five o'clock. My colleague Smith dined with us in the evening and at eight o'clock went out with Mr. Frye.

THURSDAY, 21. Correspondence in the morning. Committee met at half-past nine o'clock. We took up a number of matters from the docket relating to the Sundry Civil Bill and acted upon them. In the House after the reading of the Journal proceeded with the Post Office Appropriation Bill and passed it. A separate vote was taken on making reports on agriculture free, but we were beaten by the flatterers of farmers.[100] We then took up the Pension Bill and passed it. The Speaker was absent for the first two hours of the day attending the wedding at the President's. I think the girl makes a great mistake in marrying an Englishman. Foster made his speech on the Sanborn contracts, which was very clear and manly. The bill for the admission of New Mexico was then taken up and passed. In the evening worked on correspondence and called on the Ass't Secretary of State.

FRIDAY, 22. Committee met at half-past nine, and finished the consideration of the Senate amendments to the Legislative Appropriation Bill. The Sec'y of State and Mr. Orth, Chairman of the Com-

[99] The Moiety Bill contained amendments to the customs-revenue laws and provided for the repeal of moieties, which were payments made by the Treasury Department to informers whose reports of violations of revenue laws resulted in the collection of deficiencies.

[100] The reference is to an amendment which provided that "the Monthly and Annual reports of the Department of Agriculture shall pass free through the mails." It was approved, 134–71, with Garfield voting against it.

mittee on Foreign Affairs, were before us and were heard in regard to the reorganization of the State Department as proposed by the Senate. Committee agreed to the arrangement and finished the consideration of the bill and prepared a report for printing and delivery to the House. In the House the day was consumed on private bills. During the day went to the Post Office Department on business. At six o'clock had Mr. Robinson, my colleague, to dinner. In the evening went with Foster to visit Sheldon.

SATURDAY, 23. Correspondence in the morning. Committee did not meet. House met at eleven o'clock and immediately after the reading of the Journal, I called up the Committee report on the Senate amendments to the Legislative Bill and after a struggle with the Committee on War Claims, worked a little over an hour on the amendments. The rest of the day was given up to the Committee on Military Affairs. Mr. Monroe took dinner with us and spent a little time in the evening.

SUNDAY, 24. Did not attend church today, but took more rest than on any day since the session began. After dinner rode with Mr. Howells and Isaac Williams to Arlington. Went over by the way of Georgetown and the Aqueduct Bridge, and returned by way of Long Bridge. A very pleasant drive.

MONDAY, 25. Correspondence in the morning. Committee met at nine o'clock. Considered several propositions connected with the Miscellaneous Appropriation Bill. Also disposed of the proposition of making an appropriation to pay mail contracts in the Southern States prior to the War. The proposition was voted down in the Committee by my casting vote. In the House the day was spent in the usual manner of Mondays, and at three o'clock the death of poor Mr. Mellish[101] was noticed. He died Saturday in the Insane Asylum. At half-past three o'clock the House adjourned. He devoted himself almost exclusively to the study of the currency, became fully entangled with the theories of the subject and became insane. His public life was a terrible strain upon his nervous system. Howells left us this evening after passing a successful examination for the Consulate at Quebec—for which I secured his appointment.

---

[101] David Batcheller Mellish (1831–1874) was a Republican member of the House from New York, 1873 to his death on May 23, 1874.

TUESDAY, 26. Correspondence in the morning. Mr. Gallaudet, President of the Deaf Mute College, called and drove me to the Capitol. It is a lovely day and I long for the time to look at it and think of the bright world clothing itself in the beautiful garments of Spring. I hardly have time to look up to the skies or down at the earth. Committee heard the Secretary of the Navy and settled the appropriations for the Navy Yard. We concluded to concentrate our chief expenditures upon four, League Island, Norfolk, Pensacola, and Mare Island. Agreed to appropriate half a million for general repairs of all the arsenals. In the House the Committee on Ways and Means took the day. I am surprised to find what a change two years of occupation has wrought in the topics which interest me. Three years ago I was alive to all questions of taxation and cared but little for appropriations. Now I hear a tariff bill discussed with but little interest but am wide awake to any question of appropriation. At four o'clock the House closed its business and the funeral of Mr. Mellish took place in the Hall. A committee was appointed to accompany the remains to New England, the place of his birth.

WEDNESDAY, 27. Correspondence in the morning. At half-past nine o'clock Committee met; an argument by Mr. Lowry [Grosvenor P. Lowrey], a New York lawyer, on the Postal Telegraph Bill; it was not completed. He advanced the idea that the original purpose of the Post Office, as provided for in the Constitution, was to send parcels and packages and not to send intelligence and asserted that the telegraph was not an incident to the power of establishing post offices and post roads. In the House we acted on the Currency Bill. The amendment proposed by the Committee on Banking and Currency, which was a compromise between the two extremes, failed to be adopted by five or six votes.[102] The Senate amendments were rejected and a committee of Conference called for. The House met on the Tariff Bill and we had a weary and profitless session.

THURSDAY, 28. Correspondence in the morning. Committee met at nine o'clock, heard General Babcock on the public buildings and grounds, and then heard Mr. Mullett on the buildings under the

[102] This action on the Currency Bill occurred on May 28, when the House defeated the substitute amendment of the Committee on Banking and Currency by a vote of 118–111.

supervision of the Treasury Dep't. Had a long and workful session. In the House the day was spent on the Army Bill with but little profit. Gen'l Coburn does not seem to be a happy organizer and his bill is a striking example of his method of disjointed and inharmonious work.[103] During the day I had some leizure and went to the Library and got the last volume of Jane Austen's *Sense and Sensibility*, which I read and shortly after my return home in the evening finished the work. I shall notice more fully in some other place the impressions which Jane Austen's works make on me. George Alfred Townsend. Walked in the park with Crete and remained home very tired. Crete nearly sick.

FRIDAY, 29. Crete is quite ill and I fear is threatened with chills and fever. Went for the Doctor who came just as I was leaving for the Capitol. Committee listened two hours and a half to Mr. Lowrey on the Postal Telegraph. In the House at two o'clock I antagonized the private bills and succeeded in getting the House to work on the Senate amendments to the Legislative Bill. We completed them at half-past five, after much debate and many votes. Find that Crete has been in bed all day. The Doctor says she has chills and a kind of dumb ague. Am reading an advanced copy of Warden's *Life of Chase*.[104] The absurdest piece of egotism and biographic indecency I have ever met. The reading of that book leads me to doubt the propriety of any man's keeping a diary— "But ah what fools may come, when we have shuffled off this mortal coil, must give us pause." Warden is what Jane Austen would call a "Strong, Natural, Sterling" Ass.

SATURDAY, 30. Correspondence in the morning. At ten o'clock went with Mrs. Riddle and Sheldon to see the President and to recommend the appointment of General Thomas[105] (a native of Ohio but now a resident of New Orleans) to a South American Mission.

---

[103] The bill reported by John Coburn, chairman of the Committee on Military Affairs, provided for a gradual reduction of the size of the army. It was passed by the House the next day.

[104] Robert Bruce Warden, *An Account of the Private Life and Public Services of Salmon Portland Chase* (1874).

[105] The editors have not been able to identify this man, whose name may have been written incorrectly by Garfield's copyist.

Thomas is a queer specimen of an adventurer, having been filibustering with Walker and in connection with kindred operations since. He is a man, however, of fine ability and a good deal of culture. The Sec'y of War was present at the interview. On coming out from the President's room I met Mr. Bristow who is soon to be Secretary of the Treasury. In the evening read Warden's *Life of Chase* and became deeply interested in that part that is biographical. Read until after midnight. There is much in the early life of Chase that I deeply sympathize with. His mother's letters are very touching looked at from this distance. Although Chase had to make the fight with poverty, as I did, yet he had powerful friends to take the guide of his education and give him culture at an earlier age than I had any. Before he was sixteen he was delivering a Greek Oration at Worthington, Ohio, in the presence of his Uncle, the Bishop. At sixteen I had never seen a Greek book. I think I can see the good effect of uniting the early Western influence to the influence of his Eastern life. But oh what a biographer.

SUNDAY, 31. I am not well. Read too late last night and the fierce heat of today has kept me indoors. Read till a late hour, going over several hundred pages of Warden's bulky book. The interest deepens as I go through the biographical portion relating to his anti-slavery life. His experience in the office and family of William Wirt, in 1828–1830, must have been very valuable in laying the foundation of his knowledge of society and in acquiring the cultivation which society produces. In that respect his early advantages were greatly beyond mine. I was almost alarmed for him when I read that he applied to his Uncle Senator Chase of Vt. for a clerkship, but delighted to find that that sturdy old man answered, "Samuel [Salmon] I will give you fifty cents to buy a spade with, but I would not for anything get you a clerkship." [106] Chase thought this harsh at the time, but I have no doubt that he afterwards blessed the memory of his Uncle for it thousands of times. I think

---

[106] On page 121 of Warden's biography the reply of Chase's uncle appears as follows:

" 'Salmon,' said he, 'I once obtained an office for a nephew of mine, and he was ruined by it. I then determined never to ask one for another. I will give you fifty cents to buy a spade with, but I will not help to get you a clerkship.' "

I discover one reason why he chose Warden as his biographer. The event of his life most criticised was his election to the Senatorship in 1848. Warden was the Champion of the Pew[Pugh]-Pierce Party in the legal proceedings which led to that result, and I can see why Chase was desirous of having a biographer who would do justice to that transaction.[107]

MAY, 1874. For convenience I turn back to the vacant space of this volume [Diary of 1873, under the entry for May 22], and note a few points in reference to the course of my recent reading. I have found that the best [relaxation] is not idleness but a change of work, and in the heavy load of overwork and weariness I am carrying this session, I find great relief in the change and rest which reading brings. A few weeks ago my old classmate, Ass't Att'y Gen. Hill, was visiting me, and in the course of the evening spoke of the English novelists of the early part of this century, and related the circumstances that at a dinner party of nine distinguished Englishmen, each agreed to write down the name of the best novel he had read, and that six of them (Lord Macaulay among the number) wrote *Mansfield Park*.

This was high praise. I reread what Macaulay says of Jane Austen in his essay on Madame d'Arblay, and the next day sent to the Library for the preferred book. I read it, and then read *Pride and Prejudice* and *Sense and Sensibility*.

This reading has been restful and delightful and has opened a new field of enjoyment. It show[s] how far the public tast[e] has drifted in the last half century. The novel of today is highly

[107] As a result of the election of 1848 in Ohio, two seats from Hamilton County in the Ohio House of Representatives were contested. Two Independent Democrats (Free Soilers) in the House joined with the Democrats to organize the House and to seat George E. Pugh and A. N. Pierce, the Democratic claimants of the two seats in dispute. Ohio's Black Laws—laws restricting Negroes—were repealed and Salmon P. Chase was elected to the U. S. Senate. The Whigs charged that a corrupt bargain had been made, with Democratic votes going to Chase and for repeal of the Black Laws in return for Free Soiler support for Pugh and Pierce and in the organization of the House. The situation was complex since the contest over the two Hamilton County seats resulted from a reapportionment of the county by Whigs which Chase and others believed to be unconstitutional.

spiced with sensation, and I suspect it results from the general tendency to fast living, increased nervousness, and the general spirit of rush which seems to pervade the life and thought of our time.

June

MONDAY, 1. Committee met at half-past nine and finished the estimates for public buildings and reduced the aggregate including repairs, etc., to $6,800,000. The Choctaw Claim was voted on the bill by one majority against my wishes. Ordered a bill introduced to give half a million to the sufferers by the Mississippi overflow. I fear this precedent will trouble us. Still it seems to be necessary. Committee sat two or three hours into the day and paid but little attention to legislation in the House. We have brought the great Miscellaneous Bill near to completion and will be able I think to introduce it on Wednesday. In the evening attended the exhibition of the Kindergarten School and Jimmy and Mollie and Harry did very well in their pieces. Their advantages are far greater than mine were at their time of life.

TUESDAY, 2. Had a long session of the Committee on the Miscellaneous Bill. Session extended into the time of the session of the House several [hours]. Committee accomplished a large amount of work which left me but little time for paying attention to the business of the House. At seven o'clock dined at Bancroft Davis', Ass't Sec'y of State. The dinner was given to Mr. Bunsen, son of the great author.[108] Besides him there were present, Senator Anthony, Judge Hoar, Gen'l Parks [Parke] [109] and myself. We had a very

[108] Christian Karl Josias von Bunsen (1791–1860), Prussian diplomat, orientalist and theologian, was secretary of the Prussian mission to the Vatican while Barthold Georg Niebuhr (1776–1831), distinguished historian, headed the mission, 1816–23; he succeeded Niebuhr as minister. His son, Theodor von Bunsen, was a member of the German legation in Washington.

Davis was about to be appointed minister to Germany as successor to his uncle George Bancroft.

[109] John Grubb Parke (1827–1900), a brigadier general during the Civil War, was now a major in the regular army and assistant chief of engineers.

pleasant evening. Bunsen speaks English with but little accent. His conversation about his father, who was for a time Secretary to Niebuhr, was very interesting. Mr. Davis showed us a mask taken from the face of Oliver Cromwell after his death. The historic wart over the right eye is there and the strong nose tipped to one side.

WEDNESDAY, 3. The Committee finished the Sundry Civil Bill. In the House the day was spent on a bill for the improvement of the mouth of the Mississippi. I have at last finished Warden's bulky octavo of the life of Mr. Chase. Notwithstanding my disgust at the author's method of treating the subject, yet so much of the volume is autobiographical that I have [been] deeply interested in its perusal. My old love and admiration for Mr. Chase is on many accounts strengthened and renewed by the reading of this book. His early life, indeed his life up to 1860, is very dear to me and much of it after that time. I think the Presidential passion was the great mistake of his life and from it resulted almost all the blunders of his life. Conference Committee on the Legislative Appropriation Bill met in the room of the Senate Committee on Appropriations and worked two hours. House conferees were Kellogg of Conn., Randall of Pa., and myself. Senate conferees, Morrill of Me., Sargent and Davis.[110]

THURSDAY, 4. Gallaudet of the Asylum [Deaf Mute College] called and drove me to the Capitol before ten o'clock. Committee acted on 44 amendments of the Senate to the Deficiency Bill and I had a report of the results prepared for the House. Later in the day we also acted on the Senate amendments to the Consular and Diplomatic Bill. At one o'clock Conference again met on the Legislative Bill and worked until four o'clock. We settled a large number of differences but some were passed over on which we could not agree. At half-past four o'clock reported the Sundry Civil Bill to the House to print. Also during the day got concurrence in the Senate amendments to the West Point Bill which now goes to the President. Conference Committee again met about two o'clock and spent about three hours on the Legislative Appropriation Bill.

[110] Henry Gassaway Davis (1823–1916) was a Democratic senator from West Virginia, 1871–83.

Some of the differences between the House and the Senate are very sharp, and I apprehend trouble in reaching a satisfactory conclusion. I am invited to go to Norfolk tomorrow with the Sec'y of the Navy in his yacht but do not think it will be possible to get away. Mr. Howells was confirmed as consul to Quebec [a] few days ago.

FRIDAY, 5. Committee acted on the amendments to the Indian Bill. There were over a hundred amendments. Spent much of the day in reading proof and perfecting the text of the Sundry Civil Bill. The House devoted the first half of the day to bills for opening the mouth of the Mississippi for navigation. I offered a substitute for the two pending bills which looked to postponement until next Winter but was beaten by a small vote. The [Fort] Saint Philip Canal then beat the Jetties and passed by a strong majority.[111] A day or two since two bills were passed which had been passed in the early part of the session—which fact has been severely commented upon by the newspaper press. The[y] were reported from the Committee on ——.

SATURDAY, 6. Correspondence in the morning. After the reading of the Journal in the House, I brought up the Senate amendment[s] to the Deficiency Bill and spent two hours in acting upon them. Carried all my points but one. Had a sharp debate with Holman[112] in regard to the general question of expenditures.

SUNDAY, 7. Did not attend church, suffered intensely from the weather. Called on Mr. Willard[113] of Vt. and made arrangements for Mother to go with his family on Thursday next as far as to the corner of New Hampshire. She goes with Harry to visit her birthplace. In the evening dined at Wormley's with Messrs. Hooper,

---

[111] The "Jetties" bill provided for the deepening of one of the outlets of the Mississippi River into the Gulf of Mexico. A second bill provided for the construction of a canal to extend from some point below Fort St. Philip to the Gulf of Mexico. The latter passed by a vote of 146–80, with Garfield voting against it.

[112] William Steele Holman (1822–1897) was a Democratic member of the House from Indiana, 1859–65, 1867–77, 1881–95, and 1897 to his death. He was known as "the watchdog of the Treasury."

[113] Charles Wesley Willard (1827–1880) was a Republican member of the House from Vermont, 1869–75.

Wells and Allison. After dinner Judge Black went with us—Crete, Miss Ransom and myself—to Senator Jones's[114] where we visited.

MONDAY, 8. Committee met at ten o'clock and heard a delegation of printers from the Government Printing Office, who protested against any reduction of their pay. Our questions drew out from them the facts concerning the tyrannical spirit of that organization [National Typographical Union], which restricts the number of apprentices that may learn the trade and then arrogates to each chapter of the organization the right to fix the rates in its own city. This puts employers absolutely at their mercy. In the House the day was spent in the usual manner of Monday. After two o'clock we held another session of the Conference Committee on the Legislative Appropriation Bill. The Louisiana case[115] came up for consideration in the House and was continued until seven o'clock. Got my dinner at the Restaurant and waited until eight o'clock for the Joint Caucus of the Republicans of both Houses which was held in the Hall. Judge Kelley opposed the reformation of the Committee but it was done nearly unanimously.

TUESDAY, 9. Committee met at 10 and heard a continuation of yesterday's discussion from the Printers' Union and also heard the Binders' Union. Their organization is quite like that of the Printers. In the House the day was mainly devoted to the Geneva Award.[116] Had another session of two hours and finally completed the Conference report on the Legislative Bill. This has been the most uncomfortable day I have ever known in Washington. At half-past four o'clock the thermometer ranged 101 in the shade and the signal reports show that there was but one place in the Union, Norfolk, where it was higher. It was nearly impossible to sleep. Crete and I took a mattrass down in the parlors and laid under the open window. During the day was called to the U. S. District Court to try the case of *Driggs*

114 John Percival Jones (1829–1912) was a Republican senator from Nevada, 1873–1903.

115 P. B. S. Pinchback unsuccessfully contested the election of George Augustus Sheridan (1840–1896), who was a Liberal member of the House, 1873–75.

116 The House was considering a bill which provided for the disposition of money received from Great Britain under the decision of the Geneva Tribunal, established by the Treaty of Washington, 1871.

vs. Daniels. I succeeded in effecting a settlement satisfactory to both parties.

WEDNESDAY, 10. Called at the Treasury Dep't and saw the new Secretary, Bristow; thence to the Post Office Dep't on business for my district; thence to the House where the day was spent in discussing the Geneva Award. Went to the Senate and perfected the details of our conference on the Legislative Appropriation Bill. Home in the evening working up correspondence and preparing a brief speech on my Sundry Civil Bill which I hope to get up tomorrow. The political pot is again boiling in my district. The *Cleveland Leader* has published some articles in my favor and my old enemies are raging over it. The little digs and little assaults of little men who attribute low motives to whatever is beyond their reach forms one of the chief features of this class of assaults. I tire of such a warfare, but I think I will test my strength with them once more.

THURSDAY, 11. Called at the Treasury Department on business; thence to the Committee where we settled some additional matters that had come before us. In the House at half-past twelve got the Sundry Civil Bill up for consideration. Had a struggle over the wages of the printers and binders in which the Committee was defeated.[117] Got through with eleven pages of the bill and adjourned at half-past five. At half-past eight took Mother and Harry to the depot and got them on the train for N. Y. They go to New Hampshire to visit Mother's early home. When I was ten years of age I had never travelled fifteen miles from home. Such a trip as Hal is now taking would have been a great thing to me.

FRIDAY, 12. Called at the Treasury in the morning on business; then went to the Capitol. At 11 o'clock the House met. Soon afterwards got into Committee of the Whole on the Sundry Civil Bill and kept up the work until half-past 5. Made 32 pages of progress. There is something peculiar in the temper of the House. A clear strong statement of a case, if made too soon or too late, fails. If well made at the right time it is effective. It is a nice point to study the right time. I sometimes strike it and sometimes fail. I failed yesterday in striking

[117] For various reasons congressmen opposed a clause in the bill which provided that wages paid to government printers and binders should not exceed the average wages paid for similar work in Philadelphia, Baltimore, and New York City.

it on the Printing House question. I hit it today on several amendments to the bill, especially on Coburn's amendment to appropriate $10,000 for testing Mr. Lee's gun.[118] I said let us have fair play and treat all inventors alike. Congress should not advertize one man to the exclusion of others. I could see the consent of the House as I spoke. Home in the evening.

SATURDAY, 13. Called at the Engineer Department in the morning and also at the Post Office Dep't on business for my District. Soon after House met, the conference report on the Currency [Bill] was made and the vote taken. With much reluctance I voted for the report but it was beaten by a large majority. I cast my vote mainly for the sake of harmony in our delegation, but not until I was certain that the bill could not pass. At twelve o'clock got into Committee on the Sundry Civil Bill and nearly finished the first section. Adjourned at half-past five, in a jangle over the civil service clause. The House is determined that no further effort shall be made to reform our civil service. Came home very tired and got what rest I could in the evening.

SUNDAY, 14. Attended Church and after dinner sent the children and the girls to Arlington. Read Shakespeare's *Pericles of Tyre* for the first time. I do not believe that Shakespeare wrote the whole of the play. I can see his hand in it, but it is too artificial to be his creation. In it, however, he strikes a blow at the finished utterances of dramatic unity. At 6 rode with Sherman, Foster and Smith to Rock Creek, Brightwood and home. Crete and I called on Donn Piatt in the evening.

MONDAY, 15. Committee met at ten and settled some straggling matters that have come in since our last meeting. I resolved upon a defeat of the Choctaw Claim if possible, and soon after the House got into Committee, opened the fight, which lasted for an hour and a half. Considering the fact that six out of the eleven members of the Committee on Appropriations were in favor of it, and that the House had by a two-thirds vote suspended the rules to make it in order, the case looked hopeless. But I believe I have never conducted a contest more successfully and we beat them by ten or twelve majority

[118] John Coburn moved to appropriate $10,000 for the manufacture of Lee's breech-loading musket which would be tried in the field. The amendment was defeated.

on a square vote on the merits and at half-past five o'clock passed the bill. Servis came during the day and is looking better than I have ever seen him. The air of Montana is doing him good. The House met at half-past seven in the evening to consider bills from the Committee on Public Buildings and Grounds. The most outrageous measure I have seen for many years was up when I reached the House. A combination of public buildings and sites for buildings for some twenty-five cities were thrown together in one bill with a purpose of combining enough force to pass it. After three hours' struggle this bill also was killed and the House adjourned. Reached home at half-past eleven. Revised my speech of today upon the general results of the Sundry Civil Bill. Retired at ½ past 12.

TUESDAY, 16. Committee met at half-past ten and heard Mr. Brisbane a short time on his pneumatic tube. Immediately after the meeting of the House got up the Indian Appropriation Bill and acted on the 134 Senate amendments. The rest of the day was spent in miscellaneous legislation. We took care however to allow as little done as possible. My Committee has so far finished its business that it is not at all crowded. Servis took dinner with us. The House met in the evening on pension bills. I staid but a little while and being very tired returned home at ten o'clock. I do not believe the appropriation bills were ever so well worked up as they have been this session.

WEDNESDAY, 17. Called with Servis at Senator Sherman's and the Attorney General's. At ten o'clock went to the Senate side and met the Conference Committee on the Deficiency Bill. Sat until two o'clock and settled most of our points of difference. The Indian Appropriation for Arizona however still divides us. Later in the day finished and signed the Conference on the Legislative Bill. In the House the Conference on the Pension Bill was agreed to and I reported the Legislative Conference after it had been adopted in the Senate. House also passed bill of the Investigating Committee on the District Affairs. It abolished the Legislature and Board of Public Works and provides for a reorganization of the District. At home in the evening, was very tired and did not do much.

THURSDAY, 18. In the morning completed the Conference report on the Legislative Bill and before the day was over introduced it into the House and carried it after considerable debate. I am each day sending back to the Senate everything in the way of appropriations they send to us. In other words I manage to clear our decks each day. The House is ahead of the Senate in its business, and my committee has never had its work so well up and so thoroughly in hand as now. House met this evening and I remained for about an hour, then came home and got a little rest. There seems to be a mania for increasing the number of public buildings and I fear before the session ends we shall have to pay considerable in the line of new buildings. No one has yet gone through with my consent and indeed none has yet become a law.

FRIDAY, 19. Correspondence in the morning. Committee met at ten and took up and completed the consideration of the Senate amendments to the Post Office Department Bill. Many of them are important in that they establish the rates of newspaper postage and enlarge the express feature of the Post Office Department. In the House we took up the bill and continued its consideration until half-past five o'clock, completed it and asked for a Committee of Conference. I made a speech of fifteen or twenty minutes on the original objects of the Post Office Dep't, which I think was of some value.[119] When I got through, my colleague (Smith) sent me a note saying it was one of the most clear and comprehensive arguments he had ever heard delivered in the House.

We defeated the Senate proposition to increase newspaper postage but the House voted the express feature, increasing the amount to four pounds allowed to be sent by mail. This I believe will prove disastrous to the postal business, being a very great increase in the bulk of our mails. Session in the [evening] when Butler made one of his characteristic speeches defending himself and attacking his enemies generally. He was sharply overhauled by Foster, Roberts, and others. Home at eleven o'clock. Wallace, who was out when we got in, did not come home till very late; when he reached the house we did not hear him ring and so he stopped at the Hotel.

SATURDAY, 20. Finished conference on the Deficiency Bill after a long struggle, reported it to the House and carried it. The Conference on the Indian Bill was defeated in consequence of the appro-

[119] In a speech opposing any increase of newspaper postage, Garfield argued that the original object of the Post Office would be changed if the Senate had its way. He maintained that the Post Office was established to convey intelligence and not, as some believed, to carry packages.

priation for the Apaches. House sat until twenty minutes before midnight before finishing its work. Got the Senate to order the printing of the Sundry Civil Bill with the Senate amendments. Also the River and Harbor Bill which they did not get completed until near three o'clock in the morning. I reach[ed] home at half-past twelve too tired to sleep.

SUNDAY, 21. Committee met at eleven o'clock and worked four hours on the 124 Senate amendments to the Sundry Civil Bill. At three o'clock the Committee on Rules met in the Speaker's parlor on the rules. Cowles of the *Cleveland Leader* called on me in the afternoon. In the evening Crete and I called at Riddle's.

MONDAY, 22. House met at half-past ten, and I immediately called up the Sundry Civil Bill in order to act on the Senate amendments. Nearly the whole day was spent in debate, and I had many sharp passages, especially on the proposition to make an appropriation to the Little Sisters of the Poor. I opposed it on the ground that the Government should have nothing to do with any sect, creed, or denomination as such.[120] Some four hours was spent on the bill when I move[d] to non-concur on all the remaining amendments and send the bill to a committee of conference. House resumed its sitting and at half-past eight Conference Committee met. Morrill of Maine and Sargent and Stevenson of the Senate and Hale and Niblack and myself worked until two o'clock in the morning and settled all points save three, when Hale and Sargent flared up and the conference ended for the night. Walked with Sargent and before he reached his residence he concluded to concede to our views and sign the report. Got to bed at half-past two in the morning.

TUESDAY, 23. Conference Committee met at half-past nine, and settled the remaining differences and signed the report. Before eleven o'clock both Houses had agreed to it. The Conference Committee cut down the amount of the appropriation about one million dollars, but still the amount of the bill is considerably increased over the bill as it

---

[120] The Senate amendment appropriated $25,000 for a building for the Little Sisters of the Poor of Washington. Garfield argued that only Catholics could belong to the organization, whose very name was "descriptive of an order within the Catholic Church," and he stressed the importance of upholding the principle of separation of church and state. The House approved the amendment, 102–43.

passed the House. Got through both reports—Post Office Appropriation Bill and River and Harbor Bill. The time of adjournment was extended to six o'clock in order to give the enrolling clerks time to finish their work. All legislative action was substantially completed when the last of my appropriation bills got through. I made a speech for half an hour stating what had been done by the appropriation bills during the session. They show a reduction of $27,000,000 over the corresponding bills of last year. Dawes followed with a very handsome notice of what the Appropriation Committee had accomplished.[121] At six o'clock the House adjourned and left me very, very, tired. Thomas Phillips, who came this morning, took dinner with us and spent the night. Did not retire until midnight.

WEDNESDAY, 24. Finished up correspondence, went to the various departments and to the Capitol and spent the day in working as hard as I could to get ready for leaving town. Also completed notes of my speech on the cheap transportation problem. At nine o'clock in the evening took the train for N. Y., too tired to travel and almost too tired to sleep.

THURSDAY, 25. Reached New York at seven in the morning, stopped at the Saint Nicholas and spent the day in giving an examination to the proposition of the Phillips Bros. to sell oil lands in Europe. They offer to pay my expenses and in case of success a handsome commission, say 10 percent. If I can possibly get away from the District I shall accept their proposition. Lunched with David A. Wells at half-past one o'clock. He has just been tendered the degree of D.C.L. by Oxford University of England. Call[ed] on ex-Governor Morgan.[122] At 9 o'clock took the train for Washington. Hot, uncomfortable night.

FRIDAY, 26. Reached home from N. Y. at 7 A.M. and commenced a hard day's work to get ready to start for Hiram with the family. Be-

121 S. S. Cox, echoing the sentiments of Democratic members, scoffed at Republican claims of economy and financial responsibility, and denounced Garfield and Dawes for making what amounted to stump speeches for the coming campaign. He said that such speech-making was unfair, for with Congress adjourning the opposition was unable to reply.

122 Edwin Denison Morgan (1811–1893), wealthy New York businessman and political leader, governor of New York, 1859–62, U. S. senator, 1863–69, chairman of the Republican National Committee, 1872–76.

sides bringing up correspondence I closed up my work in the case of *Driggs vs. Daniels*, and got my fee, $500. Paid various bills, read the proofs of my speech on Transportation and Railroad[s], and revised the stenographic report of my speech on the appropriations of the late session. I have been able to show a reduction of more than $25,000,000 below the laws of last year. Failing to get time to see the Hon. Eugene Hale, my next in rank on the Appropriation Committee, I wrote him a note congratulating him on his appointment as Postmaster General, but expressing my doubt of the wisdom of accepting it. The place is less independent than his place in Congress—will be more involved in the antagonisms and intrigues of the next presidential campaign and may compromise his friendship for Blaine. Still I think he will accept. A place in the Cabinet to a man of thirty-seven and comparatively new to politics is not often offered nor declined. At 8.45 took the Baltimore and Ohio R. R. for Pittsburgh via Cumberland and Connellsville and spent a pleasant evening, *luna plena imminente* [a full moon shining overhead].

SATURDAY, 27. I did not sleep well. The old discomfort of the stomach returned and tossed me about most of the night. Reached Pittsburgh before 9 A.M., where I met Ford, who comes from the Phillips Bros. with an urgent request that I go with them to Europe. Before 10 A.M. we were on Pittsburgh, Ft. Wayne and Chicago R. R. and a little after noon reached Leetonia, where we took dinner and waited until 3.20 P.M., when we took the train for Garrettsville. Emma Redfield left us at Niles. At Warren, Austin and Morgan came on board and rode with us to Windham giving views of the political situation of the District. Reached Garrettsville at six. Drove home, a baggage wagon following, and rested sweetly under the maples, taking my first full night's rest for eight days.

SUNDAY, 28. No meeting today. Wrote letters, lay on the grass, sweltering under a sun that seems to have been brought from Washington, and [in] the evening got at my journals of 1851–4 and read till after midnight. I am amazed at the gush and slush of those days. I was a very pulpy boy till I was at least 22 years old. But with all the rudeness and crudeness of those times, I was very dead in earnest and was working by the best light I had. In looking over it now I am not ashamed of the most of it.

MONDAY, 29. Every bone and muscle of my body is tired and my mind is equally jaded. I have done all the resting I could, but am too tired to rest. I have mitigated the situation by reading Lucretius' *De Natura Rerum*. It opens with a noble and beautiful protest against the crushing tyranny of religion as he knew it. He points out the crushing effect of religion upon intellectual freedom. He says this terrorism must be dispelled by the aspect and law of nature—and to effect this he has "watched the clear nights through" in scanning the hidden things of nature. In the afternoon Burke came, and we talked and communed with each other many hours.

TUESDAY, 30.   Arose at half-past four and went with Burke and Prof. Hill[123] to Garrettsville, and thence to Cleveland. Spent the day in business, purchasing furniture, etc., for cottage at Little Mountain. Took dinner at Dr. Robison's. Saw several friends from Ashtabula County. Went to the City Library and looked at the history of the Regiments that are to hold reunion at Painesville on the Fourth. Took the 3.55 train for Solon, and went to Sister Mary's. Two hours after I arrived Crete and Mollie came, and we visited in the evening. Sister Hitty came down.

July

WEDNESDAY, 1.   Crete and I took the morning train for Garrettsville. Spent an hour at Dr. [E. B.] Lee's playing croquet, and then came home by hack. Letters and papers till three P.M. when Crete and I went to Mr. Stanhope's and staid to tea with a party of neighbors and friends. Ford came and spent the night with us. He is very anxious that I go to Europe and help the Phillips Bros. in their business. I am still too tired to do much work on any subject.

THURSDAY, 2.   Arose early to see Ford off. After breakfast felt unfit for work and slept two hours. My mind is like a becalmed schooner— it does not draw nor feel the rudder of the will. Isaac Williams came from Edinburgh and took dinner with me. When he left I tried to work on my Painesville speech, but my mind has no grip since the session has ended. It must have rest. Wrote letters, read a little, and

---

[123] Osmer C. Hill, principal of the commercial and chirographic departments at Hiram College.

afterwards set up the croquet set and played a few games. Several friends called in the evening. Later I made some notes for my Painesville address. Got three ideas in line, viz.: the object of the War of Independence; and the spirit of the late war; and their relation to each other. But my mind scratches over them like a comb full to the points of the teeth. Retired early.

FRIDAY, 3. Crete and I took the 5.20 A.M. train for Cleveland, where we spent some time shopping, and, at 11 A.M. took the Lake Shore train for Mentor, and went thence to Little Mountain. Visited our new cottage and made some arrangements for fitting it up. Went by 6 o'clock P.M. train to Painesville and stopped with Horace Steele, where a party of friends met us at tea. In the evening went with the Steeles to General Casement's[124] where was a large party of soldiers and citizens. Returned to Steele's little before midnight.

SATURDAY, 4. Slept until a late hour. Have made only the slightest preparation for a speech. Shall use some old material for part of it. Immense concourse of citizens in procession. At 11 A.M. I spoke for 40 minutes, and did better than I expected to. After speech saw a large number of citizens. State of feeling towards me seems good. Dined at Horace Steele's. At 4.15 we took train to Burton, and after tea at hotel Hoadley took us (Ford, Crete and me) to Hiram, where we arrived at 9 P.M., with the comet blazing brightly at our backs. Oh! how utterly exhausted I am.

SUNDAY, 5. After a good night's rest, I feel a little more alive, but the tire has struck deep into my fiber. Went to church and heard the usual story of poverty in reference to employing a pastor. Spoke ten minutes on the importance of this church keeping itself in active working order. In the afternoon Hon. George H. Ford and wife of Burton came to see us. Had a pleasant visit. In the evening Alvah Udall came and had a long visit. Have concluded to take Jimmie with me to New Hampshire, partly for his own pleasure and partly

[124] John S. Casement, a native of the Isle of Man, was a wealthy railroad contractor of Painesville; he was a Union officer during the Civil War. In 1874 he was living "in a splendid and extensive new mansion," which was lighted and heated with gas. He was a member of the Ohio Senate, 1872–73. In 1876 he became the candidate of the Democrats and anti-Garfield Republicans for Garfield's seat in the House; he received more votes than any other opponent of Garfield ever obtained.

to relieve his mother of the heavy care of so many. I find myself more and more averse to leaving home.

MONDAY, 6.   Went with Ford and Jimmie to Garrettsville and thence to New Castle, Pa. Dinner at Ford's. In the afternoon, Isaac, John and Charles Phillips called and talked over their project. I regretfully declined their offer to pay my expenses to Europe and back, and a large contingent fee for aiding Thomas to sell oil property. I need the trip and the money. But my friends in the District are timid and think I ought not to be absent during the anti[ante]-convention campaign. In the evening took tea and played croquet at Isaac Phillips'. Spent the night at Ford's. Jimmie has a bad cold.

TUESDAY, 7.   After breakfast went to the Bank and spent a few hours with the Phillips Bros. in reference to their European business. At noon Isaac Phillips went with us to Pittsburgh. Stopped at the Monongahela House until evening, when Jimmie and I took the train for N. Y. I declined to go to Europe, but did it very reluctantly. I have lost a fine opportunity to rest and perhaps to make some money.

WEDNESDAY, 8.   We took breakfast in West Philadelphia, and at ten o'clock were in the Brevoort House, N. Y. Mr. Ward was there and took charge of Jimmie by sending him to see Barnum's Hippodrome. I went to see several business men in reference to the Phillips business, and made arrangements with Mr. [Henry A.] Smythe, President of the N. Y. State Loan and Trust Company, to write to Thomas and help him. At six dined with Ward and Hurlbut [Hurlbert]. During the day saw several leading editors and talked over the political situation. At Brevoort over night.

THURSDAY, 9.   At ten Jimmie and I took the New York and New Haven R. R. for Springfield and went thence North to South Vernon, Vt. and thence on the Keene R. R. to Winchester, N. Y. [N. H.] There took carriage to Richmond and found Harry at Mr. Bardon's [Barden's] and Mother at Mr. Newell's.[125] Harry cried with joy to see me. We spent the night at Mr. Newell's. This is the place where we stopped first when I was in Richmond in 1872.

FRIDAY, 10.   Mr. Barden, Mrs. Newell, Mother, Harry and I, went to

125 Eliza Ballou Garfield was engaged in a sentimental pilgrimage to the scenes of her early childhood. She was born in Richmond, New Hampshire, near the Massachusetts line.

Royalston, Mass. to see Russell Whipple, and visited several houses. Stopped at a house built by Russell Ballou, Mother's uncle. On the farm north, Silas Ballou,[126] the poet, lived and died. He was buried there in 1837. On the same road, and a mile north of the Russell Ballou place, now occupied by Silas Whipple, is "Ballou Hill" where the family originally settled, and where Mother was born. We went there and found the cellar, the well, and a few stones that formed the basement of the house. It is on the road that runs north and south, parallel to the Richmond Centre Road, and about one mile east of it. The site of the house is on the south slope of the hill, and about one mile north of the Mass. line, on the farm now owned by a Mr. Harkness. After supper at Mr. Barden's we took stage to Keene, and at nine P.M. took train for the West.

SATURDAY, 11.   After two hours' delay at Bellows Falls, and a change of cars at Rutland, we reached Troy at 5 A.M., waited an hour, and then took train to Schenectady, where we breakfasted, and at 9 A.M. got train for Buffalo. It was a slow train and a dull day. Read part of Bristed's *Five Years at an English University*.[127] But I was sleepy and dull, and the day dragged wearily. Supper at Buffalo, and took the boys down to the dock to see the shipping. We waited until an hour past midnight, when we took the sleeping car on the Lake Shore Road for the West.

SUNDAY, 12.   Reached Cleveland in time to catch the Mahoning train, and went to Garrettsville. Thence took carriage to Hiram. Planted in Joe's yard the maple bough from Mother's birthplace.

MONDAY, 13.   Capt. Henry and his wife, who came before I returned, remained most of the day. We visited, played croquet, and I read a large accumulation of mail. I have not yet had a good and full night's rest since the session closed. I have been too tired to rest. In the afternoon our guests left, and in the evening I retired early.

TUESDAY, 14.   Spent the day in writing letters. Correspondence has become the great drudgery of my life. There seems to be no end to it. An average of twenty letters to be answered is not a pleasant prospect

---

[126] Silas and Russell Ballou were brothers of Eliza's father, James.

[127] Charles Astor Bristed, *Five Years in an English University*, 3rd ed., rev. (1873). Bristed, who lived in Washington during much of his later life, died there in January, 1874.

when it stretches away indefinitely into the future. In the evening Burke came, and spent several hours. Also many friends dropped in during the afternoon and evening. Again retired early to take in a part of the rest of which the session has defrauded me.

WEDNESDAY, 15. Worked on correspondence until noon. Mrs. Servis of Canfield came to visit us. At one I took carriage for Ravenna. Visited Halsey Hall and other friends and talked over the political situation of the District. Paid my county and state taxes; made several calls; got copy of the new Constitution from Horton,[128] our member of the Convention; took the six o'clock P.M. train to Cleveland, and went to Dr. Robison's. Ed. Cowles called in the evening. Had him contradict the Private Secretary story started in the papers against me.[129] Staid at Robison's over night.

THURSDAY, 16, Took the early train to Columbus. On the way found Judge Griswold,[130] Senator Sherman, Foster, Sherwood and John Hopley.[131] After dinner at the Neil House, went as per invitation to meet the Republican Central Committee. Eight or ten of us spoke on the political prospects. I was very pleasantly received by those assembled. This was in striking contrast with their bearing towards me last year. After the meeting, took the five o'clock train for Cleveland. Foster went with me as far as Shelby. He is a good friend. Reached Cleveland at ten and a half P.M., and spent the night at the Weddell House.

FRIDAY, 17. Took the morning train to Warren in answer to a request

[128] Joseph D. Horton represented Portage County at the Ohio Constitutional Convention which met in 1873. The constitution which it made was rejected by the people.

[129] Some of the newspapers, including the New York *Evening Post*, reported that Garfield's private secretary had been on the payroll of the House Postmaster for several years without performing any work for the government. Garfield's main reliance for secretarial service was on George U. Rose, who was in government service, but aided Garfield in his spare time.

[130] Seneca O. Griswold, a Cleveland lawyer, was a judge of the Cuyahoga County Court of Common Pleas, 1873–75. In 1859 he and three other prominent lawyers served as counsel for the defendants in the Oberlin-Wellington rescue affair.

[131] John Hopley was the proprietor and editor of the *Bucyrus Journal*, Crawford County, Ohio.

from Harmon Austin. Jones[132] had sent to the *Chronicle* an attack on me, on some points of which my friends wanted my help to answer. I went to Judge Kinsman's, where I staid to dinner. Austin and Morgan called and the latter read his reply to Jones's attack. They are feeling hopeful and full of fight. Austin took me to the Depot and I went to Garrettsville by the two P.M. train and thence to Hiram. Wrote letters and got affairs in readiness to take the family to Little Mountain. Loaded Stocking's wagon with goods and baggage for an early start.

SATURDAY, 18. Mr. Stocking and the two oldest boys started at 4 P.M. [A.M.] and the rest of us followed in a carriage at seven across the country to Little Mountain. The day was pleasant and the ride agreeable. We reached the Mountain at half-past twelve and found the cottage and furniture in a tumble. The afternoon put all to rights and the evening was pleasant in our summer home. Since last season I have bought a share in the Little Mountain Club, and have built a little cottage of Crete's planning. Share, cottage and all cost $965. To this I have added about $150 of furniture purchased and some more brought from Hiram and Washington.

SUNDAY, 19. Awoke after a full ten hours' sleep. More rest than I have had for many months. Several Cleveland gents called and I spent the forenoon in conversation. Rested and read in the afternoon and evening.

MONDAY, 20. Spent the day in little odds and ends of work in and around the cottage. Harry and I made a crib for Abram, and arranged for a little grading before the cottage door. In the afternoon the usual fate of letter writing. The mails find me here with fatal facility. But still the change is restful and it relieves Crete from the pressure of household cares. Read Dr. Clarke's *Sex in Education*.[133] It is a masterful paper and strikes a powerful blow at the folly of the Woman's Movement.

TUESDAY, 21. Crete and I drove to Painesville and stopped at Geo.

---

[132] Lucian C. Jones, a Warren lawyer, was a member of the Ohio Senate, 1872–74. He won 17 delegates to the Republican Congressional Convention in 1874, but they cast blank ballots since it was obvious that Garfield would easily win the nomination.

[133] Edward Hammond Clarke, *Sex in Education; or, a Fair Chance for the Girls* (1873).

Steele's. After dinner we did some shopping in the village, and I held a consultation with several political friends. Jones of Warren and his skirmishers are in the field, busy with new forms of scandal against me. He was in Painesville tomorrow [yesterday?] and is in Chardon today. Crete called at Horace Steele's, and after I had finished my consultations, we went to George Steele's for supper and thence to the Mountain. Many new members of the Club arrived this evening.

WEDNESDAY, 22. Today has been devoted to visitors. Hon. Geo. H. Ford and wife; Neil Ford and wife, of Burton; and Hon. Mr. Gowey,[134] of Champaign Co., (guest of the Fords), came early in the forenoon and staid till evening. We had a pleasant ramble among the rocks and a fine visit. During the day also came Thomas Clapp of Mentor, and President Pendleton of Bethany College, [West] Va.; also two carriages full of friends, who are attending a Sunday School convention at Mentor. What with children, and visitors, and household cares, Crete was nearly tired out.

THURSDAY, 23. Took early hack for Mentor; stopped at Thomas Clapp's; and, at 9 A.M. attended the Sunday School Convention. Made an address of twenty minutes, which was I think rather successful. Went home with Henry Clapp and took lunch and then took train for Cleveland; whence to Solon by four P.M. train and went to Larabee's. Found Mother and Mollie well, but Sister Mary is not well and has gone to Wellington to see Hattie and to rest. Went to see Sister Hittie. How hard and relentless is the struggle for bread. If the contest gets too hard for one, he pays the forfeit by a life of hard struggle. Staid at Larabee's one [over] night.

FRIDAY, 24. Took Mother and Mollie to Cleveland by morning train. Went to Dr. Boynton's and spent most of the day visiting his family and Aunt Alpha Boynton. Mother is on her way to Wellington to see Sister Mary. Mollie and I took the 5 P.M. train for Little Mountain, which we reached in time for tea. Family reunited at last. Congressional Committee of the 19th District met in Cleveland today, and fixed August 13th as date for Convention. The Beecher-Tilton Scandal the theme of all tongues. I believe in Beecher.

---

134 John F. Gowey, Urbana lawyer, was a member of the Ohio House of Representatives, 1874–75; he was a delegate in 1880 to the Republican National Convention which nominated Garfield.

SATURDAY, 25. The day brought with it a great mass of letters to be answered and papers to be read. I have read the mass of horrible stuff in reference to the Beecher-Tilton Scandal, which is so agitating the country. I can understand how terribly Beecher is suffering under the savage assault of private malice and public opinion. Though the attack of Tilton is formidable, and adroitly put, yet it has not shaken my confidence in Beecher. Especially in view of the enormous amount of apparently cheerful work Beecher has done with this thunderbolt impending. Beecher may be a bad man, but I don't yet believe it. I have had no confidence in Tilton since I saw him in Washington six years [ago]. He seemed to be overfull of himself.

SUNDAY, 26. Walked and rested and read. In the afternoon started to go to the Lake View House; but it began to rain and we abandoned the visit. Several Cleveland gentlemen sat and talked with me a long time *de omnibus et singulis* [about everything and anything]. Much discussion of the Beecher scandal.

MONDAY, 27. Took Harry with me and drove to Chardon. Called on D. W. Canfield and visited with a number of gentlemen who were at his office. Among others with Judge ——— who thinks I am wrong in my views of the currency. I hit upon a new method of presenting the case, by showing that a national man should not become the special advocate of the Creditor class as against the Debtor class, nor *vice versa.* But that we should try to reach a solid basis of specie, so that it shall not be in the power of Congress to injure any class by tampering with the currency. Took dinner and tea with D. W. Canfield. After dinner O. S. Farr[135] told me that Canfield is a candidate for Congress. D. W. C. tried to explain his position into friendliness to me but he has not been frank. He is making a mistake and I am almost compelled to distrust him. Harry and I reached to [the] cottage at 8 P.M.

TUESDAY, 28. Drove to Painesville and made some purchases for the cottage there. Found that George Payne [Paine][136] and Probate Judge Tuttle were making a raid upon me in regard to my services in the Chicago Pavement Case. Invited friends to meet me at the parlor of the Stockwell House where I stated the facts in the case and

135 Orrin Smith Farr (b. 1835), a Chardon lawyer.
136 George Paine, Painesville lawyer.

[answered] any questions they chose to ask. A raid is evidently to be made on me to prevent my nomination. Took the two o'clock train for Geneva where I was met by a large number of friends. Stopped at the Tuller House for tea. In the evening attended the Garfield Club (an organization of my friends lately formed) and responded for a short time to a complimentary address. Answered questions in reference to the Salary Act and apparently satisfied the inquiries. I spent the night at Thorp's the artist.

WEDNESDAY, 29. Went to Ashtabula by the morning train and arrived at the depot, meeting Captain Henry, who informed me that D. W. Canfield's name is announced as a candidate for Congress. This tends to confirm the suspicions noted in this journal for Monday last. Took dinner at the Fisk House and then went with a company of gentlemen and visited the Ashtabula Harbor. Took a trip of an hour on the lake in a yacht. Tea at the Fisk House in the evening, after which I was serenaded by the band and made a short address, not political. Spent the night at Henry Hubbard's. The enthusiasm and cordiality of my friends is some—yes, a great compensation for the rascality and injustice of the assaults made upon me. Henry Hubbard and nephew, E. H. Fitch, have been heroic and faithful friends in all this row.

THURSDAY, 30. Went to Warren by the Ashtabula, Youngstown and Pittsburgh Railroad, reaching there about noon. Stopped at Austin's in the afternoon and wrote letters. In the evening held a consultation with several active friends in regard to the campaign. The young men who specially impressed me with their vigor and ability, were Messrs. Kennedy and Brierly. The opposition against me in this place is very bitter and very determined, but the best men in the town are my friends. The enemy has so long been at work against me, that their influence has soaked down through the laboring class and created much prejudice against me. Spent the night at Austin's, who for the past two years has carried me about in his heart as few men ever carried a friend. I doubt if he has given any deeper thought to his family and business than he has to me.

FRIDAY, 31. Took the morning train to Garrettsville and drove thence to Hiram, where I spent three hours. Took dinner at Father Rudolph's; transacted some business; wrote some letters and returned to Garrettsville; took the three o'clock train for Cleveland. I then took the five o'clock train to Little Mountain, reaching the cottage in the evening. Found a great mail awaiting me.

How unlike my dreams this summer has been! I had hoped to spend a few months in Europe reviving my soul, and reawaking my love of art and classic history. But after serving the country with all my strength, almost with my life, and achieving an honorable renown for the 19th District, I return to be nibbled and kicked at by a little-souled set of men who would besmirch one whom they cannot hope to overthrow. I make this last fight against them.

August

SATURDAY, 1. Spent most of the day in answering letters. I have determined to make no personal effort to secure the nomination, beyond answering suggestions from my friends. In the evening J. H. Rhodes and family came to visit us. We spent a pleasant evening in visiting.

SUNDAY, 2. A beautiful day spent in the cool woods with old friends. J. N. Austin, Disciple, preached at the Lake View House. He married a niece of Alexander Campbell. They visited us after the service. He is bitten with Episcopacy and will probably leave our church. In the evening O. S. Farr came from Chardon with indubitable proof that Canfield has turned against me and will run as a candidate. This is a strange commentary on my visit with him last Monday.

MONDAY, 3. Rhodes and family left us this morning. The opposition against me in Painesville has culminated in a public meeting to be held tonight and to be address[ed] by Tuttle and Paine who will assail me in reference to the Pavement Contract, Credit Mobilier and Salary. I arranged with George and Horace Steele to attend the meeting and if they think the assault formidable to give notice that I will reply tomorrow evening, but if the meeting is a fizzle to give notice they will answer by nominating me for Congress. I see the evidences of a concerted attack upon me by various ambitious candidates throughout the district, and I think there are parties outside of the District who are egging on the attack. I suspect the printers' union of Washington and some discharged clerks are sore at the economy I tried to enforce last winter.

TUESDAY, 4. Word was brought me today of the nature of the Painesville meeting. The speeches of Paine and Tuttle were very rambling and very bitter. They have overdone the business and have weakened their influence by their foolishness. I am satisfied that there is some force behind them. Men do not start out in a crusade of that sort without some motive beneath the surface. My friends concluded their effort was too much a failure to require notice from me and so we let them wriggle; still they will poison some minds. Telegram came from Kirtland to let me know of Canfield's and Stevenson's [Stephenson's][137] opposition there against me. They say these efforts will be thwarted in that town. I think Canfield began as my friend; but becoming impressed with the belief that there was likely to be a successful raid upon me, he thought best to place himself in a position where he could catch his share of the splinters. He has shown himself not the highest type of friend, and has hurt himself.

WEDNESDAY, 5. Took the early train for Cleveland. Hearing that Judge Glidden was to be brought out as a candidate, telegraphed to Austin that I was coming to Ravenna and desired to know the facts. Remained two hours in Cleveland, wrote several letters answering inquiries concerning the movements of the campaign and took the 11 o'clock train for Ravenna. Hall met me at the Depot. After dinner we drove to the Atlantic Depot and met Austin and spent some two hours in consultation of the situation of the campaign. Portage is standing up to me with great unanimity. Austin says we shall have 21 of the 38 delegates in Trumbull. Glidden wants to run but dare not. He answered the Painesville bolters evasively so as to get the advantage of running without having to bear any of its responsibility. Austin returned to Warren in the evening. I spent the night at Hall's.

THURSDAY, 6. Returned to the Mountain by way of Cleveland. At Cleveland wrote a number of letters in the office of J. H. Rhodes. The District is very thoroughly aroused and we shall have large primary meetings. My enemies are bitter and noisy, my friends more active than ever before, and full of fight. My Lake County opposition will try to run Glidden, but it is too late for him. His timidity has lost him all the chance he had. To bring out so many candidates is a confession of weakness by the opposition—particularly of their

[137] James E. Stephenson, a Chardon lawyer, was a delegate to the Republican Congressional Convention which was to meet in Painesville on August 13 to nominate a candidate for the House.

leaders. They are puzzled at my silence—and annoyed that I am not alarmed at their noise. Probate Judge Tuttle appears to be acting for somebody who does not appear on the scene, and who that somebody is I do not yet know. For himself, he does not amount to much. George Paine and he are working together.

FRIDAY, 7. Answered letters and reading Dr. Clarke's *Sexes [Sex]* *in Education.* By 11 o'clock J. B[V]. Whitney,[138] of Montville, called on me, having driven twelve miles to see for himself what the situation is. He has been hostile to me on the salary matter but is satisfied with me now. We had a long and confidential talk concerning the character and conduct of D. W. Canfield in reference to this and other campaigns. Whitney took dinner with us and left about the middle of the afternoon. He thinks Montville will send a delegate in my favor. A large mail came this evening with reports from various parts of the District.

Whitney is a man who has long been a teacher and school examiner, and keeps himself above the ordinary level of intelligence by study and thoughtfulness. The old teaching tie is still strong with me, and I find myself in ready sympathy with one of that line of life.

SATURDAY, 8. My mail is daily increasing in size but it relates mainly to the canvass. The primary meetings are held this evening in all the townships of the District. At half-past nine o'clock I went to the Telegraph Office at the Lake View House, where I was until midnight receiving dispatches. Fifteen telegrams came from different points showing that the primaries were very large and enthusiastic and that a very large majority of all the delegates elected are for me. Warren gave three to Jones and three to me. Lake County, solid, Geauga, all but Chardon, Portage, solid. Ashtabula and Trumbull gave me a majority.

SUNDAY, 9. Rested and reading, no preaching on the Mountain today. At night more reports came which confirmed those of last evening.

MONDAY, 10. A large mail and many telegrams giving still further

---

[138] John V. Whitney, a nurseryman of Montville, Geauga County, of whom it was said that "he has been a successful teacher, is a good farmer and arboriculturist; a man of unusual intelligence, good judgment, and great force of character." *History of Geauga and Lake Counties, Ohio* (1878), p. 205.

accounts of the primary meetings. All concur that the primaries were much more largely attended than ever before in this District. Hodges came from Concord and gave me a full account of Judge Tuttle's attempt to get himself elected a delegate hostile to me. He made a speech and assailed me with great bitterness, but he lost it by six majority. The opposition in Mentor completely broke down, and did not attempt to run a candidate for delegate when they saw the strength of my friends. There were 108 votes for me and none thrown against me. In Painesville, where Tuttle and Paine had made so much noise, there were 464 votes polled (only 5 less than Noyes' whole vote) and all but 62 were for me. Grant's story of the prairie wolves is applicable to this case.[139]

TUESDAY, 11. A large number of visitors called on me today and bring further news from the primary meetings. The assaults upon me have developed an unusual amount of enthusiasm. The newspapers speak of the primaries as matters of national importance. The members of the Little Mountain Club, though mostly Democrats, congratulate me cordially on the result. Even H. B. Payne, the President of the Club, a life-long Democrat, says if I will move to Cleveland, they will elect me without distinction of party. My friends are very jubilant over the result of the primary meetings, and say it is without doubt the greatest political victory of my life. But there will be an ugly opposition at the polls. The foolish clamor against me in reference to the Salary vote of March 3, 1873, made a deep impression on the popular mind, and will not easily be erased.

WEDNESDAY, 12. R. W. Hall and wife, W. H. Beebe[140] and wife, J. C. Beatty[141] and wife and children, and Mrs. Mason, all of Ravenna, came this evening to visit us. Our friends of the Club very kindly placed at our disposal the Perkins and Rhodes cottages, so that our guests were all provided for, and we spent a pleasant evening in the moonlight under the trees visiting. The news from

[139] See entry for October 19, 1872.

[140] William H. Beebe, a former student at the Western Reserve Eclectic Institute, was cashier of the Second National Bank of Ravenna.

[141] John C. Beatty, the proprietor of a clothing store in Ravenna, was a member of the Republican Congressional Convention of the nineteenth district, which met in Painesville on August 13.

Portage County is especially gratifying. Scarcely an opposing vote appeared at any of the primary meetings. In many instances strong resolutions were passed in my favor. The blank 34 votes at the Painesville convention probably represent the sourness and envy, together with the salary indignation, of this District. There is a touch of Yankee narrowness in the people of this District which I do not at all admire, and which seems inconsistent with their general intelligence. I shall not do any thing to flatter or recognize it.

THURSDAY, 13. At nine o'clock the gentlemen of our party took the Little Mountain hack which had been placed at our disposal and drove down the Mountain and along the Mentor road to Painesville which we reached a little before eleven. A large assembly of gentlemen and ladies were awaiting us at the Stockwell House. They came from various parts of the District. Nearly all of the opposing candidates broke down before the convention assembled. Jones of Trumbull had seventeen delegates from his own county, but eight of them were obtained by the aid of Democratic votes and could have been contested had it been necessary. [Stephen A.] Northway had considerable strength from Ashtabula, but not nearly a majority of his own county and none elsewhere. Portage and Lake were solid for me and I had all the delegates from Geauga except the two Chardon delegates. At the convention all these opposing elements threw blank votes, so that I received the votes of 100 delegates and 34 voted blank. I waited in the Stockwell House for the result and when I got before the convention I was prepared for peace or war according as the opposition behaved. Winship[142] of Pierpont moved to make the nomination unanimous and this carried with the exception of a few malignants from Trumbull Co. A committee called on me at the Stockwell House and I went to the Convention and made a short address which I think was fairly successful. The convention was very enthusiastic and composed of as good men as ever met in a district convention here. Many friends went back with me to the Mountain, among them Hinsdale, Rhodes, Harmon Austin, Capt. Henry, Isaac Williams and the same party that came down in the morning. Twenty-one guests took tea with us and spent the night.

[142] T. S. Winship, a Pierpont merchant.

355

FRIDAY, 14. Awoke with a severe cold caught last night while visiting under the trees. A portion of our friends left on the morning train, but most of them staid until the noon train. Burke staid over night. In the evening I read aloud to Burke and Dr. Streator and wife, Beecher's Defence,[143] which is a most masterly production of his kingly intellect and confirms me in my inception of the truth in the case and of his character. It shows some weakness in his judgement of men and it amazes me that he should have trusted himself to such a man as Moulton,[144] but no one is great all around. I have been made deeply indignant at the low sneers and insinuation (of men who ought to be above such baseness) against Beecher. *"Puris omnia pura sunt, sed defilatis* [To the pure all things are pure, but to the unclean]," etc. Perhaps the unjust attacks from which I have recently suffered have given me a bias in favor of one accused.

SATURDAY, 15. Burke and I took a long walk among the rocks and took a long stroll in the woods, talking over our life's experiences in the old intimate way. Among other things he gave me a full account of the struggle through which his father had been passing in reference to surrendering the management of his affairs. How shall we in advance learn the lesson to grow old sweetly and accept the inevitable as it comes. Burke leaves in the evening to go to Painesville, where he speaks tomorrow. Dr. Robison and his wife came by the evening train and with them Streator and wife. We had a long visit after supper.

[143] In June, 1874, Henry Ward Beecher had appointed a committee of members of his church to investigate Theodore Tilton's charge that Beecher had committed an offense against him. The offense, it soon appeared, was adultery with Mrs. Tilton. Beecher made his defense before the committee on August 13. On August 20, before the committee issued its report exonerating Beecher, Tilton had brought suit against Beecher for $100,000 for alienation of affections.

[144] Francis Moulton, a Brooklyn merchant, became famous during the Beecher episode as "the mutual friend" of Beecher and Tilton. He claimed that Beecher had confessed to him that he was guilty of adultery with Mrs. Tilton, a claim which Beecher denied. He was much in the news in connection with the church investigation of Beecher and the suit of Tilton against Beecher.

SUNDAY, 16. Intended to make up a party and attend the Church at Mentor, but we did not go. In the afternoon the Universalists held an annual meeting at the western foot of the Mountain in the grove and Dr. Robison, Streator, and myself attended. O. S. Farr and Judge Smith[145] of Chardon called to see me and explain how it was that he, Smith, voted blank. He would have voted for me but that Canfield claimed that he could control Smith and should now have it thrown for me and that he was not a candidate. Smith was not willing to be a party to this dissimilation on the part of Canfield. Today has been excessively hot, but the evening was pleasant.

MONDAY, 17. Dr. Robison and wife left us on the early train. After working on my correspondence for a few hours I took the 11 o'clock train to Cleveland in company with several members of the club and went thence by the afternoon train to Hiram where I spent the night. Heard many interesting details of the primary meetings in this part of the District. In Hiram they had the largest primary meeting within my knowledge and no vote was thrown against me. Tomorrow is the election to determine the vote on the new Constitution. I am persuaded that there is much that is valuable in the instrument, but no adequate effort seems to have been made to lay it before the people and it is not likely to be adopted.

It requires some effort to retain one's respect for the people. I frequently think of Lieber's chapter in his *Civil Liberty*[146] on "*Vox populi Vox Dei* [The voice of the people is the voice of God]."

TUESDAY, 18. Cast my vote, visited a few minutes with Burke, and, about 10 o'clock, took the carriage that had just brought him, drove to Chardon where I am to deliver a lecture this evening before the Institution. Took tea at O. S. Farr's, whose wife was a Miss [Cynthia] Nash, an old student of mine; after which played croquet until the time for the lecture. The Court room was crowded to its utmost capacity with an intelligent audience. I spoke half an hour on the personal influence of a teacher over his pupils and

---

[145] Henry K. Smith, a Chardon lawyer and probate judge of Geauga County.

[146] Francis Lieber, *On Civil Liberty and Self Government*, 2 vols. (1853).

the necessity of studying character as a means of succeeding in the management of school. Although I found it no easy task, I found it much easier to draw on my old stores gathered in my teaching days, and I believe I succeeded very well. By special invitation of Mr. Canfield spent the night at his house. It requires some self control to behave well in his company just now.

WEDNESDAY, 19. After breakfast Mr. Canfield drove me to Chardon. I felt not a little embarrassed at accepting his hospitality in view of his recent conduct toward me. But he has been for many years my friend and I was willing to hear his statement of the case. He insists strongly that he has not been treacherous to me, but that he was putting himself into a position where he could best head off the efforts of Jones. I half think he deceives himself as to his motives and that from an effort to defeat Jones he drifted into an effort to defeat him for his (Canfield's) own sake. I think I can never feel towards him as I formerly did. A friend that turns in the hour of battle is not my type of friend. Worked on letters until evening. I perhaps ought to have added that it is easier to be magnanimous now that I have been successful over my assailants.

THURSDAY, 20. Rested and read and wrote and played billiards and passed an eventful day. In the evening Birdie Hall and her brother came—he as her escort. She was to visit us some days. She is a pretty child of fifteen and we were glad to receive her for her parents' sake, as well as our own.

FRIDAY, 21. Left the Mountain by the 11 o'clock train for Cleveland. Went to Ryder's and had photographs taken to answer the request of Mr. Everts, the historian of Portage, who desires my portrait in his Historical Atlas.[147] Took the 4 o'clock train for Warren. Large concourse of people met me at the depot and Judge Kinsman took me to his house. After supper a committee of young gent[lemen] called on me and escorted me to the hall where I had agreed to address the Teachers' Institute of that county. A large audience was in waiting and I delivered I think a more effective lecture than I made in Chardon three days ago, though in the main I followed the same line. After the lecture, I was serenaded at Judge Kinsman's,

[147] L. H. Everts, *Combination Atlas Map of Portage County, Ohio,* . . . (1874). Page 16a has a portrait and biographical sketch of Garfield.

a large concourse of citizens called on me and I made a brief speech in answer to the serenade. Spent the night at Judge Kinsman's.

SATURDAY, 22. Judge Kinsman had planned to take me to Holland Springs, but the weather was threatening and we spent the forenoon in town. At two o'clock he invited a large party of gentlemen to dinner. The party was composed of both the friends and those who had been hostile to me in the primary meetings, and several gentlemen who had been opposed to me gave in their adhesion in a cordial way. Yet Warren is still the headquarters of the opposition against [me]. Judge Glidden was there but did not seem cheerful. E. B. Taylor had more the appearance of cordiality than any of the leading opponents. Mr. [Daniel] Camp, the flax mill man, was very cordial and spent an hour with me after the other guests had left. Senator Jones, who was invited, but did not come, sulked on his porch across the street. In the evening a large party of citizens called on me with a band and gave me a serenade. They called on me for a speech and I made a short address to them, after which a large number of ladies and gentlemen visited me on the porch of Judge Kinsman's house. Burke Hinsdale and Harmon Austin came and spent some time after the crowd had gone. Spent the night at Judge Kinsman's.

SUNDAY, 23. Attended the Disciple Church and heard a good sermon from Burke. Kinsman and I took dinner at Austin's. In the afternoon called on Colonel Taylor for the first time in two years. In the evening took a drive on the banks of Mahoning and along Lovers Lane.

MONDAY, 24. Took the morning train to Garrettsville and went to Hiram. In the afternoon went to Cleveland and took the 4 o'clock train for Little Mountain. In the evening there was a large party and an amateur club from Cleveland performed *Les Voyageurs*. It was very cleverly done. Mollie Payne, the daughter of Henry B. Payne, was one of the performers and is very bright. Young Chisholm is a genius in the way of comic singing and acting. On Saturday evening this party performed a German play which was said to have been very well done. They are members of the German Club in Cleveland and have cultivated themselves in that language.

TUESDAY, 25. Crete and I went to Painesville about noon and spent some hours at George W. Steele's. Took the afternoon train for

Cleveland and thence by the Mahoning train [to] Newburgh. Took Mollie with us. We stopped at Uncle Thomas' over night preparatory to the Reunion of the Forty-Second here tomorrow. Fuller reports from the primary meetings are still coming in with additional evidences of the good state of feeling among my friends in the district.

WEDNESDAY, 26. At an early hour members of the 42d began to arrive, and at ten o'clock the meeting was called to order in the Town Hall, where in the midst of a ball 13 years ago I made a speech and called for recruits and began the raising of Company G of the 42d Regt. Captain Gillett [Charles P. Jewett] was the first to enlist. At one o'clock the members of the regiment took dinner at the Cataract House. The dinner was managed by my cousin, Capt. George Garfield. At two the Regiment re-assembled and Captain Mason read two chapters of the forthcoming history of the Regiment. The Society greeted me as their President, and the former Colonel of the 42d, with all the enthusiasm I could have desired. The attendance was large all the field officers being present. Dined late in the afternoon. The General Sheridan Party and myself with some others attended the Regimental Ball for a short time and spent the night together at the Cataract House.

THURSDAY, 27. Mother and Harry, Sister Mary and Nellie, came from Solon. Harry sprained his ankle seriously at Henry Boynton's a few days ago and is still lame. Crete, Mother and I went to Cleveland in company with Sheldon and Pardee and met their wives at the Forest City House. We spent the day in visiting, and discussing the affairs of the South, which look very threatening. Sheldon is not renominated and thinks the experiment of Negro government a dangerous one. Crete, Mollie and I went to Little Mountain on the five o'clock train and found all well at home.

FRIDAY, 28. Correspondence during the day. In the afternoon Father Rudolph and wife came to visit us. In the evening G. H. Kent and wife, accompanied by some citizens of South Kirtland, came to see me in regard to the Post Office difficulty there. The smaller the Post Office, the bigger the row it makes. I have been led to recommend a change in the Post Office there, and am now satisfied that the movement was made by a minority of the people to gratify some revenges growing out of a neighborhood quarrel. I shall have the matter investigated, which will probably reverse my

action. I have long been inclined to the opinion that the offiice
of local postmaster ought to be an elective one. I know there are
difficulties in the way, but I think it would remove from the field
of politics one of the chief causes of heart-burning among the
people.

SATURDAY, 29.   Father and Mother Rudolph, Crete, Mary and I, went
to Mentor to visit Thomas Clapp and his family. We spent a pleasant
afternoon. We have been intimately acquainted with his family for
many years. Their eldest son was first a student and then a soldier
under me. After a while he became Adjutant Gen'l of the Regiment. I afterwards had him put in the Regular Army and he is
now on duty at Nashville. His sister Eliza, who was a bright student
at Hiram, married another Hiram student, Harry Glasier, who has
[had] labored in the ministry for a number of years. Took Father
and Mother Rudolph to James Clapp's and they spent the night.
Crete and I returned in the evening.

SUNDAY, 30.   Hot, sultry day. Read. Rested. Rambled in the woods.

MONDAY, 31.   Prof. H. W. Everest, late President of the Eureka
College, but now Professor in the Kentucky University, visited us
today with his wife and children. He and I were students at Chester
twenty-five years ago. He was afterwards my associate in the school
at Hiram. His wife also was a Hiram student. Professor Amzi
Atwater and wife (née Mason) and Eliza Clapp came at the same
time. They were all from Hiram and it was a pleasant reunion.
Everest's boys are older than mine. We visited the caves and rocks
with them. It is delightful to see their young enthusiasm. How
curiously Everest's life and mine have drifted on in different chan-
nels, still with many things in common. Birdie Hall left us today.
Father and Mother Rudolph also went home.

September

TUESDAY, 1.   Left the Mountain at 11 o'clock, in company with
J. H. Devereaux [Devereux] [148] and wife and several other moun-
taineers. Took the afternoon train to Columbus in company with

[148] John Henry Devereux, of Cleveland, president of the Cleveland,
Columbus, Cincinnati and Indianapolis Railroad, and general manager of
the Atlantic and Great Western.

several friends. I had been appointed a delegate from Portage County. Halsey Hall and wife joined me on the Columbus train. My reception here this year is in marked contrast with that of last year, when the control of affairs was in the hands of Governor Noyes and his satellites, who were determined to run the campaign in their own way and for their own objects. Met the Congressional Delegation in Senator Sherman's room and had a long conversation over the situation.

WEDNESDAY, 2. Delegates from the 19th District met at the Controller's Room in the State House and made our arrangements for committees for the convention. I was unanimously chosen as a member of the Committee on Resolutions. The convention organized at 11; committees were announced and on the adjournment the Committee on Resolutions met at the Treasurer's office in the State House. As the result of four hours' work, the platform was agreed to. I wrote the financial resolutions, which were received unanimously. This was no small triumph for me, who have for so many years stood alone against repudiation, inflation and such like. The report was received with enthusiasm. Noyes was not made permanent Chairman of the Convention! ! After the adoption of the resolutions I was called out and made a short speech on some new issues which seemed to me imminent.

I was invited to speak on the State House steps in the evening but declined. Sherman and Noyes had been informed in advance and had their speeches in writing. This has been done to me once or twice before and I declined to accept the invitation. Took the 5 o'clock train for Cleveland in company with Foster of Fostoria. Spent the night at the Weddell House.

THURSDAY, 3. Took the morning train for Painesville and found George Steele and O. L. Wolcott in the cars. Stopped at Steele's where I found Crete awaiting me. Spent the day there visiting. In the evening went to the Hall to hear some speeches by members of the Dress Reform Convention.[149] Heard Mrs. Bibbert, Parker Pillsbury[150] and others and listened to about as much radical non-

---

[149] The American Free Dress Association met in Painesville on September 2 and 3.

[150] Parker Pillsbury (1809–1898) was involved in many of the crusades of the nineteenth century, including those against slavery and war and in behalf of women's rights.

sense as I have heard before in one evening. There is sense to some of the Dress Reform, but the drift of all their work is an assault on the marriage contract, only another branch of the free-love army whose doctrines I detest. Spent the night at George W. Steele's.

FRIDAY, 4. Spent most of the day visiting Painesville. We took dinner at Harry Steele's, where we had a very pleasant party. From the top of his house saw the bal[l]oon "Buffalo" sweep Northeastward over the Lake. This is one of the most striking events in ballooning and goes far to illustrate the doctrine of the cyclone. At 3 o'clock young Ferris, who lives at the foot of the Mountain, to[ok] us in his carriage to the Mountain, where we found that the Club had adjourned and the Mountain was deserted. Got tea at the Fairview House and prepared to leave in the morning. About nine o'clock at night Stocking came with his wagon and took our goods.

SATURDAY, 5. Finished loading Stocking's wagon and he left us at six. About half-past six, after taking breakfast at the Lake View House, we shut our cottage and bid good-bye to the Mountain for this season at least. Went to Cleveland and stopped at James Mason's, where we spent the day and night very pleasantly. I am strongly impressed with the purpose to make Cleveland my future home. Talked with Mason about the price of lots and real estate. He has a pleasant family and has the joy of being with them in his own home. He is a cousin to Crete's mother and stands very high here at the bar.

SUNDAY, 6. Attended the Congregational church with Mason and his wife. Crete remained with the children. Crete and I took dinner at J. H. Rhodes on Gates [Case] Avenue.

MONDAY, 7. Did shopping and miscellaneous work during the forenoon. Called at Dr. Boynton's and took dinner and arranged with him to come and join us tomorrow on a visit to Warren. In the afternoon Mason drove us to several points in the city to look at lots and discuss the future. Spent a pleasant evening with Mason in visiting and playing whist.

TUESDAY, 8. Took the early train to Solon, where I was joined by Dr. Boynton and his wife and baby Amos. At Solon engaged carriage to drive us to Orange. Called at Sister Mary's and took Mother in with us and made arrangements for Mary to follow. Drove to Orange over the old familiar ground. Found the friends and spent one of the pleasantest days of the year in rambling over the old fields and showing the children the spot where the old house stood in which I was born. In the evening sang some old favorite songs and hymns. The day has renewed my health and helped to restore my faith in life. Spent the night at Cousin Henry's.

WEDNESDAY, 9. In the morning went to the Pioneer picnic at Solon (North). Here was an assemblage of several thousand people in honor of the Pioneers. A meeting was held in Burch's Grove, adjoining the field where I once worked a month or two for Stephen Mapes when I was a boy, and across the way was a field where I helped Harry Donewell log—clear over several acres. Spoke for thirty minutes at the request of my neighbors and friends and we had a pleasant dinner in the grove. Rode to Chagrin Falls with Sheldon Wilkinson, an old schoolmate, and had a pleasant time. Harry and Jimmy and I drove to Burton fourteen miles away and spent the night with George H. Ford.

THURSDAY, 10. This is the day of the Reunion of the soldiers of the late war who resided in Geauga County. They held a general muster and made last night and today hideous with skirmishes and sham battles. I have no taste for sham war. Let it be peace or war in earnest. At one o'clock I spoke for an hour to over a thousand people in the Fair Grounds. I was then driven to Burton Station on the narrow gage road and took the train to Warren where I arrived in the evening. Stopped at Harmon Austin's where several friends met me. The Democratic district convention which met here today nominated Dr. Woods[151] of Canfield. He was my first opponent in 1862. An anti-Garfield Convention also met here and made an attempt to coalesce with the Democrats, and failing in that met and nominated Rev. H. R. Hurlburt of Erie, the Presiding Elder of the Methodist Church in this District. Judge Tuttle of Painesville made a bitter speech against me at the Court House this evening.

FRIDAY, 11. Left on the morning train for Hiram where our family has at last assembled. Spent the day in putting affairs in order and getting ready for a month's campaign. The weather is beautiful and I ought to have an opportunity to enjoy a clear month in the

---

[151] Daniel B. Woods, a physician of Warren.

country. It will be a month of battle and discomfort to me. Perhaps I need the discipline of this kind of assault upon me, still I have had a long siege of it for the last two years.

SATURDAY, 12. Continued the work of clearing up my desk and room and putting the household in order. Also prepared a speech for the evening. At 4 o'clock took Harry with me in the buggy and drove to Newton Falls, stopping at Dr. Applegate's. The Town Hall was crowded with citizens and I made a speech of an hour and a half on the general topics of the year and then for three-quarters of an hour discussed the personal features of this campaign. I talked severely and without disguise of those who have assaulted and attempted to injure me with the people. I felt something of the spirit of battle in me and found that the response from my friends was ardent and enthusiastic. Then had a consultation at the hotel with a large number of friends and went to A. B. Merrill's[152] and spent the night.

SUNDAY, 13. After an early breakfast at Merrill's Harry and I drove to Hiram, stopping at Garrettsville Station and taking Brother Joe home with us to Hiram.

MONDAY, 14. Worked during the day on correspondence and preparing for the campaign. Took the evening train for Warren where I had requested the Congressional Committee of the five counties of the 19th District to meet me to-morrow. The local committee of Trumbull County having refused to appoint meetings for me, I made this call to circumvent their purposes. Spent the evening in visiting and consultation with friends.

TUESDAY, 15. Committee met me at the Thompson House and we had a full discussion of the affairs of the District and they agreed to appoint meetings for me in the several counties. I had received a letter from Thompson and a letter from Taylor of Painesville challenging me to debate. I do not propose to allow these fellows to get up meetings and take up half the time throwing mud at me. I therefore stated that all my enemies are at liberty to ask questions at any of my meetings, but that I should discuss national questions in my own way. Further arranged the meetings of the Committee and I took the one o'clock train for Akron and at Freedom met

[152] Auren B. Merrill, of Newton, a farmer and local office holder, was a leading Republican.

Crete and her mother and Mollie, who went with me to Akron, where we stopped at Rockwell's and visited Sister Nellie, who was leaving for her new home in Saint Louis. Spent the night at Rockwell's.

WEDNESDAY, 16. Took the 6 o'clock express for Galion, where I caught the express from Cleveland to Columbus. Found a number of acquaintances on the train. Was there for the first time introduced to Governor Wm. Allen.[153] He is a genial old gentlemen and seems to take to me very kindly. Stopped at the Neil House and met a crowd of delegates and old acquaintances. There is a prospect of a large majority in this town. At the Columbus Depot we were met by a delegation of soldiers of the Army of the Cumberland which escorted us to the Neil House where we dined. Immediately after attended the Army of the Cumberland Reunion at the Opera House. A great number of the leading soldiers were present. Sherman, Sheridan and many of my old comrades were there. I was called on for a speech and addressed the assemblage for a short time. In the evening attended Sherman's reception at Mr. Miller's[154] at the mansion formerly belonging to Judge Swaim [Swayne]. The last time I was there I visited J. D. Cox while he was Governor of the state. Capt. Henry and I spent the night at Capt. [Andrew] Gardner's of the 42nd.

THURSDAY, 17. Served as Chairman on a Committee for the nomination of officers for the ensuing year. Reported Phil Sheridan as President. In the afternoon we were driven to the various public institutions, and among other things witnessed a very pleasant Exhibition at the Deaf and Dumb Asylum. General McDowell came in the afternoon and I had a long visit with him. Banquet in the evening at the City Hall which continued until after midnight. I was called upon to respond to the toast to General Thomas, which

---

[153] William Allen (1803–1879) emerged from a political retirement of nearly a quarter of a century to be elected governor on the Democratic ticket in 1873; he served one term, being defeated for re-election in 1875 by Rutherford B. Hayes. He was a member of the U. S. House of Representatives, 1833–35, and of the Senate, 1837–49.

[154] Thomas Ewing Miller, one of the most prominent merchants of Columbus; he bought the house because it was there he met his future bride when she was visiting the Swaynes.

I did with more than usual satisfaction to myself. The chief point of my address was that General Thomas' life was a striking example of the value of culture and discipline. Took the two o'clock train for Cleveland where I soon met Judge Pardee and, in company with Carson and Capt. Henry, visited the Northern Ohio Fair. Dined on the Fair Grounds with Dr. Robison. Visit[ed] some of the more prominent shows about the fair and took the evening train for Hiram.

FRIDAY, 18. [No entry]

SATURDAY, 19. Made careful preparations for a speech at Warren, where, tonight, I shall discuss exclusively the present issues of this campaign. Have arranged for a shorthand reporter to get my speech in full to the press. Stopped at the Thompson House where several friends met me. The enemy have attempted to divert me from my path by challenging me for debate, probably with the braggart Tuttle. Let my enemies draw their own crowds. I draw mine. A terrible rainfall just towards evening and the audience was small though it filled the Court House. I spoke for two hours, pausing at each point for my enemies to put their questions. But few were asked and those few were answered promptly and conclusively. I let these gentlemen know that during this campaign it was to be blow for blow and those who struck must expect a blow in return. It was a painful kind of speech for me to make, but I did it thoroughly to the satisfaction of my friends. Spent the night at the Thompson House.

SUNDAY, 20. Spent the day revising the reporter's notes of my speech. Took dinner at Austin's. Took the evening train for Cleveland and spent the night at the Forest City House.

MONDAY, 21. Returned to Hiram on the morning train. Spent the day in answering letters and completing the revision of my Warren speech. Took the evening train for Niles where I was met by Josiah Robbins[155] and went with him to his house for supper. After supper

---

[155] Josiah Robbins, Jr. (1830–1893), son of Garfield's longtime friend, was an iron manufacturer in Niles. "The Robbins family," Garfield once wrote, "have always been the firmest and most powerful of my friends in Niles, and Josiah, Jr., has perhaps more influence than any man in Niles." Garfield to Charles Henry (typed copy), December 14, 1873, Garfield Papers.

went to the hall where a large audience was awaiting me. A number
of persons had driven down from Warren and I discussed national
topics for an hour and a half by explaining my votes on the currency and tariff, which had been shamefully misrepresented here in
Niles. I showed the people that I was opposed as much to a pro-
hibitory tariff on the one hand as to free trade on the other. I then
spent three-quarters of an hour in discussing personal issues and
referred them to my Warren speech which will soon be in print.
On the whole I think the meeting was a successful one. There has
been much bitterness and misrepresentation in Niles and the people
have been made to believe that the financial panic which swept this
town last fall was largely due to me for my opinions on the tariff
and currency. Was introduced to Tydvill Davis, a Welshman, who
has written several articles in the Welsh papers in my defence.
Spent the night at Josiah Robbins'.

TUESDAY, 22.   Took the morning train for Ashtabula which I reached
at 12 o'clock. Was met at the depot by Henry Hubbard, who took
me to his house where a large and select company of gentlemen
met me and dined with me. After dinner we drove to the Harbor
and spent several hours in examination of its situation and prospects.
Major Henry Hubbard is a striking illustration of what faith and
persistent work will do. Eight years ago he and I visited this
desolate place. I became satisfied that he was right in his views of
its future. Since that time we have worked together and secured
government aid in perfecting the harbor and now we have the
satisfaction of seeing two railroads discharge their coal and receive
their iron here from the numerous schooners and propellers that
lay at their docks. Returned in the afternoon and in the evening
made a speech of an hour and three-quarters at the Opera House,
at which I felt myself in full sympathy with the audience. I believe
this town will give me a good vote in the coming election. Spent
the night at Major Hubbard's.

WEDNESDAY, 23.   After visiting Mr. Fassett and other friends and
writing a number of letters, I took the train for Madison where I
was met by a committee who took me to the hotel. A large number
of friends called to see me and after dinner Mr. Ervine Ensign[156]

[156] Ervine Ensign, a Madison businessman, was a delegate to the Republican Congressional Convention which had recently nominated Garfield.

and two other friends drove me among the beautiful farms in the neighborhood. Made a pleasant call at Ensign's house and returned to the hotel in the evening. Played croquet a little while at a house next to that of a leading merchant of the town, whose name I regret to say I have forgotten. There is a good deal of bitterness against me here caused by the active efforts of a few disappointed spirits. In the evening their large hall was crowded to repletion and I spoke for two hours more successfully than I have yet done any where else. I think I carried conviction to nearly all my hearers. A large delegation from Geneva attended and I was told that more than one hundred people were obliged to leave for want of room. Spent the night at the hotel.

THURSDAY, 24. Took the six o'clock train for Painesville. Took breakfast at the Stockwell House in Painesville, and at 8.30 took the Narrow-Gage for Middlefield. J. F. Scofield, Editor of the *Telegraph*, accompanied me. He informs me that Thorp has challenged Tuttle for debate at Painesville and thinks it a bad thing. At Middlefield, C. A. Brigdon [Brigden][157] met me and took me to his house at Mesopotamia where I dined. At two o'clock addressed a large audience in the Congregational Church. Squire Udall came from Hiram and drove me across the country, sixteen miles, home, where I found a large mail awaiting me.

FRIDAY, 25. Spent the forenoon in writing letters, took the six o'clock train at Garrettsville for Solon. Then rode with Mr. Williams to Chagrin Falls. Stopped at Sister Mary's on the way. Dined at Mr. Douglass', where a Disciple Mite Society was in session. A large number of neighbors and friends called on me. Among others Moses Lowe whom I have not seen since we were boys of fifteen. In the evening the audience was too large for any hall in town and I spoke from the steps of Champion Hall. I had not been in the building since 1858 when I debated with Denton. Spoke nearly two hours to a large and attentive audience. Rode home to Pond Station with Captain Henry and his brother Samuel [Simon?]. On the road called a moment to [see] Chauncey Niece, who was my teacher when I was eight years old. Spent the night at Capt. Henry's.

[157] C. A. Brigden, a merchant and prominent Republican of Mesopotamia, Trumbull County.

SATURDAY, 26. Took the morning train for Garrettsville, where I engaged Goff's black ponies and drove twenty miles to Deerfield, stopping at N. L. Wann's. At two o'clock addressed several acres of people on the Fair Grounds, discussing transportation and its relations to agriculture. Went to Wann's and after two games of croquet drove back to Garrettsville, making the distance in little more than two hours. Then Goff drove me to Hiram where I arrived very weary.

SUNDAY, 27. Read a large mail and heard a good solid sermon from Burke.

MONDAY, 28. Spent the day in answering letters and visiting with Burke and making out the deed for my Iowa land,[158] which I have sold. In the afternoon went to Garrettsville in the hack and played two games of croquet. Took tea at Dr. Lee's. Just before going in I received a copy of the N. Y. *Sun* extra, headed "The Record of James A. Garfield," and containing twenty-eight columns.[159] Made, I think, an effective speech to a large audience and after the conclusion of the general discussion, reviewed the character of the assaults upon me and exposed the character of the N. Y. *Sun*. Right here near at home there is a set of men bitterly opposed to me; for what reason I do not know. Halsey Hall and wife and John Beatty came from Ravenna to see me. Father Rudolph and Jimmy came down and took me home after the meeting.

TUESDAY, 29. Took the morning train for Warren, where I stopped over one train and called on Henry B. Perkins for a short time. Took the nine o'clock train for Baconsburgh, where Squire Barnes, of Gustavus, met me and drove me home to his house. It was a raw autumn day and I really suffered with the cold. Squire Barnes's son, R. B. Barnes, who has been lukewarm and hostile to me, seemed

[158] Reference is to the sale of 320 acres of land near Iowa City. Garfield had purchased it in 1865 for about $5 an acre. He received for it a draft for $772 and four notes for $1,175 each, carrying 10 percent interest. In 1880 he said of the investment that he had made about 50 percent after taxes.

[159] The four page *Sun* extra, picturing Garfield as utterly corrupt, was brought into his district in large numbers. According to the *Painesville Telegraph* the extra was the result of the visit to Lake County by a *Sun* reporter at the instance of a small ring of anti-Garfield Liberals there.

inclined to be cordial. His wife is an intelligent, matronly lady and his daughter Phoebe is a very pleasant person. At two o'clock we proceeded to the place of meeting, where a large audience was in waiting whom I addressed for two hours. Spent the night at Barnes's. I think the impression made on this town is very good and I shall be disappointed if the defection here is not small in consequence of my visit.

WEDNESDAY, 30. Barnes drove me to Kinsman; where we stopped and took dinner at Thomas Kinsman's, and then drove on to Andover in the midst of a heavy rain. Reached Andover half an hour late. Found Northway awaiting me. Also, found parties distributing large quantities of the N. Y. *Sun.* There were only enough people to fill the Hall. Northway spoke about thirty minutes, when I followed, speaking an hour and a half in replying to some of the questions which were put by the enemy, continued my speech for about three-quarters of an hour longer. It was about as dreary and cheerless a day's meeting as I have ever had. At the conclusion Mr. Morey [Morley] [160] drove us (Northway and myself) to Jefferson sixteen miles—a cold dreary ride. After getting tea at the Thompson House, went to the Court House, which was filled with an audience provided [presided] over by Senator Wade. I spoke for two hours. For the first time in my life I felt a chill come up to me from a Jefferson audience—although Wade appears cordial and denies emphatically the story in the *Sun* that he is hostile to me.[161] Thorp came and reported the results of his Painesville debate, which seems to have been rather disastrous.[162] Spent the night at the Thompson House.

[160] J. S. Morley, described as "a wheel-horse of the Republican party," was postmaster of Andover for many years. He also published the short-lived *Andover Enterprise*, 1872–75.

[161] In a letter to Freeman Thorp dated September 29, 1874, and printed in the *Painesville Telegraph,* Benjamin Franklin Wade denied that he had said that the *Sun's* charges against Garfield were true, and declared that he would vote for Garfield.

[162] According to the *Painesville Telegraph* both Probate Judge Tuttle and Freeman Thorp spoke to a group of 50 to 75 people, but whereas the judge was heard without interruption, Thorp was constantly interrupted.

October

THURSDAY, I. Took the morning train for Ashtabula, where I spent an hour and a half. Dined with James Reed. Found that not only Wade and Kellogg[163] but also Sherman and Hall have denied the truth of the *Sun*'s statements about their feelings towards me. Took the one o'clock train for Conneaut. Stopped at the Hotel. Mr. Smith[164] drove me to the Harbor, where I spent some two hours in looking over the landmarks and reflecting that there was the beginning of the settlement of the Western Reserve. Also considered the construction of the Harbor and am satisfied that there has been much folly and waste on the part of the engineers for want of a uniform policy in the management of the harbor construction.

Returning to Conneaut, I called at the *Reporter* office and also at my former friend's, Haywood's [Hayward's]. He has grown hostile, but received me cordially and I think showed some symptoms of regret for his attitude. Dined at Smith's and had a pleasant visit with his family. Addressed a large audience for nearly two hours and succeeded fairly well. Left the Hall in the midst of a drenching rain and went home with Mr. ——————[McCalmont],[165] Principal of the Geneva schools. He is a stanch friend. Went to bed and rested what little time I could before taking the train.

FRIDAY, 2. Was awakened a little before two o'clock and took the express train for the West and awoke about eight o'clock as we neared Norwalk. Mr. Gardiner[166] met me at the Station and drove me to his house, a very pleasant residence surrounded by large and beautiful trees. After breakfast he drove me to the Fair Grounds,

163 Abner Kellogg, a lawyer of Jefferson, Ashtabula County, was a member of the Ohio legislature, 1843–44, 1864–65, and 1866–67.

164 Sagito J. Smith, a Conneaut merchant.

165 J. D. McCalmont, principal of the grammar and preparatory school in Geneva.

166 John Gardiner (b. 1816), Norwalk banker, railroad official, and landowner.

and on our returning to dinner Hon. Charles Foster met us. We had a pleasant visit. Thirty years ago he was a student in this town and boarded in this house. At one o'clock we were escorted to the Fair Grounds by the band and at two I delivered an address of about one hour on the future of agricultural life in this country. I succeeded better than I have ever before done on that subject. After wearily watching the races and the sights about the Fair Grounds, returned to Gardiner's where we had a pleasant tea with a large number of gentlemen. In the evening Foster and I addressed an audience of about three thousand people. Foster's speech was the first I have listened to this campaign. He is fighting a hard battle but I think will win it. Spent the night at Gardiner's.

SATURDAY, 3. Took the 9 o'clock train for Cleveland and found Crete and Jimmy awaiting me at the Forest City House. They brought a large mail which I hurriedly read and after assisting them a little in their shopping and sending a few telegrams, I took the two o'clock train for Ravenna. Halsey Hall met me at the station and took me to his house. I am very weary and feel certain that I am speaking once too much if I speak again today. After supper Hall and his wife and invalid child went with me to Conneaut [Kent]. A very large audience has [had] filled the Hall to overflowing and I spoke effectively for nearly two hours, but I felt during it all that I was using up about the last supply of power I had. When I concluded the vocal chords seemed to relax and I grew very hoarse. Went to the hotel and spent the night with General Pardee and two or three others and sat up till near midnight, when I retired so hoarse that I could scarcely speak above a whisper. I have rarely been so tired as I am tonight.

SUNDAY, 4. Rose at six o'clock and Reuben Cannon took Captain Henry and myself to Aurora. I reached the station just in time for the morning train which had been telegraphed to and stopped for me. Went thence to Garrettsville, where Brother Joseph met me and we went home. I lay during the day like a log scarcely able to feel.

MONDAY, 5. Wrote letters and doctored my throat until two o'clock in the afternoon. At two o'clock I went to the College in pursuance of an old engagement to address the Teachers' Institute. For about an hour my voice served me better than I expected. My lecture was the elaboration of two ideas. First: The value and the necessity of culture. Second: The power of personal influence in teaching. On the first I drew my illustrations from John Stuart Mill's *Autobiography* and the life of John Adams. At four o'clock Brother Joe drove me to Troy, where the Town Hall was crowded to overflowing. I spoke two hours by taking a lower key than usual. My voice stood it very well. Then rode with George and Nellie [Neil] Ford to Burton and spent the night at George's house. I feel very anxious that my voice shall hold out for tomorrow, which is to be a field day.

TUESDAY, 6. Took the morning train by the Narrow-gage[167] for Painesville, where I was met by the band and a large concourse of citizens who escorted me to the Stockwell House. After dinner a large number of citizens called on me. At two o'clock went to the Opera House, which was densely packed. Mr. Perkins,[168] a venerable gentleman, presided, and I spoke for an hour and a half on public questions, more satisfactorily than I have yet spoken during the campaign. I then turned to the personal issues that have been made upon me and discussed them thoroughly for three-quarters of an hour. I felt that I had the audience in my hands. I then challenged my enemies to propound questions. Judge Tuttle rose, backed and seconded by J. B. Burrows, and propounded a series of questions. I answered him promptly, and each answer brought forth a storm of applause. He persisted in repeating the same questions and I finally opened up on him with a furious attack which everybody seemed to feel was crushing him. The meeting lasted three hours and broke up with tremendous cheers. I believe I have broken the back of the opposition in Painesville and that Judge Tuttle's career is substantially ended. By the kindness of Mr. [G. R.] Crane, Superintendent of the Narrow Gage Road, a special train took me to Chardon, where W. S. Fury [Furay] [169] is to speak. At the conclusion of his speech in the Court House I was called upon and spoke an hour. Spent the night at the Chardon House.

WEDNESDAY, 7. In company with O. S. Farr, Judge Smith and D. W.

[167] The Painesville and Youngstown Railroad, with a guage of three feet, was in operation from Painesville to Niles in 1874.

[168] William L. Perkins, of Ashtabula County, was in both the Ohio House and Senate during the 1840's.

[169] William S. Furay, Ohio editor of the *Cincinnati Gazette*.

Canfield, drove to Canfield [Thompson] where the "World's Fair" is in progress. After sauntering about the Fair Grounds for an hour or two found that Judge Tuttle and Rev. Mr. Hurlburt were on the grounds. The former mounted a wagon and commenced an assault upon me. I decline to be present or condescend to notice a man so indecent as to use an agricultural fair grounds for the purpose of a political speech. Towards evening we drove to Canfield [Montville], stopping at Whitney's Hotel. After tea went to church where a large audience awaited me. Spoke for nearly two hours and was followed a short time by O. S. Farr. Two strenuous efforts have been made in this town to make capital against me, but I think this meeting has done much to counteract these efforts. Mr. Hurlburt has been visiting his Methodist brethren to awaken ecclesiastical prejudice in his favor. I am informed that several converts to my honesty were made at this meeting. Spent the night at Seth Whitney's.

THURSDAY, 8. J. F[V]. Whitney, the man who visited me at Little Mountain in August, drove me to Chardon. We had a long visit and I am satisfied his friendship for me is confirmed. Reached Chardon before ten o'clock and took the morning train to Painesville. Dined at Harry [Horace] Steele's[170] and spent the afternoon in visiting. The effects of my Painesville [speech] were even more than I had anticipated. My friends were greatly elated and my enemies furious. In [It] has drawn the lines very sharply and a fight is made on well defined grounds. Took tea at George W. Steele's, after which he drove me in his carriage to Willoughby, twelve miles away. It rained heavily on the way and I feared it would spoil our meeting. But on arriving I found the town full of people and thoroughly aroused. The Methodist College building was illuminated from basement to cupola with a candle at each pane of glass. As this was the home of Mr. Hurlburt, the demonstration was a pleasant surprise. A Mr. Clements [George W.

---

[170] Horace Steele and his brother George, businessmen of Painesville, were long-time personal and political friends of Garfield. George was the representative of Lake County in the Ohio House of Representatives, 1870–73. In 1881 Horace was president of the Painesville Savings & Loan Association.

Clement],[171] a leading Methodist of the Hurlburt Church, presided and the great Hall was filled to overflowing. There must have been 3,000 persons present. There had been loud threats of questions and interruptions, but if the enemy were on hand none of them ventured to put any questions. I spoke two hours. At the conclusion Mr. Steele and I took tea at the hotel and then drove back to his house in Painesville, reaching there a little after midnight. The night was very dark and stormy.

FRIDAY, 9. Took the 8.30 train on the Narrow Gage for Warren, which we reached nearly an hour behind time. Judge Kinsman and Hon. T. J. McLain were waiting with a carriage and we drove thirteen miles to Brookfield, where I addressed a mass meeting for an hour and a half and was followed for about three-quarters of an hour by McLain. We took tea at Mr. Hamilton's,[172] a sturdy friend of mine, and then drove to Brookfield [*sic*] where a crowded audience were awaiting me. I spoke two hours and was followed for half an hour by McLain. Hurlburt had been here peddling the N. Y. *Sun,* and here for the first time during the campaign I made allusion to him by expressing the hope that it was not possible that he could be lending himself to so base a proceeding. We spent the night at the hotel in a miserable room and more miserable bed.

SATURDAY, 10. Took the morning train for Warren. Went home with Judge Kinsman where we had breakfast about nine o'clock. Toward noon heavy showers came on which promises [promised] bad for our meeting. Senator Sherman came from Mansfield by the early train and we dined together at the Thompson House. At half-past one o'clock Sherman spoke to a large audience in the Opera House and made very handsome mention of my personal character and public services. At the close of his speech, I spoke about three-quarters of an hour, devoting about two-thirds of the time to general topics and the last third to a condensed and scornful notice of those Republican enemies who were peddling the N. Y. *Sun.* I think I have never struck a more effective blow at the enemy than the last fifteen minutes of this speech. At five o'clock

[171] George W. Clement, a Willoughby businessman and a member of the Lake County Republican Committee.

[172] Henry Hamilton, who was born in Ireland, was a Brookfield, Trumbull County, Disciple, furniture dealer, justice of the peace, and coal prospector.

Senator Sherman and I took the Atlantic train, he for Mansfield and I for Ravenna. Halsey Hall met me at the Ravenna Depot and took me to his house. After tea went to the ————— and addressed the largest indoors meeting I have ever seen in Ravenna. This is my tenth speech for the week and I was jaded almost to the point of falling down. I did not satisfy myself in this evening's speech for my stability seemed almost gone. Still the audience appeared to be reasonably well pleased. Spent the night at Halsey Hall's.

SUNDAY, 11. Isaac Williams drove me home to Hiram. I am greatly exhausted, though I feel better than I did a week ago today.

MONDAY, 12. At home resting and reading Goethe's *Autobiography*. It is a great relief to turn from the turbulence of this campaign into the quiet of the beautiful German life in Frankfort and the serenity that filled the childhood of Goethe. As I read his life I compare it with the singular *Autobiography* of John Stuart Mill. It is a dreary rainy afternoon, but as I have agreed to speak at Nelson tonight, I go in spite of the weather. Went to Garrettsville on the hack. Took tea at Mr. Foot's[173] after which he drove me in the dark and alone to Nelson. Notwithstanding the storm the Hall was pretty well filled and I spoke nearly two hours. In a familiar conversational way answered many questions and I think satisfied those who heard me. But the township has been pretty thoroughly poisoned by the active efforts of two or three enemies. Mr. Foot drove me back to Hiram which I reached about eleven o'clock. I have spoken 28 times since the 17th of September, and I think have done much to turn back the tide of opposition which industrious enemies have started. Still the old anger about my salary vote will reduce the vote more than all other things combined.

TUESDAY, 13. Read Goethe's *Autobiography* with keen enjoyment. It is a good foil to my campaign work. The election passed off quietly here as it always does on the Western Reserve. A large vote was polled. I estimate that Hurlburt will receive about two thousand Republican votes. Some Democrats may vote for him, in which case his vote will be larger. I tell my friends today that I shall be satisfied with six thousand majority over the Democratic ticket.

[173] C. O. Foot, a Garrettsville, Portage County, carriage maker.

Took the evening train for Cleveland and stopped at the Forest House. Spent the evening at the *Leader* Office until midnight when the returns indicated a general defeat of the Republican Party in Ohio and Indiana. Payne carried the Cleveland District. It is not yet possible to say what my majority will be.

WEDNESDAY, 14. Spent the forenoon with J. H. Rhodes looking at some lots on Euclid Avenue with a view to a future home. I am in doubt about the wisdom of buying such expensive lots as those we looked at—still it may be best in the long run. Returns from the state come in worse and worse. The chief causes that have worked against us are the Temperance Crusade, the hard times resulting from the panic, and the indiscriminate attacks upon the party made by the newspapers within the last two years. Took the afternoon train to Solon. Went to Sister Mary's and purchased one-quarter of an acre of land from her to widen the front of the land I bought last year. For her sake I paid a big price. Took the evening train to Garrettsville and reached home at ten o'clock.

THURSDAY, 15. Read Goethe and answered correspondence. Returns slowly coming in from the district. Hurlburt received nearly a thousand Democratic votes which gives him an aggregate of about three thousand four hundred—a little more than I expected he would receive. My vote reaches about twelve thousand six hundred. I am twenty-eight hundred behind the state ticket. This marks the extent of the bolt. I have between six and seven thousand majority over the Democrats and some three thousand over both. I took supper with Burke and attended his lecture at the College on "The relation of College Students to the Faculty." I spoke ten minutes at the close of his lecture.

FRIDAY, 16. Read Goethe with great pleasure. The unfolding of his poetic nature is as beautiful as the growth of a rose. Commenced collecting up my accumulation of documents at [and] letters. Took tea with Burke and then listened to the reading of a long chapter in his forthcoming [work] "The Doctrine of Evolution Applied to Theology." The chapter he read was on Jesuit [Jewish] Christianity, and is a very able presentation of the growth of the Christian idea in the Jesuit [Jewish] mind, and the effect upon it of Jesuit [Jewish] thought. It is the ablest summary of the leading points in the Book of Acts I have ever seen. I made a number of suggestions and criticisms, most of which he adopted. Burke has grown steadily and solidly during the last ten years. He has a high degree of intellectual honesty and faith in the investigation of any subject.

SATURDAY, 17. The day was passed with Goethe and correspondence and clearing the docket of the year, preparatory for leaving to go to Washington. In the evening Dr. Robison and wife and Harmon Austin and wife came to visit us. We spent a long evening in conversation, discussing political and religious questions, and reviewing the old memories of our early acquaintances. Twenty years ago Dr. Robison was here at the Commencement, and took a walk with me which was really the commencement of our college [association] and which threw me with him. From that day forward he has believed in me and stood by me with an enthusiastic and unwavering friendship. I became intimately acquainted with Austin a few years later.

SUNDAY, 18. This was one of the most perfect days I have ever seen. The woods are in their full Autumn splendor and color, and a delicate haze of blue vails the Indian Summer and was spread over the landscape. With our visitors attended church. Burke delivered a powerful sermon on —————. He and his wife took dinner with us. Dr. Robison and wife left on the evening train.

MONDAY, 19. Austin and wife left us. I wrote letters, settled up my dues in the neighborhood with the various trades people. Spent several hours in overhauling and arranging my books. The growth of my library is one of the pleasant things of my life. At no period have I brought a large number of books and I have rarely bought any book except to meet some immediate intellectual want. My library is therefore typical of my intellectual growth and I can trace the different eras of developement by the dates on the books purchased. Sent two boxes of goods to Garrettsville for shipment to Washington.

TUESDAY, 20. Purchased our Winter's supply of butter and potatoes. Settled with Brother Joseph for board with family in Hiram and took the evening train with Harry and Jimmy for Cleveland. A few days ago I made out a deed to Hinsdale for my home in Hiram. This almost completely severs my business connection with Hiram. I shall probably never return here except as a visitor. We were delayed an hour and reached Dr. Robison's, where I had been

379

invited to supper with his friends and brother directors of the Second National Bank. The party had been waiting for us over an hour. Had a very pleasant supper. Met Henry B. Payne and had a long and pleasant conversation with him. After supper played euchre with Payne, Wade and Ely[174] until nearly midnight. I came to Hiram as a student twenty-two [twenty-three] years ago and it has been my home ever since.

WEDNESDAY, 21. Telegraphed to Crete to stop with the family at Newburgh, where I would meet them. Took the boys in a carriage and drove to Newburgh. Met Crete and the family at the Mahoning Station. Took them to Uncle Thomas', where we staid one-half an hour and then took the train for Pittsburgh. Reached Pittsburgh at 6 o'clock. Found no room in the Monongahela House. Stopped at the Saint Charles, where we were badly accommodated but spent the night. I always feel a sense of suffocation and of gloom in this City of the Cyclops. I. N. Phillips and W. J. Ford met me and we had a conversation in regard to the affairs of the Phillipses. They are greatly embarrassed, and I am likely to lose the amount I have invested with them, which will be to me a very considerable loss. I am not a little surprised that Ford has not known of this situation sooner.

THURSDAY, 22. Took the morning train on the Pittsburgh and Connellsville Road and passed a dreary sultry day on the cars. Crete thought it would be better to spend the night at Pittsburgh and take two days on the cars, rather than a day and a night. This day satisfied her of her mistake. Children very restless and the day far more uncomfortable than the night would have been. We got dinner at Cumberland and passed through Harpers Ferry and the Point of Rocks before night. Told the children the story of John Brown as we stood on the bridge overlooking the old arsenal and engine house. Reached our home in Washington about seven o'clock where we found that Daniel[175] and Mary had prepared us a good

174 Probably George H. Ely, a handler of iron ore in Cleveland. During the presidential campaign of 1880, as president of the Cleveland Republican Men's Club, he headed a large delegation of Cleveland businessmen who called on Garfield at Mentor.

175 Daniel Spriggs, a Negro servant in the Garfield household; he later served the family of Garfield's daughter Mollie.

supper. After dinner bathed the children and washed off many ounces of dirt from the family. Then went to rest as weary as travellers often are.

FRIDAY, 23. Continued the work of putting the house in order. Commenced a thorough system of cleaning and overhauling the bills and books and documents that have long encumbered my library. Dictated a portion of my long-neglected journal. Several friends called in the afternoon and evening. The weather is as sultry as it was in September.

SATURDAY, 24. It is amazing how much dirt will accumulate in a house during a few months of solitude. The forces which tear down are silent but remorseless in their operations. Crete and I went shopping and purchased a carpet for the library and another for the upper stairs. I engaged the men to put down both the new and the old carpets on Monday next. I found that my friends here were greatly elated at my success in the election. They had been led to suppose I was in serious danger of defeat. My old classmate Rockwell called on me in the evening and we had a delightful meeting after seven years of separation. He has been doing seven years of faithful service as Captain A. Q. M. in the Regular Army. He has been on duty at Fort Sill, Fort Gibson, and Fort Yuma and has really been living out of the great world. He comes back to serve here in Washington and I promise myself great pleasure in his society during the Winter.

SUNDAY, 25. Mother and I attended our church and heard a sermon from young Bela H. Hayden, a graduate of Bethany and former student of Hiram.

MONDAY, 26. Crete and I started out early to settle Harry and Jimmy in school. We have determined to keep Mollie at home this Winter and teach her a little of housekeeping and something of books. Harry and Jimmy need the hand of a master at school and after much discussion of the subject, we concluded to send them to Mr. Young's private school on the west side of Franklin Square.[176] Terms, twenty dollars each for ten weeks. Completed the cleaning out of my library and sent off a large package of pamphlets to the Congressional Library. Went to the Capitol and got some books

[176] Charles B. Young's Emerson Institute.

from the Library and attended to a few little matters of business. In the evening commenced the reading of Auerbach's *Waldfried*.[177]

TUESDAY, 27. Dictated additional entries for the Journal. Answered some letters and in the afternoon directed the putting down of the carpets. Also, had the plumbers overhaul the gas and water works through the house and the glazier repair some broken windows. In the afternoon went to see Daniel, our colored servant, who is seriously sick with the pneumonia, or as he calls it, the pneumonium. Called on the President and had a pleasant conversation. Went to the Treasury Department and spent an hour and a half in looking over the receipts and expenditures of the year thus far and the estimates of appropriations for the next year. Read further in *Waldfried*, answered some letters, and continued the work of putting things to rights.

WEDNESDAY, 28. Finished *Waldfried*. It is an interesting story of the late wars of Prussia against Austria and France and full of the sweet German home life. It is of the Pre-Raphaelite style of writing, but it lacks in condensation and compactness of plan. He dwells too much on little things and do[es] not make the plot stand out so vividly as he ought to. Still on the whole, the book delights me and has been a great rest. Went shopping with Crete and made some necessary purchases for the Winter. In the evening Capt. Rockwell called and spent two hours in reviewing our intellectual growth since we separated seven years ago. I feel a return of my stomach troubles of last Winter. It hurts me to lie on my left side too since the appearance there of the stomach troubles which leads me to fear neuralgic dyspepsia.

THURSDAY, 29. Had men to work on the carpets and we still continued the business of cleaning up and putting the house in order. Went to the Treasury Dep't during the day and had some further conversation with the Ass't Secretary in regard to the estimates of appropriations and to general Department business. Also went to the Capitol and spent some time in the Congressional Library. In the evening dined at Welcker's with my old classmate Capt.

[177] Berthold Auerbach, *Waldfried: A Novel*, translated by Simon Adler Stern (1874).

Rockwell of the Army and had a delightful reunion after seven years of separation. The Captain presented me with a beautiful matchbox of gold—gold quartz and moss agate—with this inscription, "From an old fellow to another." At the conclusion of our dinner we played several games of billiards.

FRIDAY, 30. Finished the carpets and at last got the house in pretty fair order for Winter. There are some things a man cannot afford to be ignorant of. I have all my life been coming across references to the Cid and have had only the vaguest notions of what it was. Yesterday I got Southey's translation of the *Chronicle of The Cid*[178] from the Library and made myself acquainted with the leading points in his history. I have resolved to remove at least this one block of ignorance out of my way; so today I have spent some time on this Spanish romance. Some history but much legend. The usual crowd of clerks hunting for office is upon me day and evening.

SATURDAY, 31. After an early breakfast, took the eight o'clock train in company with Senator Sargent for Cumberland, Maryland. We had a pleasant visit comparing our ideas and opinions on literary and religious subjects and reached Cumberland at one, where a Committee of gentlemen met us and took us to the hotel. After dinner, we were driven to the narrows, a mountain gorge through which Wills Creek flows. Through this gorge runs a national road.[179] Through here, also, Washington went on his way to Fort Pitt, to the scene of Braddock's defeat. In the evening a crowded audience, and we were compelled to have two meetings. I spoke for a short time to the crowd out of doors. I then returned into the hall and spoke for an hour. This is the home of Lloyd Lowndes, Jr.,[180] who is the Republican Candidate for Congress in this district. The prospect seems fair for his re-election. At two o'clock we took the train for Washington.

[178] Robert Southey's translation of Pierre Corneille's *Le Cid* (1636 or 1637) appeared under the title *Chronicle of the Cid* in 1808.

[179] The old Cumberland or National Road, which was opened from Cumberland, Maryland, to Wheeling, Virginia, in 1818 and later extended as far as Illinois.

[180] Lloyd Lowndes, Jr. (1845–1905) was a Republican member of the House from Maryland, 1873–75, and governor of Maryland, 1895–99.

November

SUNDAY, 1. Reached home at seven o'clock, a good deal jaded and with a bad cold. Attended Church and heard a sermon from my old friend Dr. Beldon [Belding], whom I have not seen for many years. He and Bela Hayden came home with us to dinner. Mr. Riddle called in the evening and we had a long visit.

MONDAY, 2. Worked on correspondence in the forenoon and read Emanuel Deutsch's discussion of the Talmud as published in the London *Quarterly Review* for October, 1867. It is a powerful piece of writing and the subject is one that I have long desired to understand. It throws a good deal of light on the Jewish character. Towards noon went shopping with Crete and made permanent arrangements for our Winter supplies. In the evening Crete and I called on Colonel Rockwell and wife and upon Gen'l McKibbin and wife, who were stopping at Rockwell's. We had a pleasant visit with these friends. The Colonel has kept up his culture during his frontier life and I mention it to his credit that he has since he joined the Army owned four parlor organs. He even took one to Fort Sill in the Indian Territory. While we were there General [Louis H.] Pelouze came and we played a rubber of whist.

TUESDAY, 3. Worked on correspondence. Read the Talmud, and worked up miscellaneous business. In the evening attended church with Mother. Heard a sermon from Dr. Beldon [Belding]. Over two hundred members of Congress are to be elected today. I have no doubt we are to suffer a general defeat. Only two days ago, the *National Republican*, which professes to be the organ of the Administration, assaulted me as having been so niggardly in the appropriations that, if the elections were lost, it would be because I refused to make large appropriations to give the people work. It is just this infatuation and folly of our public journals that has brought on the reaction. Called on the Secretary in the evening who expressed his indignation at the course taken by the *Republican*. He told me that the President disapproved of it, but he feared that there were some people near the President who were hostile to me. I suppose probably he meant Shepherd and Babcock who were of that way of thinking and probably inspired the article.

WEDNESDAY, 4. Usual work during the day. Went shopping with Crete to make arrangements for our winter's supplies. A number of gentlemen called during the day. The returns from the election show that the defeat was more sweeping than even the first accounts. This election is very much like that of 1862, when I received a smaller majority than this year. If the South had then been represented in Congress, the House would have been heavily Democratic. In the evening dined with my classmate Hill at Wormley's. His party consisted of Judges Miller[181] and Davis[182] of the Supreme Court and Philip Phillips,[183] with young Mr. Winthrop of Boston—brother of Theodore Winthrop,[184] the author—and another Boston man, whose name I forget. We had a long talk over the defeat and its causes. It is my opinion that the Republicans will carry the Presidential Election more certainly because of this defeat. There is a fickleness in the public mind that loves to express itself in changes. But I think the oscillation of public sentiment will bring us back to Republican ideas again. In fact I do not think this has been a revolution of ideas but rather an expression of discontent at the present situation. The city is filled with Democratic rejoicing—bonfires and speeches.

THURSDAY, 5. Worked on correspondence in the forenoon, then went to the Post Office Dep't and settled a number of pending questions and answered letters relating to the same. In the afternoon went to the Capitol and spent two hours in the Crypt of the Library, looking over the duplicates stored there. I am impressed with [the] ephemial [ephemeral] character of the vast mass of literary work. The cords of forgotten books packed away in the subterranean vaults of this library made me feel as though I were in a neglected grave-

[181] Samuel F. Miller (1816–1890), an associate justice of the U. S. Supreme Court, 1862–90.

[182] David Davis (1815–1886), an associate justice of the U. S. Supreme Court, 1862–77, and a senator from Illinois, 1877–83.

[183] A prominent Washington lawyer who sometimes appeared before the Supreme Court.

[184] Theodore Winthrop (1828–1861), a Connecticut writer who was killed in the Civil War, was the author of a number of novels published after his death, including *John Brent* (1862), *The Canoe and the Saddle* (1863), and *Life in the Open Air* (1863).

yard. In the evening Scofield of Pennsylvania called and spent several hours. It is pleasant to me to listen to his half-cynical philosophizing on men and events.

FRIDAY, 6. Wrote letters in the morning. Received a letter from Knox[185] of N. Y. retaining me in two cases for the N. Y. Mutual Life Insurance Company. I went to the Clerk of the Supreme Court and entered my name in the two cases and spent most of the day in ascertaining the situation of the hostile motion about to be made by the counsel on the other side. Met Senator Morrill of Vt. at the Capitol and spent some time with him talking over the political situation and looking over the improvements being made at the East front of the Capitol, in pursuance of the plans of Fred Law Olmsted.[186] The tree known as the Washington Elm is about to be removed if its removal is possible, which I doubt. In the evening read Dr. Clarke's book on *The Building of a Brain*,[187] which is in the line of his work on *Sex in Education*.

SATURDAY, 7. Spent the forenoon in correspondence and adjusting my accounts, and also in making some further examination of the two N. Y. Insurance cases. In the afternoon went shopping with Crete. She is adjusting her purchases for the family to cover the next two months. On our return I found Rockwell awaiting me and we went out and played a few games of billiards. Rockwell took dinner with me. Accepted the invitation of Senator Morrill of Vt. to spend the evening with him, and Senator Edmunds, Dr. Baxter and myself played euchre until half-past ten o'clock. I find my old

[185] Henry E. Knox, a Williams College classmate of Garfield, was a member of the New York City law firm of Fullerton and Knox. During this period Garfield and Knox were drawn closer together as a result of a mutual interest in certain insurance cases. During the campaign of 1880 Knox rendered some service to Garfield, and in 1881 was appointed U. S. marshal for the Southern District of New York; he resigned the following year.

[186] Frederick Law Olmsted (1822–1903), landscape architect, was commissioned in 1874 to design the grounds of the U. S. Capitol. He was also the author of a number of books dealing with his travels in the South, including *A Journey in the Seaboard Slave States* (1856).

[187] Edward Hammond Clarke, *The Building of a Brain* (1874).

stomach troubles return with a good deal of force. This is surprising considering how well I have passed the summer.

SUNDAY, 8.   Attended church. Sermon by Bela Hayden. Spent the afternoon in reading Goethe's *Autobiography* and in connection with it Lewes's biography of Goethe.[188] The development of the Poet's mind is among the most wonderful things I have seen. I shall try to write a brief summary of the impressions this book has made upon me, when I have finished it. Hill called in the evening, and he and I spent two hours in a very pleasant conversation on books and authors. I know of few men of his age who have done so much thorough reading.

MONDAY, 9.   Correspondence as usual in the morning. J. Edmond Mallet, a Canadian Frenchman by birth, a clerk of the 6th Auditor's Office, called on me with a Mr. Blanchard, who is the famous "Riel"[189] of Manitoba notoriety, travelling under an assumed name. He desires to see the President. At ten o'clock I went to the Law Library and worked on the Insurance Case No. 463 for three hours, and there satisfied myself that it could not be dismissed because of informality in the record. Every case I have convinces me anew that I need a more thorough knowledge of the technical parts of

[188] George Henry Lewes, *The Life and Works of Goethe, with Sketches of His Age and Contemporaries, from Published and Unpublished Sources* (1855).

[189] Louis Riel (1844–1885) was the leader of the metis (French-speaking half-breeds) in the Red River area of Rupert's Land who opposed the incorporation of their territory into the Dominion of Canada. A short-lived provisional government established under Riel's leadership collapsed in 1870 with the arrival of a Canadian military force. On three occasions during the 1870's Riel was elected to the Canadian parliament but was not permitted to take his seat. In 1874 he was outlawed. In November he arrived in Washington from St. Paul. Edmond Mallet had been urged by a friend of Riel's to aid the insurgent. Although the expansionist-minded Grant Administration would have welcomed the annexation to the United States of all or part of Canada, it was not interested in supporting Riel. During the 1880's he headed a second provisional government, and when forced to surrender was condemned for treason and hanged. See George F. G. Stanley, *Louis Riel* (1963) and Alvin C. Gluek, Jr., *Minnesota and the Manifest Destiny of the Canadian Northwest* (1965).

the law and of case law. Went to the Agricultural Department to get the statistics of the crops, with a view to ascertaining how our revenues are likely to come in. Called on the President on several matters of business. Told him of my interview with "Riel." The President agrees to have an interview with him tomorrow morning, by the name he is now travelling under. In the evening read until a late hour in Goethe. His *Autobiography* and Lewes's *Life of Goethe* attract me powerfully.

TUESDAY, 10. Awakened at daylight with a sharp distress in my stomach. Rose and read Goethe for an hour. Wrote a long letter to W. J. Ford, forwarding my note against Phillips of May 9th, 1874, for $3,706, due in six months, and payable at the First National Bank in New Castle. In accordance with previous appointment went to the Committee at 12 o'clock, where three members met me, namely, Starkweather, O'Neill[190] and Swann. We reviewed the general situation of our estimates and spent an hour in conference on our approaching winter's work. Committee adjourned until 12 o'clock tomorrow. Called at the Post Office Department and transacted some business. Then worked up correspondence at home until three, when Dr. Thompson sent his horse around to me and for my stomach's sake I took a long ride, by the way of the New British Legation building, Meridian Hill, Soldiers' Home, and N. Y. Avenue.

In the evening helped the boys with their lessons. They are doing better than ever before in their studies and I remark a much better effect in the tone of their mind. Read Goethe until a late hour.

WEDNESDAY, 11. Worked on correspondence in the morning. Committee met again at 12 o'clock. Loughridge and Tyner arrived, making a quorum. Spent an hour discussing the general features of our work and determined to take up the Legislative Bill as our first work. I distributed portions of it to the several members present and we adjourned until Friday with a view to spending Thursday at the Departments preparing the several sections of the bill. At the close of our session went to the Appropriation Committee Room of the Senate and had a long conversation with Senators Morrill and Sargent in regard to some reforms which we think can be made

---

[190] Charles O'Neill (1821–1893) was a Republican member of the House from Pennsylvania, 1863–71, 1873–93.

in the public expenditures. I am very desirous of reforming the Customs Department so as to make the expenditures depend upon specific appropriations by Congress, rather than as now upon perma[nent appropriations] to be disposed of at the discretion of the Secretary of the Treasury. At three o'clock took a horse-back ride along the river bank behind the Naval Observatory to Georgetown under the Aqueduct Bridge and under the canal one-quarter of a mile above. Back through Georgetown home. I thus saw a portion of the city I had never before visited—old delapidated warehouses and shipping stores, where once there was thriving commerce. Home in the evening. Read Goethe. This is the 16th anniversary of my marriage. Crete and I reviewed the past years and their events and blessed epoch.

THURSDAY, 12. Correspondence until 11 o'clock when I went to the Treasury Department and worked on the estimates for appropriation for several hours. During my visit there Secretary Bristow invited me into his private room and read a considerable portion of his forthcoming report. It is very clear and strong on the subject of specie payment for which I am grateful, but I fear the obduracy and madness of the people will prevent a return to specie payments. The Secretary gave some very confidential views of the internal condition of the party, as exhibited in the Ca[binet.][191] I am satisfied that Grant made a great mis[take] in not reorganizing his Cabinet on his sec[ond] election. He has done more than any other [Presi]dent to degrade the character of Cabinet office[rs] by choosing them on the model of the military staff, because of their pleasant personal relation to him and not because of their national reputation and the public needs. In reference to the integrity of some of them, I have serious doubts, which at this time I do not choose to specify. At three o'clock took my horseback ride, going from the South Front of the President's [House] down the river bank to the arsenal, thence by the way of the Capitol home. Read Goethe in the evening.

FRIDAY, 13. After the usual forenoon's work, went to the Capitol,

---

[191] The bracketed parts of the words in this sentence and the two which follow were all at the ends of lines and were obliterated when someone removed a pasted strip that had covered them.

where the Committee met at 12 o'clock. Hale was there and for nearly three hours we worked on the Legislative Appropriation Bill. Took a horseback ride through the grounds of the Soldiers' Home. After dinner Rockwell came and visited for an hour. At seven o'clock went to Senator Sherman's, where were Senators Morrill of Maine and Sargent of California. We visited and played euchre until 11 o'clock. A pleasant party. I am forcing myself to some form of recreation, to see if I cannot better the condition of my stomach. It would please me better to spend the evenings in study. And particularly this evening, for this afternoon I received from the Library of Congress 26 volumes of Goethe and his works.

SATURDAY, 14. Soon after breakfast J[oseph] W. Robbins, late a Graduate of Hiram, but now of Columbus, Mississippi, called to tell me that he was under arrest and likely to be indicted for conspiracy to defraud the revenue. I went with him to Commissioner Douglass[192] and made an arrangement for the hearing of his case, after the papers should be examined. He came back at two o'clock saying that the Commissioner declined to interfere in his favor. I went again to the Department and ascertained that he was badly involved with Collector McClure. I am afraid he will come to grief for what he has done. Worked on correspondence and read Goethe until evening. At half-past seven in company with Hale and E. B. White [Wight] visited Starkweather at Willard's and spent a portion of the evening.

SUNDAY, 15. Attended Church with Mother and heard a very stupid sermon from Bela Hayden. At half-past two o'clock took a horse-

192 John W. Douglass, commissioner of internal revenue. Henry B. McClure, collector of internal revenue for the second district of Mississippi, was charged with accepting a bribe; he was tried and acquitted. Joseph W. Robbins, a member of the class of 1872 of Hiram College, and deputy collector in McClure's district, who was involved in the same incident, appeared before a grand jury but was not indicted. He wrote to Garfield on November 14, 1874: "Let me say that I believe this deliverance of mine is due to your unselfish and generous sympathy which prompted you to use your time and powerful influence in my behalf." After another period in the internal revenue service, he became a correspondent for the Chicago *Inter Ocean.*

back ride and went to the Reform School some six miles away and made a short address to the boys. Goethe in the evening.

MONDAY, 16. Correspondence in the morning. The Committee met at 12 and continued work on the Legislative Bill until half-past three o'clock. Horseback ride until dinner. In the evening went with Rockwell to hear James T. Fields's[193] Lecture on Sidney Smith. It was scholarly and well considered, but it did not strike me as so masterful a presentation of Smith's career as could have been made. The lecturer undertook to make too many points. He should have heeded the exhortation *Multum in* [*non*] *multa* [Much, not many things]. After the lecture Rockwell and I played a few games of billiards. I have a sore throat tonight which brings a suggestion of diptheria. General Sherman called in the evening and we had a pleasant evening. I regret his departure to Saint Louis, for he is a delightful addition to the social life of Washington.

TUESDAY, 17. At nine o'clock, by previous arrangement, the Committee went in carriages with General Babcock to visit the water works and examine the various offices, reservoirs and culverts, including the great Union Arch at Cabin John Bridge, and reached the Great Falls of the Potomac at ½ past 12 o'clock. Examined the dam and the site of its proposed extension—also, the Falls. After a pleasant dinner at the Hotel drove back, reaching home at six. Enjoyed many pleasant reminiscences of Washington life as given by Governor Swann during the journey. In 1830 he rode from the Hermitage to Washington with General Jackson, and in default of a barber shaved the General. The Governor's father was Washington's lawyer and also the lawyer of Lord Fairfax, and he has a great mass of interesting papers.[194] Swann's father was intimately ac-

---

[193] James Thomas Fields (1817–1881), a member of the Boston publishing firm of Ticknor & Fields, and editor of the *Atlantic Monthly* from 1861 to 1870, lectured and wrote on literary subjects. His writings include *Yesterday with Authors* (1872). During this visit to Washington, in addition to the lectures on Smith and Tennyson which Garfield heard, he spoke on Charles Lamb and Henry W. Longfellow.

[194] Governor Swann's father, Thomas Swann, a Virginian, became a prominent lawyer in the District of Columbia. He may have done legal work for George Washington although he seems not to have been a corre-

quainted with Washington and was with him as a fellow student of Wm. Wirtz [Wirt].[195] He once entered his father's room and found his father fiddling with Wirt dancing. He remembers to have seen Jefferson, Madison and Monroe walking up arm in arm to the University of Va. when he was a student there.[196] In the evening attended the Presidential Levee given in honor of his son, Colonel Grant,[197] and bride, whom I knew nine years ago as Miss Honoré. A large and elegant party were present and a collation was served in the State Dining Room about 11 o'clock. The East Room has been handsomely refitted by General Babcock and its hall-like appearance broken up by pillars into a more homelike looking place. General Sherman is here on business, but has removed to Saint Louis.

WEDNESDAY, 18. Finished Lewes's *Goethe,* and also the two volumes of autobiography. Commenced Eckerman[n]'s *Conversations*[198] and am making points of Goethe's peculiarities that impress me most. The Committee met at 12 and substantially finished the Legislative Bill. Agreed to take up the Naval Bill tomorrow. Horseback ride by way of the Smithsonian, Agricultural Grounds, and the new State

---

spondent of Washington. The editors have not been able to discover the location of the "great mass of interesting papers" preserved by Governor Swann.

[195] Either Garfield did not understand what Governor Swann said or he did not make it clear to his secretary, who wrote the entry in the diary. The reference to Washington is perhaps to the city and not the man. William Wirt (1772–1834), a distinguished lawyer who became U. S. attorney general, read law under Thomas Swann, Sr., in Virginia for five months during the early 1790's. The elder Swann and Wirt were intimate friends in Washington. Governor Swann, like Wirt, studied law with the elder Swann, but the two students were about 35 years apart.

[196] Governor Swann attended the University of Virginia, 1826–27. Thomas Jefferson died on July 4, 1826.

[197] Frederick Dent Grant (1850–1912), an officer in the U. S. Army, married Ida M. Honoré, daughter of Henry Hamilton Honoré, a Chicago businessman, on October 20, 1874.

[198] Sarah Margaret Fuller's English translation of Johann Peter Eckermann's *Gespräche mit Goethe* . . . (1836) appeared in 1838 under the title *Conversations with Goethe.* . . . John Oxenford's English translation of the same work appeared in 1850 under the title *Conversations of Goethe.* . . .

Department. Worked on correspondence in the evening until eight o'clock, when Colonel Rockwell and I attended Thomas' concert.[199] Twenty violins and forty other instruments sounding in harmony make a great volume of melody. This [There] is much in the concert that delighted me, but I do not sufficiently understand the language of music to be able to translate its meaning. Its riddles pique me and I sometimes doubt whether it has any meaning at all. I wish I could converse with some great master of music and learn something of his mental processes.

THURSDAY, 19. Dictated correspondence and notes on Goethe in the forenoon. Committee met at 12 and sat until a late hour. Completed the Naval Appropriation Bill and adjourned over till Monday. Today completes my 43d year. I have passed all the dates which superstition had fixed in my mind as the limit of my life. How far it now is to the other shore I make no guess. While my life has been a very busy one, I feel keenly that I have accomplished but little. So many fields of thought I have left untouched; so many plans of culture begun and unfinished. The fact is that nearly all my plans of culture are "asides" in which I attempt to do something outside of my regular work. Thankful for what the past has given me, yet remembering its storms, I must say with the mariner "*Cras ingens iterabimus aequor* [Tomorrow we shall embark again upon the mighty sea]."

FRIDAY, 20. Spent the forenoon in bringing up correspondence and adjusting accounts. At noon went to the Interior and Post Office Departments on business and on my return dictated more letters. Rained in the afternoon and I did not ride. In the evening went around to Hill's and took him with me to hear James T. Fields lecture on Tennyson. It was very enjoyable and valuable for some of the items of personal knowledge which Fields gives concerning the poet. But he did not show that grasp of Tennyson's poetry which I expected. He did not attempt to give us an analysis of Tennyson's characteristics, nor did he describe the field which Tennyson occupies in history. In his rendering of the Bugle Song, he missed

[199] Theodore Thomas (1835–1905) during a long and distinguished career conducted orchestras in Brooklyn, New York and Chicago, and on tour.

the spiritual meaning of it altogether, namely, the contrast in the last stanza between the external beauty of the bugle notes which die and the higher beauty of the spiritual echoes which "roll from soul to soul" and grow forever.

SATURDAY, 21. Spent the forenoon in correspondence and in dictating notes of my readings of Goethe. I am making notes of the leading points which impress me in his life, character, and work. I long for more leizure to follow up the bent of my mind in literature. Yet if I had abundant leizure, I might fritter it away. Perhaps that study of literature is fullest which we steal from daily duties. In the afternoon went to the Treasury and had a long interview with the Secretary in regard to revenues and expenditures. Played billiards with Rockwell for a couple of hours before dinner. Spent the evening in reading Goethe.

SUNDAY, 22. At home—not well—did not attend church. Read two of Carlyle's essays on Goethe. Read also Goethe's *Iphigenia in Tauris*. It is very powerful and strong enough to escape the destruction of translation. How much I regret I cannot readily read it in the original.

MONDAY, 23. Worked on correspondence until noon. Committee met at 12, heard the Commissioner of Patents, the Commissioner of the General Land Office, and received several communications from other officers in reference to the Legislative Appropriation Bill— then took up the Fortification Bill. Came home in the evening and worked on correspondence and dictated some more notes on Goethe until time for the train, when I went to the Baltimore and Ohio Depot and took the train for Pittsburgh. A few minutes after I was seated in the car I opened my carpet bag to take out *Wilhelm Meister*, which I had promised myself the enjoyment of on the journey, but was greatly disgusted to find I had taken instead Mrs. Holmes's *Dora Deane*,[200] which I [had] never before seen and out of spite mentally resolved never to read.

TUESDAY, 24. Reached Pittsburgh at 8.45 and after breakfast, while awaiting for the train to New Castle, concluded to read *Dora Deane*, which I did. The work was pleasant until I reached the two chap-

[200] Mary J. Holmes, *Dora Deane, or the East India Uncle*; and *Maggie Miller, or Old Hagar's Secret* (1858).

ters before the last, where I was infinitely disgusted and where I found the authoress planning a petty revenge on the erring Eugenia by making the good people in her work meaner than Eugenia herself had been. Took the one o'clock train for New Castle, and after riding about thirty miles the Conductor brought me a telegram requesting me to stop at the next station and come back with Ford, who was coming down. This I did. At half-past three Ford and I took the train up the Allegheny River for Butler, which we reached a little before seven in the evening. Spent several hours with Phillips discussing the situation of his affairs, with the hope of saving him if possible from going into Bankruptcy.

WEDNESDAY, 25. Spent the day in interviews with lawyers and others connected with Mr. Phillips, and made some calls, among others one on Judge McJunkin,[201] a member of Congress. Late in the evening I discovered a method of closing up Mr. Phillips' chief trouble, that in relation to the Starr Farm, which was to have him confess judgment in the suit for ejectment and thus deliver back the farm which carried with it the contract for purchase and the seventy-five thousand dollars of unpaid purchase money.

THURSDAY, 26. Had the papers made out in reference to confession of judgment, and arranged for filing them tomorrow morning. This being a holiday it was not deemed safe to make the transaction of this day. Took the train at half-past two to Pittsburgh. Ford and Phillips accompanied me as far as Freeport. On the way to Pittsburgh I read the only remaining literature I had with me, the second story of Mrs. Holmes in the volume I had taken with me. The story was entitled *Maggie [Miller]; or, Old Hagar's Secret*. It has not the glaring faults of *Dora Deane*, but both are perhaps popular among sentimental young people. The book shows marks of having been much read. Took tea at the Monongahela House and at eight P.M. took the Connellsville train for Washington. There I met Thorp, the artist, of Geneva, who came through with me.

FRIDAY, 27. Reached home at 7.45 in time for breakfast. Family all well. A large mail awaited me. Went to the Committee meeting at ten, but no quorum was present. Spent an hour in the Library and

[201] Ebenezer McJunkin (1819–1907), a Republican member of the House from Pennsylvania, 1871–75.

found out to my disgust that Mrs. Holmes has written eleven novels and is still blazing away. Spofford tells me that her books are constantly called for. This verifies the soldier's maxim, "Aim low." Spent the rest of the day in answering letters, in reading Carlyle and having the headache. I find in Carlyle's speech of 1866 as Lord Rector at Edinburgh University that he has stated quite fully his views of Goethe, which exhibit his very high appreciation of the great German thinker. There is much in the Edinburgh Address which agrees with my notions about books and work. The article has furnished me several passages for my Index Rerum.[202]

SATURDAY, 28. In the morning took Harry, Mollie, and Jimmy to the Dentist and had their teeth examined. Both Harry and Jimmy had some teeth filled. It is surprising that at their age they should need to have this work done. I have lost but one tooth and that a double tooth. I lost it when I was 16 years of age. My sister, Mrs. Larabee, came today to spend some time with us.

Correspondence and Goethe in the forenoon. Called on Governor Dennison and the other members of the District Commission on business connected with my taxes. In the evening called on Rockwell. We read together awhile and then played billiards.

SUNDAY, 29. Attended church and listened to a sermon from Mr. Cutler of Va., a man who is evidently in the Sturm and Drang period —only in his case it is difficult to see against whom his crusade is. In the afternoon called on the Earl of Rosebery, who is spending a few days in Washington. In the evening told my children the story of *The Rape of Helen* and the tragedy of *Iphigenia in Aulis,* which I have just read in Wodhull's translation of Euripides. I was pleased to see how strongly the story touched the hearts of the little ones. Jimmy left the room crying when he thought Iphigenia would be sacrificed. Several other members of the family were shedding tears before the story was completed. This suggests to me that it might be possible to work a large share of ancient and modern literature and history in[to] the minds of these little people.

MONDAY, 30. Worked on correspondence and Goethe in the forenoon. The Committee met at twelve and after disposing of a large

202 During his lifetime Garfield kept two Index Rerums, volumes of blank pages in which he copied quotations from his readings, wrote comments and miscellaneous notes and pasted printed items. They are in the Library of Congress.

number of miscellaneous communications from the Executive Departments, took up the Army Appropriation Bill and worked on it for three hours and nearly completed it. Arranged for a joint meeting with the Senate Committee on Appropriations tomorrow. Took my horseback ride of an hour in company with E. B. White [Wight] of the *Chicago Tribune.* After dinner worked on correspondence and Goethe. Also, at the request of General Cist[203] of Cincinnati, wrote out the speech I delivered at the last Reunion of the Army at Columbus. It is somewhat difficult six months after delivering speeches extemporaneously to reproduce them, but I believe I am able to do it successfully in this case. After the boys had finished their lessons, the family came into the Library and I told them the story of *Iphigenia in Tauris* as I had read it from Euripides. I found the little ones very much interested in the story, but after the boys had gone to bed Harry came down crying, saying he could not go to sleep for he was thinking of the dream of Iphigenia—so I told him some other stories which toned him down and let him go to sleep. I took occasion to tell the boys that all these stories of gods and goddesses which were believed in by the ancients were untrue and that Jesus came to sweep away all the myths and goblins of ancient mythology and teach men the story of the true God and Beneficent Father, that now the shadows of night were not filled with horrors but with the sense of sweet peace. Jimmy said he was glad of this. He did not believe in the Gods that Orestes and Iphigenia talked of but he did believe in Jesus. But after stopping a moment he said, but how do we know that the story of Jesus is true? I gave him some of the plainer evidences, which seemed to satisfy him.

December

TUESDAY, 1. Worked on correspondence until ten o'clock, when at the request of Secretary Bristow I called on him at the Treasury and consulted with him in regard to some portions of his Annual Report

[203] Henry Martyn Cist (1839–1902), a Cincinnati lawyer, was assistant adjutant general of the Army of the Cumberland during the Civil War. His extensive publications on the war included *The Army of the Cumber land* (1882).

which is just now finished. At 12 o'clock the Committee on Appropriations of the Senate met our Committee and consulted on some matters of reform in the public service. The result was the appointment of two joint committees, one to consider the cost of collecting the revenues for customs and the other to consider the expenses of the Post Office Department. After the conference ended the Committee considered some miscellaneous matter before it, and adjourned at two o'clock. Took my usual ride at four. Mr. and Mrs. Rockwell called in the evening. After they were gone, read the *Electra* of Sophocles.

WEDNESDAY, 2. Worked on correspondence and miscellaneous business until ten, and then went to the Treasury Department. Had a long interview with the Supervising Architect, Mullett, who has resigned. Mullett tells me the authority that he cares most for in architecture is Inigo Jones. He does not believe in classic or Gothic styles, but in the spirit of the renaissance adapted to American ideas. Committee met at 12 and considered the condition of the Land Office and also revised the Legislative Bill. Took my horseback ride to the Soldiers' Home.

THURSDAY, 3. In the evening read the *Electra* of Sophocles. These plays exhibit the difference between Greek morals and the morals of Christians. It is hard for us to understand how lying of the most outrageous sort can be put into the mouth of a hero in a great work of art and not be considered a blemish. In the forenoon worked on correspondence and finished my notes of readings on Goethe, which make between fifty and sixty pages of manuscript. At eleven o'clock started on a round of business at the Departments which kept me until three. Then for two hours took a horseback ride with Colonel Piatt across Rock Creek to Brightwood and home. Had long talk on political and literary questions. Piatt expressed the opinion that women do not as a general rule marry for love—that men marry for love more than women. Miss Ransom, the Cleveland Artist, came this evening and will visit us some time.

FRIDAY, 4. After finishing correspondence went to the Interior and Post Office Departments on business and thence to the Capitol. The Committee met at twelve and made a careful examination of the appropriations for the mints and assay offices. Heard Dr. Linderman very fully, and finished many details of the bill. At half-past three o'clock joined Colonel Piatt on horseback and rode until half-past five. E. B. White [Wight] of the *Chicago Tribune* joined us on the way. At half-past seven went to a party at Senator Morrill's. There were present Chief Justice Waite, Justice Miller, Senator Morrill of Maine, Edmunds, Sargent, Bristow and Jewell,[204] Hale, of the House, and myself. Spent a pleasant evening. Bristow tells me that the President had in his message this morning a recommendation for large expenditures on public works, with a view to employing the laborers. Bristow succeed[ed] in getting a portion of it out. This would be a fatal policy.

SATURDAY, 5. After morning correspondence called at the several Departments on business. Committee met at ten and worked on bills until about two o'clock. Washington is rapidly filling up by Members of Congress and others arriving for the Winter. At three o'clock took my usual ride and worked on correspondence in the evening. Had many callers. Among others my old friend Smalley called and spent an hour in conversation on the general aspects of public affairs. He has drifted a good ways off from his old Republican feelings, and yet shrinks from becoming a Democrat. I doubt if he can ever satisfy himself with being of that party.

SUNDAY, 6. Did not attend church. Went to the Capitol with Miss Ransom and helped her put up her picture of General Thomas in the Rotunda.[205] Took my horseback ride as usual. In the evening Crete and I read Tennyson till a late hour.

MONDAY, 7. Correspondence in the morning. Committee met at 11 o'clock and revised our bills and made them ready for introduction. The House met at 12. Eleven years ago this morning, and it was

[204] Marshall Jewell (1825–1883), a Connecticut manufacturer who served three terms as governor of his state during the early 1870's, was appointed postmaster general by President Grant in December, 1874. His honesty and efficiency won him enemies, and the President was persuaded to ask for his resignation in 1876. He was chairman of the Republican National Committee, 1880–83; his letters to Garfield during the campaign of 1880 are in the Garfield Papers.

[205] Caroline Ransom hoped that Congress would appropriate money to buy her large portrait of General George H. Thomas. When this hope was disappointed despite the help of Garfield (see entries for February 15, 17 and 26, 1875) she presented the painting to the government.

then Monday, I took my seat as a member of Congress. After the reading of the President's Message, I introduced the Legislative Bill, other members then followed with the Naval, Army, Indian, and the Fortification bills, and Mr. Tyner put through a small appropriation for scales for the Post Office Department, after which the House adjourned. Happily the President was induced to keep out of his message his scheme for employing the laborers of the country by large appropriations. I rejoice that he holds firmly in favor of specie payments. At half-past six dined with Clarkson Potter, S. B. Chittenden[206] and Professor Bonamy Price. Had a long and delightful visit with the Professor. He is of Norman extraction, born on the Island of Guernsey, is vivacious and chatty, brilliant and opinionated. He was personally acquainted with Wordsworth and thinks the poem on "Immortality" the greatest English poem since Milton. Gave several reminiscences of Wordsworth—one showing Author's meaning of that passage in "Immortality" which thanks God for the "fallings off and vanishings," saying that Wordsworth illustrated them by stepping to the gate and grasping a bar, then saying that at one period of his life he frequently was compelled to seize hold of something to assure himself that matter existed. Thus he thanked God for his power of ideality which could make matter vanish.

TUESDAY, 8. Correspondence in the morning. Committee met at eleven, spent an hour in arranging business for future meetings. In the House, on the call of Committees, a debate sprang up on Kelley's currency bill[207] and he and Butler exhibited their inflation doctrines in full blast. I replied for fifteen minutes, apparently with good effect. My speech seemed to be well received. Did not take my

[206] Simeon Baldwin Chittenden (1814–1889) was a Republican member of the House from New York, 1874–81.

[207] The measure authorized holders of greenbacks to purchase convertible U. S. bonds, bearing an annual interest of 3.65 percent, and required the secretary of the treasury to apply the greenbacks received from such purchases to retire U. S. bonds, many of which were in foreign hands. Believing that the costly "foreign debt," carrying "gold interest," was the basic cause of the nation's economic ills, Kelley said the object of his bill was to make American taxpayers, instead of foreigners, the creditors of the government, and to vindicate the honor of the government by acknowledging the integrity of greenbacks.

horseback ride today. At six o'clock dined with Donn Piatt, General Benét and another officer of the Ordnance Corps, whose name I have forgotten. Spent two hours in discussing the military armament of our fortifications. Returned home at half-past eight and worked on correspondence till a late hour. Sheldon from Louisiana called and brought me a box of oranges picked from his orange trees two days ago.

WEDNESDAY, 9. Correspondence as usual in the morning. Committee met at eleven and heard the three Commissioners of the District of Columbia in regard to some necessary legislation for the District. But little was done in the House and we adjourned at an early hour. There is a general feeling of depression among the leading Republicans in consequence of the hopeless division on the great question of the currency. It was mortifying to me to notice that while Kelley and Butler were making their astonishing speeches yesterday, they were listened to by the Right Honorable Mr. Forster,[208] Member of the late British Ministry. I felt a sort of national shame at the exhibit they were making of themselves. At three o'clock went with Col. Rockwell and played billiards for two hours instead of taking my usual horseback ride.

THURSDAY, 10. Correspondence in the morning. Called on the President in company with Sheldon and asked the appointment of Pardee to the vacant Judgeship in New Orleans. Committee met at eleven and finished the Consular and Diplomatic Bill. In the House Mr. Dawes continued his speech on the Kelley bill. After him Phelps and Boardman Smith. I think the discussion is doing good. Ford took dinner with us and staid until half-past 8 o'clock. Called on Chas. Foster, then talked over the prospects of resuming specie payments.

While Dawes was speaking in the House, I had Bonamy Price sitting by me, and he passed me a slip of paper on which he had written the following. "No good can be done, unless people are brought to understand that all currency only moves goods; wealth is a cart and not the things in it."

[208] William Edward Forster (1818–1886) was a member of the British House of Commons, 1861–86. He was appointed to the Privy Council by Gladstone in 1868; after the dissolution of the ministry in 1874 he paid a visit to the United States. He was chief secretary for Ireland, 1880–82.

FRIDAY, 11. Correspondence in the morning. Called at the Post Office Department on business. Also called on the Att'y General in reference to the appointment of Don Pardee to the vacant Judgeship in New Orleans. House met at twelve and consumed most of the day in the discussion of private bills. I called the attention of the House to the article in yesterday's *Tribune* charging the Committee on Appropriations with having introduced an additional half million subsidy for the Pacific Mail in the Post Office Appropriation Bill.[209] Answered the charge by the statement that the bill had neither been introduced nor taken up by the Committee for consideration. It is a curious specimen of the recklessness of our journalism of today. The two *Tribunes* for the preceding days had stated in its Associated Press Report all the appropriation bills which had been introduced in the House, and the Post Office Appropriation Bill was not one of them. In the evening dined at Gov. Swann's with the Appropriation Committee, together with Judge Niblack and Gen'l Latrobe of Baltimore.[210]

SATURDAY, 12. Worked on correspondence, and finished writing out

[209] Under a contract with the federal government the Pacific Mail Steamship Company had received an annual subsidy of $500,000; but in 1873, the company having failed to fulfill its contract, the postmaster general excluded the item from his budget recommendation for the fiscal year ending June 30, 1875. In 1874, however, newly-appointed Postmaster General Marshall Jewell, on advice from the attorney general, requested the subsidy for the fiscal year ending June 30, 1876. James N. Tyner, chairman of the sub-committee on Post Office appropriations, explained to the House during the discussion of the *Tribune* editorial that he had secured a copy of the attorney general's opinion and, with permission from the Committee on Appropriations, had asked the House to approve an order to print it. The House had passed the order and a number of copies had been printed. Apparently it was that document which led the *New York Tribune* to conclude that the subsidy (the paper called it a robbery) had been recommended in the Post Office Bill reported to the House by Garfield's Committee on Appropriations, when in fact the committee had not yet considered the bill.

[210] Ferdinand Claiborne Latrobe, a Baltimore lawyer and politician who had been judge advocate general of Maryland. He was elected mayor of Baltimore in 1875 and three times thereafter. His first wife was the daughter of Garfield's friend Thomas Swann.

my speeches delivered at the meeting of the Army of the Cumberland, at Columbus, in September last. Spent some time at the Departments working up materials for the appropriation bills. Had long interview with Secretary Bristow in reference to a bill for specie payments. Drove out with Crete shopping in the afternoon. Spent a portion of the evening with Sheldon and Foster. The King of the Sandwich Islands[211] arrived in the City today and has been received as the guest of the Government. This is the first instance of a reigning king visiting the U. S.

SUNDAY, 13. Church at eleven o'clock. Horseback ride at three. Several people called during the day. At six dined with Secretary Fish. There were present his wife, daughter and son, Senators Anthony and Conkling, Mr. Stoughton[212] of N. Y., Mr. Orth of Indiana and myself. A pleasant party. Severe criticisms were made on the manners of Prof. Bonamy Price. He is an inveterate talker and seems to have offended the ladies by his volubility at the table. At a recent dinner he asked each of the guests to write down their idea of heaven. Sec'y Robeson responded that he thought of heaven as a place "without money and without price." It is said the English Professor did not appreciate the joke. At the close of the dinner the Secretary of State consulted with Mr. Orth and myself in regard to the proper attention to be paid to the King Kalakaua. Crete has read Goethe's *Hermann and Dorothea* today. Says it is a pleasant story but not very profound.

[211] David Kalakaua (1836–1891), king of Hawaiian Islands, 1874–91. was in Washington from December 12 to December 23. He came to the United States at the urging of American sugar interests in Hawaii to promote a reciprocity treaty between the two countries. Such a treaty was signed by President Grant in January, 1875, and approved by the Senate in March.

[212] Edwin Wallace Stoughton (1818–1882), a New York lawyer. In 1876 at Grant's request he went to New Orleans to report on the Hayes-Tilden election in Louisiana. He observed the canvassing of the state Returning Board and later represented the Republican cause before the Electoral Commission. All of the disputed Republican electoral votes were honored by the Electoral Commission on the basis of his legal reasoning that Congress could not go behind the decision of a state and must accept the election certificate if signed by the proper state authorities. Stoughton was minister to Russia, 1877–79.

MONDAY, 14. Committee met at eleven o'clock and worked on several matters before them. The usual wash of resolutions and bills filled the day. Horseback ride in the afternoon. Correspondence again in the evening and then worked until eleven o'clock preparing the materials for a speech on the Appropriation Bill. I am not certain that I will deliver it until I reach the end of the bill. But it may be necessary and so I have prepared the materials for an extemporaneous speech of an hour, if necessary. I am pleased to find that the statement made in my speech of March 5th, '74, that the total appropriations for the year ending June 30th, 1875, would not, if my recommendations were carried out, exceed 270 millions, has proved strikingly true. The actual appropriations made were about 270 millions eight hundred thousand dollars.

Considering the large reduction of thirty-odd millions below the estimates and over twenty millions below the appropriations of the year before, these figures are rather remarkable.

TUESDAY, 15. After breakfast called at Welcker's and had a visit with Messrs. Duncan[213] and Nordhoff[214] of N. Y. on the financial situation. Committee met at eleven and made up the statements of the amounts recommended for the six bills already introduced, as compared with the estimates and appropriations of last year. In the House, Mr. Dawes tried to get through a resolution of adjournment for the Holidays.[215] I thought it was premature to adjourn for so long a time, and resisting it, succeeded in beating his resolution by 8 votes. Then got into Committee of the Whole and took up the Legislative Bill—going through sixteen pages of it. I made no general speech, but will wait till the bill is reported back from

[213] William Butler Duncan (1830–1912), a banker and businessman of New York City. He was closely associated with the Baltimore and Ohio Railroad, and in 1877 he retained Garfield as a lawyer in a suit which he and others had brought against the railroad company.

[214] Charles Nordhoff (1830–1901) was the Washington correspondent of the *New York Herald*, 1874–90, and the author of a number of books, including *The Communistic Societies of the United States* (1874).

[215] Dawes's resolution called for a recess from December 23, 1874, to January 5, 1875. The resolution was adopted, but on a motion by Garfield the House decided to reconsider the vote, 128–120. On December 21 the Dawes resolution was passed by a vote of 121–93.

the Committee of the Whole to the House. Horseback ride and at five took dinner with Col. Piatt, [William] Neely Thompson of N. Y., General Banning of Cincinnati and Gen'l Lamar of Mississippi. Lamar is a very brilliant thinker. Correspondence in the evening.

WEDNESDAY, 16. Captain Henry came to the City yesterday and took dinner with us. Went with him to the Post Office Deaprtment and at eleven o'clock went to the Committee meeting. Soon after the reading of the Journal in the House, got into Committee of the Whole and spent four hours on the Legislative Bill. Got through with twenty-seven pages, leaving off at the bottom of the 43d page. This was an extraordinary good day's work. Capt. Henry took dinner with us. We have succeeded in getting Colonel Pardee appointed U. S. Judge of La. This evening I wrote a letter to Judge Edmunds, Chairman of the Judiciary Committee of the Senate, in favor of his confirmation. It is very gratifying to be able to help my noble old friend and comrade to this honorable position which he will probably hold during the remainder of his life. Had some interesting reflections on the change from foetal life to the life that we now live. It is certainly as great as the change from this life to the next.

THURSDAY, 17. Correspondence in the morning. Committee met at eleven o'clock and worked on miscellaneous matters until twelve. Got into Committee of the Whole immediately after the reading of the Journal and put in four hours' effective work on the Legislative Appropriation Bill. Dined with Hill and three other classmates at six. They were Captain Rockwell, Reverend G. B. Newcomb[216] of New Haven, and Gilfillan of the Treasury. We had a delightful reunion. Of forty-two graduates in our class in 1856, more than half were in the Army, and yet up to the present time only four are dead.[217] Lamberton died of consumption only a few months after graduation, Robbins was drowned two years after graduation, and Baxter was killed in battle. Bronson died two years ago. On the

[216] George Benton Newcomb (1836–1895) was a Congregational minister in New Haven, 1869–78, and professor of philosophy in the College of the City of New York, 1879–95.

[217] According to the report on the Williams class of 1856, published in 1898, five of Garfield's classmates had died by the date of this entry—William R. Baxter, Isaac Bronson, John E. D. Lamberton, Nathan B. Robbins, and Lemuel P. Webber.

whole the class have done remarkably well as a body and are a noble set of fellows.

FRIDAY, 18. Correspondence in the morning. Went shopping with Crete for an hour. Had a Committee meeting of fifteen minutes, before twelve, on a few items in the Legislative Bill. Long before the hour of meeting the galleries were crowded to overflowing and all the approaches to the Hall were packed with people desirous of catching a glimpse of the King of Hawaiian Islands. At one-quarter past 12, the Senate, headed by the Vice President, entered the House, and soon after the Committee on Introduction, headed by Senator Cameron and Mr. Orth, brought in His Majesty, who was introduced by Senator Cameron and welcomed by the Speaker in a speech. The King replied through his Lord Chancellor in writing. The King himself was so hoarse that he could not speak. He is a large, well-built, tawney-complexioned man and very much resembles Mr. Cook,[218] the colored collector of this District. After the visitors withdrew the House went into Committee of the Whole and finished the Legislative Bill. During the day Speer[219] of Pa. made a series of snappish attacks upon the Republican Party and I replied to him with more vehemence than I have usually done. I was warmly congratulated by a large number of members at the close of the speech.

[218] John F. Cook, register of the District of Columbia.
[219] Robert Milton Speer (1839–1890), a Democratic member of the House from Pennsylvania, 1871–75, asked Garfield whether the attorney general had submitted, as required by law, an itemized account of his expenditures of a contingent fund of $21,000. Garfield evaded the question and accused Speer of making attacks against appropriations which were too vague and general to be answered. He then launched a general attack against the Democratic party, accused it of having plunged the nation into the depths of bankruptcy and protest, and concluded by declaring that the Republican party "saved the country from this degradation and slavery and ruin, from treason and rebellion, and lifted it out of war . . . and made its public credit and name great in the world." In reply Speer upbraided Garfield for failing to answer a proper question and objected to his party's being lectured by a gentleman "who stands in the mists and clouds of suspicion, if not of guilt." He accused Garfield of being supercilious toward members of the House, saying that "it may be well for him to be taught, here and now, that however we may stand with reference to length of service and official position on this floor, as Representatives of the people we are equal."

At four o'clock the Committee rose and reported the bill to the House, and at one-quarter before five the bill passed. This I believe is the first time in the history of the Government that the great appropriation bill has passed before the Holiday vacation. At six o'clock dined with William Orton in company with Hale, Tyner, and Loughridge. At half-past nine attended the President's Reception given to King Kalakaua. A large company were present, among others the Japanese Minister and his wife. This is the first time I have seen a Japanese lady in a public assemblage.

SATURDAY, 19. Correspondence until half-past ten o'clock, when I went with Crete and spent three hours among the Holiday goods to find Christmas gifts for the family. At one o'clock went to the Departments and had a long conversation with the Secretary of the Treasury, who informed me of the intrigues of Delano, Shepherd and Babcock against him. It is not impossible that a crisis will soon occur which will drive either him or Delano from the Cabinet. I trust Bristow will not be the victim. Called at the Pension Office and secured a place for Ferry and for King of Bloomfield at the Land Office.[220] At three o'clock went with Col. Rockwell and played billiards until five P.M. I am very much wearied with the work of the week.

SUNDAY, 20. A rainy, dreary day outside. Did not attend church but wrote and read until six o'clock, when I dined with David A. Wells, Senator Bayard and William Orton.

MONDAY, 21. Committee met at eleven o'clock and worked on miscellaneous matters. In the House the day was spent with the usual Monday work, except that Richard B. Irwin was ordered to be brought before the House for refusing to answer a question put to him by the Ways and Means Committee in reference to the Pacific Mail Subsidy.[221] In the course of this discussion an interesting

---

[220] The names of the men should be in reverse order: L. King's job was in the Pension Office and Lemuel A. Ferry's in the Land Office.

[221] Richard B. Irwin of New York was employed to procure a federal subsidy for the Pacific Mail Steamship Company. For this assignment, which he accomplished, the company paid him $750,000. Subsequently a charge was made that the subsidy had been procured by corrupt means, whereupon the House Ways and Means Committee conducted an investigation. Irwin was called before the committee to testify but refused to disclose the names of persons he had employed to help him. On January 6, 1875, he was

question was raised by Alexander Stephens, who insisted that the House had no power to punish a recusant witness. It could turn him over to the Courts of the District of Columbia, in accordance with the Statute of 1857, to be tried and punished. I am inclined to think Stephens is right, at least, to this extent, that the House may hold a witness in custody until he answers even if that be to the end of the Congress, but cannot punish him other than by detention. Still I am in doubt whether it may not have a power to punish for contempt, as a Court may.

TUESDAY, 22. Took Mother, Sister Mary and Crete in the carriage and drove to the War Department, and thence to the Interior Department, where, after transacting some business, I went to the Capitol. Committee met at eleven, as usual; went over the Military Academy Bill and reported it to the House. In the House at one o'clock, got into Committee of the Whole on the Naval Appropriation Bill, which after some sharp debate, was passed with but one amendment and that I offered.[222] It seems impossible to keep the members here to do any work very near the Holidays. Thirty or forty obtained leave of absence before we adjourned. Two leading appropriation bills before the Holidays is good work. I tried to pass an appropriation for paying the expenses of the King of the Hawaiian Islands, but Hereford[223] of West Va. objected. Home in

---

brought before the bar of the House, where he continued to be contumacious. He was then held in contempt of Congress, placed in custody of the sergeant-at-arms, and imprisoned in the common jail of the District of Columbia. A short time later the sergeant-at-arms, in obedience to a writ of habeas corpus, presented the body of Irwin before Judge Arthur MacArthur of the Supreme Court of the District of Columbia. After completing his inquiry MacArthur dismissed the writ and remanded Irwin to the custody of the sergeant-at-arms. Irwin then decided to answer questions asked by the committee, did so, and was released from custody.

[222] Minor amendments by Samuel Jackson Randall and John Holmes Burleigh were also adopted.

[223] Frank Hereford (1825–1891) was a Democratic member of the House from West Virginia, 1871–77, and of the Senate, 1877–81. He opposed Garfield's motion (it provided for an appropriation of $30,000) on the ground that no account had ever been made concerning the disposition of an earlier appropriation of $25,000 for the Japanese embassy of 1872.

the evening. Call[ed] on Mr. Parsons of Cleveland in the evening.
WEDNESDAY, 23.   Called on the Attorney General in reference to his
appropriations. Stopped a moment at the Institute of Mr. Young to
attend his exhibition before the recess. I think Harry and Jimmie
are doing well in the school. Committee met for half an hour
before the meeting of the House and distributed work for the
Recess. In the House there was a slim attendance—not more than
a quorum. The Finance Bill came from the Senate and we tried to
get it up for action. The Democrats resisted, and we were compelled to adjourn without action. The bill makes steps in the direction of specie payments, and though the measure is not a very
decisive one, yet it does something and I shall probably favor it,
as it promises something that approaches to a union in the Party.
Spent the afternoon and evening at home. A number of people
called. I worked for a while on Case No. 124 in the Supreme Court,
which is to be argued on the eighth of January.

THURSDAY, 24.   Correspondence in the morning. At eleven o'clock
rode on horseback. Stopped on the way to purchase some Holiday
Gifts. Went to the Capitol and transacted some business there. At
one o'clock went with Rockwell and played billiards for three or
four hours. Early in the evening worked on correspondence and later
read several Christmas poems, among others Milton's Hymn of
the Nativity. It is a poem of wonderful grasp and full of grand
music. For many years on Christmas Eve I have read passages from
Tennyson's "In Memoriam," and they come back to me each year
with singular power and sweetness. Among other things this evening, read Mrs. Browning's poem of "Mary to the Child." The children went to bed early, flushed with the expectations of Christmas
morning.

FRIDAY, 25.   At an early hour we listened to the exclamations of delight from the children at the presents which had been distributed
during the night. I am glad to notice that Harry and Jimmy have
this Winter awaked to the love of reading. Their desire for the
street, and the crowd of boys that throng it, has happily decreased,
and they spend the most of their evenings in reading. I am trying
to direct them into the better class of stories, *Robinson Crusoe*,
Cooper's *Leather Stocking Tales*, etc. Rockwell spent two hours with
me before dinner. In the evening called with Carrie at Mr. Riddle's.

Also read again the story of Cupid and Psyche and Mrs. Browning's "Paraphrase of Apuleius." The story of Cupid and Psyche is one of the most beautiful of the ancient Legends and is to me very significant of the power and triumphs of love. Read also Homer's Hymn to Venus. The Greek conception of beauty is very wonderful to me. All forms seem to stand out clear and luminous in the bright air of Greece. I have such a longing to see that country, as Goethe had to see Italy, when he wrote *"Kennst Du Das Land?"* Will the time ever come when I can gratify this passion and make it useful to those dependant upon me?

SATURDAY, 26. Worked on Correspondence in the morning. I was invited by Secretary Robeson to go with him on an excursion down the river, but the hourly expectation that Crete would be confined kept me from going. I remained at home and worked on Case No. 124, which is to be argued in the Supreme Court on the 7th of January. Feeling depressed in spirits, I determined to tone myself up by reading one of Shakespeare's plays that I had never read, and took up *King John* and read and admired its marvelous wealth of language and imagery. I read it aloud to Crete late this afternoon and while I was reading in Scene 2, Act 3, the following words:

> "But on, my liege; for very little pains
> Will bring this labor to a happy end,"

she said, "Let us hope so," and at that moment felt her first pain. The pain passed away and she went down to dinner with us. It returned later in the evening. She went to bed at one-quarter past eight. The Doctor came at half-past eight, and at five minutes after nine a boy was born.[224] She was assisted in this labor by taking chloroform for the first time. She only took enough to dull the pain a little. I think it was very efficacious. I am filled with a deep sense of thankfulness for her safe deliverance from this danger.

SUNDAY, 27. As the children came down one by one, their curious and varied exclamations of delight and surprise at the arrival of the new boy were amusing. Mollie burst into tears because he was not a girl. The rest seemed satisfied that it was a boy. Attended

224 Edward Garfield (1874–1876).

church at eleven and listened to a very rambling and sophomoric sermon. On my return read three odes of Horace. Took a long walk in the afternoon. In the evening Piatt and several other friends called. I read to the children from Charles Lamb's *Shakespeare's Tales*[225] the story of the *Midsummer Night's Dream*. The children understood it and were delighted with it. I believe in this way I can give them a hint of what is contained in Shakespeare and create a taste for the great Dramatist. Crete got through the day quite comfortably.

MONDAY, 28. Worked on correspondence until ten o'clock. Then went to the Interior and Post Office Departments on business for nearly two hours. Met Blaine and Hale and went with them to Blaine's to lunch. At 3 o'clock settled up several bills and made several purchases. In the evening worked on correspondence. Several people called. Among others, Colonels Rockwell and Pelouze. Crete had been doing finely, but the day is warm and sultry and almost enough to suffocate one. Worked to a late hour on Case No. 124, examining the authorities referred to in Mr. Burke's brief.

TUESDAY, 29. Worked on correspondence in the forenoon until ten o'clock, then drove with Mr. Gallaudet to the Deaf Mute Asylum to examine the necessity for further appropriations for buildings. Went from there to the Capitol and transacted some business at the Committee room. Spent an hour among the law books. Then I went to the Post Office Department on business. Home at four. Worked on correspondence until nine o'clock, when I took the train for N. Y. Regret leaving Crete at this time, but cannot avoid it.

WEDNESDAY, 30. Reached N. Y. this morning and drove to Neely Thompson's, No. 235 Madison Avenue. After breakfast Col. Piatt and I went down town and I spent the most of the day in shopping. During the afternoon called on Dr. Slade[226] and witnessed some of

---

[225] Charles and Mary Lamb, *Tales from Shakespeare* (1807).

[226] Henry Slade was one of many "mediums" of this period who claimed to be able to communicate with the "spirit world." Among his techniques at his seances was the use of slates, on which messages appeared, purportedly the work of "spirits." In 1876 he introduced slate-writing into England, but was soon convicted in court of deception; when the conviction was set aside on a technical point, he left the country before a new summons could be served. During 1877 and 1878 he attracted the attention of

his remarkable performances which he calls spiritual manifestations. In the evening attended the theatre and listened to the *Gilded Age*,[227] a piece whose stupidity is only equaled by the brilliant acting of Colonel Sellers. The play is full of malignant insinuations and would lead the hearer to believe that there is no virtue in the world, in public or in private life. Spent the night at Thompson's.

THURSDAY, 31. After breakfast went to General McDowell's. Visited with him for an hour and then called on my classmate Knox and spent some hours with him in reference to our insurance case in the Supreme Court. We visited the N. Y. Life Insurance Co. and had a long talk on the cases. Dined at 6 with General McDowell and sat up until midnight with him. Had a pleasant review of his public and private affairs and enjoyed his society exceedingly. I regard him as one of the noblest and truest of men. He gave me some good ideas in regard to family expenses and showed me his methods of keeping his accounts. This closes 1874.

---

a number of professors in Germany, and a subsequent report by one of them lent support to his claims. In 1885 he appeared willingly before a committee appointed by the University of Pennsylvania to investigate spiritualism. In its preliminary report the committee declared that "however wonderful may have been the manifestations of his Mediumship in the past, or elsewhere, we were forced to the conclusion that the character of those which passed under our observation was fraudulent throughout." He was a tall man of striking appearance, with dark eyes with very dark circles around them. See Frank Podmore, *Modern Spiritualism*, 2 vols. (1902)—republished as *Mediums of the 19th Century* in 1963—and *Preliminary Report of the Commission Appointed by the University of Pennsylvania to Investigate Modern Spiritualism in Accordance with the Request of the Late Henry Seybert* (1887).

[227] *Colonel Sellers*, a drama in five acts by Mark Twain, was based on *The Gilded Age* (1873) by Mark Twain and Charles Dudley Warner. Garfield witnessed the 108th performance of the play at the Park Theatre; on December 23, Mark Twain had spoken at the 100th performance. John T. Raymond played the part of Colonel Sellers.

APPENDIX

During the years covered by this volume Garfield usually wrote his entries on note paper to be copied into his diary by his secretary, George U. Rose, or by someone else, or he dictated the entries. On occasion, however, he wrote in the diary himself, sometimes writing an entire entry but more often concluding words or sentences. Listed below are the parts of the diary for the years 1872, 1873 and 1874 which are in Garfield's hand (with the exception of an occasional correction made by him).

1872

January 11.	Last two sentences.
April 18.	Last sentence.
April 22.	Beginning "and was recommitted" to end of entry.
April 23.	Second paragraph.
April 24.	Last sentence.
April 25.	Last sentence.
April 27.	Last five sentences.
May 1.	Last two sentences.
May 2.	Last sentence.
May 4.	Last sentence.
May 9.	Last sentence.
May 11.	Last two sentences.
May 14.	Last sentence.
May 15.	Second paragraph.
May 16.	Last sentence.
May 17.	Last fifteen words.
May 19.	Entire.
May 25.	Last four sentences.
June 13.	Second paragraph.
June 14.	Last three sentences.
June 15.	Last two sentences.
June 16.	Entire.
June 17.	Entire.
September 16.	Beginning "Wilson gave me" to end of entry.

September 17.	Second paragraph.
September 18.	Second paragraph.
September 22.	Entire.
September 23.	Last two sentences.
September 24.	Last three sentences.
September 25.	Second paragraph.
September 26.	Last three sentences.
September 27.	Beginning "among other[s] Mr. Plants" to end of entry.
September 28.	Second paragraph.
September 29.	Beginning "and heard a very solid sermon" to end of entry.
September 30.	Beginning "but I will not use it against him" to end of entry.
October 1.	Second paragraph.
October 2.	Last two sentences.
October 7.	Last sentence.
October 9.	Last sentence.
October 10.	Last two sentences.
October 14.	Last sentence.
October 15.	Last two sentences.
October 17–21.	Last three sentences.
October 24.	Last five sentences.
October 26.	Entire.

1873

May 3.	Last twelve words, with exception of "until."
May 14.	Last two sentences.
May 15–22.	All of these entries appear to be in Garfield's hand.
May 23.	Last sentence.
May 24.	Second paragraph.
May 25.	Last sentence.
May 26.	Last two sentences.
September 5.	Last ten words.
October 27.	Second paragraph.
October 31.	Last four sentences.
November 17.	Second paragraph.
December 14.	Last three sentences.

1874

May (undated).	Entire entry at the end.
July 29.	Last two sentences.
July 30.	Beginning "who, for the past two years" to end of entry.
July 31.	Second paragraph.
August 3.	Beginning "and I think there are parties" to end of entry.
August 4.	Last two sentences.
August 6.	Last four sentences.
August 7.	Second paragraph.
August 10.	Last four sentences.
August 11.	Last three sentences.
August 12.	Last three sentences.
August 14.	Last three sentences.
August 17.	Second paragraph.
August 18.	Last sentence.
August 19.	Last sentence.
August 28.	Last two sentences.
October 21.	Last three sentences.

Index

417

Colorado statehood 145; education 15, 16, 17; election (KuKlux) 55, 59, 61, 62; fisheries 154; navy 121; Oklahoma territorial 139; postal card 39–40; postal telegraph 44, 45, 49, 126; printing of Congressional debates 154; rivers and harbors 39; St. Croix land grant 24–25, 30, 31; St. Louis public building 30; shipping commissioners 38; steamboat inspectors 36, 38; tariff 20, 36, 37, 41, 42, 47, 48, 49, 52, 53, 54, 55, 56, 59, 60–61; two percent 126; William and Mary College 20, 22; Yerba Buena 34–35

committees: appropriations (Garfield chairman) 6–63 *passim*, 104–105 *passim;* commerce 140; District of Columbia 121; education and labor 13; judiciary 29, 138; pension 9; Poland (investigating Credit Mobilier) 89, 90, 134, 138, 142–143, 153–154, 155, 156; rules 44, 119; Wilson (investigating Credit Mobilier) 153

Congress, Forty-third (1873–1875) bills: appropriations 258–340 *passim*, 388–408 *passim;* army 328; bankruptcy 268; centennial 320, 321; civil rights 264, 274, 275; Choctaw Claim 323, 325, 331, 336; *Clara Dolsen* 323; currency 304, 305, 306, 307, 309, 310, 312, 315, 316, 327, 336, 400, 401, 409; District of Columbia reorganization 337; Louisville and Portland Canal 318–319; military prison 292; Mississippi flood relief 331; Mississippi River improvement 332, 333; Modoc Indian 290; moiety 325; naturali-

zation 318; New Mexico statehood 325; postal telegraph 327, 328; public buildings and sites 337; rivers and harbors 332, 339, 340; salaries 252, 254, 257, 258, 259, 262, 263, 277; steamboat inspection 323; tariff 327; tax 289; transportation 297, 302, 303, 304, 305

committees: appropriations (Garfield chairman) 257–339 *passim*, 388–409 *passim;* rules (Garfield member) 255, 262, 280, 339

miscellaneous: bills, increase in number introduced 288; caucus of Ohio delegation in House 251; caucus of Republicans of both houses 334; caucus of Republicans of House 251; committee appointments 255; drawing of seats in House 252; District of Columbia, investigation of affairs ordered 286; effort to restore franking privilege 298; Garfield member of committee to wait on President 253; Garfield's forebodings concerning new Congress 243; inflation, triumph of 304; possible solutions of financial problem 261; reception of King Kalakaua 406; retrenchment 273, 274–275, 277, 280, 281, 183–184, 286, 287, 289, 302, 303, 340, 341, 384; rumors concerning House organization 248, 250, 252; rush to introduce bills repealing salary increase 254; work load of members increasing 224–225

Congressional Convention (St. Louis, 1873) 179, 184

Congressional Library. *See* Library of Congress

Russell, M. T. 276
Russel, Thomas: sketch of 267; 269
Russian bath 130, 162
Rutson, Albert O.: sketch of 260; 287
Ryder, Symonds 203
Ryder, Symonds, Jr. 171
Ryder's (Cleveland) 358

St. Clair, Arthur 250
Saint Croix and Bayfield Railroad 24–25, 30, 31
St. Ignatius Mission (Jocko Reservation, Montana Territory) 82
St. Mary's Mission (Bitter Root Valley) 79
Salaries, increase of (Salary Grab, 1873): Garfield's views on adoption of proposal 156, 157; his letter of explanation to his constituents 168, 169, 170, 171; as issue in the campaign of 1873 228, 229; Republican caucus on 252; rush to introduce repeal bills 254; debate on repeal 258, 259, 262; repeal of 277; as issue in campaign of 1874 350, 351, 354, 355; mentioned 159, 160, 161–167 *passim*, 172, 173, 176, 181, 182, 183, 192, 263
Sale of arms to France: controversy over 21, 24
Salter, Francis: sketch of 115
Sanborn, John D. 300
Sanborn contracts 300, 325
Sanders, Wilbur F.: sketch of 77; 78, 84, 153
Sands, Alexander: sketch of 247; 250
Sanford, Charles 302
Sanford, Henry: sketch of 287
Sanford, Solomon N.: sketch of 215
Sandy Valley Campaign 189

Sargent, Aaron A.: sketch of 12; tells ghost story 48–49; mentioned 25, 123, 126, 130, 133, 158, 252, 255, 276, 278, 332, 339, 383, 390, 399
Sartoris, Algernon C. F.: fiance of
Sartoris, Adelaide Kemble 319
   Nellie Grant 319; wedding 319, 325
Saunders, William 40
Sawyer, Frederick A. 44, 284
Sawyer, Philetus: sketch of 43
Schaefer, Gottfried H.: editor of Pliny's *Works* 207
136
Schenck, Robert C. 301, 319
Schurz, Carl: sketch of 21; 60, 121, 316, 386
Scofield, Glenni: sketch of 46; 52, 133, 155, 252, 253, 288, 293,
Scofield, Jonathan F.: sketch of 98; 230, 369
Scott, George S. 297
Scott, John: sketch of 128
Scudder, Samuel H.: sketch of 256
Sears, John 94
Seaton, William W.: biography of 133
Second Ohio Cavalry: reunion of 219–220
Sedgebeer, Eugene H. 182
Seguin, Mrs. 315
Senatorial election in Ohio (1872) 4, 7, 8
Sergeant, John 278
Sermons: Garfield on 5, 60, 92, 97, 107, 109, 112, 150, 171, 173, 192, 194, 198–199, 200, 205, 210, 212, 218, 220, 222, 227, 232, 240, 241–242, 256, 260, 265, 273, 359, 370, 379, 390, 396, 411
Servant problem: Garfield and the

445

Venus, transit of: Garfield discusses with Simon Newcomb 38

Verdi, Tullio: sketch of 16

Viall, Jasper A.: sketch of 78; 84

Vickers, George: sketch of 128

Victor, chief of Flathead Indians 66, 79

Victoria, Queen 63

Vienna Exposition 126, 163, 165

Vigilantes, Montana Territory 85

Virginius Affair 249, 254–255, 257, 259, 260, 261

Vokes Family (performers) 317

Voorhees, Daniel W.: sketch of 54

Voyageurs, Les 359

Wade, Benjamin F. 29, 96, 288, 371, 372, 380

Wade, Decius S.: sketch of 77; 84

Wade, Henry P. 288

Wade, Jeptha H.: sketch of 208

Wade, Randall P.: sketch of 208

Waite, Morrison R.: sketch of 296; sworn in as Chief Justice 297; mentioned 399

Wakefield, Edmund B.: sketch of 109; 157, 200, 219, 220

Walker, Amasa: sketch of 24

Walker, Francis A.: sketch of 32; 65, 111, 252, 309

Walker, William 329

Wallace: Wallace J. Ford

Wann, N. L. 228, 370

War Department: Garfield calls at 59, 62, 67, 250, 265, 325, 408

Ward, Jasper D.: sketch of 292

Ward, Samuel: sketch of 23–24; 24, 27, 30, 37, 49, 136, 139, 142, 254, 257, 263, 286, 292, 344

Ward, William Hayes 105

Warden, Robert Bruce: author of *Life of Chase* 328, 330, 332

Warmoth, Henry C. 10

Warner, Sidney: sketch of 94

Warren (Ohio) *Chronicle* 170, 184, 347

Washburne, Elihu 9

Washington, D.C.: beautification of 105; desirable place of residence 190; Garfield in 3–67, 70–71, 91–92, 103–106, 110–117, 118–159, 161–169, 175–186, 188–189, 206–207, 225–226, 233–234, 238–240, 243–266; 269–341, 380–411; improvements in 122, 180, 181; social power of and its effects on public events 133; weather in 25, 63, 334 and *passim*

Washington, George 250, 307, 383, 391

Washington *Capital* 27

Washington *Chronicle* 64, 283

Washington Elm 386

Watterson, Henry: address on journalism 175

Wayne, Anthony 250

Weather Bureau 35

Weaver, Aaron W.: sketch of 163

Webber, Lemuel P. 405

Webster, Daniel 129, 201

Welch, Charles A. 268

Welcker, John 17

Welcker's Restaurant: sketch of 17; mentioned 27, 34, 65, 70, 139, 150, 179, 206, 254, 279, 292, 301, 317, 319, 382, 404

Wells, David Ames: sketch of 23; mentioned 24, 69, 117, 118, 136, 234, 256, 257, 269, 297, 317, 334, 340, 407

Wells, Erastus: sketch of 124

Wells Brothers 203

Welsh, William: Garfield critical of letter of in regard to Indians 82–

PRESIDENT OF THE UNITED STATES

INAUGURATED
MARCH 4
1881